Greek and Hellenic Culture in Joyce

R. J. Schork

D1542968

University Press of Florida
Gainesville/Tallahassee/Tampa/Boca Raton
Pensacola/Orlando/Miami/Jacksonville

03 02 01 00 99 98 6 5 4 3 2 1

Library of Congress Cataloging-in-Publication Data

Schork, R. J., 1933–
   Greek and Hellenic culture in Joyce/by R. J. Schork.
      p.   cm.—(The Florida James Joyce series)
   Includes bibliographical references and index.
   ISBN 0-8130-1609-6 (cloth: alk. paper)
   1. Joyce, James, 1882–1941—Knowledge—Greece.   2. Greek literature—
Appreciation—Ireland.   3. Philosophy, Ancient, in literature.   4. English
fiction—Greek influences.   5. Mythology, Greek, in literature.   6. Hellenism in
literature.   7. Greece—In literature.   I. Title.   II. Series.
PR6019.09Z79436   1998
823'.912—dc21   98-20340

The University Press of Florida is the scholarly publishing agency for the State University System of Florida, comprising Florida A & M University, Florida Atlantic University, Florida International University, Florida State University, University of Central Florida, University of Florida, University of North Florida, University of South Florida, and University of West Florida.

University Press of Florida
15 Northwest 15th Street
Gainesville, FL 32611
http://nersp.nerdc.ufl.edu/~upf

Greek and Hellenic Culture in Joyce

The Florida James Joyce Series

The Florida James Joyce Series

··

Edited by Zack Bowen

Dedicated to the Zürich James Joyce Foundation:

Its director, staff, friends, and benefactors

Contents

Foreword

R. J. Schork has written the most complete reference guide to Greek and Hellenic culture in Joyce ever attempted. No previous reference book or guide has ever come close to it. As companion volumes, our already published *Latin and Roman Culture in Joyce* and *Greek and Hellenic Culture in Joyce* constitute a complete classical guide to Joyce's works. The contribution of these two books to Joyce studies is inestimable, and the present volume may be the last among the primary texts for Joyce studies ever to be published. Classical allusion in Joyce's work in all-pervasive, and this work fills in the final major gap in Joyce explication. I know of no other scholar with Schork's depth of knowledge of both Joyce and classical culture and literature, an assertion based on Schork's intimate knowledge of Joyce's letter, essays, notebooks, drafts, publication history, and biography, as well as principal and ancillary works. It all comes once more into fruition in this book.

As the title implies, Schork covers the whole gamut of greek classical studies as they impinge on Joyce's thought processes as well as his work. He devotes chapters to Greek history, the several historians who wrote it, the Greek gods and mythology, Plato and Neoplatonism, Aristotle, the minor philosophers and sophists, Greek tragedy, comedy (Aristophanes), miscellaneous writers (including Aesop's fables), *The Iliad, The Odyssey,* modern Greek language, and classical Greek language.

In doing so Schork never diverts interest from Joyce, explaining only what is relevant to the Joyce texts but doing so in an uncomplicated, lucid style accessible to any literate reader—translating everything, giving the entire context of the Greek allusion, taking nothing for granted in terms of classical background even as he speaks to an audience of sophisticated Joyceans. Regarding Joyce scholarship, Schork's knowledge of all material relevant to his topic is as complete as his knowledge of the classics. Schork's research into Joyce archives produced information about his life and writing of which I personally was unaware, as well as covering the relevant scholarly bases.

Despite the length of the text, the writing itself is so lively and full of good humor that I was never bored by any chapter or the length of any etymological explanation. Through it all, Schork for the most part carefully avoids making claims for nonexistent or dubious parallels between the Greeks and Joyce and freely admits the rare occasions when he is on suspect speculative grounds. There is no doubt that the manuscript is more than a mere contribution to Joyce studies; rather, it is one of a relative handful of texts that most Joyceans will want/have to consult for years to come.

Zack Bowen
Series Editor

Preface

This book is the Greek companion to my *Latin and Roman Culture in Joyce* (1997). The classical venue has shifted, but my objectives and methods remain centered on texts and the archival data that lie behind them. The primary focus of this book is the influence of ancient Hellenic civilization—its history, mythology, language, and literature—on the the literary life and fiction of James Joyce. Its primary locus is the Greek-speaking world of the eastern Mediterranean as it impinges on Dublin, Trieste, Zürich, Paris, and the universe of Joyce's intellect and imagination. Not all of the people and places involved, however, fit quite so neatly into the parameters defined by Homer and Plotinus, Athens and Alexandria. Characters as diverse as, for example, Paul Phokas and Paul Ruggiero (fellow exiles and Joyce's neo-Hellenic tutors), Johannes Scotus Erigena (a ninth-century Irish philosopher and heterodox theologian), and H. Rider Haggard (the English novelist) occasionally participate in the discourse. And locales as far spread as an enchanted isle in Lago Maggiore, a street in the capital city of the ancient Persian Empire, and an "Academy" of pseudo-Platonists at the National Library in Dublin also appear on the contours of the critical map that I trace.

The organization of the diverse material is straightforward. After introductory discussions of ancient Greek history and historians, there is a long chapter on gods, goddesses, and Heroes (the reason for the eccentric capital *H* will be explained). Homeric epic is next, with an examination of the influence of the *Iliad* and considerably more attention to the ways and means by which the *Odyssey* left its polytropic mark. Then come three chapters on Plato, Aristotle, and minor philosophers, followed by treatments of tragedy and comedy (almost exclusively Aristophanic) and a brief review of the roles of several other ancient authors. The book concludes with two chapters on the Joyce's use and abuse of the language of the modern and classical Greeks.

The term *etymology* (the accurate derivation of words) occurs frequently in my discussions, even in those sections that are not specifically linguistic in orientation. Given Joyce's dedication to dictionaries and his cultivation of exotic lexical hybrids, that emphasis is natural. Many of the examples come from *Finnegans Wake,* because that is where the major etymological action is. The process, however, is not limited to Joyce's last work, as demonstrated by the following excerpt from Molly Bloom's final monologue in *Ulysses.* She is curious about the meaning of "Arsenic," the poison of choice used by Mrs. Maybrick in a notorious late nineteenth-century murder. Molly wonders if she should approach Leopold to find out what he knows about "why they call it that if I asked him hed say its from the Greek leave us as wise as we were before" (*U* 18.241–42). Since I have spent many years hanging around with teachers of Greek, I understand Molly's hesitation. But her expectation of obfuscation is not the necessary outcome. The etymology of *arsenic* is complex, but clear: It ultimately derives from the Persian *zar* (gold; bright yellow), a word similar to the Hebrew *zarniq;* in Greek the noun *arsenikon* refers to a yellowish ointment. That term was, however, confused with the unrelated adjective *arsenikos,* which means "male," "masculine," "strong." In English *arsenic* refers to a highly poisonous chemical element, often used in compounds for the disposal of unwanted spouses, male or female—a thoroughly practical piece of toxicoetymological information.

Throughout this book, whenever points of complex Greek cultural or linguistic data need to be explained, I make every effort to ensure that readers are not left as wise as they were before. All terms or citations (ancient or modern) are immediately translated; the use of Greek script is kept to a minimum. In that regard, classical readers are warned that Joyce did not know or care about the principles of accentuation that were once the hallmark of an expensive education. Moreover, since he learned his Greek from speakers of the unaspirated neo-Hellenic evolution of the ancient language, he rarely bothers with breathing marks. Whenever I reproduce a word or phrase in Joyce's (or one of his informant's) Greek script, I print what was written, a procedure that is bound to cause some raised eyebrows, if not a "blepharospasmockical" (*FW* 515.16) epidemic. My usual mode is to avoid all but the most essential citation of actual Greek, unless it encapsulates a clever or off-color verbal finesse. The evidence I have examined leads me to conclude that Joyce's manipulation of the classics in general and Greek in particular was done primarily for comic or scatological purposes. So much for the ethical energy purportedly absorbed from grappling with the conjugation of -μι verbs or meditating on the grandeur that was Hellas.

I emphasize from the start a warning repeated several times in the text: James Joyce could not read ancient Greek; he never studied it at school or on his own. During his stay in Zürich in 1915–19, he learned the rudiments of Modern Greek, and at that time he could have carried on a basic conversation in it. There is no evidence that Joyce engaged in correspondence that involved more than a few phrases of Greek, nor is there any record that he read anything in neo-Hellenic literature. On the other hand, Joyce's formal training in Latin was extraordinarily thorough, and he would have had no difficulties in transferring the similar grammatical-syntactical procedures from the one language to the other. That is, with a commentary (or a literal translation) and a dictionary, he could have made remarkably sophisticated deductions about the structure or the figurative force of a Greek word or phrase even in the most difficult of authors. If someone who knew classical Greek—like Stuart Gilbert—had made a pointed observation about a text of Homer, Plato, or Herodotus, Joyce could have followed the explication with ease. In my discussions of Joyce's use of ancient Greek literature, there are very few occasions when I suggest direct reference to the original text. When that procedure is indicated, Joyce must have had the sort of assistance, personal or bibliographical, that I have just described.

As for technical matters of transliteration, I use the forms of names and places in ancient Greek history, mythology, and literature that should be most familiar to most readers. I have generally followed the example of *Crowell's Handbook* cited in my list of basic references. Thus, the belabored mighty Hero is Heracles, not Herakles or the Latinate Hercules. For common nouns I transliterate *kappa* as *k* (not *c*) and *upsilon* as *y* (except in diphthongs: *kyklos, autokinēton*); *eta* is *ē, omega* is *ō*; the diphthong αι most often appears in English as *ae*. Sometimes Joyce (who liked the spellings *Eschylus* and *esthetics*), his correspondents and critics, or translators whom I cite employ slightly different conventions, but readers (who have learned not to expect absolute consistency in matters Joycean) should have few problems coping with names, technical terms, or the occasional transliterated citation. Both ancient and Modern Greek use the same alphabet, but the conversion of the neo-Hellenic version into languages that use the Latin script is based on erratic phonetic principles that cause all sorts of variation in contemporary transliteration. I discuss this phenomenon, which Joyce sometimes exploited for comic effect, in my chapter on Modern Greek.

A caveat from my *Latin* book is also appropriate here: Interpretations that hinge on moments or figures from Hellenic history or the manipulation of the Greek language are not meant to foreclose other explanations of source or application. The phrase "the kerl he left behind him" (*FW* 234.7–8) seems to me to be indebted equally to the title of a popular song and to the dramatic recognition device that Orestes placed on Agamemnon's tomb. Evidence—whether archival, compositional, or thematic—is the basis for claims of classical allusion or verbal legerdemain involving Greek elements; but such claims, by themselves, in no way negate the validity of other interpretations supported by persuasive argument. There is no grand unified theory to explain the *Wake*.

I take for granted that readers are familiar with Gifford and Seidman's *"Ulysses" Annotated*, McHugh's *Annotations to "Finnegans Wake,"* and Glasheen's *Third Census of "Finnegans Wake."* None of these guides is complete or infallible, but each is a necessary resource and a source of useful information of every kind. This book usually does not repeat material covered fully and accurately in these works, although in some instances I expand or redirect their data. The *Classical Lexicon* by O Hehir and Dillon is invaluable for most word derivations, but its scope (almost exclusively the etymology of single words) precludes thematic explication. Their appendices A (on classical names) and C (on the marginal names at *FW* 306–308) are useful but incomplete; the "Supplementary Notes" on linguistic and phonological matters seem far too complex, even pedantic, to me. At the same time, a Greekless reader of the *Wake* or *Ulysses* will usually profit from glancing at the tricolumnar format (Joyce's "word"/Greco-Latin "source"/English "translation") of their accessible glossary.

In addition to my primary attention to the texts (as opposed to, say, biography, theory, or postcolonialism), I have brought archival research into the critical process. For *Ulysses* this means taking notebook VIII.A.5 and the British Museum notesheets into account; for *Finnegans Wake* the VI.B and VI.C series of Notebooks (distinguished hereafter by the capital *N*) are essential. A cluster of VIII.A notebooks (now in the Joyce collection at Buffalo) and a few related manuscripts provide most of the evidence for my discussion of Joyce's exercises in Modern Greek. I occasionally trace the relevant draft stages of a passage to help determine the propriety of a claim for classical allusion or the roots of exuberant wordplay. Research in this mass of genetic material, especially the detection of documentary sources, offers fascinating glimpses of Joyce's creative imagination at work during the prelude to and process of composition. Attention to the notesheets and the *Wake* Notebooks is, however, only a necessary preliminary step in interpretation of the text. Evidence from archival entries should support—not obfuscate with overexpansive conjecture—the plausibility of critical insight, but the mere citation of a note or source is no substitute for clear exegesis.

Readers interested in an accessible survey of the pertinent ancient history might look at *Greece and the Hellenistic World,* edited by John Boardman, Jasper Griffin, and Oswyn Murry, in *The Oxford History of the Classical World;* an older and far more detailed work is Russell Meiggs's revision of J. B. Bury's *A History of Greece.* I strongly recommend *Crowell's Handbook of Classical Mythology,* edited by Edward Tripp, for reliable treatment of that vast topic. Arthur H. Armstrong's *An Introduction to Ancient Philosophy* is old-fashioned but very accessible. For basic information about every aspect of ancient Greco-Roman civilization, readers should consult the 1996 third edition of the *Oxford Classical Dictionary,* edited by Simon Hornblower and Antony Spawforth. The primary authors—Homer, Herodotus, Aristophanes—are cited from standard editions, usually the appropriate Oxford Classical Text. Those who wish to see more of the original literary landscape may consult a volume of the Loeb Classical Library, with its facing Greek and English pages. Unless specifically noted, all translations are my own, and designed to help the reader see the linguistic point (or its Joycean distortion) of the ancient text. Throughout this *Greek* volume, I make frequent cross-references to my previous *Latin* volume in the Florida James Joyce Series, since the two are meant to complement each other.

Acknowledgment is due to the *International Journal of the Classical Tradition,* in which a version of chapter 10 appeared. The firm of B. G. Teubner, Stuttgart and Leipzig, granted permission to reproduce a figure from its edition of the Greek text of Euclid. Copies of archival material were kindly supplied by the Beinecke Rare Book and Manuscript Library at Yale University; the Carl A. Kroch Library, Rare and Manuscript Collections, at Cornell University; the Harry Ransom Humanities Research Center at the University of Texas at Austin; the James Joyce Tower in Dublin, and the James Joyce Foundation in Zürich. The staff in the Interlibrary Loan, Archives, Serials, and References divisions of the Joseph P. Healey Library at the University of Massachusetts–Boston were unfailingly efficient and courteous in keeping up with my sometimes exotic requests. Professor Dia Philippides of Boston College and Angela Sawyer, one of my former Greek students, generously supplied a copy of an essential monograph. Colleagues Emily McDermott, Kenneth Rothwell, Robert Green, John Tobin, Martin Andic, Walter Weibrecht, and Bobby Kartsagoulis at UMass, as well as Ted Ahern at Boston College, were always willing to answer questions, offer suggestions, and exorcize wild notions. I have also benefited from the discoveries and comradeship of several fellow laborers in the genetic field, Vincent Deane (Dublin); Geert Lernout, Inge Landuyt, and Dirk Van Hulle (Antwerp); and Wim Van Mierlo (Miami). Peter Hartshorn (Showa Institute, Boston) supplied information about the Greek community in Trieste. The participants in the Zürich 1995 Summer Workshop ("Homer/Joyce/Homer") bristled with ideas that helped to define and refine some of the points in this book.

Thanks to the Smithsonian Study Tours, I have been fortunate to visit—far too often and too luxuriously, some claim—Greece itself, the islands, and many classical and Byzantine sites in Crete, Cyprus, Asia Minor, and Egypt. Ellynn Packard was a tremendous help with word processing. Once again Gillian Hillis of the University Press of Florida provided fine-toothed and collegial editorial assistance. My daughter, Heidi, supplied several perfect graphic images and, at the last moment, a little Wisdom. Betsy Boehne assisted throughout by showing me how to call down a superscript, by appreciating my jokes and rough drafts, and by tolerating the conversion of our study into Cloudcuckooland while I tried out some of the para-Aristophanic "Great Ideas" that generated this book. Finally, in my dedication I acknowledge Fritz Senn and *his* dedication, for almost forty years, to Joyce and Joyceans throughout the world.

Abbreviations

For almost all of the following abbreviations (cited parenthetically in the text), I have followed the standard conventions of the *James Joyce Quarterly*. I add several other items that are frequently cited.

CP   Joyce, James. *Collected Poems.*

CW   ———. *The Critical Writings of James Joyce.*

D   ———. *Dubliners.*

E   ———. *Exiles.*

EB   *Encyclopaedia Britannica,* 11th ed.

FW   Joyce, James. *Finnegans Wake.*

GJ   ———. *Giacomo Joyce.*

JJII   Ellmann, Richard. *James Joyce.*

JJA   *The James Joyce Archive.* I follow the *JJQ* guide for citing volumes and pages.

Letters   Joyce, James. *Letters of James Joyce.*

P   ———. *A Portrait of the Artist as a Young Man.*

Scribbledehobble   *James Joyce's "Scribbledehobble": The Ur-Workbook for "Finnegans Wake."* Citations refer to page in this book followed by original workbook page in brackets; for example, 95 [511].

SH   Joyce, James. *Stephen Hero.*

SL   ———. *Selected Letters of James Joyce.*

U   ———. *Ulysses.*

UNBM   *Joyce's "Ulysses" Notesheets in the British Museum.* Citations refer to page and line number; for example, 142:94.

1

History

In this chapter there is more emphasis on dates, places, and events than is found in the rest of the book. The information is designed to establish a historical-political context for subsequent discussions of cultural, literary, and linguistic matters. This survey of the facts of ancient Greece is not comprehensive; it covers only those periods and persons that grabbed Joyce's attention in his fiction.

Standard histories of Greece begin with an acknowledgment of the debt that the ancient Hellenic world owes to more advanced civilizations in the Middle East, Crete, and Egypt. Thanks to his readings in Victor Bérard's *Les Phéniciens et l'Odyssée,* Joyce was acutely aware of this cross-cultural influence. Indeed, he includes a brief reference to the totally mythological Phoenician origin of the Irish language in the introduction to a 1907 lecture in Trieste (*CW* 156). In a compact paragraph in the introduction to his study of *Ulysses,* Stuart Gilbert summarizes these traditions: "Phoenician thalassocracy, Peoples of the Sea, Minos, Cadmus the Tyrian, Danaos the Egyptian."[1]

According to legend, the connection between Greece and Egypt can be traced to Io, a priestess of Hera in Argos. She was one of the many mortal women who attracted the attention of Zeus. Some say that Hera transformed Io into a heifer to thwart her husband's lust; others claim that Zeus changed the maiden into that form to hide his infidelity. At any rate, Hera sent a hundred-eyed gadfly to sting the heifer-maiden on her trip beyond the borders of civilization: past the oak-oracle at Dodona, through the land of the Amazons, across the Bosphorus, and beneath the crag in the Caucasus to which Prometheus was chained. She finally lay exhausted beside the Nile, where Zeus's Olympian caress restored her to human shape and begot a son, Epaphus (Touch). Generations later twin sons,

Danaüs and Aegyptus, were born to the ruler of Egypt. The former had fifty daughters, the latter fifty sons. Since his daughters refused marriage to their cousins, Danaüs fled with them to Argos, the Greek homeland of their distant ancestor, Io. Later, when Aegyptus's sons came to Greece to claim their brides, forty-nine of the women obeyed a pledge to their father and killed their husbands in their marriage beds. The other bride, Hypermnestra (Super Suitor), spared her mate.[2] Eventually father, daughter, and the surviving son-in-law were reconciled, and Danaüs's rule of the Argives was long and prosperous.

Joyce injects several items from this episode in Greek prehistory into *Finnegans Wake*. It would be pushing allusion to the limits to claim that "cowrymaid" (*FW* 164.8) refers to the metamorphosis of Io. There can be no doubt, however, that the Argive maiden is meant to be present in a list of love-satellites of the planet Jupiter (the Latin name for Zeus): "The datter, io, io" appears just two lines before "Bossford" (*FW* 583.10–12). That word is a literal translation of the name *Bosphorus* (ox, or cow, ford), the straits between Europe and Asia Minor that owe their name to Io's crossing. The son that Zeus formed in Io by means of his touch may exist (side by side with the Flying Dutchman) in "flyend of a touchman" (*FW* 327.23). The case is strengthened by "flyend," a compounded reference to Zeus's final freeing of Io from the torments of the gadfly in Egypt. "Egyptus" (*FW* 263.6) is both the land of the Nile and one of the twin descendants of Io in that land. His rival twin brother is commemorated by his extraordinarily subservient daughters, the "timid Danaides" (*FW* 94.14); with a single exception, they carried out their father's command to murder the alien cousin-husbands on their wedding nights.[3] Finally, the area of Greece into which Danaüs and his daughters fled is cited in a list of places that claim to be Homer's birthplace, "Argos" (*FW* 481.22). Its inhabitants—and those of all Greece—also put in an appearance in "Danaan" (*FW* 381.6), a designation formed from the name of their immigrant ancestor, Danaüs.

When Europa, princess of Tyre (or Sidon) in Asia Minor, was carried away by Zeus, the king of her native city ordered her brothers either to find her or never to return home. All failed this task; none of them learned of Zeus's disguise as a bull or of their sister's abduction to Crete. On his search one son, Cadmus, eventually founded the city of Thebes in northwest Greece.[4] His marriage to Harmonia was fruitful, but most of their children (for instance, Semele and Actaeon) were destroyed in close encounters with the Olympian gods. The most significant act in Cadmus's career was the introduction of his native Phoenician alphabet to Greece. This mythological tradition is supported by literal fact: The Greek script was indeed adapted from a northwest Semitic model. Joyce acknowledges this gift of far-reaching orthographic consequence in "Night Lessons." There *"Cadmus"* is entered in the margin beside the essay question "Should Spelling?" (*FW* 307.L and 25). In section I.6 of the *Wake* Shem asks Shaun to respond to a series of twelve questions, the answers to which reveal the work's characters and the book itself. The Fourth Question is divided into four parts, labeled "a," "b," "c," and "d." Shaun requires his brother to "harmonise your abccedeed responses" (*FW* 140.14). That request converts the name of Cadmus's wife, Harmonia, into a verb, the object of which is his greatest gift to the prehistoric Greeks, the alphabet.

After Princess Europa, bull-borne from Asia Minor, arrived in Crete, she gave birth to Zeus's son Minos. He ruthlessly assumed the throne of the new island kingdom, but angered Poseidon by refusing to sacrifice a magnificent bull to the Lord of the Sea. The god caused Minos's wife, Pasiphaë, to fall in love with the bull, and Daedalus's hollow wooden cow enabled the queen to gratify her lust. The result was the Minotaur, whose compound name (*tauros, -us* means bull in Greek and Latin, respectively) proclaims the king's shame. The monster was enclosed in the Labyrinth, another of Daedalus's marvelous constructions on Crete.

Joyce, of course, was well aware of the basic details of Minoan mythology, as is demonstrated by the Stephen's surname in *Portrait* and *Ulysses* and the Ovidian epigraph to the first novel. There are, however, surprisingly few references to Crete in Joyce's later works. In "Scylla and Charybdis" Stephen Dedalus recites a list of "incests and bestialities" from the "criminal annals of the world." The catalog includes "queens with prize bulls" (*U* 9.850–54). An expanded version of that prehistoric scandal occurs in "Circe": "*Et exaltabuntur cornua iusti.* Queens lay with prize bulls. Remember Pasiphae for whose lust my grandgrossfather made the first confessionbox" (*U* 15.3865–68). The Latin quotation is from Psalm 75:10 (74:10 in the Vulgate); it means "And the horns of the just man shall be raised up." The Minoan analogue to the "confessionbox" is Daedalus's receptive wooden cow. One of the participants in the wide-ranging discussion in "Oxen of the Sun" sustained "the theory of copulation between women and the males of brutes"; his authority was "fables such as that of the Minotaur" (*U* 14.991–94).

In the *Wake* I have been able to detect only two faint allusions to tales involving Crete. The Minotaur's maze appears in a passage in which "Big Maester Finnykin" is invoked to lead his stepchildren "through the labyrinth of their samilikes and the alteregoases of their pseudoselves" (*FW* 576.28–33). Minos's posthumous appointment as one of the judges in Hades seems to be behind the threatening title "old Minace" (*FW* 95.1). Another of Europa's children by Zeus was also selected to judge the souls of the dead; the name of the Cretan Prince "Rhadamanthys" appears in an archival list of Underworld items (VIII.A.5.49).

Since most of the adventures—and the tragic flight—of Daedalus and Icarus are thoroughly discussed in the "Ovid" chapter of my book on Roman culture as found in Joyce,[5] Cretan details from the *Metamorphoses* are not repeated here. There is, however, an additional important episode in Greco-Minoan mythology that has left some traces in the work of Joyce. While it was reeling from an outbreak of the plague, the prominent mainland city-state of Athens was attacked and conquered by King Minos. He demanded that every nine years thereafter, the Athenians send fourteen young citizens as tribute to Crete. There, after performing in ritual games with bulls, the teams of bull leapers were fed to the caged Minotaur. Prince Theseus of Athens volunteered to lead one of these sacrificial groups in an attempt to put an end to the horrible form of tribute. While watching him perform in the games, Princess Ariadne fell in love with the enemy youth, and she told him how to penetrate the maze and navigate his way out again with a spool of thread. Theseus then killed the monster at the heart of the Labyrinth. Ariadne sailed to Athens with him, but they became separated (perhaps by Theseus's design) on the island of Naxos. Later Theseus, then king of Athens, married Ariadne's sister Phaedra, whom Aphrodite bewitched into falling in love with her husband's son, Hippolytus.

These details are a bare outline of the legendary adventures of the greatest hero of prehistoric Athens. Although Prince Theseus's destruction of Minoan power is central to the tales, his victory in Crete does not seem to have attracted Joyce's allusive attention beyond the reference to the labyrinth already cited. In fact, the only other reference is embedded deeply in a marginal note in "Night Lessons" in the *Wake*: "*Bet you fippence,* *any*thesious, *there's no* pugatory, *are yous game"* (*FW* 266.L; my emphases). The covert presence of Theseus's name and a truncated suggestion of "purgatory" are intended as a reference to the Athenian king's journey into the Underworld to kidnap the goddess Persephone, queen of Hades. Theseus was bound by pledge to his devil-may-care comrade Pirithous to undertake this suicidal mission. Hades was not amused by their bravado and caused the two mortals to become permanently attached to stone seats in his infernal court. Theseus was eventually rescued by Heracles; Pirithous never escaped.[6]

According to some accounts Theseus participated in another adventure with Pirithous. They attacked the kingdom of the Amazons on the southern shore of the Black Sea. There Queen Antiope either fell in love with the Athenian king or Theseus carried her off by force. Before the Amazon died, she bore Theseus his only son, Hippolytus. The tragedy of Hippolytus and Phaedra is not mentioned by Joyce, but there is a clear indication, in an emphatic position in the *Wake,* that he was aware of the etymology of *amazon.* The term is derived from the Greek word for breast (*mazos,* sometimes spelled *mastos*) and the negative prefix *a-* (not, non-). Thus, *amazon* literally means "without a breast." One explanation of the origin of the term is the reputed custom by these legendary warrior-women of cutting off their right breasts so that they could more effectively shoot bows and throw spears. Just before she merges with the sea, ALP makes the following comments: "I can seen meself among them, allaniuvia pulchrabelled. How she was handsome, the wild Amazia, when she would seize to my other breast!" (*FW* 627.27–29).

There is one final aspect of Theseus's life and deeds that has left a faint trace in the *Wake:* the story of his birth. King Aegeus of Athens, concerned because was childless, wisely consulted the oracle at Delphi and was told that he would father a child "if he did not unloose the foot of his wineskin" until he returned home to his wife. On the way back to Athens, Aegeus visited King Pittheus of Troezen and told him about the oracle's strange advice. Pittheus realized the significance of the message and connived to have his unmarried daughter sleep with the royal guest. Thus, the "wineskin" was loosened and Theseus was conceived.[7] Later the prince made his way to Athens to claim his birthright. Joyce rephrases the oracular reply as "and reloose that thong off his art" (*FW* 224.35), although I am not sure about the force of "art" here.[8] There are, however, nearby references to a ready penis ("bandished" [*FW* 224.34], from the

French verb *bander*, to have an erection) and an untimely emission ("pricoxity" [*FW* 224.36], from the Latin adjective *praecox*, premature).

Since this book devotes separate chapters to the *Iliad* and the *Odyssey*, there is no section on the Trojan War–Mycenaean Period.[9] Joyce's works have no discernible references to the Dark Ages through the Orientalizing Period (around 1100–625 B.C.). Thus my survey of Greek history leaps ahead to the Archaic and Classical Periods (625–336 B.C.).

The standard political-military unit in Greece during this period was the *polis*. This noun is usually translated as city-state. The English words *politics* and *polite* are derived from it; both terms have something to do with life in an organized community. Aristotle's famous dictum "Man is a political animal" thus means that the natural habitat of a human being is a city-state. The urban center of the area, with its walls, markets, temples, was the titular city; adjacent agricultural-pastoral territory was also part of the unit. An overpopulated or commercially ambitious polis would frequently found colonies. Several of the more important city-states, such as Athens and Sparta, developed mutual defense leagues—or, in the eyes of their enemies, forced less powerful states into their empires. In short, although the Greeks spoke a single language, honored the same gods, and participated in more or less the same culture, they organized themselves into independent (sometimes fiercely so) political entities.

Joyce certainly knew the dimensions of this term and its historical context, but in the *Wake* he uses the word *polis* as a synonym for *city*. The Latin motto of Dublin, for example, is *Obedientia Civium Urbis Felicitas* (The Happiness [or Prosperity] of a City is the Obedience of Its Citizens). Joyce turns this into "the hearsomeness of the burger felicitates the whole of the *polis*" (*FW* 23.14–15; my emphasis). In "Night Lessons" the term appears in the only complete ancient Greek sentence in the *Wake*: οὐκ ἔλαβον πόλιν· ("ouk elabon polin"; "I/they did not capture the city" [*FW* 269.L2]). The words are not a fragment taken from an ancient historian; they are a bilingual schoolboy pun, which I discuss in my chapter on classical Greek.

Although the process by no means always took some sort of teleogenic line of evolution, in the ancient Greek world there was a general pattern of political movement from monarchy through various forms of oligarchy (aristocracy, plutocracy), interrupted by periods of tyranny, to democracy. Because there is more documentary evidence about Athens during this period, standard textbooks naturally emphasize the constitutional history of that *polis*. According to tradition the first written code of laws in Athens was composed by Draco in 621 B.C. The penalties imposed under this code were extremely harsh, as might be deduced from the name of its author: *drakon* means serpent or dragon in Greek. Joyce, perhaps adopting a Bostonian pronunciation of "law," briefly alludes to that ancient legal landmark in *"Draco on the Lour"* (*FW* 343.2).

The next step in Athenian political process was a thorough and liberal-izing revision of the laws and the political-judicial process by Solon, who was elected as the city's chief magistrate in 594 B.C. The "Night Lessons" essay topic assigned to his marginal name is "The Thirty Hour Week" (*FW* 307L and 18–19). That reference is a utopian synopsis of the many social and economic reforms that he initiated, especially the abolition of slavery for debts. The Athenian lawgiver is also linked with Solomon, the wise judge-king of the ancient Hebrews: both are pictured "around their old traditional tables of the law like Somany Solans" (*FW* 94.26–27). There are several relevant legal and political terms in the following passage: "My *phemous themis* race is run, so let *Demoncracy* take the highmost! . . . I'll beat you *so lon*. . . . *My unchanging Word* is sacred" (*FW* 167.24–28; my emp-hases). The Greek word *themis* means law or custom; "phemous" contains the Greek root *phē/a* (speech, decree), thus implying that Solon's law was meant to be *the* word in Athens and that his decrees have achieved a measure of historical fame. "Demoncracy" and "so lon," though typically distorted, are obvious in derivation. The final, italicized phrase makes perfect contextual sense given that, after he formulated his code, Solon exacted a promise from his fellow citizens that they would not attempt to modify its provisions. He then went into voluntary exile for ten years so that he himself would not be tempted (or forced) to amend his decrees. There is another allusion in "solons and psychomorers" (*FW* 476.14–15); the second element is composed of the Greek word for spirit or soul (*psychē*) and the Latin word for custom or behavior (*mos, moris*). If the roots of both parts of "psychomorers" are taken as Greek, however, then the lawgivers are teamed up with some foolish (*mōros*) souls.

The siglum in a *Wake* Notebook entry links the Four Old Men (X), who act as prosecutors and judges in the kangaroo trial of HCE, with the early Athenian proponent of civic justice "Solons X" (VI.B.8.201). Another archival entry involves Solon as a character in Plato's dialogue *Timaeus*. In that work Critias tells a story about the lawgiver's voluntary exile from Athens, when he traveled to Sais in Egypt. In that ancient city a senior priest of the temple chided the visitor for his narrow view of world history: "O Solon, Solon, you Greeks are always children. There is no such thing as an old Greek" (*Timaeus* 22b). This ethnic "immaturity" is explained by the tale of the primeval destruction of the civilization of Atlantis, which set off decades of disasters in Greece and eradicated its inhabitants' memory of the past. One of the notes for *Ulysses* reads "O Solon you Greeks— / there is not among you" (VI.C.7.137).

In the early fifth century, all of Greece faced invasion by the massive forces of the Persian Empire. After Shah Darius had swept through the Greek city-states in Asia Minor, he was stopped on the mainland at Marathon (490 B.C.). Ten years later King Xerxes overpowered the Spartans at Thermopylae, only to be decisively defeated by the combined Greek fleet under the command of the Athenian general Themistocles, at the Battle of Salamis (479 B.C.). Some of the events of the Persian wars are discussed in my treatment of Herodotus's *The Histories* (see chapter 2); as for the presence of Themistocles in the *Wake*, it seems likely that Joyce's source of information was not Herodotus, but Plutarch. That second-century A.D. Greek author (the authority for the story of Theseus's strange conception) is best known for his *Lives of the Noble Grecians and Romans.* Some of the *Lives* are arranged in pairs, and a number of parallel figures are compared, for example, as "founders" (Theseus-Romulus), or as "orators" (Demosthenes-Cicero).[10]

Both appearances of the politician-general Themistocles in *Wake* involve his burial: "*Themistocles* . . . Eu" (*FW* 307.L and 26) and "under geasa, Themistletocles, on his multilingual tombstone" (*FW* 392.24–25). The key to the significance of these cryptic passages lies in the final pages of Plutarch's biography. Despite his great naval victory at Salamis, Themistocles was later ostracized from Athens.[11] He wound up promising to serve Greece's deadliest enemy, the king of Persia. According to Plutarch, during his banishment Themistocles learned the Persian language well enough to speak to the shah without an interpreter. When it seemed as if he would have to fight against the Athenian ships that were roving in Persian waters, Themistocles committed suicide, supposedly by drinking bull's blood.

Plutarch also reports that there is a splendid sepulcher of Themistocles in Magnesia in northwestern Greece. He dismisses any claim that there is a tomb in Piraeus, the port and naval base of Athens (*Lives* 154). Themistocles died and was buried in exile. Thus, Joyce's collocation of the name of the Athenian general and the town of Eu on the Normandy coast of

France pivots around an event in medieval Irish history. St. Laurence O'Toole, archbishop of Dublin, died and was buried outside Ireland, at Eu in 1180. There may also be a hint of treason in the collocation of Themistocles and the Irish prelate. Some claim that St. Laurence collaborated too eagerly with the invading King Henry II of England and acceded too willingly to the provisions of the bull *Laudabiliter* issued by the only English Pope, Adrian IV. Another citation adds to the notion of burial in exile. "Libera, nostalgia! Beate Laurentie O'Tuli, Euro pra nobis!" (*FW* 228.25–26). On a liturgical level those appeals are meant to sound like invocations in Latin from the Litany of the Saints: "Deliver us from pain! Blessed Laurence O'Toole, pray for us!" (The English word *nostalgia* is composed of two Greek nouns, *nostos* [home-coming, return] and *algos* [pain, suffering]; a literal translation of the compound would be home-sickness.) The French town in which the saint was buried is also present in the initial letters of "Euro", as is the entire continent: "Euro pra." In short, that brief prayer in the *Wake* is directed to someone who, like Themistocles, lies in a foreign tomb, rejected by his own people.

Joyce's second reference to Themistocles confirms an Irish connection. According to McHugh, the Irish word *geasa* means magical injunctions or taboos; Joyce's "geasa" reflects Themistocles' death away from his home in Athens, "under a ban." He was not, however, placed under a "multilingual tombstone" (*FW* 392.24–25). There is no such information about a burial monument to Themistocles in Plutarch, Nepos, or any other source. I suspect Joyce has conflated the reports of Themistocles' fluency in Persian and his death in exile to produce this minor error in Greek sepulchral epigraphy.

The period between the Persian wars and the Peloponnesian War (479–431 B.C.) is sometimes called the Golden Age of Greek civilization. More frequently this era of classical productivity in the arts is known as the Periclean Age, after the Athenian politician who guided the city during most of those years. It is surprising that there are no Joycean references to Pericles, perhaps the most famous name in ancient Greek history. A partial exception is the Parthenon (Virgin's Place). This temple on the Acropolis was completely rebuilt, with its pedimental sculpture, frieze, and monumental statue of Athena, under Pericles' direction. The building is mentioned in a list of faraway places that have special meaning to Leopold Bloom: "the Parthenon (containing statues of nude Grecian divinities)" (*U* 17.1984–85). Bloom is, however, characteristically mistaken here—there were no nude statues in the Parthenon. It is likely that he confused the Athenian temple to the virgin-goddess Athena with the Pantheon (Place of All the Gods, or Totally Godlike Place) in Rome. That first-century B.C. structure housed statues of the chief gods, goddesses, and the deified Julius Caesar, but it is unlikely that any of them were nude. (Other significant landmarks in literature and philosophy, such as the tragic and comic dramatists of the Periclean Age and the new directions in rational inquiry under Socrates, are discussed in chapters 6 through 10.)

In "Oxen of the Sun" a comrade reminds Stephen of his schooldays at Clongowes. Then he asks "about Glaucon, Alicibiades, Pisistratus. Where were they now ?" (U 14.1110–12). While there is another possible link for "Pisistratus" (see chapter 5), each of these names can be associated with Athens. Glaucon was the primary questioner of Socrates in Plato's *Republic,* a dialogue about a utopian polis. Peisistratus was one of the tyrants who assumed intermittent power in Athens during the mid-sixth century B.C.[12] Alcibiades played a significant part in the military and political events of the Peloponnesian War. That tragic conflict between Athens and Sparta took place in 431–404 B.C. During the *Wake's* tour of the "Willingdon Museyroom" (*FW* 8.10) and its relics of many famous battles, there is a reference to Lord Wellington's "pulluponeasyan wartrews," and a bit later to the "Delian alps" (*FW* 8.20–21, 28). The first phrase is a phonetic representation of the Greek war, its short-lived cessation of hostilities, and a reference to the Duke's ready-for-combat trousers; the second phrase commemorates the Athenian alliance, the Delian League, so called because its ritual headquarters were on the island of Delos, the sacred birthplace of Apollo and Artemis. Another connection between the Peloponnesian War and Wellington is found in the margins of "Night Lessons": "*Hoploits and atthems*" (*FW* 272.L2). Hoplites were heavily armed Greek infantrymen; "atthems" recalls both Athens and the Iron Duke's battle cry, "Up, guards, and at them."

Alcibiades, the brilliant but mercurial pupil of Socrates, was accused of sacrilege during a crucial phase of the Peloponnesian War when he was about to assume command of the truce-breaking Athenian expedition to Sicily (415 B.C.). He fled to Sparta but later returned to his native city and was elected a general. After another Athenian defeat, he went into exile for a second time. This bizarre political career and the fickle swings of Athenian democracy are commemorated in the *Wake.* There a marginal

"*Alcibiades*" is balanced by the essay topic "Do you Approve of our Existing Parliamentary System?" (*FW* 306.L2 and 28–30). A Spartan victory over a revived Athenian navy at Aegospotami (Rivers of the Goat) in 405 B.C. was the city's final blow; it surrendered the next year. In "Aeolus" the bombastic philhellene Professor MacHugh laments this ancient loss "of the empire of the spirit . . . that went under with the Athenian fleets at Aegospotami" (*U* 7.566–68).

Dionysius the First was the ruler of Syracuse, the most important Greek polis on Sicily. He was universally regarded as a consummate tyrant, a cruel, dissembling, debauched, suspicious autocrat. Both Wakean references to this despot involve the "whispering gallery" that he constructed in his palace so that he could eavesdrop on what guests and officials were saying about him. That chamber was called "the ear of Dionysius," as is confirmed in "Night Lessons": "*Dionysius* . . . How to Understand the Deaf" (*FW* 307.L and 20–21). The hero of the *Wake* is also reported as having the same paranoiac curiosity: "Earwicker, that pattern-mind, that paradigmatic ear, receptoretentive as his of Dionysius" (*FW* 70.35–36).[13]

In the fourth century the most important figures in Greek—and world—history were King Philip II of Macedon and his son Alexander the Great. The changes brought about by their conquests mark the beginning of the Hellenistic Age. Historians use this term to designate the period of wide expansion and adaptation of Greek culture, under Alexander and the monarchs who succeeded him, as they divided up control of the Mediterranean world and that of the Middle East as far as India.

Philip II, the ruler of Macedon, a petty kingdom on the northwest limits of civilized Greece, was notorious for his excessive drinking. Plutarch reports the following comment by Alexander when his father fell in a drunken rage: "See there the man, who makes preparations to pass out of Europe into Asia, overturned in passing from one seat to another" (*Lives* 807). In another story, a woman who has been unfairly judged by the king tells him that she will appeal the decision of Philip drunk to Philip sober. That anecdote explains the presence in "Circe" of "*The Siamese twins, Philip Drunk and Philip Sober*" (*U* 15.2512–27). In scrambled form the pair reappears in the *Wake* as HCE boasts of one of his feats: "I made sprouts fontaneously from *Philuppe Sobriety* in the coupe that's cheyned for noon *inebriates*" (*FW* 542.9–10; my emphases). In his nine-book *Factorum et Dictorum Memorabilium* (Of memorable deeds and words) of the first century A.D., the Roman rhetorician Valerius Maximus reports that "a foreign woman, who had been unjustly judged by the drunken Philip, said that she would appeal the decision. When the king asked to whom she would address the appeal, she replied 'To Philip, but a sober Philip'."[14] The king then shook off his drunkenness and rendered a just verdict. The woman's boldness passed into a proverb—and into Joyce's final two works.

In the same paragraph as the previous citation from the *Wake*, Joyce invents a new verb: "demosthrenated my folksfiendship, enmy pupuls felt my burk was no worse that their brite" (*FW* 542.18–19). The Greek *dēmos* means the people; *thrēnos* is a wail, a dirge. The combined terms are meant to sound like the name Demosthenes, the Athenian orator whose *Philippics* warned his fellow citizens that the Macedonian king was the deadly enemy of their city and their liberty. Hence, Demosthenes almost literally bewailed the semibarbaric "fiend" who would subjugate the "folk" of Athens. The lightly disguised names of two English statesmen reinforce the oratorical thrust of the passage: Edmund *Burke*, who supported home rule for Ireland, and John *Bright*, who opposed it. (Another indicator of the multiple levels of allusion here is the Norwegian title—*En folkefiende*—of Ibsen's play *An Enemy of the People*.) The Athenian patriot also plays a cameo role in a Ulyssean list of famous statesmen who spoke out for liberty, "Henry Grattan and Flood and Demosthenes and Edmund Burke" (*U* 7.731–32.) The *Philippics* themselves are relocated and considerably reduced in stature by being assigned to Skin-the-Goat in "Eumaeus," who airs "his grievances in forcible-feeble philippic anent the natural resources of Ireland or something of that sort" (*U* 16.986–87; also note *UNBM* 384:68). In the *Wake's* re-creation of the Wellington Museum, we hear "me Belchum sneaking his phillippy" (*FW* 9.1).

In his life of Demosthenes, Plutarch writes that the young orator overcame his naturally inarticulate and stammering delivery by practice in speaking with pebbles in his mouth (*Lives* 1028). In other reports he declaims at the seashore so as to build up the strength of his voice by making himself heard over the sound of the surf. Joyce was aware of the Athenian statesman's youthful speech defect: "Demosthenes stammered" (*Scribbledehobble* 96 [511]). At times of stress—and there are many of them in the *Wake*—HCE also stammers. Joyce alludes to the ancient orator's speech problem and surfside therapy in HCE's exclamation during his rebuttal of charges pressed by the Four Old Men: "(rookwards, thou seasea stamoror!)" (*FW* 547.25–26). An archival index clarifies another Wakean reference to Demosthenes: "at sea pebbles—/ mouth . . . / . . . climb / ᵇtreadmill / . . . / Demosthenes lives underground" (VI.B.17.35). When Yawn confesses HCE's sins in the text, several of these entries are combined into "[t]he treadmill pebbledropper haha halfahead overground" (*FW* 494.23–24).[15]

Philip II's son and successor, Alexander the Great, plays a decidedly minor role in the works of Joyce. His name is collectively embedded in "*giving* allasundery *the bumfit of the doped*" (*FW* 339.25–26) and "I'd burn the books that grieve you and light an *allassundrian* bompyre" (*FW* 439.34–35; my emphases). The primary allusion in the second citation is to the (incorrectly) alleged burning of the library at Alexandria during its siege by Julius Caesar.[16] The Egyptian port city, founded on the delta of the Nile, is one of fourteen places to which the world conqueror lent his name. In fact, the fame of its Museum and collection of texts was so enduring that Stephen Dedalus fantasized about sending copies of his epiphanies "to all the great libraries of the world, including Alexandria" (*U* 3.142–43). Alexander's wife Roxana appears in a list of Issy's handmaidens in "Anna Livia," where she is given a riverine surname, "Roxana Rohan" (*FW* 212.11).

After Alexander's death in 323 B.C. his empire was divided up by various Macedonian generals. The dynasty that established itself in the kingdom of Egypt was the Ptolemies: "you born ijypt. . . . Well, ptellomey soon" (*FW* 198.1–2). The ruins of the mausoleums of these kings are mentioned (along with megalithic dolmens) in the *Wake:* "the remains of the outworn gravemure where used to be blurried the Ptollmens" (*FW* 13.10–11). An unlikely Semitic member of this royal line is suggested in "Bar Ptolomei" (*FW* 529.34). Here the king's name is preceded by the Aramaic word *bar* (son of) to yield an apostolic "Bartholomew"—or perhaps "Partholan." The latter (also note "parth a lone" [*FW* 15.30]) was a legendary Greek adventurer who is supposed to have colonized Ireland around 1500 B.C. Some say he also invented the letters of the Hebrew, Greek, and Irish alphabets.[17]

Another association is a second-century A.D. astronomer and geographer, Claudius Ptolemaeus, who worked at Alexandria. His eight-book geography is cited several times by Joyce, since the writings of this

Ptolemy mention Ireland. In "Cyclops" the Citizen instructs Bloom: "Where are the Greek merchants that came through the pillars of Hercules . . . with gold and Tyrian purple to sell in Wexford at the fair of Carmen? Read Tacitus and Ptolemy" (*U* 12.1248–51). In his description of Ireland the geographer called Dublin "Eblana," as in *Ulysses* 14.205 and 16.237. In the *Wake,* Dublin's "famous river, called of Ptolemy the Libnia Labia, runneth fast by" (*FW* 540.7–8).

Cleopatra (Father's Glory) is the name given to many of the princesses and queens in the Ptolemaic dynasty. The most famous is Cleopatra VII, the last member of the royal line; after her suicide in 30 B.C. Egypt was annexed as a province of Rome. She is most famous for her love affairs with Julius Caesar and Mark Antony, each the subject of a play: one by Shakespeare, the other by Shaw. In his disquisition on *Hamlet,* Stephen naturally tries to find some biographical analogue in Shakespeare's family: "Who Cleopatra, fleshpot of Egypt, and Cressid and Venus are we may guess" (*U* 9.883–84; also see *U* 9.252). In a burlesque catalog of "Irish heroes and heroines of antiquity," "Cleopatra" is separated from "Julius Caesar" by "Savourneen Deelish" (*U* 12.188). That "heroine" is not a name but the Irish phrase for "My Precious Darling"—the title of a popular song about a soldier who returns from war only to be brought to the cold grave of his beloved.[18] In the *Wake's* "Night Lessons" a marginal "*Cliopatria*" is aligned with "Jeallyous Seizer" and "Malthouse Anthemy" (*FW* 271.L and 3, 6). Mark Antony was notorious for his indiscreet behavior and wild drinking bouts, as is suggested by the nickname and the gist of the following passage: "A cleopatrician in her own right she at once complicates the position while Burrus and Caseous are contending for her misstery by implicating herself with an elusive Antonius, a wop who would appear to hug a personal interest in refined chees of all chades at the same time as he wags an antomine art of being rude like the boor" (*FW* 166.34–167.3).[19]

The Greco-Egyptian queen also appears disguised as an Irish Christian bishop, "Cliopatrick" (*FW* 91.6; see also *FW* 508.23), not far from "Markarthy" (*FW* 91.13). The latter name may represent Mark Antony, or the Phoenician god Melqarth (there is an adjacent "Baalastartey" [*FW* 91.14]), or some unspecified Mr. McCarthy. In the nineteenth century, European powers took many obelisks from Egypt as decorations for their own cities; one of them rises in the *Wake* as "*Cleopater's Needlework*" (*FW* 104.20; also note VI.B.18.191).

Another Hellenistic queen of Egypt is part of the Joycean pageant of Greek history: Berenice, whose name is the Macedonian form of Pherenikē (Bearer of Victory). She was the wife of King Ptolemy III (247–222 B.C.). When her husband went off on a military campaign, she vowed a lock of her hair for his safe return. On his arrival, Berenice deposited the tress in the temple of Arsinoe/Aphrodite.[20] The offering disappeared from the altar, infuriating the king and causing him to suspect the integrity of the donor. The royal astronomer found a solution to the imputation of queenly impiety by claiming that the lock had been supernaturally transported into the sky, where it remains as a constellation. In one of the learned catechetical replies in "Ithaca," Joyce alludes to "the stargroup of the Tress of Berenice" (U 17.1212–13). There is another reference to this legend in "her savuneer dealinsh and delicate her nutbrown glory cloack to Mayde Berenice" (FW 243.25–26). In that passage the faithful queen is conflated with the "Precious Darling" of the Irish song mentioned previously, and her votive offering is identified with the auburn hair of Livia Schmitz, the wife of "Italo Svevo." On several occasions Joyce apologized for stealing the Triestine signora's locks so as to rechannel them into the undulant flow of the River Liffey in Dublin (Letters I.212; III.133, 435).

The opening scene in "Nestor" pivots around an ancient history lesson at Mr. Deasy's school. A student remembers that King Pyrrhus of Epirus in Greece defeated the Romans in "279 B.C.," but he forgets the place. Stephen supplies "Asculum," which jogs the boy to repeat Pyrrhus's comment: "*Another victory like that and we are done for*" (U 2.1–14). Stephen then asks about the end of Pyrrhus, and a bit later wonders what would have happened if the king had not died after having been hit on the head by a roof tile thrown by an old woman. This theme appears again in "Aeolus" (U 2.48–53 and 7.568–75). (Since the famous "Pyrrhic victory" was more significant for Roman than for Greek history, I discuss the details elsewhere.)[21] The ultimate source for the life and deeds of the ill-fated king of Epirus is Plutarch (Lives 467–93).

As the final topic in this review of a Joycean slant on Greek history, the Seven Wonders of the Ancient World go on exhibit here, items that would be most appropriate in a section on ancient geography or on tourism in the last three millennia B.C. Yet there is considerable justification for their inclusion in this chapter, since five of the monuments were located in the Greek-speaking Mediterranean basin; two of these were famous statues in honor of gods of the Hellenic pantheon, and another was a temple of epiphany consecrated to a revered goddess. Moreover, the two non-Greek Wonders were first described in *The Histories* of Herodotus. During his research expedition to Egypt, Herodotus visited the marvels at Giza and thoroughly described the pyramids of the pharaohs Cheops, Chephren, and Mycerinus (*Hist.* 2.124–34). The father of Greek history also made a trip to Babylon, where he saw and later recorded his impressions of the city's great wall of brick and bitumen. There is no mention of the Hanging Gardens in his work, but the riverside esplanades and flood control measures of Queen Semiramis receive considerable attention (*Hist.* 1.178–86).

In the *Wake* Joyce presents two versions of the Seven Wonders of the Ancient World. One occurs in the summary-conclusion of HCE's description of his many marvelous construction projects. The Master Builder laid out a city "with chopes pyramidous [1] and mousselimes [2] and beaconphires [3] and colossets [4] and pensilled turisses [5] for the busspleaches of the summiramies and esplanadas and statuesques [6] and templeogues [7]" (*FW* 553.9–12).

Another list of these prodigious monuments is cleverly built into the start of "Night Lessons," as the twins seek to locate, perhaps as part of a geography project, their tavern-home in Chapelizod. They arrive at that site in a state of alliterative wonder and relief, "having conned the cones [A] and meditated the mured [B] and pondered the pensils [C] and ogled the olymp [D] and delighted in her dianaphous [E] and cacchinated behind his culosses [F], before a mosoleum [G]" (*FW* 261.9–13).

The numbers and letters that I have interpolated into both of those excerpts are designed to facilitate identification and discussion of some of the less evident Wonders. Cheops's pyramid, even when viewed as a cone, cannot be missed (1/A). The funeral monument of King Mausolus at Halicarnassus is combined with a twentieth-century Italian dictator (2/G). The Lighthouse at Alexandria appears only in the first list (3). The Hanging Gardens of Babylon (which Joyce seems to have confused with Queen Semiramis's esplanades) appear in both lists (5/C), signaled by the Latin adjective *pensilis* (hanging). The massive Walls of Babylon rise only in the second catalog (B), where their presence is marked by a term derived from the Latin noun *murus* (wall).[22] The rest of the Wonders are commemorated in both passages in the *Wake:* the Colossus at Rhodes

(4/F), a giant statue of the sun god Helius; the seated ivory and gold statue of Zeus at Olympia (6/D); the temple at Ephesus, where an apparition of the goddess Artemis/Diana was seen in the pediment window (7/E).

Two of the Wonders also appear in other venues in the *Wake*. The passage "Collosul rhodomantic not wert one bronze lie" (*FW* 241.8) refers to the fate of the Colossus; after being toppled by an earthquake about 226 B.C., it lay in ruins until it was carried away as scrap bronze by Arabs who plundered Rhodes in A.D. 654.[23] The Colossus may be present in another passage, "And a capital part for olympics to ply at. Steadyon, Cooloosus" (*FW* 625.21–22). But here I suspect that Joyce or, more likely, ALP has confused the giant statue at Rhodes with the Colosseum in Rome, since the passage clearly envisions a park in which it would be possible to erect a stadium for the revived Olympic Games. Biblical and Mesopotamian attractions are relocated to London in "the flushpots of Euston and the hanging garments of Marylebone" (*FW* 192.29–30; also note VI.C.8.107).

Finally, even though the Walls of Babylon have not made the cut in contemporary lists of the Seven Wonders and even though they appear in only one of Joyce's clusters, these Middle Eastern marvels are prominently placed in another significant passage. The First Question in section I.6 of the *Wake* seeks to uncover the identity of the epic hero Finn MacCool. The last clause in the monumentally long thirteen-and-a-half-page inquiry introduces a Mesopotamian element into the mass of clues: "and an he had the best bunbaked bricks in bould Babylon for his pitching plays he'd be lost the want of his wan wubblin wall?" (*FW* 139.11–13). We need not be archaeologists to detect the kiln-baked bricks and the bitumen mortar of the Walls of Babylon in that thematically alliterative clause.

"Nestor," the second chapter in *Ulysses,* opens in a classroom in which Stephen Dedalus is conducting a review of ancient history. The teacher checks a student's answer with a quick glance at "the name and the date in a gorescarred book" (*U* 2.12–13). This futile exercise in academic "chaps and maps" can be seen as Joyce's narrative statement on the discipline of history in action. A more theoretical judgment is offered near the end of the same chapter: "—History, Stephen said, is a nightmare from which I am trying to awake" (*U* 2.377). Be that as it may, from Danaüs's fifty daughters to a pair of Ptolemaic queens, Joyce displays an impressive command of ancient Greek history. He naturally places special emphasis on the major moments and figures in the political evolution of the premier polis, Athens, with oblique glances at the judicial sobriety of King Philip II of Macedon, Demosthenes' stammer, and two Irish versions of the Seven Wonders of the Ancient World.

2

Historians

Herodotus

For its time and place, *The Histories* of Herodotus is a work of remarkably expansive scope. To set the stage for the wars between Greece and Persia (490–479 B.C.), Herodotus describes the geographical and cultural background and reviews the political history of Lydia, Media, Babylon, Egypt, Persia, Scythia, Libya, Ionia, and various Greek city-states in Asia Minor, on the Aegean islands, and on the European mainland. To record the results of his "research" (*historiē*, in Greek) with the greatest vigor and accuracy, Herodotus traveled to many of these places and gathered firsthand data from native informants. Examples of this on-the-spot methodology include a graphic summary of the methods and various grades of mummification in Egypt (*Hist.* 2.85–90); reports of the circumnavigation of Africa by Phoenician and Carthaginian fleets (*Hist.* 4.42–43); a fantastic description of the giant digger ants of northern India, which mine gold-rich sand and pursue the camels ridden by men who steal their treasure (*Hist.* 3.102–5). For this type of research, in the words of a modern commentator, Herodotus merits the title not only of the father of history; he is also "the father of comparative anthropology."[1]

Ulysses, on the other hand, takes place in a single, quite homogeneous city, over the space of less than a day. Perhaps this difference in narrative compass is the reason why Herodotus shows up only once in Joyce's picaresque history of Bloom's Day. He appears—and there seems no logical explanation for the placement—near the end of the catalog of "the tribal images of many Irish heroes and heroines of antiquity . . . Boss Croker, Herodotus, Jack the Giantkiller" (*U* 12.175–97).

That eccentric citation does not mean that Joyce gave no consideration to other options for accommodating Herodotean material in the process of composing *Ulysses*. Stuart Gilbert reports that Joyce learned from Bérard that the Phoenicians had established a commercial settlement in the Asia Minor city of Miletus, as recorded by Herodotus (*Hist.* 2.112). Bérard strongly suggests that Miletus, with its mixed Semitic and Hellenic population, was the birthplace of the Homeric poems. Gilbert also mentions Herodotus as a source of both information on the morphology of the lotus plant (*Hist.* 2.96, 4.177) and suggestions that Pan was the son of an unchaste Penelope and the god Hermes (*Hist.* 2.145).[2]

There are also several references to the Herodotus in the notesheets that Joyce prepared while composing *Ulysses:* "Herodotus opens hist with Phen. version of rape of Helen" (*UNBM* 106:31). *The Histories* does, in fact, begin with a "Phoenician version" of the origins of East-West problems, namely, the four abductions (two by Europeans, two by Near Easterners) of important women: Io of Argos by Phoenician traders, Europa of Tyre by Cretans, Medea of Colchis by Greek adventurers led by Jason, Helen of Sparta by Prince Paris of Troy. The Persians and the Phoenicians claimed that stealing women was not a serious matter—until the Greeks launched a fleet of ten thousand ships to avenge the rape of Helen (*Hist.* 1.1–4).[3]

Another note, "Story of Darius" (*UNBM* 202:35), may refer to the famous anecdote that Herodotus uses to illustrate how each people regard their own customs as the best and those of foreigners as outlandishly grotesque (*Hist.* 3.38). The king of Persia, Darius, asked some Greek visitors to his court what sum of money would induce them to eat the corpses of their fathers. The Greeks said they would not do it for any amount of money. Then the shah asked some Indian Callatians, who customarily eat their parents' remains, what their price would be for burning their dead fathers. The point Darius made was taken by both groups. Another highly dramatic narrative, as retold by Herodotus, is that of Darius's rise to the throne. The "Story" in the archival entry may refer to the entire Darius-tale, one significant element in which I discuss later. Two additional archival entries in the notesheets merely make the same pun: "ʳDairy arse darius" (*UNBM* 97:117) and "Dairy arse Darius" (*UNBM* 197:82).

The archival note "ᵇCroesus" (*UNBM* 319:146) refers to the fabulously rich king of Lydia, who appears at the beginning of Herodotus's narrative of the Persian assumption of power in the Middle East. The oracle at Delphi told Croesus that if he attacked the forces of Cyrus, he would destroy a mighty empire. He launched his attack but was defeated by the Persians. When challenged, the oracle defended its answer by pointing out that the Lydians had assumed that the empire to be destroyed was their enemies', not their own (*Hist.* 1.46–71, 86). (The story of Croesus's son, who plays a role in the capture of his father by Cyrus, is discussed later in this chapter.) The king's name does appear in *Ulysses*, as a component in a minor catalog in "Circe": ". . . Henri Fleury of Gordon Bennet fame, Sheridan, the quadroon Croesus, the varsity wetbob either from old Trinity" (*U* 15.3003–4). Herring notes the high probability of a textual error here, since the previous notesheet entry is "Sheridan the Quadroon" (*UNBM* 319:145). In all editions of *Ulysses* the comma seems to have been misplaced so that it is not Richard Brinsley Sheridan, but the Lydian king who is labeled a quadroon. A passage in *Finnegans Wake* calls attention to the splendor of the king's riches: "Do you ever heard the story about Helius Croesus, that white and gold elephant in our zoopark?" (*FW* 564.4–6; note VI.B.19.22). Here Joyce is playing with the term *chryselephantine,* an adjective applied to objects made of gold (*chrysos*) and ivory (*elepas, elephantos* in Greek).

Joyce commemorates Herodotus early in the *Wake.* Just before a review of some significant dates in Irish history, the name of the father of history is incorporated into a reference to the *Annals of the Four Masters:* "saith our herodotary Mammon Lujius in his grand old historiorum" (*FW* 13.20– 21). The Greek writer's penchant for recording unfamiliar customs and exotic rituals is acknowledged in two other citations: "hairyoddities" (*FW* 275.N5)[4] and "horodities" (*FW* 614.2).

The names of several of the Persian shahs also appear in the *Wake.* "Darius" (*FW* 138.27) and "Artaxerxes" (*FW* 337.36) do not seem to have any thematic purpose. "Egyptus, the incenstrobed" and "Cyrus" appear in a list of traditional enemies in "Night Lessons" (*FW* 263.6–7); Xerxes can be detected at the end of a commingled list of geometric-ethnic terms in the same section: "anymeade or persan, comic cuts and series exerxeses" (*FW* 286.7–8). Yawn is described as an Oriental potentate or a Persian provincial governor: "asprawl he was laying too amengst the poppies . . . far more similar to a *satrap* he lay there with unctuous beauty" (*FW* 476.19–23; my emphasis [note also VI.B.1.150]).

Several of the battles between the Persians and the Greeks, first reported by Herodotus, twist their way into the *Wake.* The victory at Marathon (*Hist.* 6.110–17) is mixed into the feats of Wellington and

Bismarck: "This is the bissmark of the marathon merry of the jinnies they left behind them" (*FW* 9.32–33). Perhaps Joyce felt that the campaigns of the Iron Duke and the Iron Chancellor were as momentous for the course of European history as the Greek defeat of the Persians in 490 B.C. The presence of "jinnies" in the passage just quoted is puzzling. I know of no account, in Herodotus or elsewhere, that mentions any use of donkeys (jennies) at Marathon—or any leaving behind of their pack animals by either side before the battle. In the absence of such historical evidence, prudence would dictate labeling the term *jinnies* an allusion to the eighteenth-century popular song "The Girl I Left behind Me."[5] Yet there is a crossed Notebook entry that does in fact link the two elements, at least in Joyce's archival imagination: "ᵗdonkey marathon" (VI.B.2.143). The momentous Greek victory is also mentioned in *Ulysses* by Mr. Simon Dedalus. It is part of his dismissal of the florid prose of the archbishop's letter that has been delivered to the newspaper office: "And Xenophon looked upon Marathon . . . and Marathon looked on the sea" (*U* 7 254–55).[6]

There is another reputed reference to the battle of Marathon in the essay-topic section of "Night Lessons." King Darius's name is keyed to the maxim "If You Do It Do It Now" (*FW* 307.L1 and 27). McHugh glosses this combination with the comment that the "Persian King [was] defeated at Marathon because the Greeks attacked immediately." Historically speaking, it was the Greek forces under Miltiades who *delayed* committing themselves to battle (*Hist.* 6.110), while Darius is depicted as a man of almost immediate action (*Hist.* 3.135, 7:1). Thus, it would be more accurate, in purely Herodotean terms, to ascribe the dilatory Persian reaction at Marathon to the Persian field commander, not to the shah. The commander of the Greek forces is commemorated in the same section of the *Wake*. "*Miltiades Strategos*" appears immediately after "*Pompeius Magnus*" in the marginal list of names; the suggested topic for this pair is "The Roman Pontiffs and the Orthodox Churches" (*FW* 307.L1 and 17–18). Pompey the Great was an outstanding Roman general; in the entry just cited, the term in apposition to Miltiades is the Greek word for general (*strategos*). In the *Wake* such references to the military prowess of ancient Greece and Rome are typically applied to the later religious conflicts between the Roman Catholic Church led by the pope and the Greek Orthodox Church led by its patriarch.

During the second Persian invasion of the Greek mainland by King

Xerxes, the first notable battle was the glorious defeat of Leonidas and the Spartan rear guard at Thermopylae (480 B.C.). The defenders were overwhelmed when the Greeks' position and a secret way around the mountain pass were revealed to the Persians by Ephialtes (*Hist.* 7.212). Joyce characterizes the traitor with a distorted phrase from the *Odes* of Horace: "Ephialtes . . . *simplex mendaciis*" (*FW* 493.23–24). As noted previously in regard to Danaüs's disobedient daughter, a literal translation of the Latin is "simple in her/his betrayals"; Joyce obviously intends his readers to think that the traitor was "simply mendacious."[7] In "Night Lessons" the commander of the brave Spartan forces at Thermopylae is mentioned, "*Leonidas*" (*FW* 307.L1), but the adjacent essay topic, "The Kettle-Griffith-Moynihan Scheme for a New Electricity Supply" (*FW* 307.9–10), is puzzling. The relevance of Arthur Griffith would appear to be tangential, since the founder of Sinn Féin, while having significant military experience, did not die heroically in battle. McHugh suggests that the patriot's name has been conflated here with that of the engineer Griffith who was involved with Kettle and Moynihan in a plan to provide hydroelectric power to Dublin in the 1920s. Perhaps the source of that electric power was a thermal spring, which might, in Joyce's demythologizing imagination, supply a tenuous connection with Thermopylae (Greek for "hot [spring] gates").

One of the most detailed of Herodotus's ethnographic surveys is his description of Egypt, which comprises all of book 2 of *The Histories*. At the very start of that review, Herodotus reports a scientifically controlled experiment conducted by the Pharaoh Psammeticus (seventh century B.C.). Prior to his reign, the Egyptians believed that they were the most ancient race on earth. Seeking empirical proof of that presumption, the pharaoh ordered two newborn babies to be placed in an isolated cottage. The infants were to be given goat's milk by a shepherd, who was strictly forbidden to speak in their presence. When the pair were two years old they repeatedly begged for βεκός (*bekos*). The pharaoh inquired and learned that those syllables were the Phrygian word for bread. Thus, the ruler of Egypt conceded the superior antiquity of the Phrygians—and their language. The priests of Ptah/Hephaestus at Memphis told Herodotus about this royal experiment in comparative linguistics (*Hist.* 2.2). In "Night Lessons" Joyce reveals that Shem was an infant prodigy in mathematics, who had learned very early to count on his fingers: "manual arith . . . which was the *bekase* he knowed from his cradle" (*FW* 282.8–10; my emphasis). In the italicized word, which is lifted from Mark Twain's *Huckleberry Finn*, I detect an echo of the primitive staple of Phrygian life, *bekos*.

A Notebook entry signals an ultimately Herodotean source for a common geographical point. In his introductory comments on Egypt the Greek historian writes that that land is "a gift of the river" (*Hist.* 2.5). Joyce transposes the fluminal benefit of the Nile to Ireland in a note that surges with Wakean force, as ALP is explicitly merged with the Liffey: "Dublin gift of Δ" (VI.B.35.98).

The most knowledgeable of Herodotus's native informants were the priests in Heliopolis at the Temple of the Sun (*helios*, in Greek) (*Hist.* 2.3). The *Wake* alludes to that city at least twice: "Heliopolitan" (*FW* 530.16) and "Heliotropolis" (*FW* 594.8). A Latinate form of the god's name appears along with the name of the superrich king of Lydia, "Helius Croesus," who is connected with a gilded statue in Dublin's great "zoopark" (*FW* 564.5–6). That place is Phoenix Park; its primary monument is topped with a representation of the phoenix, the sacred bird of ancient Heliopolis. Herodotus gives the earliest account of the flight from Arabia to Egypt by the phoenix. It arrives once every five hundred years for the purpose of embalming its phoenix progenitor in a myrrh egg, which is deposited on a funeral pyre at the Temple of the Sun (*Hist.* 2.73). That exotic ornithological detail is thematically relevant, since phoenixes, in every shape and form, hover over all the *Wake*.

The Roman historian Tacitus includes more specific information about the miraculous life cycle of the phoenix. The mature bird prepares the body of its parent phoenix for sacred burial and immolation on the altar of the Sol (Sun) at Heliopolis. Moreover, when a phoenix realizes that the time of its own death is near, it builds a nest on the ground and infuses into it the force to make life (*vim genitalem*). From this creative deposit a new bird rises to perpetuate the tradition of filial piety, flight, fire, and renewal (Tacitus, *Annals* 6.28). Joyce mixes the Herodotean and Tacitean versions of the tale: "the phoenix be his pyre, the cineres [Latin for "ashes"] his sire" (*FW* 128.34–35; also note *FW* 265.8–9 and 621.1–2 and "ᵍPhoenix" [VI.B.13.16]).

Herodotus indicates that some of his information about Egypt came from pharaonic records, compiled by temple priests, covering a long span of time. These documents include "the names of three hundred and thirty monarchs, in the same number of generations" (*Hist.* 2.100). Joyce may have intended a contrast between the pageant of these dynasties and the traditional Greek method of designating time periods in terms of Olympic years: "olympiading even till the eleventh dynasty" (*FW* 84.31–32).[8] That citation appears in a passage in which HCE's crime is alleged to be as infamous as any deed in the annals of world history.

A bit later in the *Wake,* among the idiosyncratic habits recited in the "First Question" is the claim that HCE "eats with doors open and ruts with gates closed" (*FW* 129.19–20). There is nothing particularly odd about this domestic behavior, but the formulation of the contrast brings to mind a similar list of strange (by Greek standards) customs that Herodotus observed in Egypt. In the midst of a long catalog of such "reversals," he reports that "to ease themselves the Egyptians go indoors, but eat outside in the streets, on the theory that what is unseemly but necessary should be done in private, and what is not unseemly should be done openly" (*Hist.* 2.35).

In *Ulysses* Joyce alludes to another aspect of ancient Egyptian history that has its ultimate source in Herodotus. As Bloom wanders through Dublin on his way to lunch in "Lestrygonians," he contemplates the impermanence of even the greatest construction projects: "Piled up in cities, worn away age after age. Pyramids in sand. Built on bread and onions" (*U* 8.489–90). The two foodstuffs named were staples in the diets of ancient slaves; Herodotus stresses (mistakenly, in the opinion of modern historians) that the great pyramid of Cheops was constructed by the forced labor of the pharaoh's enslaved subjects. In his account of the project, Herodotus explicitly mentions a hieroglyphic inscription on the pyramid that records the immense amount spent on "radishes, onions, and leeks" for the laborers—in addition to the sum for their rations of "bread and clothing" (*Hist.* 2.125). The most famous of the pyramid builders is mentioned twice in the *Wake:* once with an appended pseudo-Byzantine title in an HCE acrostic, "first pharoah, Humpheres Cheops Exarchas" (*FW* 62.20–21); then with an acknowledgment of his achievements, "chopes pyramidous and moussilimes" (*FW* 553.10). That last phrase also acknowledges another of the seven wonders of the ancient world, the Mausoleum at Halicarnassus, Herodotus's birthplace.

The final example of Joyce's recycling of Herodotean material in the *Wake* can be seen only after a microscopic examination of the text. Near the end of HCE's scrutiny by the Four Old Men, they pose a series of incriminating questions to the defendant. My case for Herodotean allusion depends on three primary phrases, with several adjacent supporting items, in this interrogation. The evidence strongly suggests that Joyce included in his exposé of HCE's career some material that is derived from Herodotus's narratives of the lives of three Middle Eastern potentates, one Lydian and two Persian.

The first analogue is King Croesus. Herodotus reports that one of his sons was a deaf-mute (*kōphos* in Greek; *Hist.* 1.34). An oracle promised that the son's first word would be spoken on a day of sorrow, as happened when an invading Persian soldier penetrated the defenses of the Lydian palace and was about to cut the king down. The terrified son cried out, "Do not kill Croesus, man!" (*Hist.* 1.85). In the report of the offenses of HCE, there is mention of "that surdumutual son of his" (*FW* 530.10), and "surdumutual" evokes *sourd,* the French word for deaf. HCE's son's handicap is expressed more crudely in the nearby "deffydowndummies" (*FW* 530.3). The king's name is thinly disguised as "Cruses" (*FW* 530.13), and his fabulous riches are modestly displayed in "wealthy" (*FW* 530.9).

The second analogue is King Cambyses, the Persian ruler who first invaded Egypt. On an inspection tour of his conquests he mocked the temple priests and fatally wounded the sacred Apis-calf at Memphis. To avenge this sacrilege the Egyptian god destroyed the shah's already unstable mind (*Hist.* 3.27–29). Herodotus characteristically offers a more rational explanation for these events: Cambyses suffered from a "great sickness, which some people call 'the holy disease'" (*Hist.* 3.33). In other words, the king had epilepsy. In the *Wake* this Herodotean account is cryptically transferred to the indictment of HCE: "to see the fallensickners aping the buckleybackers" (*FW* 530.1–2). A common term for epilepsy is "the falling sickness." The participle "aping" in the *Wake* citation is, in Greek, four-fifths of the accusative case of the name of the god Apis—just as it appears in the Herodotean text that assigns supernatural retribution as the reason for Cambyses' madness: *dia ton Apin* (because of Apis) (*Hist.* 3.33).

The third analogue is King Darius. After the death of the childless Cambyses, a group of seven noble Persian conspirators overthrew the power of the priestly Magi. The members of the cabal then decided how to determine which one of them would be their new leader: As they rode into the city on the following day, "he whose horse first neighed after dawn would have the throne" (*Hist.* 3.84). Darius's clever groom circumvented chance by leading his master's horse to a spot along the route where the stallion had mated with a mare on the night before the test.

When the horse came to that location on the outskirts of the city the next morning, he neighed. Others say the groom had rubbed his hand on a mare's genitals, then when the sun rose, put his hand on the nose of Darius's horse, who neighed at once (*Hist.* 3.86–87). The nearby phrases "rampaging the roads" (*FW* 530.15) and "under the noses" (*FW* 530.16) refer, respectively, to the alternative versions of the groom's ploy. In either case, in the same Wakean passage as all the previous citations, there is a forceful allusion to this piece of Persian trickery: "by offers of vacancies from females in this city, neighing after the man and his outstanding attractions" (*FW* 530.6–8). In this account of HCE's indiscretions, Joyce has cleverly reversed the direction of the sexual energy: The females neigh after the male.

One must grant the extreme improbability of the proximate presence of the key phrases concerning three Herodotean potentates in the compass of ten Wakean lines. Equally improbable, however, is the chance that the allusions to Croesus's deaf-mute son, Cambyses' divine madness, and Darius's aroused stallion are the result of some cosmic accident or creative coincidence. There is no acknowledgment of a source here, nor are there any archival references to these topics. The essential—and the only common—element in each of these anecdotes is its source in Herodotus. This is not to claim that Joyce necessarily had a text and a translation of that work on his desk when he composed various drafts of section III.3 of the *Wake*. Perhaps one of his "helpers" supplied the information; perhaps the incidents were picked up from a popular book or article on memorable Middle Eastern rulers. It is not likely that a classical scholar would have had a reason for connecting these odd moments in ancient history; rather, the selection and emphasis are characteristic of a novelist's eye for gripping detail. At any rate, *The Histories* of Herodotus, with its vivid dynastic color, must be the ultimate source of the royal Lydian-Persian elements so brilliantly woven into the indictment of HCE's distinctly commonplace indiscretions.[9]

Thucydides

A second great name in the list of ancient Greek historians, Thucydides, seems to have left no mark whatsoever on the works of Joyce. The subject of the historian's *Peloponnesian War* is the momentous conflict between Athens and Sparta (431–404 B.C.). This work is packed with episodes and speeches that might have been exploited—the plague, Pericles' funeral oration, the Melian dialogue, the disaster of the Sicilian expedition; but I cannot detect any Joycean references that point to this source. Nor are there any Thucydidean entries in the notesheets or Notebooks.

Xenophon

On the other hand, there is clear evidence that Joyce was familiar with the author, title, and at least one famous phrase from Xenophon's *Anabasis*. This work, often titled *The Persian Expedition* in English, is an eyewitness account of the retreat of ten thousand Greek mercenaries after the unexpected failure of Cyrus's expedition to place himself on the throne of Persia. Their trek through the plains and mountains of Mesopotamia and along the shore of the Black Sea finally brings the survivors to civilization. As has been mentioned previously, Simon Dedalus linked "Xenophon" with "Marathon" in his dismissal of archepiscopal prose (*U* 7.254). His reason for doing so has far more to do with a desire to parade a smidgeon of misinformation about ancient Greek history than with any hidden connection between the Dublin churchman and the ancient battle. The names in his statement, two words of the same rhythm in near-rhyme, form a pseudoantique jingle; moreover, the historical Xenophon never turned the postmodern gaze of his narrative toward Marathon.

In the *Wake's* "Night Lessons" there are two references to Xenophon. The first is the marginal presence of a pair of distinctly Greek-rooted nouns, "Catastrophe and Anabasis" (*FW* 304.L2). The literal translation of these terms is "down-turn and up-going." In a Xenophonic context (signaled by *Anabasis*), these words summarize the content of the historian's narrative: the *catastrophic* isolation of the Greek mercenary soldiers in the heart of Persian territory and their heroic *march upcountry* to safety. In the adjacent text of the *Wake*, the word "retorting," which contains the Latin root for "turn" (*tort*) and the nearby "reborn" (*FW* 304.27), is also meant to suggest *Anabasis*. Shortly thereafter "*Xenophon*" himself appears in the list of classical and biblical heroes; the concomitant essay topic seems to overlap with that for Darius: "Delays are Dangerous. Vitavite!" (*FW* 308.L1 and l). I interpret the second element to mean "Avoid [from the Latin imperative *vita*] quickly [the French adverb *vite*]!" During the dangerous march from the Tigris to Thrace, Xenophon and his fellow

Greek commanders constantly urged the troops to move with speed, avoiding delay in both attack and flight.

Early in *Ulysses* Buck Mulligan tries a bit of linguistic one-upmanship with a Homeric apostrophe to the "wine-dark sea"; that epic formula is followed by the most memorable words from Xenophon's *Anabasis:* "Thalatta! Thalatta!" (*U* 1.80). After months in the snow and mountains of Armenia, the Greek troops arrived at Mount Thekes, from which the Black Sea is visible. They shouted *"thalatta, thalatta"* (the sea, the sea [*Anabasis* 4.7]). This cry is repeated throughout the *Wake,* frequently in aquatic contexts: "The letter! The litter!" (*FW* 93.24); "The latter! The latter!" (*FW* 100.2); "ye seal that lubs you lassers, Thallasee" (*FW* 324.9); "(tha lassy! tha lassy!)" (*FW* 328.29);[10] "Galata! Galata!)" (*FW* 547.32; cf. Vl.B.4.124); "kolassa kolassa!" (*FW* 551.35); "The leader, The leader!" (*FW* 593.13); and "Sea, sea" (*FW* 626.7).

After that cascade of marine references, it is probably anticlimactic to point out a final allusion to Xenophon's history. No one who has read the *Anabasis,* however, can forget the recurrent Persian term for a land-measure of approximately three and a half miles, *parasang*. The word is frequently left in its native form in English translations, as it is in the Greek text. Since the ten thousand soldiers marched so relentlessly toward the sea, *parasangs* are all over the place in Xenophon's narrative. Joyce acknowledges their ubiquity with a formulaic Ulyssean translation, "Thence they advanced five parasangs" (*U* 14.1450), and a Wakean echo, "parasangs" (*FW* 586.27).

With a single extraordinarily cryptic exception, Joyce's use of the major ancient historians is unremarkable. In his archival notes and in the texts of his last two works, there are occasional allusions to names and material that ultimately stem from Herodotus and Xenophon (but not Thucydides). The exception to this largely mediated information is the staccato reference to crises in the lives of three Middle Eastern potentates within thirteen lines of the *Wake*. I have found no Notebook entries on the son of Croesus, the madness of Cambyses, or the stallion of Darius; but the specific detail and diction in this compact cluster of exotic allusions preclude narrative coincidence.

3

Gods and Mythology

As he makes himself comfortable with a full pipe and a half glass of whisky at the bar of the Ormond Hotel, Simon Dedalus muses, "By Jove, . . . I often wanted to see the Mourne mountains" (*U* 11.219). At the National Library Buck Mulligan warns Stephen Dedalus to be on guard against Leopold Bloom: "O, I fear me, he is Greeker than the Greeks. His pale Galilean eyes were on her mesial grove. Venus Kallipyge" (*U* 9.614–16). Those two remarks, each uttered at an archetypical Ulyssean site—a library and a bar—echo the standard forms of mythological vocabulary in turn-of-the-century Dublin. The gods and goddesses of the ancient classical world were traditionally invoked by their Latin names (Jove/Jupiter, Venus) rather than the Greek forms (Zeus, Aphrodite), even though an ostentatiously Greek epithet, *Kallipyge* (having beautiful buttocks), is appended in the second case. The custom of using Roman terminology was widespread in the English-speaking world during the Victorian and Edwardian eras. In schools and in museums, as well as throughout the classics of English literature, Mars was better known than Ares, Minerva than Athena.

Joyce's preference in mythological nomenclature conforms to local usage. Even in jotting down bits of exotic information in his pre-text notes, he almost always selects a Latin form. That practice, faithful to his sources and times, is reflected in his fiction. As a consequence, a significant number of Joyce's mythological allusions are identified and discussed in my *Latin and Roman Culture in Joyce*. Its long chapter on "Gods, Goddesses, and Ritual" covers some of the same Olympian and Infernal ground as this book. In the previous volume the detail and the emphasis are usually derived from the Ovidian or Vergilian versions of the traditional tales; in this book the principle of inclusion is the presence of a distinctly Greek slant in terminology, geography, or cultural idiosyncracy.[1]

One of the most engaging features of classical mythology is the fluidity of its content. Within broad perimeters, none of the details of the Olympian or Heroic tales was fixed; there was no official version from which it would be heretical to depart. Various artists, in different times, places, and media, re-presented the myths, giving them their own twists. The Greek tragedians, especially Euripides, kept their audiences alert to unexpected manipulation of the traditional plots of their plays. In selecting a model version of a myth for this chapter, then, I emphasize those elements that most closely correspond to Joyce's version. But neither he nor I can be definitive on this turbulent aspect of ancient culture.[2]

During the period of Greece's grandeur and Rome's glory, Zeus/Jupiter occupied the Olympian throne as the Father of Men and Gods (*Iliad* 1.544, *Odyssey* 1.28). Such was not always the case. Even among the immortals there had been several dynastic upheavals, with attendant depositions, celestial civil wars, royal exiles, attempted coups, and Olympian paranoia.

The first divine king and queen of the world were Uranus (heaven, sky) and Gaia (earth). The primary function of this transparently cosmogenic royal pair (she was his mother-wife) was to begin the process of populating the world with immortal progeny. This activity continued at a furious pace. Uranus, however, started to imprison his huge and sometimes monstrous children within Gaia. She retaliated by inducing a son, the Titan Cronus, to castrate his godly but abusive father. Glasheen suggests that the first-dynasty divine king is nominally commemorated in Shaun's cry, "—Horraymost! . . . Heavenly blank!" (*FW* 413.32–33). Here the Latin exhortation *oremus* (let us pray) is balanced by a wish for celestial thanks. The planet named after Uranus can also be glimpsed in the midst of a highly astronomical setting in which Wakean events "will be known through all Urania soon" (*FW* 583.16; also see *U* 17.1095). Queen Gaia is more obviously situated in "the attitude of Gea-Tellus" (*U* 7.2313). Molly Bloom's position in bed is described as being like that of the great Earth-Mother whose name is given in both Greek and Latin.[3] That etymological title of honor is also applied to ALP in the *Wake:* she is "Gran Geamatron" (*FW* 257.4–5) and the "eternal geomater" (*FW* 296.31–297.1). The exclamation "Gam on, Gearge!" (*FW* 599.18) appears to be Joyce's unscientific attempt to create a feminine version of the name George (farmer). Its genuine Greek components are *geō-*, the combination form of the noun meaning earth, and the verbal root *ergō* (to work).[4]

After his castration by his son Cronus (in mythology, punishment usually fits the crime), Uranus disappears from the heavenly scene. The avenger-usurper, Cronus/Saturn, assumed the throne and married his sister, the Titan Rhea. Cronus had been warned that one of his offspring would overthrow him. The new royal pair thus conceived children at a more moderate pace than their first-dynasty parents. Just to be sure, however, Cronus swallowed each of Rhea's babies as soon as the immortal infant was born. In this manner, Hestia, Demeter, Hera, Hades, and Poseidon were effectively imprisoned in their father's stomach-womb (see VIII.A.5.26). Queen Rhea resented this mockery of her female reproductive power and the maltreatment of her children. When Zeus was born, she hid him in a cave and presented Cronus an oblong stone wrapped in swaddling clothes. He swallowed it. The site of the cave is either Mount Dicte or Mount Ida, both on Crete; there a goat (*aix, aigos,* in Greek) named Amaltheia suckled the hidden godling among her own offspring. All of these details of Zeus's infancy are recorded in the *Wake:* "Ida" (*FW* 276.F4), "amaltheouse" (*FW* 338.20), "Cave of kids" (*FW* 261.15), *"For all us kids under his aegis"* (*FW* 276.L3). When Zeus matured, he confronted his father and forced him to vomit forth the imprisoned siblings. In a battle of cosmic proportions, the younger gods triumphed over Cronus and his second-generation allies, the Titans. Zeus assumed the throne of Olympus and assigned to his brothers and sisters the rule of various parts of the world. Their parents, the deposed king and queen, were sent into perpetual exile in the Islands of the Blest, far out in the Ocean.

The grotesque events surrounding the rise and fall of Cronus are cryptically summarized in a phrase that immediately follows a reference to his deposed father, Uranus: "Like jealously titaning fear" (*FW* 583.17). The suggestion that that passage refers to the anxiety for his crown that gripped Cronus is reinforced by an adjacent phrase: "like rumour rhean round the planets" (*FW* 583.17). Here mythology combines with astronomy (Rhea is a satellite of the planet Saturn) so as to encapsulate the paranoia of King Cronus and the fame that Queen Rhea won by concealing Zeus and helping to free her immortal children. They became the senior members of the extended royal family of the third Olympian dynasty.

Even in ancient times, Cronus's name was confused with the similar-sounding Greek word *chronos* (time). That etymological blur between an initial *kappa* (*c/k*) and *chi* (*ch*) is responsible for naming one of the *Wake's* Four Old Men "the old croniony" (*FW* 390.6–7) and "the poor old chronometer" (*FW* 391.15). In a May 28, 1929, letter to Miss Weaver, Joyce suggests a graphic representation of the glide in divine identity: "I have also proposed to a young Dublin artist to do an illustration for the old earwig's funeral (Time, Saturun [Cronus])" (*SL* 342). A bit later in the *Wake's* narrative we learn that "O'Cronione lags acrumbling in his *sands* but his *sunsunsuns* still tumble on" (*FW* 415.21–22; my emphasis). Joyce's mythological arithmetic is absolutely correct here: Cronus's three *sons* (Zeus, Poseidon, Hades) still rule, although only the youngest, Zeus the Deliverer, reigns in the solar system.

Zeus (Jupiter/Jove)

Greek gods and heroes are frequently known by a patronymic, a name derived from that of their fathers—even if the paternal-filial relationship was less than ideal. Zeus, for example, is sometimes called Cronion (son of Cronus). Another form of the divine patronymic appears in one of Joyce's Zürich notes for *Ulysses:* "Zeus Kronides" (VIII.A.5.26). As mentioned before, the name of the second-dynasty king is often merged with that of Chronus (time). Joyce perpetuates that confusion: "And so time wags on: but father *Cronion* has dealt lightly here" (*U* 14.1336; my emphasis). An ancient Greek would have understood Zeus to be designated by the italicized word, and Joyce clearly implies the presence of Father Time in the passage. The same etymological error is found in "Bester-farther Zeuts, the Aged One" (*FW* 414.35–36). Here, however, the Olympian's initial epithet takes on a competitive dimension with an abbreviated version of the modern Olympic motto, "Higher, Farther, Faster." The first Olympic Games were founded by Heracles to honor Zeus in 776 B.C. A late archival note "ᵍolympic games" (VI.B.47.56) was placed in the text near the conclusion of Anna Livia's monologue, alongside two possible venues for the competition: "And a capital part for olympics to ply at. Steadyon. Cooloosus" (*FW* 625.21–22; also note VI.B.16.31).[5]

As king of gods and men, Zeus is invoked on at least two occasions in the *Wake*. In their interrogation of Yawn, the Four Old Men demand to hear what he knows "about our sovereign beingstalk, Tonans Tomazeus.

O dite!" (*FW* 504.18–19). That is, what did the divine rod of existence ("being-stalk") have to say as the lord of the universe ("sovereign being's talk")? The Four know that Zeus may well reply by thundering (*tonans* in Latin), and they suggest that he has the same power as the Babylonian god Tammuz, whose name means "the son who rises." Finally, they simultaneously order that Yawn "speak" (*dite* in Italian) and command that all must "listen" (*audite* in Latin). Zeus's words are especially worthy of attention because, in addition to all his other spheres of activity, he was the oracular god at Dodona. At that hallowed site the god's answers to requests for supernatural information were given by the wind rustling through the leaves of his totem trees, giant oaks. Joyce recorded this fact (but apparently never used it in *Ulysses*) in a Zürich notebook: "Zeus Dodonaios" (VIII.A.5.5). In a second interrogatory context in the *Wake*, Yawn calls upon the chief Olympian to back up some particularly salacious testimony about "bisectualism": "zwelf me Zeus" (*FW* 524.36 and 30). Here Joyce elides the English expression "So help me God" and alludes (*Zwölf* means twelve in German) to the number of Olympians over whom Zeus is the High King.

In *Finnegans Wake* a truncated alphabetical list of the ancient gods begins with "ardent Ares" and ends with "zealous Zeus" (*FW* 269.17–18).[6] There is no activity in which Zeus displayed more zeal than in his ardent pursuit of women, human and divine. None of his most notorious amorous adventures seem to have left a discernible trace in Joyce's fiction, but there are several extended archival indices on this topic. In the notesheets for *Ulysses* the following entry appears: "Golden rain: Jove fucked Alcmene as Amphitryon (Helios) for 3 long days when he came she knew. Tiresias revealed last mortal fucked by Jove. Amph. burned her Jove sent rain dies in Thebes, Jove and Hermes to bring to Elys. Hermes put stones in coffin. Herocleades [*sic*] couldn't carry" (*UNBM* 282: 125–29).[7]

In that long note, the first item, "Golden rain," refers to the disguise adopted by Zeus to outwit the guardians of Danaë's chastity. Her father, King Acrisius of Argos, had been warned by an oracle that his grandson would kill him. To avoid that outcome he imprisoned his daughter in a tower of bronze, watched by teams of sentries. Zeus first laughed at the mortal attempt to block destiny, and then converted himself into a shower of gold, which penetrated the fortress and impregnated Danaë. The bulk of the note deals with the most ingenious of the many disguises that Zeus used in his earthly love affairs.[8] When he wanted to possess Alcmene (whose husband, Amphitryon of Thebes, was on a military campaign), Zeus assumed her husband's mortal form. Helius cooperated in prolonging what Alcmene thought was a legitimate night of reunion; he delayed the rise of the sun for three days. When Amphitryon actually did return, he was amazed that his wife already knew all the details of his adventures. Alcmene, also puzzled, explained to Amphitryon that he had told her everything in their bed the night before. The famous seer Tiresias finally cleared up this situation by revealing Zeus's disguise. In due course, twins were born to the pair: Iphicles, a mortal, and Heracles, the god's son.[9]

The last two and a half lines of the note refer to the variant epilogues to Zeus's visit to Alcmene. Some versions say that Amphitryon tried to punish his wife by burning her to death. Zeus rescued his temporary mistress by sending a violent thunderstorm that extinguished the blaze. When Alcmene died, Zeus dispatched Hermes to take her to eternal rest in Elysium, which in early Greek mythology is often associated with the Islands of the Blest. To conceal Zeus's extraordinary gift of divine assumption, Hermes filled Alcmene's coffin with a large stone. At her funeral, her son's sons (the Heraclids) could not lift the coffin, discovered the substituted stone, and set it up in a shrine to their family in Thebes.

These details and Joyce's notes on them testify to the fascinating variety of the seamy tales about Zeus's loves. With a single possible exception, however, none of the mythological material discussed here was actually used in *Ulysses*. The exception appears to be a conflation of classical and nineteenth-century Irish myth: Some of his most ardent supporters claimed that Charles Stewart Parnell did not die in 1891. They said that "he is not in that grave at all. That the coffin was filled with stones. That one day he will come again." The speakers in this latter-day speculation are Paddy Dignam's mourners on a visit to "the chief's grave" in "Hades" (*U* 6.923–24 and 919).

Two other archival notes for *Ulysses* refer to the text of Homer's *Odyssey*. They indicate that during the process of gathering material for his book, Joyce made occasional reference not only to the Butcher and Lang translation but also to a text in which the original Greek forms are printed. As it stands in transcription, Joyce's note reads "ὁδόν / Zeus" (*UNBM* 120:50). An annotation ("The Greek word is an epithet for Zeus, meaning 'farsighted'") strongly suggests that a second Greek word has been accidentally omitted in Joyce's composition or in Herring's transmission of the entry.[10] In Homer's text the essential part of the line is ὁδόν εὐρύοπα ("farseeing [Zeus devised] a path") (*Odyssey* 14.235). The epithet, significant for its odd grammatical form, is what attracted Joyce's attention—and that of countless other commentators. A second note reads "ᵇloosened many a man's thighs" (*UNBM* 391:155). This seems to me to be a variation on one of the epic formulas that emphasize the success of a warrior in battle: "[the combatant] loosed the knees of many a man." A Homeric source for Joyce's note is *Odyssey* 14.236, a single line after the phrase quoted in the first notesheet entry discussed here. The "combatant" in this Homeric instance is Zeus himself. Odysseus has returned to Ithaca and, still disguised as a beggar, is telling the loyal swineherd, Eumaeus, a trumped-up tale of the battles at Troy, where, as Zeus willed, many men met their fate. Joyce substituted "thighs" for Homer's formulaic "knees." When that crossed archival note was used in the novel (*U* 16.1355), the context is definitely erotic—and dangerous for the man involved. The feminine pronoun in the line cited, as well as the placement in the plot, also suggest another Homeric source (see chapter 4 for a review of the role of Helen of Troy in the *Iliad*).

There is a final suggestive phrase from the *Wake* that deserves to be cited concerning Zeus and his zealous loves. The thighs in this case are not those of an Achaean or Trojan warrior but those of an unspecified goddess (*thea* in Greek): "her theas thighs" (*FW* 613.22). The awesome king of the gods is also nearby: "The folgor of the frightfools is olympically optimominous" (*FW* 613.28–29). The Latin *fulgor* means stroke of lightning, Zeus's favorite weapon; one of his Latin titles is *Juppiter Optimus* (the best). In this case he is ominously brandishing, on Mount Olympus, his maximum divine threats (*minae* in Latin), or perhaps he is poised to strike from the highest Olympian battlements (also *minae* in Latin).

Hera (Juno)

Hera was the third-dynasty Queen of Heaven. As the sister-wife of philandering Zeus, she had a domestic life that was none too happy. Most of her mythological adventures are attempts to prevent or, more frequently, to get revenge for her husband's amorous insults. Her hidden and repeated name in the following sentence is Joyce's way of putting that situation in the best possible light: "She is my bestpreserved wholewife, sowell *her a*s *hera*fter" (*FW* 533.4; my emphases).

Hera's most memorable stratagem in the *Iliad* is her seduction of Zeus,

who had forbidden the gods to meddle in the battles being fought
between the beachhead of the Greeks and the ramparts of Troy. She
resorts to this extreme measure so that, while the king is taking a post-
coital nap, Poseidon can help to defend the Greek ships from a furious
Trojan attack. In this episode, called the *Dios apatē* (the deception of Zeus),
the goddess makes elaborate preparations in her Olympian boudoir:

> With ambrosia first did she cleanse every stain from her winsome
> body, and anointed her with olive oil, ambrosial, soft, and of a sweet
> savour. . . . Therewith she anointed her fair body, and combed her
> hair, and with her hands plaited her shining tresses, fair and ambrosial,
> flowering from her immortal head. Then she clad her[self] in her fra-
> grant robe that Athene wrought delicately for her, and therein set
> many things beautifully made, and fastened it over her breast with
> clasps of gold. And she girdled it with a girdle arrayed with a hundred
> tassels, and she set earrings in her pierced ears, earrings of three drops,
> and glistening, therefrom shone grace abundantly. (*Iliad* 14.170–83)[11]

This description is capped by Hera's appeal to Aphrodite for her magic
sash, "wherein are all her enchantments; therein are love, and desire, and
loving converse, that steals the wits even of the wise" (*Iliad* 14.216–17).
These preparations work, and Zeus is overcome with desire. After the
immortal couple make love, he sleeps. While the Olympian king is curled
in bed, Poseidon leads the Greek counterattack against Hector and the
Trojans. Zeus awakens in time to prevent a premature Greek victory.

Although the narrative context in the *Wake* contains no hint of deception, seduction, or divine combat, Joyce composed a paragraph that is
remarkably similar in detail to the Iliadic scene. In the "Anna Livia"
episode, the washerwomen describe ALP's preparations to go out and
defend the reputation of her husband, HCE:

> First she let her hair fal and down it flussed to her feet its tevoits wind-
> ing coils. Then, mothernaked, she sampood herself with galawater and
> fraguant pistania mud, wupper and lauar, from crown to sole. Next she
> greesed the groove of her keel, warthes and wears and mole and itcher,
> with antifouling butterscratch and turfentide and serpenthyme. . . .
> Peeld gold of waxwork her jellybelly and her grains of incense anguille
> bronze. And after that she wove a garland for her hair. She pleated it.
> She plaited it. . . . Then she made her bracelets and her anklets and her
> armlets and a jetty amulet for necklace of clicking cobbles. . . . That
> done, a dawk of smut to her airy ey, Annuskha Lutetiavich Pufflovak.
> (*FW* 206.29–207.9)

The best commentary on Joyce's lines is a rereading of the model scene from the *Iliad*. Minor details that tidy up a few items in this description of an epic toilette can be picked up from a fast glance at McHugh. I am not entirely convinced by Glasheen's suggestion that Hera's name is embedded in "*her a*ry ey" (*FW* 207.8; my emphasis), but there may be a Homeric echo in the phrase. In the *Iliad* the entire seduction-deception episode begins when "Hera . . . stood on the peak of Olympus, and saw with her eyes" that Poseidon was violating Zeus's commands by helping the Greeks. Perhaps the heavenly venue of those lives (*Iliad* 14.153–54) contributed to Joyce's description of ALP's application of mascara to her "airy" eyes. Be that as it may, there is, in addition to the basic Homeric tone of the passage, an appropriately Nilotic contribution. When Anna Livia washes her body, she is thorough: "*wupper and lauar* from crown to sole" (*FW* 206.31–32; my emphasis). Two of the best genetic scholars, Landuyt and Lernout, have discovered a source for the italicized phrase: Léon Metchnikoff's *La civilisation et les grands fleuves historiques*.[12] The relevant Notebook entry, which occurs in a long index, concerns the impact of the River Nile on Egyptian civilization: "ᴿUpper Nile made Lower Nile / Lower Nile made history" (VI.B.1.33). When Joyce combed the Notebook index for appropriately riverine terms for this celebrated section of the *Wake*, he ingeniously converted the "Upper" Nile to "wupper," which is a river in western Germany; the "Lower" Nile became "lauar," which encompasses the "Laua" (one of three rivers—Lowa, Lua, or Luvua—all in the Congo) and phonetically suggests the French verb *laver* (to wash) or its Latin root *lavare* (to wash).

Poseidon (Neptune)

When Poseidon was liberated from Cronus's belly, Zeus made his older brother Lord of the Sea. Poseidon plays quite a significant role in both Homeric epics. He is a staunch enemy of Troy in the *Iliad* and the father of the Cyclops Polyphemus in the *Odyssey*—and therefore the immortal enemy of the adventurer who blinded his son. But the god of the ocean scarcely puts in an appearance in Joyce's fiction. I have found no allusions whatsoever in *Ulysses*, nor is he named in either of the schemata for that work. In the *Wake* there is a fairly obvious play on his name and his sphere of divine activity: "Posidionius O'Fluctuary" (*FW* 80.28–29), which incorporates the Latin noun *fluctus* (sea, waves).

A slightly more expansive reference appears in the passage "the *tridont* sired a *tritan stock, farruler,* and I *bade* those *polyfizzyboisterous seas* to *retire* with hemselves from os (*rookwards,* thou *seasea stamoror*!)" (*FW* 547.23–26; my emphases). Each of the italicized words contributes to the complex classical allusion. Poseidon's symbolic weapon was the Latin *trident,* which Joyce spells with the Greek root for tooth (*odont*). In mythology Triton is a son of Poseidon who can calm the seas by blowing his horn, a conch shell. The German *Stock* means a stick, a Latin synonym for which is *ferula.* Because he presides over the globe-girdling seas, one of the epithets of the far-ruling Poseidon is *eurysthenēs* (with might that reaches far and wide) (*Iliad* 8.201; *Odyssey* 13.140). In both Homeric epics the sea is *polyphloisbos,* or "loud-sounding" in traditional translations (*Iliad* 1.34; *Odyssey* 13.85). The allusions from classical mythology are combined with an English legend. When the Danish King Canute invaded England he is reported to have *bade* the *sea* to *retire,* to fall back (*rückwärts* in German). To emphasize the point, Joyce re-creates the royal command in Latin: "seasea stamoror" (*FW* 547.25–26), which can be translated as "The sea, the sea must halt [*sta* in Latin]; I, Canute, cause it to delay [*moror* in Latin]." Finally, the repeated motif of "Thalatta! Thalatta!" (Greek for "the sea, the sea") appears in distorted but recognizable form six lines below the primary passage: "Galata! Galata!" (*FW* 547.32).

Athena (Minerva)

Athena is sometimes called Pallas Athena; that epithet is derived from the verb *pallō* (I brandish, I whirl), probably referring to her function as the warrior-maiden with a poised spear. In Greek mythology, the tale of the goddess's birth is bizarre. She is born, a mature woman, from the head of Zeus, either because he swallowed his pregnant mate Metis (Thought) or by parthenogenesis as the incarnate form of divine reason and prudence. Buck Mulligan alludes to this odd bit of mythological obstetrics in *Ulysses.* Near the end of the *Hamlet* debate in the National Library, he cries out, "I have an unborn child in my brain. Pallas Athena! A play!" (*U* 9.876).

In Homer's *Odyssey* Athena is the most significant of the Olympian gods. She is Odysseus's divine patroness, frequently appearing to him and his son, sometimes without the customary disguise.[13] This exception to the traditional mythological form of face-to-face immortal-human communication is seen as an indication that Odysseus's careful strategy on earth vibrates sympathetically with the goddess's primary Olympian qualities. It is strange, then, that Athena plays a very minor role indeed in *Ulysses*. Perhaps Joyce, like many post-Homeric imitators of the epic genre, decided to omit the divine apparatus, at least its overly Greek aspects—messengers, omens, sacrifices, and transformed gods.

Under the heading "Persons" for the "Telemachus" chapter in the Gorman-Gilbert schema, "Mentor" and "Pallas" are bracketed together; under the "correspondences" heading the "Milkwoman" is linked with "Mentor."[14] When Athena appeared to Telemachus in the second book of the *Odyssey*, she disguised herself as Mentor, a comrade of Odysseus. Although Ellmann and others have heard an echo of the schematic parallel in the Joycean text, I have difficulty finding anything in common between the Milkwoman, an old, ignorant crone, and Athena, even in her mortal disguise.[15] In fact, the only hint of Athena's presence in "Telemachus" that I can detect is a pair of the goddess's characteristic "grey searching eyes" *(U* 1.186)—but here they belong to Buck Mulligan. Not only does the schema cast him as Antinous, the cruel ringleader of Penelope's suitors, but that role also suits his arrogant behavior in the opening chapter of *Ulysses*.

Another of the epic epithets applied exclusively to Athena is *glaukōpis* (bright-, flashing-, grey-eyed) (*Odyssey* 1.44ff). The post-Homeric word for owl, Athena's wise totem, is *glaux, glaucos,* a reference to its glaring eyes.[16] Joyce frequently noted this epithet: "ᵇγλακῶπις" (*UNBM* 482:31); "Pallas squint ?g[lau]coma" (VI.A.2.40:16);[17] "Pallas Athena—her eyes are shaded by a peak [of her helmet] (γλαυκῶπις) iridectomy" (*Scribbledehobble* 86 [381]). In that jumble of archival data Joyce has obviously connected the Homeric epithet with the clinical term for a serious optical problem, glaucoma (grey-gleam-swelling), the opacity of the lens of the eye. This condition can be exacerbated by iritis, from which Joyce suffered acutely. His first attacks occurred in Zürich while he was working on *Ulysses*. An iridectomy is the surgical removal of part of the eye's iris. None of these annotated philological-ophthalmological speculations about the eyesight of the goddess Pallas Athena worked its literal way into the texts of Joyce's works. On the other hand, there is much evidence that the author's own eye problems affected both *Ulysses* and the *Wake*.[18] In a March 11, 1923, letter Joyce reported the following odd but personally relevant example of long-range medical diagnosis: "he

[Homer] went blind from glaucoma according to one of my doctors, Dr. Berman, as iridectomy had not been thought of" (*Letters* I.201).

Apollo

Apollo, the son of Zeus and Leto, has the same name in both Greek and Roman mythology. (See my *Latin,* 88–90, for discussion of Apollo's infrequent appearances in Joyce's work.) One allusion worth repeating here is "O Phoebus! O Pollux!" (*FW* 431.35–36). The first exclamation is the standard transliteration of Apollo's primary epithet, *phoibos,* a Greek adjective meaning brilliant, shining. The second exclamation encapsulates the name of a tragic mortal twin, Pollux, and an acoustic approximation of Apollo.

Another item is an unused note for *Ulysses:* "Pythian Apollo of Delos" (*UNBM* 309:59). That entry brings together Apollo's two most important ancient cult centers, his birthplace on the Aegean island of Delos and his oracular shrine on the Greek mainland at Delphi. At Delphi the priestess (the Pythia) went into a trance to deliver the god's cryptic advice. She is so named because, when the Olympian gods of the Sky first established themselves in the Greek world, Apollo defeated and slew the Python, the dragon-goddess who once protected the site. From primeval times Delphi was sacred because it was thought to be the center of the earth (*omphalos* in Greek).[19] Some say that the oracular priestess was so named because, after he killed the original goddess-guardian, Apollo left her corpse to rot (*pythō* in Greek). In historic times, the sanctuary at Delphi, on the slopes of Mount Parnassus, became a center of Panhellenic importance. Temples, shrines, and a theater were constructed there, and every four years the Pythian Games were celebrated in the stadium at Delphi to honor Phoebus Apollo. Throughout ancient history a steady stream of suppliants visited Delphi to consult the oracle. Joyce acknowledges this in an archival note: "Apollo's job—that's telling things" (VI.B.25.73). An inhabitant of that ancient prophetic sanctuary is momentarily merged with a citizen of the American City of Brotherly Love: "foul a delphian" (*FW* 378.36).

In one of the *Wake* Notebooks is an index of terms associated with Apollo. It appears immediately after the entry "Greek mycology," which is an indication either that Joyce was interested in ancient fungi and mushrooms (*mykos* in Greek) or that he was playing on the word *mythology.* That item is followed by: "Apollo / Phoebus / Paean / Hyperboreans / apples" (VI.B.21.258). A chain of mythological logic connects the items in that cluster. Apollo's most important epithet is Phoebus; he is often associated with Paeëon, the divine healer of the Olympians (the third entry might also be a reference to the *paean,* a thanksgiving hymn sung to the god); Apollo spends the three months of winter among the Hyperboreans (those who live beyond the North Wind); the apple trees guarded by the Hesperides (Daughters of the Evening) were planted in the far west, perhaps in the land of the Hyperboreans. On top of the next page of the Notebook, the entry "Apollo " is repeated, followed by "bk[Apollo] and abbles" (VI.B.21.259). The mythological fruit reappears in the text as "ivvy's holired abbles" (*FW* 5.30), where the god's name is replaced by "ivvy," selected instead of his favorite laurel to create a play on "holly and ivy" and to suggest Eve's not so holy apple.

An entry in one of the *Ulysses* notebooks shows how thoroughly Joyce went through the handbooks in search of mythological detail: "fervor of Apollo at Megara" (VI.C.7.242). Legend tells that the god helped King Alcathous of Megara rebuild his city's walls. The king then built a temple to Apollo and was offering a sacrifice there when one of his sons interrupted the ritual to report the tragic death of another son. Incensed at this act of apparent impiety, Alcathous killed the youth on the spot, using a burning log from the sacrificial fire. That was the acme of Apollonian fervor at Megara.

Artemis (Diana)

Artemis, the daughter of Zeus and Leto, was the twin sister of Apollo, born on Delos. She was the virgin goddess of wild things, whom she both protected and hunted in the deep forests. One of the most detailed myths associated with the goddess is an amalgam of a number of traditional motifs. Zeus fell in love with Callisto (Most Beautiful), a mortal maiden who was a member of Artemis's virginal entourage. To seduce her, the king of the gods first disguised himself as Artemis; even in female form, his Olympian strength overcame the young woman. Months later Callisto and Artemis stripped to bathe in a mountain stream. The goddess saw that Callisto was pregnant and expelled her from her troop. Soon a son, Arcas, was born. Zeus's jealous wife, Hera, also learned of Callisto's delivery of the child, deduced its divine origin, and transformed the mother into a bear. Years later, while hunting in the forests, Arcas came upon his bear-parent. Just as he was about to drive a spear through her shaggy side, Zeus lifted both mother and son into the heavens, where even today Callisto is called Arctos (Big Bear) and Arcas is known as Arctophylax (Bear's Guard). There are several casual and multilingual allusions to Callisto's metamorphosis into a constellation in Joyce's works: "Ursa Major" (Latin for Larger Bear) (*U* 17.1993, 1996); "*The Big Bear bit the Sailor's Only*" (*FW* 267.L2); "Dah! Arcthuris comeing!" (*FW* 594.2). In English-speaking countries the star cluster is frequently called Charley's Wain (*FW* 426.25) or the Big Dipper; the latter appears as a "consollation" from the "blue-funkfires of the dipper" (*FW* 581.13–14).

Artemis's status as Lady of Wild Things is also evident in the ritual performed in her honor at Brauron, a shrine near Athens. The accounts of the origins of this ceremony differ in details, but it is clear that it was intended to appease the goddess, who was enraged at the killing of a bear. A number of young girls, once clad in bearskins, later in saffron-colored robes, danced the *arkteia* (bear liturgy).[20] Selection as a "bear" for the annual festival was a great honor from the city. Joyce's eye for uncanny detail, even in antique Athenian ritual, was attracted to this event: "8 yearly dance[r]s (bear) to Artemis / in crocus chlamys [short cloak]" (*UNBM* 354:61). This archival note was prepared for the "Circe" chapter of *Ulysses*, but the ancient ceremony seems to have left no mark on any of the impromptu dancing at Bella's brothel.

The holy island of Delos, Artemis's birthplace, is also commemorated in several passages in the *Wake*. The geographical epithet itself appears as the fourth name in an alphabetical list of Issy's female companions: "Delia" (*FW* 147.11). Issy herself is referred to as "the dowce little delia" (*FW* 208.29). In an improbable setting for the adamantly virginal goddess and an epithet of her twin brother (Apollo), "Dehlia and Peonia" are described as "druping nymphs, bewheedling" their father, Zeus (*FW* 414.36–415.2); she is more properly associated with mountains in the "Delian alps" (*FW* 8.28).

The "logic" of mythology links the maiden Artemis with the moon, based on the similarity of the length of human menstrual cycles and lunar cycles. Thus, Artemis is often identified with a more primitive moon-goddess, Selene. Joyce includes an invocation to "Selene, sail O!" (*FW* 244.26) in the midst of a passage that swirls together elements from classical and biblical stories of floods. In the fantasy world of "Circe," Leopold Bloom announces majestically that we "have bestowed our royal hand upon the princess Selene, the splendour of night" (*U* 15.1506–1507).

Aphrodite (Venus)

One of the few direct references to the Greek goddess of sexual rapture is a baldly etymological phrase that spotlights her genesis. Buck Mulligan declares that he has been to the National Museum, "where I went to hail the *foamborn* Aphrodite" (*U* 9.610; my emphasis). As one might expect from the novel's self-proclaimed Hellenizer of Ireland, Mulligan's Greek etymology is correct: *aphros* means foam or froth, and the unrooted suffix *–dite* has traditionally been interpreted as an indicator of origin. In mythology, Aphrodite's place of birth is the sea, and several of her most hallowed shrines are on Aegean islands. But the circumstances of her birth are far more grotesque than a mere marine venue. They are compactly narrated by Hesiod in his *Theogony* (*The generation of the gods*). When it became obvious to the offspring of Uranus, the first king of the gods, that he was determined to continue his practice of burying them deep in their Earth-Mother, Cronus castrated his father with a huge sickle:

> As soon as he cut off the genitals with adamant,
> he threw them from land into the turbulent sea;
> they were carried over the sea for a long time, and white
> foam arose from the immortal flesh; within a girl
> grew; first she came to holy Kythera, and
> next she came to wave-washed Cyprus.
> An awesome and beautiful goddess [Aphrodite] emerged. (*Theogony*
>   188–94)[21]

This weird tale attracted the attention of Joyce, who graphically re-created it just beneath the surface of the following passage in the *Wake:* "Mistress Mereshame, of cupric tresses, of the formwhite foaminine, the ambersandalled" (*FW* 241.14–15). The German word *Meerschaum* literally means sea-foam (it is also the name of a material for making pipes); ambergris, a grayish waxy substance secreted by sperm whales, is found floating on the sea. The concatenation of these motifs of a sea birth is certified by a late Notebook entry: "(*Venus*) ⌐Mrs. Mereshame / Venus" (VI.B.33.65). In another passage is a blasphemous juxtaposition of Aphrodite's birth and the Virgin Mary's conception of Jesus. In the Old Testament, God's sign to Gideon to lead the Israelites into battle was that a fleece on the threshing floor stayed dry while everything around it became wet with dew (Judges 6:36–40).[22] Some Christian biblical commentators have interpreted that incident as an allegorical prediction of the miraculous conception of a savior by a virgin. As is signaled by "neuhumorisation of our kristianiasation," Joyce combines biblical and the mythological elements into "the joy of the dew on the flower of the fleets on the fields of the foam of the waves of the seas" (*FW* 331.31–35).

To return to a more realistic topic, the goddess's favorite island, Cyprus, was famous for its copper mines; in the Greco-Roman world the metal took its name from the island. Moreover, the Greek word *k/cypros* also means henna, the plant from which a red-brown dye is made. In honor of her genial island, Aphrodite is sometimes depicted with tresses of copper-amber tint, rising from the sea (as in Botticelli's *Birth of Venus*). Buck Mulligan's swimming companion at Fortyfoot Rocks in "Telemachus" alludes to the reputedly wanton sexual behavior of mortal females whose hair is the same color as that of Aphrodite: "redheaded women buck like goats" (*U* 1.706).

Glasheen ingeniously detected a parody of this mythological birth tale in one of HCE's braggadocio defenses of his own manhood. While discharging his more-than-human parental duties, so he claims, he fathered Issy in a drunken Saturday-night wet dream: "I reveal thus my deepseep daughter which was bourne up pridely out of medsdreams unclouthed when I was pillowing in my brime (of Saturnay Eve . . .)" (*FW* 366.13–16). Saturn is the Roman name for Cronus, who wielded the adamantine sickle that severed Uranus's genitals. Joyce's humanized and rationalized version of the birth of Aphrodite/Issy is an example of euhemerism. This mode of interpreting mythological persons and events owes its name to Euhemerus, a late fourth-century B.C. author of the *Sacred History*. In that work he attempted to show that the bases of ancient tales were actual events that had been distorted over time, that the gods and goddesses had been distinguished humans who received divine honors after their deaths. Joyce acknowledges this ancient process in "neuhumorisation" (*FW* 331.31) and "bEuhemerismus" (VIII.A.5.31).

In his aesthetics arguments in *Portrait* Stephen offers two hypotheses to explain widely different types of ideal feminine beauty. The "eugenic" solution involves an appreciation of "the great flanks of Venus," so "she would bear . . . burly offspring"; "her great breasts" that "give good milk" are also cited (*P* 207–9). Be that as it may, the anatomical feature of Aphrodite that most excited the admiration of Joyce's characters is her buttocks. In *Portrait* Lynch irreverently refutes Stephen's contention that aesthetic emotions rise above carnal desire: "one day I wrote my name on the backside of the Venus Praxiteles in the Museum. Was that not desire?"

(*P* 205; also see *P* 208). The specific reference is to a plaster cast reproduction of the famous statue of Aphrodite of Knidos by the premier Athenian sculptor, Praxiteles.[23]

In *Ulysses* Leopold Bloom gives his full attention to the "mesial groove" of a statue in the National Museum; it was a reproduction of "Venus Kallipyge" (*U* 9.615–16).[24] The epithet means having beautiful buttocks, or "gallantbuttocked," as the two Greek roots are nicely turned in a description of Dlugacz's mare as it trotted down the street (*U* 11.885; also see *U* 15.3727). In the light of Bloom's final "melonsmellonous osculation" of Molly's rump and the consequent "proximate erection" (*U* 17.2241–46), it is appropriate to note that he seems to have considered the object from all angles. That characteristic circumspection is also reflected in Bloom's thoughts when he shows Stephen a faded photo of Molly. The husband, "being a bit of an artist in his spare time," has a classical frame of reference. He recalls that "no later than that afternoon he had seen those Grecian statues. . . . Marble could give the original, shoulders, back, all the symmetry, all the rest" (*U* 16.1448–52).

There is archival evidence that Joyce himself engaged in some research on the origins of the cult of Aphrodite of the Beautiful Buttocks.[25] Among his notes for "Circe" is the following crossed—and geographically specific—entry: "gVenus Callipyge Syracusas" (*UNBM* 344:40). This item, which occurs in the midst of several other notes concerning sexual oddities, refers to a bizarre anecdote about two mortal sisters who lived near Syracuse on Sicily. To settle a dispute over which sister had the more beautiful rear curves, they agreed to moon a passing youth. He gazed and decided in favor of the older sister. Later his junior brother repeated the viewing but decided in favor of the younger woman. The two pairs of siblings married, an event commemorated in a line of verse: "In Syracuse there was a yoked-pair of beautifully buttocked sisters." The couples dedicated a temple to the wives' patroness, Aphrodite, the goddess who shared their physical attraction. The full version of this etiological anecdote is found in a second-century A.D. collection of curiosities, Athenaeus's *Banquet of the Learned* (12.554cd).[26] Joyce probably ran across a summary of the tale somewhere, perhaps in Roscher's *Lexikon* (I.418–19).

In his stream-of-consciousness monologue in "Nausicaa," Bloom recalls a crudely obscene sketch and then muses that women recognize their sexual impact. Outward male manifestation of arousal and its effects are hard to conceal: "Women never meet one like that Wilkins in the high school drawing a picture of Venus with all his belongings on show" (*U* 13.909–910).

In "Circe" there are, not unexpectedly, several apparitions of this goddess. Her powers are cited by "MRS BELLINGHAM," who testifies that Bloom has written her letters "with fulsome compliments as a Venus in furs" (*U* 15.1045–46). Later in the same episode, the keeper of the museum appears, "dragging a lorry on which are the shaking statues of several naked goddesses, Venus Callipyge, Venus Pandemos, Venus Metempsychoses" (*U* 15.1704–6). The first epithet is an alternative English spelling (*c* for kappa) of the amply endowed statue of Aphrodite. The second reference, Venus Pandemos (Of All the People), is also supported by an archival entry, "ʳVenus Pandemos" (*UNBM* 202:45);[27] she is a vulgar manifestation of the goddess cited in Plato's *Symposium*, in contrast to Aphrodite Urania, the "heavenly" deity of purified love. The goddess's final epithet in the quote has nothing to do with Aphrodite or mythology: *metempsychosis* is the Greek term for transmigration of souls. The meaning of this word was explained to Molly by Leopold Bloom, as he brought breakfast up to her in bed in "Calypso" (*U* 4.339–42). The term reappears in the text here only because of its Greek etymology and its pseudo-Homeric ring of epic grandeur—or, at least, of polysyllabic pomposity.

In mythology Aphrodite's major function was to excite sexual activity among gods and humans. She aided Hera in her tactical seduction of Zeus by lending the queen of Olympus her enchanting sash. An archival note refers to this "Girdle of Venus" (*UNBM* 293:56). In a passage studded with astronomical allusions is a bilingual reference to Aphrodite's most significant immortal lover, Ares, the Lord of Combat: "Ers, Mores" (*FW* 494.12). Another of Aphrodite's love affairs is the subject of a brief note: "waters of Salmacis make hermaphrodite" (*UNBM* 244:43). After entreaties by the messenger-god, Aphrodite made love with Hermes; their son bore the names of both his parents, Hermaphroditus. A spring-nymph, Salmacis, fell in love with the youth and entwined her body with his when he bathed in her waters. The embrace became permanent, and the linked lovers are now neither male nor female, but both at the same time. This tale, although fully compatible with some of the metamorphoses of "Circe," does not appear in *Ulysses*.

One of the best known and most tragic of Aphrodite's mortal lovers, Adonis, is changed into a star in a passage near the previous citation:

"Nova Ardonis" (*FW* 494.10–11; also see "Venus and Adonis" [*U* 9.258]). The far more traditional metamorphosis of Adonis makes him into a blood-red flower, and except for Joyce no mythographer suggests an astral transformation. Aphrodite herself is associated with flowers and gardens; in Crete her primary cult-name is *Antheia* (Lady of Flowers). That epithet appears in the *Wake* in an Edenic setting: "When old the wormd was a gadden and Anthea first unfoiled her limbs" (*FW* 354.22–23).

A very odd mixture of superficially conventional epithets is found in a marginal note to "Night Lessons": "*Canine Venus sublimated to Aulidis Aphrodite*" (*FW* 299.L1). I know of no mythical tales, however, in which Aphrodite/Venus is associated with dogs or with the island of Aulis, from which the Greek fleet sailed to Troy. In fact, Aphrodite's Olympian opposite, the virginal Artemis, is often shown with a hunting dog, and one of her major shrines is at Aulis. I surmise that Joyce confused the two goddesses here and mistakenly entered Aphrodite for Artemis, or he may be indicating a lapse in Shaun's marginal command of mythology.

Another allusive epithet can only be associated with the goddess of physical love. In "Anna Livia" the washerwomen speculate about ALP's sexual exploits. The women report that in ALP's primeval encounter with a hermit in Wicklow, their ecstatic climax was accompanied by a firework-like rainbow of exploding colors—an "Afrothdizzying" experience (*FW* 203.27–28). That description echoes the Greek goddess's odd birth and highlights her power to excite passion.

Ares (Mars)

Ares, the son of Zeus and Hera, was not well-liked by his fellow Olympians, and mortals feared him. The reason was the same in both worlds: The shedding of blood and the panic of battle were the only activities that interested him. Yet when wounded himself during the Trojan War, Ares whined in pain and was upbraided by Zeus (*Iliad* 5.888–98). Several brief references to Ares are made in connection with his divine mistress, Aphrodite. His Latin and Greek names are also combined in "martiallawsey marses" (*FW* 64.13) and "allsfare for the loathe of Marses ambiviolent about it" (*FW* 518.2–3).[28] First, last, and always, the character of this god is summarized in "ardent Ares" (*FW* 269.17).

Hephaestus (Vulcan)

Hephaestus, another son of Zeus and Hera, was Lord of Technology and Volcanoes. His glowing forge was located either on the volcanic island of Lemnos or under Mount Aetna; there he produced lightning bolts for Zeus, mechanical objects to amuse the Olympians, and armor for important Heroes. The god's name and his work station are phonetically commemorated in "Heavystot's envil" (*FW* 514.11), but in Joyce's fiction most of the allusions to Hephaestus's mythological deeds occur in Joyce's fiction under his Latin name (see Schork, *Latin*, 83–84). Hephaestus's most ingenious mechanical device plays a part in the *Odyssey.* The god is married to Aphrodite, who characteristically betrays her lumbering husband with her fiery lover Ares. Hephaestus traps (and displays to Olympian scorn) the adulterers in a web of gold chains that envelops them in the divine couple's own marriage bed (*Odyssey* 8.266–366). Joyce alludes to this marvelous tale of revenge in *Ulysses* when Leopold Bloom contemplates various means of retribution for Molly's adultery with Blazes Boylan. One possibility is "Exposure by mechanical artifice (automatic bed)" (*U* 17.2202–2203).

Demeter (Ceres)

Demeter, the sister of Zeus and Hera, had been swallowed by Cronus and was released by her younger brother. She ruled over the earth as its Mother, the power of fertility and growth. Her most exciting mythological adventure is her search for her kidnapped daughter Persephone (Proserpina) from the clutches of Hades. The story of the goddess's bereavement and recovery was used by the Greeks to explain the origin of the seasons: When Demeter grieves, the earth lies fallow; when she rejoices with her recovered daughter, the earth blossoms. The most complete literary source for this etiological myth is the *Hymn to Demeter,* a long hexameter poem composed in Homeric style. In *Ulysses* Stephen Dedalus refers to this work while at Bella Cohen's whorehouse. Drunk and obnoxious, the young student flaunts his classical learning: "The rite is the poet's rest. It may be an old hymn to Demeter" (*U* 15.2088). Almost immediately afterward he makes a meaningful self-correction: "that is Circe's or what am I saying Ceres' altar" (*U* 15.2091–92). Within the *Hymn*'s central plot, the reunion of Persephone with Demeter, is the story of the mournful goddess's stay at the house of some kind mortals, in Eleusis, about four-teen miles northwest of Athens. To repay these people for their sympathy, Demeter established the Eleusinian Mysteries, which were celebrated, down to the fourth century A.D., in her honor.

Part of the elaborate quadrennial ceremonies was a procession from Athens to the cult center, following the Eleusinian (Sacred) Way. Joyce plays around with this pilgrimage path in "hallucinian via" (*FW* 478.13–14), within a cluster of references to ancient roads.[29] There is also some archival evidence that Joyce had consulted a scholarly reference work on the background of the Eleusinian Mysteries. When Demeter was disconsolate because of the disappearance of her daughter, one of her host's old servant-nurses attempted to cheer her up with what the stan-dard version says are "quips and jokes that made the holy lady smile, then laugh, softening her heart" (*Hymn* 197–205). Variant texts, including Athenaeus's second-century A.D. account, call the servant Baubo and report that her "jokes" involved exposing her private parts to the goddess.[30] Joyce's notesheet entry does not mince words: "Baubo shows bald cunt Ceres laughs" (*UNBM* 344:44). That note appears in one of the collections of sexual odds and ends that Joyce prepared for the composi-tion of the "Circe" chapter of *Ulysses*. It seems not to have been used in the text, nor do any of the adjacent entries deal with the Eleusinian Mysteries or other ancient rituals. On the other hand, the nearby entries "[g]Venus Callipyge Syracusas" and "waters of Salmacis make hermaphrodite" (*UNBM* 344:40, 43) suggest that Joyce was exploring topics related to the remarkable genitalia of various mythological characters. There is, then, the remote possibility that Joyce recalled this bit of classical bawdiness and incorporated it into the *Wake*'s "Night Lessons," where twins are exploring the mysteries of the female sexual organs: "if she pleats, lift by her seam hem and jabote at the spidsiest of her trickkikant (like thougsands done before since fillies calpered. Ocone! Ocone!) the maids-apron of our A.L.P" (*FW* 297.8–10).

Hermes (Mercury)

Hermes, the son of Zeus and the nymph Maia, was extraordinarily preco-cious: While still an infant he stole Apollo's cattle and invented the tortoiseshell lyre as recompense. In classical myths Hermes performs three primary functions: Olympian messenger, especially in the service of his father; patron of human travelers and traders; guide of the souls of the dead into the Underworld (see *UNBM* 304:74–87). In preparation for *Ulysses*, Joyce spent some time investigating the various facets of Hermes' divine career. The following is an extract from a 1920 letter to Frank Budgen dated September 29 ("Michaelmas"):

> *Moly* is a nut to crack. My latest is this. Moly is the gift of Hermes, god of public ways, and is the invisible influence (prayer, chance, agility, *presence of mind,* power of recuperation) which saves in case of accident. This would cover immunity from syphilis (σύ φιλις = swine-love?). Hermes is the god of signposts: i.e. he is, specially for a traveller like Ulysses, the point at which roads parallel merge and roads contrary also. He is an accident of providence. In this special case his plant may be said to have many leaves, indifference due to masturbation, pessimism congenital, a sense of the ridiculous, sudden fastidiousness in some detail, experience. (*Letters* I.147–48)

Joyce's point of departure in that rambling excerpt is the *moly,* the magic plant that Hermes gave to Odysseus to protect him from Circe's charms (*Odyssey* 10.302–6). Homer specifies that the plant has black roots and a milky-white flower; it will serve as an antidote against the witch's drugged potion (for a discussion of this topic from a different perspective, see chapter 5). Joyce's allegorical interpretations of the *moly* and its power are no more fanciful than others proposed by various ancient and early Christian commentators on the Homeric epic.[31] In fact, about a month later in another letter to Budgen, Joyce writes, "Moly could also be absinthe the cerebral impotentising (!!) drink or chastity. Damn Homer, Ulysses, Bloom and all the rest" (*Letters* I.149).

A series of pre-*Ulysses* notes on Hades (which Joyce derived from Roscher) includes the term "Psychopompos" (VIII.A.5.26). This is one of Hermes' titles; it designates him as the escort (*pompos*) of a mortal's soul *(psychē)* on its final trip to Hades. The Greek god also lent his name to the supposed author of works on alchemy, magic, and gnostic esoterica, Hermes Trismegistus, who is cited in "Circe" (*U* 15.2269) in the midst of a paragraph of mystical mumbo-jumbo. The link between an Olympian deity and the apocryphal writer of mystical treatises is the ancient Egyptian god of invention and cunning, Thoth, who was identified with Hermes and was believed to have inspired the *Hermetica.* That ostentatiously classical title was designed to add a bit of antique respectability to a collection of texts that probably emanate from the syncretistic culture of third-century A.D. Greco-Roman Egypt (see chapter 6).

In *Finnegans Wake* there are several passages into which Joyce crammed multiple allusions to ancient roads and means of transportation. For example, "milestones" are found "along the tramestrack" (*FW* 81.6–7) Among the other possible interpretations, the last word combines a modern *tram's track* with the Latin *trames* (path, foot-way). The welfare of travelers on those roads is guaranteed by "Anton Hermes" (*FW* 81.7). "Anton" is meant to commemorate St. Anthony of Padua, who ensures that messages are delivered safely and promptly, as in the pious ejaculation "Saint Anthony Guide!" (*FW* 409.7).

A related area of influence assigned to Hermes is his protection and definition of property. In ancient Greece, a *herm*, or stone column, was set up in front of houses and as a marker for the boundaries of fields. The source of the original term was the bust of Hermes that topped the marker and the representation of the god's phallus that protruded from its shaft. Joyce clearly alludes to this sort of minimonument when he refers to "the paunch of that halpbrother of a herm, a pillarbox" (*FW* 66.26–27) as one of the containers of the Letter in the *Wake*. A "herm" is also found in a paragraph that includes several other references to roads and travel markers, including a visually accurate and etymologically valid doublet, "statuemen" (*FW* 471.17, 28; also note "Statue of Mercury Hermes" [VI.B.8.104]). In Latin the noun *statumen* means prop, pillar, or support. Just a page before the appearance of these two monuments to Hermes, we learn that Jaun, traveling to visit Issy's "daughters of February," has given himself "some sort of hermetic prod" (*FW* 470.2). It is possible to detect in this instrument (or gesture) the cattle-prod used by Hermes, who rustled Apollo's herd; or the phallic protuberance on a herm; or an unspecific occult jolt to Jaun's flagging energy. Perhaps all three aspects are intended, since the self-inflicted goad is reported to have "acted like magic" (*FW* 470.3).[32]

Dionysus/ Bacchus (Liber)

Considering Joyce's fervent devotion to the pleasures of wine, it is strange that there are very few references to the Lord of the Vines in his work—and those always under the more familiar Greco-Latin form of his name,

Bacchus (see Schork, *Latin*, 88). Scholars judge Dionysus to be a relatively late addition to the Hellenic pantheon. His miraculous birth (conception as a Hero by his mortal mother, Semele; birth as a god from the thigh of his immortal father, Zeus) is an indication of his distinctly odd divine attributes—and his foreign (Near Eastern) origins. That otherness is also reflected in the frenzied rituals by which he was honored. At the same time, Dionysus was the divine patron of the quintessentially Greek art forms, ancient tragedy and comedy.

Some scholars think that the "naturalization" of Dionysus as one of the Olympians is the reason for the gender imbalance in the number of the most important of the ancient gods. In the royal family of the third dynasty, there are seven males (Zeus, Poseidon, Apollo, Ares, Hephaestus, Hermes, Dionysus) and five females (Hera, Athena, Artemis, Aphrodite, Demeter). There is some evidence that Hestia (Vesta), the goddess of the family hearth, was also once regarded as an Olympian. Joyce acknowledges her sphere of influence: "As cream of the hearth thou reinethst alhome" (*FW* 531.13). When Hestia was displaced (but not disgraced or exiled), her position was taken by the ecstatic male newcomer, Dionysus, and his entourage of Maenads, Sileni, and Satyrs.

The last of those randy creatures, half-human and half-goat, appear in several instances in the *Wake*. "A satyr in weddens" (*FW* 88.15) looks like a confused allusion to the infamous mythological occasion when a pack of drunken Centaurs (half-human, half-horse) created havoc at a Lapith wedding reception to which they had been invited. Another reference reinforces that theme: "pszozlers pszinging *Satyr's Candledayed Nice*" (*FW* 415.14). McHugh reasonably interprets that line as "sozzlers singing [Robert Burns's] *Cottars Saturday Night*." "Satyrdaysboost" (*FW* 583.19) also connects Dionysus's woodland companions with the weekend consumption of booze.

Hades (Dis)

Even though Hades was a child of Cronus and Rhea, he was not an Olympian. After being liberated by Zeus, Hades became Lord of the Underworld. The land of the dead, far from the light of the sun and the palaces of his divine brothers and sisters, was his realm. In *Ulysses* the events surrounding the burial of Paddy Dignam in Glasnevin Cemetery constitute the "Hades" chapter, an adventure for Leopold Bloom that is meant to be analogous to Odysseus's trip to the Underworld in book 11 of Homer's epic. The "Persons" and "Correspondences" in the schemata are quite a bit more detailed for this chapter than for the others. Stuart Gilbert's discussion of the episode in his study of *Ulysses* is also full of Greek and Latin (and at least one Semitic) etymologies, as well as derivations and parallels from classical mythology.[33] An entire page of Joyce's 1918 Zürich notebook is devoted to entries on Hades from Roscher's *Lexikon*. The first presents the traditional Greek explanation of the god's name: "Hades ἡ ἰδεν / un seen (maker of)" (VIII.A.5.26).[34] Another note indicates that Hades had "no children / sterile never left his kingdom but 2 to / rape P-[ersephone] / and be cured of wound of Hercules by / Paion" (VIII.A.5.26). (The abduction of Persephone is discussed previously in this chapter's review of Demeter's mythological role.) On his last labor Heracles came into the Underworld to steal the Stygian guard dog, but Cerberus's master put up a fierce fight and was severely wounded. Thus, Hades left his realm a second time, to be cured by the divine physician Paeëon (also spelled Paieon and Paean).

Two other archival entries record epithets of Hades: "'great host'" and "'all bring to rest'" (VIII.A.5.26). These terms are typical of the Greeks' euphemisms for the fearful or unpleasant, such as death or the king of the dead.[35] That principle is neatly exemplified in Hades' primary epithet: Pluto, the "rich" (*ploutos* in Greek) god into whose coffers all mortals are eventually deposited. The god's rape of Persephone (Proserpina in Latin) is summarized in the following alliterative jingle: "plutonically pursuant . . . pretty Proserpronette" (*FW* 267.9–11). On the other hand, "Hades" is cited as the source of "fresh horrors" in a *Wake* passage that catalogs the consequences of syphilis and its traditional therapy (*FW* 183.35). In a scrambled catalog of the names or topics of the "Homeric" chapters in *Ulysses,* Joyce's fairly direct "Had Days" (*FW* 229.13) incorporates the notion that a person consigned to the Underworld has "had all his days" in the sun. A Wakean equivalent of "the devil take them!" is "—Ahdays begatem!" (*FW* 506.10).

In a burlesque trial in "Circe," J. J. O'Molloy defends Leopold Bloom. One of his demands for order in the court begins with "By Hades" (*U* 15.967). In the Homeric poems the strongest oath an immortal can take is to swear by the River Styx. Joyce notes this custom with "ᵇswear by Styx"(*UNBM* 308:46). Although this entry is crossed out, it does not reappear in *Ulysses*—unless Joyce has converted the oath from ancient pagan to Dano-Hibernian usage. In the Library chapter the supercilious Protestant John Eglinton says that no critic has claimed that Hamlet was an Irishman: "Judge Barton, I believe, is searching for some clues. He swears (His Highness not His Lordship) by saint Patrick" (*U* 9.520–21).[36]

An entry in *Scribbledehobble* links the names of three of the traditional rivers in the Underworld: "Styx, Cocytus, Pyriphlegethon" (93 [481]). The first is invoked in the *Wake,* when ALP "swore on the croststyx nyne wyndabouts" (*FW* 206.4–5). According to standard mythological geography, the flow of the Styx circles Hades only seven times, so it seems that Joyce has added two laps to its "hateful" course. Nearby is another infernal river, "Spark's pirryphlickathims" (*FW* 199.35). Joyce's etymology is absolutely on the mark here: The two Greek components mean fire (*pyr*) and to burn, to blaze (*phlegethō*); also note "Pluto of fire" (VI.B.33.47). In the same general vicinity as these two hellish streams is the Acheron (Pain or Grief). Joyce has converted it into a thoroughly modern adjective, "anacheronistic" (*FW* 202.35). The ultimate source of the names of the infernal streams is the *Odyssey* (10.513–14).

Another (but post-Homeric) river in the Underworld is the Lethe (Forgetfulness); it appears at the end of the same section as the previous references, in the form "lethest" (*FW* 214.10), and later as "lethemuse" in a context that involves "forgetting" (*FW* 272.F3 and 16). A final allusion to the River Lethe has a classical documentary source. The "Myth of Er" is placed at the end of Plato's *Republic* to answer questions about human free will. According to this tale, the warrior Er was so severely stunned in battle that his soul went to the Otherworld, from which he was soon returned—still alive—to tell how all human beings choose their own lives and how souls being born into a new body must drink from the River Lethe so that they forget every past experience. The length of the cleansing period between death and rebirth is one thousand years (*Republic* 614b–621d). Joyce alludes to this period of purification and "rest" in a phrase introduced by a parenthetical HCE acrostic: "(*hypnos chilia eonion!*) lethelulled between explosion and reexplosion" (*FW* 78.3–4; Joyce's emphasis). The italicized words are a fairly close translation into Greek of "sleep for a thousand ages (*aionon*)."

According to the "Myth of Er" each soul must be judged when it reaches the Otherworld. Although Plato does not specifically name them, the three traditional judges in Hades are Aeacus, Minos, and Rhadamanthys. Eugene Jolas reports that Joyce told him about a dream in which, while walking through a large city, he meets "three men named Minos, Eaque, and Rhadamante," who threaten to hurt him. Three weeks later, Jolas continues, he read in a Paris newspaper that the police were searching for terrorists who sent bombs through the mails. The trio of fanatics signed themselves "Minos, Eaque, Rhadamante, the Judges of the Underworld."[37]

Lesser Gods

The traditional Greek tales include several fairly prominent second-level gods. They do not dwell in Zeus's royal complex on Olympus, but they are in charge of important functions in the universe.

Helius (Sol)

The Titan Hyperion and his wife were the parents of three children, Eos (Dawn), Selene (Moon), and Helius (Sun). The latter drives his four-horse chariot through the sky during the day. At night, after passing below the western limits of the world, Helius and his team are returned to their eastern starting point by the River Oceanus. His wife Perse bore the Lord of the Sun a number of children noted for their uncivilized behavior: Aeëtes, the barbarian guardian of the Golden Fleece and the father of Medea; Circe, the seductive sorceress who bewitches most of Odysseus's crew but not their master (*UNBM* 283:167–68). Helius's most famous child was the tragic Phaëthon, who asked for one day's control of the sun/chariot as a pledge of his divine origin. The immortal father offered his tears of fear as proof of paternity, but the headstrong boy demanded the chariot. When he could not manage the horses, Zeus aborted the mission (and Phaëthon's life) with a lightning bolt.[38]

Like his daughter Circe, Helius lent his name to one of the chapters of *Ulysses*. In Homer's epic the crew of Odysseus violate his order not to touch the sacred cattle of the god Helius. The punishment for their slaughter of, and six days' feasting on, these animals was the destruction of their ship, the last one remaining in the Ithacan convoy from Troy. The crew perished in the disaster, but Odysseus was finally washed ashore on the island of Calypso (*Odyssey* 12.260–453). The Joycean chapter that was meant to offer parallels to the epic crime and its consequences is "Oxen of the Sun." The schemata list a number of "Correspondences": "Hospital-

Trinacria" (Sicily: Helius's island kingdom); "Lampetie, Phaethusa-Nurses" (Helius's daughters); "Helios-Horne" (a chief physician at the maternity hospital); "Oxen-Fertility."[39]

Oxen and cattle are everywhere in this chapter, including Queen Pasiphaë's bull-child (*U* 14.993–96) and a genuinely Greek "Bous Stephanoumenos" (*U* 14.1115; also see *U* 9.939). That often-mistranslated phrase means wreathed, or crowned, ox, and it reflects the ancient ritual custom of circling the head of a sacrificial ox with garlands of flowers (also see the opening cadenza of chapter 5).[40] A note by Gifford and Seidman calls attention to a longer, direct echo of the Homeric episode in "Oxen of the Sun": when Odysseus's men prepare their feast from the meat of the forbidden cattle, the gods send portents of disaster—the flayed hides creep, the flesh on the spits bellows, and the noise is like the sound of oxen (*Odyssey* 12:395–96). Joyce links this omen and the fate of the crew with the desolation around the Dead Sea: "and on the highway of the clouds they come, muttering thunder of rebellion, the ghosts of the beasts . . . the bulls of Bashan and of Babylon. . . . They moan, passing upon the clouds" (*U* 14.1088–93).

Helius's primary function is to bring light and warmth to mortals. Early in "Circe," Bloom's cake of lemon soap is temporarily changed into the sun. As Bloom points to the east, it "arises, diffusing light and perfume." Then the soap celebrates its celestial transformation and salutes its bearer: "We're a capital couple are Bloom and I. / He brightens the earth. I polish the sky" (*U* 15.335–39). I suggest that one of the sources for Joyce's diction in that couplet is a standard Homeric epithet for the sun god, *phaeisimbrotos Helios* (Helius Who Shines on Mortals) (*Odyssey* 10.138).

The Egyptian city of On was the cult center of Re, god of the sun. In Greek, this site was called Heliopolis (Sun City). In Wakean terms, in those temples his devotees practiced "heliolatry" (*FW* 237.1; also note VI.B.8.166); *latreia* is the Greek term for service given to a god. In a paragraph packed with allusions to *The Histories* of Herodotus, who visited Egypt, Joyce refers to "the Heliopolitical constabulary" (*FW* 530.16). The deification of the sun is given a decidedly Christian and Trinitarian aspect in another passage: "in the names of the balder [Norse god of light] and of the *sol* and of the hollichrost" (*FW* 331.14–15; my emphasis). The Latin noun for the sun, *sol,* is also mentioned in the formula "old Sol" (*FW* 253.9). As a matter of comparative religious fact, the *Wake's* mixture of natural, mythological, and Christian elements was briefly anticipated in *Ulysses*. There, as a part of the Circean coronation of Bloom, the bodyguards distribute all sorts of souvenirs, including *"cheap reprints of the World's Twelve Worst Books."* One of them is *"Was Jesus a Sun Myth?"* (*U* 15.1577–70). The title of that volume quite likely suggested the side-by-side presence of three other books in the later catalog of Bloom's library at Eccles Street: *"A Handbook of Astronomy, The Hidden Life of Christ, In the Track of the Sun"* (*U* 17.1391–95).

Aeolus

In early mythology, Aeolus was a mortal king who lived on an island that floated in the sea north of Sicily. Zeus appointed him to take charge of the winds. In later tales, Aeolus was the god who performed that same function, often to please one of the Olympians by aiding or impeding the voyage of a human. In Vergil's epic, for example, Aeneas was blown to Carthage by a storm released by a clearly divine Aeolus at Juno's request (*Aeneid* 1.50–156). But it is a sympathetically human Aeolus who gives Odysseus's crew the bag of winds, which they foolishly proceed to untie (*Odyssey* 10.1–75).

In *Ulysses* Aeolus gives his name to the newspaper office chapter, with its blasts of oral and written rhetoric. Two key "Correspondences" in the schema link "Crawford-Aeolus" (Crawford is the editor of the *Evening Telegraph)* and "Floating Island-Press." Joyce transliterates the traditional Aristotelian terms for the three types of rhetoric, to be used as "Techinic" in this chapter: "Simbouleutike[41] [deliberative oratory for the Assembly], Dikanike [forensic oratory for the courts], Epideictic [ceremonial oratory for public events]." The headlines that introduce the episodes in the chapter miss no opportunity to let the reader know which way the wind is blowing: "WHAT WETHERUP SAID" (*U* 7.337), "O, HARP EOLIAN!" (*U* 7.370), "RAISING THE WIND" (*U* 7.995), "VELOCITOUS AERO-LITHS" (*U* 7.1022). The accompanying text is equally breezy, but the quoted display of diction and tropes is the only discernible role that the ancient Lord of the Winds plays in Joyce's fiction.

Prometheus

Prometheus was the son of the Titan Iapetus. Although a scion of the earliest divine generations, he refused to join any of the attempts to

depose the third-dynasty king of Olympus. His efforts to help humans—
some myths say he created the race of men from clay—also put him into
extreme jeopardy. The *Wake* includes several prominent references to
various aspects of Prometheus's immortal career, especially his alleged
rebellion and binding. Since Aeschylus's *Prometheus Bound* is the primary
source for the dramatic details, the clash of the Titan with Zeus is
discussed in chapter 9, as part of Greek tragedy.

Prometheus's mistreatment at the hands of Zeus was especially disturb-
ing because the Titan had fought as a loyal ally with the Olympian king
when the Giants and the Titans rebelled. The details of the attempts of
gods of earlier generations to depose Zeus are confused; some accounts
mix together several thwarted coups and the siege of the redoubt on
Mount Olympus. At the bottom of these divine civil wars is Zeus's arro-
gance; the new king scorned and, some say, abused the huge, often
monstrous offspring of Uranus and Gaia. Finally, these Giants and Titans
fought back: "The thundering legion has stormed Olymp that end it" (*FW*
167.22–23). Even though he was himself a Titan, Prometheus recognized
the potential benefits of the comparatively more civilized third-dynasty
king and he fought at Zeus's side against his brothers. He did not share
their resentment nor was he afraid to battle for what was right. Zeus
unleashed his celestial weapon against the rebels: "Photoflashing it far too
wide. It will be known through all Urania soon. Like jealously titaning
fear" (*FW* 583.15–17).

In the ongoing conflict of the Titans and Giants against Zeus, no single
attack is more famous than the attempt to pile Mount Pelion on top of
Mount Ossa to assault "the heave of his juniper arx in action" (*FW* 583.2).
In that last citation I see, or hear, "Jupiter" in "juniper"; *arx* is the Latin
noun for citadel, or fortified heights. The siege tactic is clearly specified in
"piles big pelium on little ossas" (*FW* 128.35–36). Some mythological
accounts name the two rebellious Giants, Ephialtes and Otos, who stacked
the mountains in their futile try to reach the sky (*Odyssey* 11.305–20).
Joyce knew about these daring twins and incorporates them in a passage
packed with classical allusion: "while the massstab whereby Ephialtes has
exceeded is the measure, *simplex mendaciis,* by which our Outis cuts his
thruth" (*FW* 493.22–24). None of the tales directly involve Prometheus in
the defeat of Ephialtes and Otos; nonetheless, the loyal Titan did deserve
Zeus's thanks for general help in stanching the revolts. Zeus's subsequent

accusation of treason and his chaining of Prometheus to the crag are not the new divine king's finest hour. In the end, however, Prometheus is unbound and reconciled. Foresight prevails.

Heroes and Heroines

Not all the participants in the pageant of Greek mythology are gods and goddesses. The category of Heroes and Heroines is equally important. The capital *H* indicates the special status of this class of beings in having one divine parent; they are the offspring of a goddess and a human male or of a god and a human female. Immortal genes, however, are recessive. All Heroes and Heroines die, but their semidivine legacy inspires them to achieve pseudoimmortality. They do so by performing marvelous deeds that ensure that the memory of their names lives forever in mythology.

Heracles (Hercules)

As related earlier, the bizarre story of Heracles' conception involves Zeus's assumption of the human shape of Alcmene's husband for three nights of love with the beautiful mortal princess. Heracles was the fruit of this union. His name reflects a common theme in tales involving the philandering of the king of the gods. When Zeus's wife, Hera, learned of her husband's adultery, she took her revenge by forcing the mighty Heracles to perform Twelve Labors for one of her favorites, the timorous King Eurystheus. Thus, in a backhanded way, every mention of Heracles redounds to the goddess's "glory," since that is exactly what his name means in Greek, being a compound of *Hera* and *k/cleos* (fame, glory).

The Labors of Heracles did not include construction of a road, but this omission does not stop Joyce from stating that "it was Hercules' work" (*FW* 81.3; also note VI.B.8.105) in a passage that deals with highway construction and transportation. The reference to the Hero occurs just after mention of the Carthaginian general Hannibal. I know of no connection whatsoever between the two, but Joyce casually links the pair in another passage. At the end of the chapter "Cyclops," the Citizen throws a tin biscuit box at Bloom. It misses, but creates epic havoc as it clatters along the street. The "*débris*, human remains, etc" must be cleared away by "the men and officers of the Duke of Cornwall's light infantry," supervised by Rear Admiral Anderson. The first two "Christian" names of that august official are "Hercules Hannibal" (*U* 12.1893).

In both the previous two citations, the name appears in its more familiar Latin form, Hercules. In the draft for this chapter of *Ulysses*, the Greek spelling "Heracles" is used, then crossed out in favor of "Hercules."[42] The Latin version of the name is also converted into an adjective and used to indicate that HCE is enjoying "strong health": "he is in taken deal exceedingly herculeneous" (*FW* 570.16–17; also note VI.B.13.134). There is a classical precedent for Joyce's usage here. One of the cities destroyed by the eruption of Mount Vesuvius in A.D. 79 was Herculaneum, near Pompeii, in the Bay of Naples. Legend has it that this small port city was founded by Heracles when he docked his fleet there on his return from Iberia after capturing the cattle of Geryon in his Tenth Labor. While on this trek Heracles also came to the Strait of Gibraltar. To memorialize the extent of his journey he set up the Pillars of Hercules, which Joyce calls "the pilluls of hirculeads" (*FW* 128.36). These stone monuments are now known on the European side as the Rock of Gibraltar and on the Moroccan side as Jebel Musa (Moses' Mountain in Arabic).

The Eleventh Labor took Heracles to the western ends of the earth to get the apples of the Hesperides, which were guarded by a hundred-headed dragon. Heracles tricked the Titan Atlas, not only into gathering the apples from the dangerous garden but also into accepting, once again, the burden of the sky on his shoulders—while the crafty Hero searched for a pad to cushion the load. In another version, Heracles himself killed the dragon and stole the apples. The constellation Kneeling Heracles outlines the Hero fighting with the sentry-snake. Joyce refers obliquely to the second tale when he has Leopold Bloom point "out all the stars and the comets in the heavens . . . : The great bear and Hercules and the dragon, and the whole jingbang lot" (*U* 10.567–69). On his Twelfth (and last) Labor, Heracles went to the Underworld to bring back Hades' triple-headed watchdog, Cerberus, as a trophy for King Eurystheus. Some versions of this adventure report that Hades, trying to protect Cerberus, was wounded by Heracles.

Heracles' suffering did not cease when he had completed his Twelve Labors. Although the chronology is very confused and confusing, all the myths include the episode of the Madness of Heracles. Some place this horrible event before the tasks; others at their end. At any rate, Hera's hostility went so far as to strike the Hero with a sudden fit of insanity. During this period of rage he killed his children (and perhaps his wife). Joyce emphasizes the means and the victim of this divine vengeance:

"—Loonacied! Marterdyed!! Madwake*miheruloss*ed!!!" (*FW* 492.5; my
emphasis). The italicized portion of the final exclamation is the phonetic
equivalent of the Latin oath *mehercules,* which can be rendered as "By
Holy Hercules."[43]

After an agonizing death (burned alive by a poisoned robe wrongfully
prepared by his wife), Heracles suffered the fate of every mortal: His shade
descended into the realm of Hades. The Heroic son of Zeus, however, was
not destined to remain in the Underworld. He was assumed into Olympus,
reconciled to Hera, and perhaps married to her daughter Hebe (Youthful-
ness). In short, after all his troubles, Heracles—unique in Greek mythology—achieved posthumous immortality. Thus, when Odysseus visited
the Underworld, he saw not Heracles (who was then with the Immortals)
but a specter, an image (*eidolon*) of the Hero (*Odyssey* 11.601–4). Joyce
probably had this Homeric scene in mind in his "Hades" chapter, when
Bloom's imagination leaps from the cemetery caretaker, John O'Connell,
to the famous Irish hero Daniel O'Connell, buried in Glasnevin: "used to
say he was a queer breedy man great catholic all the same like a big giant
in the dark. Will o' the wisp" (*U* 6.751–52). Even if O'Connell's size and
the evanescence of his spirit are not meant to suggest Heracles' "phantom"
(as the Butcher and Lang version translates *eidolon*), there is something
symbolically missing from that hero's grave site. It is a fact that Daniel
O'Connell's body is at rest "in the middle of his people. . . . But his heart is
buried in Rome" (*U* 6.643–44).

Perseus

Although he too was involved in many Heroic adventures, Perseus is
almost totally neglected in Joyce's fiction. He was the son of Zeus
(disguised as a shower of golden rain) and Danaë. His most notable feat
was the rescue of Andromeda from a horrible sea creature. With the tactical help of several gods, Perseus first slew the Gorgon Medusa, whose face
had the effect of turning into stone anyone who gazed at it. Then he used
Medusa's severed head to petrify the monster who threatened the maiden
Andromeda. In the *Wake* Medusa's baleful power is transferred to HCE,
who "acts active, peddles in passivism and is a gorgon of selfridgeousness"
(*FW* 137.33–34; also note VI.B.31.135).

Dioscuri (Gemini)

The Gemini—the Twins Castor and Polydeuces (Pollux), sons born to
Leda—have an odd genealogy. In Homer they are the human sons of King

Tyndareus of Sparta. Later writers call them the "Sons of Zeus" (*Dios-kouroi*), although Castor is sometimes considered to be fully mortal, while Polydeuces is almost always a Hero. (Their sisters, Helen and Clytemnestra, share this genetic confusion: the former is Zeus's daughter, the latter merely a mortal princess.) The Twins had their earliest adventures as Argonauts led by Jason. Castor was a tamer of horses; Polydeuces was a boxer. After Castor was killed by a rival for a woman he hoped to marry, Polydeuces begged Zeus to allow him to share in the Heroic life force of his mortal brother. Zeus permitted the Dioscuri to spend alternate days in Hades and Olympus. He also transformed both of them into the constellation known as the Twins (*Gemini* in Latin). Some say that one of the two brightest stars in this zodiacal cluster is always visible above the horizon, an astral symbol of the fraternal bond that moved Polydeuces (Pollux) to sacrifice some of his semi-immortality for his brother. Joyce included Pollux in a list of Heroes whose adventures included a "Descent into Hell."[44]

The Dioscuri do not appear in *Ulysses*, but an archival note indicates that Joyce was aware of their allusive potential: "ʳBros Guiness. 2 noble peers (Castor & Pollux)" (*UNBM* 94:13). In "Cyclops," the "brewery of Messrs Arthur Guinness, Son and Company (Limited)" (*U* 12.1453–54) commemorates only one of the founder's knighted sons (Arthur, Baron Ardilaun); the other son (Edward, Baron Iveagh) seems to have slipped beneath Joyce's referential horizon. That omission, however, is only apparent. At the beginning of the "Cyclops" chapter, Alf Bergan is ceremoniously given "a crystal cup full of the foamy ebon ale which the noble twin brothers Bungiveagh and Bungardilaun brew ever in their divine alevats, cunning as the sons of deathless Leda" (*U* 12.280–83). Here the pre-textual entry has been expanded to include the twinship of both parties in the allusion, as well as an acknowledgment of Leda, the mother of the Dioscuri.

In the "Night Lessons" section of *Finnegans Wake*, the marginal entry "*Castor, Pollux*" is keyed to the essay topic "Compare the Fistic Styles of Jimmy Wilde and Jack Sharkey" (*FW* 307L and 19–20). Here the reputation of Pollux as a Heroic boxer receives all the attention,[45] while Castor's equestrian talents are overlooked. All of the other Wakean references to the Dioscuri involve verbal play with their names: "cat's hours on the Pollockes'" (*FW* 28.5–6); "Caxton and Pollock" (*FW* 229.31); "castor and porridge" (*FW* 489.16). Another invocation links one of the Twins with Apollo: "O Phoebus! O Pollux!" (*FW* 431.36); the other is mentioned one

line later: "Castor's" (*FW* 432.1). That reference also identifies the mythological Twins with the *Wake*'s fraternal pair, Shem and Shaun, styled
"younkers twain" (*FW* 431.35). To ensure that no readers miss the allusion, there is a nearby appeal for some "oldworld tales of homespinning
derringdo and *dieobscure* and daddyho" (*FW* 431.22; my emphasis). The
italicized word is close to the Latin phrase for "on a murky day"; it also
sounds out the Twins' Greek title, Dioscuri.

Tiresias

In Greek mythology Tiresias is only marginally a Hero. Although his
mother, a minor nymph, was immortal, Tiresias's adventures are neither
epic in scope nor personally tragic, but his participation in matters human
and divine was extensive. Tiresias was the blind seer in the city of Thebes.
That location assured him a role in Sophocles' *Oedipus the King* and
Antigone, as well as in Euripides' *Bacchae*. In those dramas he acted, without saving effect, as the medium between rash mortal proposal and crush-
ing divine disposal. In Homer's *Odyssey* Tiresias instructs the voyager on
his trip to Hades and predicts a favorable outcome to his wanderings.

The primary tale of the cause of Tiresias's blindness and his prophetic
mission pivots around Olympian sexual rivalry. But even before the critical instance, he was involved in a pair of odd metamorphoses that quali-
fied him to serve as an arbiter in a divine quarrel. While a young man,
Tiresias came upon two snakes copulating on a mountain trail. He struck
and killed the female with his club—and was immediately transformed
into a woman. A number of years later, he found another pair of snakes,
also copulating. This time he killed the male—and resumed his former
masculine form. Since he had had the unique experience of personally
engaging in human sexual activity as both a mature male and a mature
female,[46] he was called upon to adjudicate a marital argument between
Zeus and Hera. The point of divine contention was whether the man or
the woman enjoyed more pleasure in sexual intercourse. Tiresias
responded in an oracular couplet: "If the joy of sex be divided into ten, /
Nine parts go to females, one for men." Hera, who had been complaining
that she and those of her gender always gave more than they got, was
infuriated. She struck Tiresias blind; Zeus compensated him with an inner
sight, the gift of prophecy.

In his Zürich notebook Joyce jotted down the details of that tale and added another "cause" for the seer's blindness: "saw Minerva [Athena] at bath" (VIII.A.5.29; also note *UNBM* 281–82:123–24 and VI.B.17.80). An adjacent entry reports that he "ʳunderstood birds speech" (VIII.A.5.29). In "Nausicaa" Leopold Bloom transfers that vatic talent to young women like Gerty MacDowell: "Of course they understand birds, animals, babies" (*U* 13.903–4). Two archival entries identify Tiresias as the one who revealed all the details of Zeus's disguise when the god became Amphitryon to make love to his wife, Alcmene (VIII.A.5.32; *UNBM* 281:123–26). A later note for *Ulysses* modernizes the seer's mission: "ᵇCirce's Tiresias, her tipster" (*UNBM* 320:19). In Homer's epic Circe tells Odysseus that he must consult Tiresias in Hades, but there is no mention that the seer was a source of information for the witch herself. Another note, taken directly from Bérard, seems to suggest a Semitic antecedent for the prophet's name and his necromancy: "Tiresias—le d.r.s. (Heb) / evokes ghosts."[47] In the "Circe" chapter of *Ulysses,* one of Bella Cohen's whores reveals that the madam is "on the job herself tonight with the vet, her tipster, that gives her all the winners" (*U* 15.1288–89). It is natural that a veterinarian, perhaps on duty at the racetrack, should be able to tip off Bella about the sure bets; it is purely mythological that the tipster should be connected with Tiresias, who understood birds and animals.

Various commentators have detected other cameo appearances of Tiresias in *Ulysses.* While walking along Sandymount strand Stephen Dedalus thinks, "Seadeath, mildest of all deaths known to man" (*U* 3.482–83); in the *Odyssey* Tiresias assures the wanderer that he will return to Ithaca, then "from the sea shall thine own death come, the gentlest death that may be" (*Odyssey* 11.134–35) (see chapter 5).

There is only one clear reference to Tiresias in the *Wake.* His marginal name in "Night Lessons" is linked to the following title of an essay: "Is the Co-Education of Animus and Anima Wholly Desirable?" (*FW* 307L and 3–4). This obvious allusion to the tale of Tiresias's alternating sex is keyed to variants in grammatical gender in the Latin words *animus, -a.* Carl Jung exploited the same distinction in formulating a pair of the technical terms for his brand of psychoanalysis.

Reversal of sexual orientation is the primary gimmick in the plot of Guillaume Apollinaire's surreal verse drama *Les Mamelles de Tirésias.* Joyce commented on this play in a July 25, 1925, letter from Paris to his brother Stanislaus in Trieste. There are several distinct echoes of this work in the

Wake, including the bi-gendered noun-adjective "Teheresiann" (*FW* 538.2) and the puzzling parentheses in which female-male bodily characteristics are confused: "(*tout est sacré pour un sacreur, femme à barbe ou homme-nourrice*)" (*FW* 81.28–29).[48]

The last items of mythological lore in this chapter are a few miscellaneous details. At the earliest level of his genealogy of the gods, Hesiod reports that "from Chaos were born Erebus and black Night" (*Theogony* 123). An archival diagram (VI.B.16.137) shows that Joyce had noted these primeval births. There is also evidence that he was aware of the root meaning of the Greek noun *chaos:* not confusion or disorder, but a yawn, gape, or division. Chaos in Hellenic mythology, then, was the start of a cosmic process of separation and arrangement, as reflected in "dividual chaos" (*FW* 186.4–5) and "every person, place and thing in the Chaosmos of Alle" (*FW* 118.21). The connection between order and chaos, paradoxical to a speaker of English, is reinforced by the following linguistic conundrums: "—Yet this was has meed peace? *In voina viritas. Ab chaos lex,* neat wehr?" (*FW* 518.31–32). Here the Latin maxim *in vino veritas* (in wine is truth) is combined with the Russian *voina* (as in Tolstoy's *Voina i mir*), with the Latin *virtus* (manly courage), and with *viritim* (man by man, separately). For the next phrase, "Ab chaos lex," read "From [*ab* in Latin] chaos comes law" (*lex* in Latin—which hints of light, *lux*). All of the paradoxes are confirmed by the formulaic German phrase *nicht wahr?* (that's correct, isn't it?), the noun *Wehr* (weapon, defense), and the adjective *wirr* (confused, chaotic)—the last item making a tidy contrast with the adjacent word in the text, "neat." Chaos's offspring, Erebus (Darkness) and Nyx (Night), also have a moment of dubious notoriety in the *Wake:* "The phay*nix* rose a sun before *Erebia* sank his smother!" (*FW* 473.16–17; my emphases).

Another Wakean motif of paramount importance, the Tree and Stone, may also owe some of its genetic force to Hesiod's poem on the origins of the gods. In a March 7, 1924, letter to Miss Weaver, Joyce announced that he had just completed the "Anna Livia" piece that would later become episode I.8 in the *Wake.* He wrote, "It is a chattering dialogue across the river by two washerwomen who as night falls become a tree and a stone" (*Letters* I.218). Throughout the last section of the women's gossip (*FW* 212.20–216.5), there are all sorts of arboreal and petrological allusions. Early in the *Theogony* Hesiod claims to have been selected by the Muses to celebrate the race of the gods and to sing of themselves, first and last. Then comes a verse that puzzles ancient and modern commentators: "But what is this of oak or rock to me?" (*Theogony* 35). It is likely that the maxim is meant to imply that the generational and dynastic conflicts of the gods were of greater significance to the poet than the lavish praise demanded by the Muses.[49] At any rate, the presence of a tree (*drys* was used generically for tree as well as for a specific oak) and a stone at the start of Hesiod's poem may have attracted enough of Joyce's attention to have been worked into the chatter of a pair of very un-Muse-like contributors to the *Wake*.

This chapter's final example of mythological allusion owes everything to the linguistic expertise of two essential first-level annotators of the *Wake*. "Night Lessons" brings the appearance of the couple "Tytonyhands and Vlossyhair" (*FW* 265.21). McHugh supplies a pair of totally unexpected glosses: *tytón* (Polish for tobacco) and *wlosy* (Polish for hair). Since HCE was a heavy smoker, his hands may have stained by nicotine; ALP fussed about the "auburnt streams" of her hair, but they were neither flossy nor glossy. O Hehir and Dillon gloss "tyton-" with Tithonus, who was immortalized as the lover of the goddess Eos (Dawn) (*Odyssey* 5.1). They also note that Homer sometimes modifies Eos by the epithet *euplokamos* (literally, "with goodly hair") (*Odyssey* 5.390). The union of this couple had a sad ending. Eos—who seems to have been flighty as well as fair-tressed—neglected to ask Zeus to grant Tithonus eternal youth along with the gift of immortality. Thus, she left his bed "when the first grey hair sprouted from his beautiful head." The goddess kept Tithonus in her heavenly house and fed him nectar and ambrosia, but Eos finally had to lock her aging mate in his room when he became too feeble to move.[50] There is no hint of such a fate in store for HCE at the hands of ALP in the *Wake*.

Thus did Joyce use divine and Heroic characters in Greek mythology. In the beginning, the transparently cosmogenic reign of the Sky King and Earth Queen gave way to a paranoid child-swallower, who was in turn deposed by the currently reigning Lord of Olympus. Some irreverent teachers have characterized many of the subsequent mythological tales as the sexual adventures of "Zeus on the loose." That judgment would certainly be supported by Hera—and by such as Danaë, Leda, Callisto, Alcmene. The weird births of Aphrodite and Athena are emblematic of their functions, the one as the goddess of sexual rapture, the other as the Lady of Prudence. The divine foils, Apollo and Dionysus, play only minor roles in Joyce's fiction, while Hermes appears frequently in several appropriate forms. The Underworld realm of Hades is more important than his personality; the Sun (Helius) and the Winds (Aeolus) are superhuman forces. Prometheus's forethought benefits mortals but exasperates Zeus.

Subsequent chapters in this book deal with the mortal participants in the Trojan War (*Iliad*) and the long trip home for the survivors (*Odyssey*). A generation before the Homeric warriors launched their ships, the mighty Heracles, in compensation for his suffering, became immortal after he died. He, the loyal Dioscuri, and blind Tiresias—as well as the epic Achilles and Helen—validate Pindar's marvelously paradoxical formulation of the test and the reward of ancient Greek Heroes: "Not all who die die."[51]

4

The Iliad

In his *Iliad* Homer sings of the wrath of Achilles and its terrible consequences for both the Greeks and their enemies on the plain outside the walls of Troy. Those events take place during the tenth (and last) year of the war; they mark the onset of the final stages of the siege. The conclusion of combat leads to the capture and destruction of the city, the dissolution of the Achaean forces, and the return home of the victors. Among the warriors who survive the battles that "hurled down into Hades many strong souls of heroes, and gave their bodies to be a prey to dogs and all winged fowls" (*Iliad* 1.3–5)[1] is Odysseus. The adventures that he experienced on his way from the war zone to Ithaca are the plot of the *Odyssey*.

The fall of Troy, then, is the necessary precedent to the tale of the many epic turns of Odysseus.[2] Fittingly enough, that same sequence of Homeric chronology and geography marked a major phase of Joyce's documentary research for his own contemporary epic. It is well known that he scoured Victor Bérard's *Les Phéniciens et l'Odyssée* for many of the esoteric details that lie behind *Ulysses*. It is almost certain, however, that Joyce first learned of Bérard's work in another volume of early twentieth-century scholarship, Walter Leaf's *Troy: A Study in Homeric Geography*. The evidence for the priority of this source was established by Rose and O'Hanlon in their reconstruction of a lost notebook.[3] The key element in their ingenious detective work is a series of three notes composed of Bérard's name, the title of his book, and a direct quotation ("loi des isthmes") from his text. These entries on page 40 of the reconstructed *Lost Notebook* come directly from Leaf's study, pages 257–59. The date for these notes is summer–autumn 1917; the place is Zürich. That venue is confirmed by an entry on the front cover verso of the reconstructed notebook: "P & ZG1116/117." The initial *P* represents the title of Bérard's two-volume work (*Phéniciens*); the second half of the entry is the call numbers for the two volumes in the Zentralbibliothek Zürich.[4] Four pages of notes from Leaf's work (41–38) are followed by more than nine pages (37–24) from Bérard's.

In terms of the actual composition of *Ulysses*, Joyce seems to have used none of the notes from Leaf that are reproduced in the *Lost Notebook*. Moreover, all of the more than sixty archival entries come from about seventy-five pages in Leaf's chapter entitled "The Allies and the War." Joyce did not bother with the central archaeological material that the scholar used to locate the site of Homeric Troy at Hissarlik, as excavated by Schliemann and Dörpfeld. The data that Joyce chose to excerpt are primarily background to the Homeric events. He noted, for example, that Troy was a mercantile center, with a late summer fair. The war itself was probably "a sordid commercial war," like the one England waged against Spain in the eighteenth century over "Jenkins's ear."[5]

Only three *Lost Notebook* entries can be directly related to the text of Homer's *Iliad*. The homeland of an important Trojan ally is commemorated in the reference to the Carian custom of staining "horses' ivory cheek-piece purple"; in the epic a simile compares the blood on Menelaus's white skin to a similar artifact (*Iliad* 4.141–47). Another item commemorates the two heroic commanders of the Lycians, Glaucus and Sarpedon, the "only [Trojan] allies not mercenary" (*Iliad* 2.876–77, 12.307–328). Third, Joyce notes Leaf's comments on the rarity and value of iron in the Homeric epics: "Achilles gave him [Polypoites] lump pigiron as the prize," since he threw this weight (made of what was then considered a precious metal) the farthest during the funeral games for Patroclus (*Iliad* 23.826–49).[6]

The two previous paragraphs are designed to illustrate a salient and abiding feature of Joyce's note taking: He rarely concentrates on material that will be used to work out his plot or to flesh out his characters. Rather, even after Homer's Odyssean patterns had long been established as a framework for *Ulysses*, Joyce took a four-page run of notes from Leaf's book on the epic geography of Troy, a distinctly Iliadic topic. And only in the course of skimming the sixth chapter of that scholarly book did he first come across mention of Bérard's work, the text that scholars rightly regard as the quintessential source of Joyce's recherché Phoenician-Odyssean lore and of the Semitic origins of its hero, Leopold Bloom. The lesson learned in examining the *Lost Notebook*'s entries derived from Leaf's study is that Joyce does not seek psychological insight, thematic relevance, or plot parallels in his documentary sources. His typical notes are random in content, with an emphasis on odd terms and exotic proper names of people and places. While it is presumptuous to make a definitive statement based on so small a sample (especially since none of the Leaf notes were reused in the text of *Ulysses*), it is safe to say that Joyce's primary interest in these source notes is lexical. In the selection of material to be entered into a notebook, the shape and sound of the words are, generally speaking, more important than their conceptual force. The same focus is found in Joyce's use of other source documents. This does not mean that he completely ignored the information and conclusions of his sources; rather, these aspects of the various documents (scholarly, popular, literary, journalistic) were not the main motive for his note taking or for his deployment of archival entries in his fiction.

So much for the notebook entries from a primarily Iliadic source. In the transfer of material from literary or secondary sources to the text of Joyce's works, I have detected only a handful of instances that can be directly traced to Homer's war epic. The longest and best-known of these passages is the description of ALP's detailed attention to her hair, skin, perfume, and jewelry before she ventures forth in the "Anna Livia" chapter of *Finnegans Wake*. The scene (*FW* 206.29–207.14) is closely modeled on Hera's elaborate preparations (*Iliad* 14.161–86) prior to her seduction of Zeus so as to divert his attention from the battlefield. While the King of Gods and Men was asleep in her arms, Hera roused her Olympian allies to assist the Greeks and to repulse the Trojan assault on their ships. This divine ruse, called the *Dios apatē* (the deception of Zeus) is discussed in more detail in the section on the goddess-queen in chapter 3. The similarities in detail, tone, and structure indicate that Joyce had a translation of the *Iliad* (again, most likely the Lang, Leaf and Myers version) directly at hand as he composed this scene in the *Wake*.

In another passage for which there appears to be a direct source in the *Iliad*, the Greek text itself is part of the evidence. In the opening scene of the epic, a Trojan priest, Chryses, comes to the Greek camp and begs to ransom his daughter, who is being held by King Agamemnon as his spearwife. When the Greek commander-in-chief rebuffs the captive woman's father, the old man retreats to the seashore and prays to Apollo. He implores the Lord of the Silver Bow to listen to him, "if I have ever *roofed over* a shrine pleasing to you" (*Iliad* 1.39). My literal, italicized translation of the central verb (*erepsa*) in the plea is based on the root meaning given for that word in the standard dictionaries of the Homeric dialect.[7] That same quite rare verb appears a second time very near the end of the epic, when Hermes has escorted King Priam of Troy to the seaside camp of Achilles. The old man is seeking to ransom the mutilated corpse of his son, Hector. The pair approach "the *lodge* of the son of Peleus [Achilles] . . . which the Myrmidons built for their commander . . . and *roofed over* (*Iliad* 24.448–50). I suggest that Joyce ran both of these Homeric passages together, and that he imitated both in a deliberately archaicizing translation of their shared verb. The *Wake* context for this epic wordplay is Shem's First Question in I.6. The Penman recites a long list of the master builder's construction projects, in one of which HCE "put a roof on the lodge for Hymn" (*FW* 136.16).

The presence of the key Homeric verb is obvious. My suspicion that *both* Iliadic instances of its use have been combined by Joyce is based on the verb's direct and indirect objects in the *Wake*'s text. There the structure that HCE has roofed over is a "lodge" (*klisēn* in Greek) not a "shrine" (*nēon*) for a god. That direct object points to the second Homeric passage as its source. On the other hand, the Wakean structure is made to please a capitalized "Hymn," and Apollo (the beneficiary of the building in the first Homeric passage) is the god of music. In fact, one of Apollo's primary epithets is Paion, since "paeans" (war cries, hymns of praise) were sung to him. Finally, there is an intriguing Notebook entry that may have something to do with these passages: "help to roof a house for Jesus / Canon Nestor" (VI.B.2.137). Nestor, the venerable host of Telemachus in the *Odyssey*, does not appear in either the first or the last book of the *Iliad;* but he, Apollo's priest Chryses, and King Priam certainly are archetypal old men. Perhaps Joyce mixed together his Homeric golden-agers, and decided to add a Christian dimension (Jesus for Apollo) to his archival revision of the Homeric motif. At any rate, in my judgment, the two Iliadic appearances of *erepsa/-an*, the dictionary definitions of this extremely uncommon verb, and Joyce's roofing of a Wakean lodge can not be a coincidence, much less one of such of epic proportions. HCE's achievement was designed to be a cryptic allusion to the pair of phrases, alpha and omega, in the Greek text of Homer.

A far more obvious use of a Homeric phrase in the original language is "Anaks Andrum" (*FW* 240.27; also note "anaxandren" [VI.B.31.226]). Again, the contextual referent is HCE, whose dubious merits are being recounted. In a translation of the phrase from the Greek, HCE is being dubbed a "battle-king of warriors." The original Homeric epithet, *anax andrōn,* is most often applied to Agamemnon, notably in the opening lines of the *Iliad* when Homer calls upon the Muse to sing of the wrath generated by the dispute between "the son of Atreus [Agamemnon], *anax andrōn,* and god-like, shining Achilles" (*Iliad* 1.7). Since the epithet is well known and used throughout both Homeric epics, I hesitate to claim that its initial Iliadic appearance, however emphatic, is unquestionably the source. Nevertheless, shortly after this adaptation of the phrase, it is revealed that HCE has a "portemanteau *priamed* full potatowards" (*FW* 240.36–241.1; my emphasis). Here the name of King Agamemnon's opposite number, King Priam of Troy, has been converted into a past participle. That lexical-grammatical metamorphosis suggests that the *Iliad* was on Joyce's mind here.

There is a final, polysyllabic instance for which Joyce—or one of his Homeric informants—must have made direct reference to the Greek text. In the first book of the *Iliad,* after Agamemnon has refused to return Chryses' daughter, the old priest of Apollo left the Achaean camp and "fared silently along the shore of the loud-sounding sea" (*Iliad* 1.34). In the original Greek the compound adjective is *polyphloisboio;* in the *Wake* the formulaic phrase memorably reappears as the "polyfizzyboisterous seas" (*FW* 547.24–25; also note VI.B.11.69). The fact that the onomatopoeic epithet occurs just five lines before Chryses reminds Apollo of having "roofed a shrine" for him strongly supports my case for immediate textual reference for the latter phrase.

The next example of Iliadic influence on Joyce does not come directly from the text of the epic; in fact, the evidence involves a comparison between the hero of the *Iliad* and the hero of the *Odyssey.* In a 1903 review of a literary study of Shakespeare, Joyce mocks the author, who wrote that both warriors delivered "'philosophic speeches during the siege of Troy. . . . They evidently turn aside from their grand object for a brief space to utter words of profound wisdom.'" The author's sentence before those remarks seems to have irritated Joyce even more: "'His noble comrade [Ulysses] fully rivals Achilles in wisdom as in valour.'" The editors of *The Critical Writings* add a note to this quotation: "For Joyce now, as later, the wise Ulysses had nothing in common with the bullying Achilles" (*CW* 137–38).

That editorial judgment is probably true, but it cannot be supported by citation from *Ulysses* or any other of Joyce's works. His only comparative comment on the two epic heroes is, as a matter of serendipitous fact, composed in Greek. While in Zürich during World War I, Joyce began a series of exercises designed to improve his basic competence in modern Greek (*JJII* 408–9).[8] A number of notebook pages—vocabulary lists; practice sentences; elementary translations of letters, songs, stories; and other instructional material—have survived from this period. On the first page of one collection of these Berlitz-like exercises, Joyce wrote the Greek sentence that I translate here: "Achilles was the most fearless [*aphobotatos*] of the Greeks, but Odysseus had circled the world [*kosmogyrismenos*]" (VIII.A.1.1). In chapter 5 I suggest that latter participle, in Joyce's own hand, was part of the process that led to the characterization of Leopold Bloom as a "cultured allroundman" (*U* 10.581). Achilles, the god-like, swift-footed sacker of cities, is also appropriately modified in the exercise, although the adjective that Joyce selected does not occur in Homer.

During the war at Troy it was destined that many "Gricks may rise and Troysirs fall" (*FW* 11.35–36). The ostensible occasion for the conflict was the rape of Helen, queen of Sparta, by the Trojan prince, Paris. That instance of wife stealing, however, had been sanctioned by the goddess Aphrodite: Helen was the bribe/prize awarded to Paris for his judgment that Aphrodite was the most beautiful of the three female Olympians who contended for the golden Apple of Discord. That fatal fruit (engraved with the phrase "to the most beautiful") had been rolled down the divine head table, at a banquet, by the goddess Eris (Discord, Strife). Eris had not been invited to the feast, and the goddess characteristically sought to stir up trouble. The occasion being celebrated was the marriage of the sea nymph Thetis to a mortal, King Peleus of Phthia. The foregoing chain of events not only outlines the steps that led to the Trojan War but also demonstrates the emphasis on detailed causality in mythology—nothing is accidental.

Additional proof of myth's demand for specific reasons for every turn of affairs is the identity of the bride and groom at the wedding banquet cited above. When Prometheus (Foresight) told Zeus that he knew who would overthrow the third Olympian dynasty, the King of Gods and Men demanded that vital information. Prometheus said he would reveal his secret if Zeus released him from the Caucasian crag to which he had been bound for alleged rebellion. Zeus agreed, the gods were reconciled, and

Prometheus identified the nymph Thetis as the potential mother of the usurper god. Armed with this secret information about the future, Zeus prudently determined that Thetis would never be allowed to mate with one of the gods—she would never bear an immortal child. Thus it was that Thetis was betrothed to the mortal Peleus, and all the Olympian gods and goddesses (except Eris), their dynasty secure, attended the wedding ceremony. The only child of Peleus and Thetis was the Hero Achilles. (It is hard to imagine what deeds he might have done had he been born an immortal, of two divine parents.) At any rate, Achilles set out to gain pseudoimmortality by performing epic feats that would guarantee that his name would live forever.

Thetis was aware that her son's drive for enduring fame would propel him into deadly situations. Thus, when he was still an infant, she attempted to make him invulnerable by dipping him into the waters of the River Styx in the Underworld. In this way, Achilles' entire body was supernaturally protected—except for the tendon of the heel by which Thetis held her infant son when she "baptized" him. In the "Eumaeus" chapter of *Ulysses,* much is made of Thetis's futile attempt to forestall fate. Leopold Bloom meditates on the perilous state of the British Empire: "The Boers were the beginning of the end. Brummagen England was toppling already and her downfall would be Ireland, her Achilles heel, which he explained to them about the vulnerable point of Achilles, the Greek hero, a point his auditors at once seized as he completely gripped their attention by showing the tendon referred to on his boot" (*U* 16.1002–1006). Later in the same episode Bloom remembers "his gentle repartee" from earlier in the day at Barney Kiernan's and lands a cross-cultural jab: "The most vulnerable point too of tender Achilles. Your god was a jew" (*U* 16.1637–41). Bloom's final application of this mythological allusion occurs as he prepares to escort Stephen away from the shelter; he skips around "to get on his companion's right, a habit of his, by the bye; his right side being, in classical idiom, his tender Achilles" (*U* 16.1715–16).

Things characteristically are taken a few steps further in *Finnegans Wake.* During the debate between the Mookse and the Gripes, the latter says he always wishes "on all my extemities"; the former counters by telling his opponent to address *his* extremities and, pointing to lifted heel, to "Ask my index, mund my achilles" (*FW* 154.18). Later in the work, Issy tries to tell Shaun that her secret color is heliotrope. Her medium of revelation is a riddle that begins "My top it was brought Achill's low" (*FW* 248.11); here the "top" is the first three letters of "*hel*iotrope," which sound like "heel."

The only other Joycean reference to the Hero-warrior of the *Iliad* occurs in the National Library chapter of *Ulysses*. As he stands in the office, the inner sanctum, Stephen contemplates the "coffined thoughts around [him], in mummy cases, embalmed in spice of words" (*U* 9.352–53). Among the desiccated remains of the past to which the librarian devotes his life are "things not known: what name Achilles bore when he lived among the women" (*U* 9.350–51). That is an allusion to another strata-gem that Thetis used to prevent Achilles from risking his life in the Trojan War. She insisted that her nine-year-old son be dressed as a girl and be kept among the daughters of King Lycomedes on the island of Skyros. Six years later Odysseus uncovered the disguise when he placed various femi-nine trinkets, along with a spear and a shield, before the children of Lycomedes' court. The girls played with the trinkets, but Achilles grabbed the weapons when Odysseus ordered a battle alarm to be sounded. That very day the son of Thetis and Peleus sailed off to Troy as one of the commanders of the Greek fleet. And, with appropriate mythological attention to onomastic detail, several ancient sources report that the name borne by Achilles while he was in disguise among the women was Pyrrha (Fire, Flame).[9]

Heroic rage and scorn for death propel the plot of the *Iliad*. Early in the epic, just after Achilles reacts to Agamemnon's insult by announcing that he will not fight, all the Greek troops are marshaled beside the ship. Agamemnon addresses the conclave and presents an ill-conceived ploy to test their loyalty. The troops believe that their battle leader is sincerely suggesting that they abandon the siege and sail home. It is Odysseus who must bring his comrades back in line. One man in the ranks babbles on, Thersites, "the uncontrolled of speech, whose mind was full of words many and disorderly, wherewith to strive against the chiefs. . . . Hateful was he to Achilles above all and to Odysseus." Odysseus shuts Thersites up by beating him on the back and shoulders with his staff. The warriors laugh at Thersites' tears, and praise Odysseus for silencing the loose-mouthed buffoon (*Odyssey* 2.211–77).

Stanislaus Joyce applies elements of the *Iliad*'s unique scene of totally unheroic behavior to his own domestic situation in Dublin. In his memoir of their early life in Dublin, Stanislaus says that James's friends accepted him as his "brother's rather taciturn henchman. My father, Thersites-like, called me my brother's jackel."[10] That judgment, even in a classical simile, is a harsh one to bring against one's father. Stanislaus, however, was probably less concerned with exact parallel than with suggesting that he frequently acted as a circumspect Odysseus by deflecting scorn aimed at his impetuous Achillean brother. At any rate, the anecdote is additional evidence that both the elder and the younger generation of Joyces were adept at epic invective and allusion. In two of his studies of *Ulysses,* Ellmann links Thersites, "the most foul-spoken of the Greek host," to Buck Mulligan and to the black-hearted narrator of "Cyclops."[11]

The most disastrous personal consequence of Achilles' withdrawal from combat is the death of Patroclus, his loyal comrade, who asks to borrow Achilles' armor and rush to the front lines. This action will rally the Greeks and terrify the Trojans, both of whom will think that Achilles has returned to the fight. During this strategic foray, the god Apollo and Prince Hector bring Patroclus down and strip off his borrowed armor. Achilles, stunned with guilt and aflame for revenge, returns to the war, slays Hector, then celebrates the magnificent funeral games in honor of his dead comrade. Joyce alludes to that episode in the *Wake.* During one of the replays of HCE's interrogation, the alleged perpetrator is addressed: "I want you, witness of this *epic struggle* . . . to reconstruct for us . . . how these *funeral games* . . . took place" (*FW* 515.21–25; my emphases; note "ᵣfuneral games" [VI.B.14.213]).[12] In the midst of this passage there is a specific reference to one of the individual contests, the archery competition in which the target was a wild dove tethered to a pole. The shot of the first competitor severed the cord. As the string hung loose, Meriones notched his arrow, invoked Apollo, hit the bird, and won the prize (*Iliad* 23.850–83). Joyce condensed the details of this contest into "homer's kerryer pidgeons, massacreedoed as the holiname rally round place" (*FW* 515.24–25; also note VI.C.1.29).

After Achilles, the most feared warrior in the Greek forces at Troy is Ajax. In the *Iliad* he goes on several rampages, but his primary function is to act as the defensive bulwark of the Achaeans. Nothing illustrates this heroic service on the battlefield better than the warrior's stand, with his tower-high shield, over the corpse of Patroclus after Achilles' comrade has been slain by Hector (*Iliad* 17.123–761). Joyce obliquely alludes to Ajax's ferocity in the "Circe" chapter of *Ulysses*. There Signor Maffei is introduced in a lion tamer's costume; part of his spiel is the claim that he "broke in the bucking bronco Ajax with [his] potent spiked saddle" (*U* 15.709).

In his postwar wanderings Odysseus meets the ghost of Ajax in the Underworld, but the fierce warrior has not died in combat. Rather, after the death of Achilles (who was hit in the heel by an arrow shot by Paris), the Hero's divinely crafted armor was to be given to the most deserving comrade. Quite naturally Ajax expected that this magnificent prize would be his. Instead, Agamemnon and the other commanders decided to signal the start of a new phase in the war for Troy—strategic maneuver before explosive onslaught. They consequently awarded Achilles' armor to a different type of hero, Odysseus, the man of many turns. Like any prudent warrior who learns that he has been declared obsolete, Ajax planted his sword in the ground and fell on it. Thus, when the specter of Ajax sees the still-living Odysseus walking through the land of Hades, he refuses to reply to his rival's conciliatory greeting and walks away amid the souls of the other dead warriors. Many commentators have detected a parallel to this Homeric scene in Joyce's final episode of the "Hades" chapter in *Ulysses*. Leopold Bloom has politely pointed out to John Henry Menton that there is "a dinge in the side of his hat." Mr. Menton "[s]tared at him for an instant without moving" (*U* 6.1015–19). The cause of John Henry Menton's epic grudge was his memory of one evening on the bowling green when Bloom spun a ball inside Menton's winner: "Hate at first sight" (*U* 6.1012).

Among the attempts to inject local color and verisimilitude into the tale of his meeting with HCE, the tramp utters a phrase that both includes an adjectival form of the name Ajax and summarizes his epic character: "all fortitudinous ajaxious rowdinoisy tenuacity" (*FW* 53.16–17). That does very nicely for the gigantic warrior to whom Homer assigned the epithet "bulwark of the Achaeans" (*Iliad* 3.229 and elsewhere). Ajax also appears in the *Wake* in the same sentence as the "polyfizzyboisterous seas"; there another Joycean epithet underscores his unflinching bravery, and his name incorporates his huge size: "quailless Highjakes" (*FW* 547.22–23). In addition to the glory he won on the battlefield, Ajax was also a fierce competitor in contests of athletic skill and strength. In the funeral games of Patroclus, Ajax entered three of the seven events: wrestling, which ended in a draw between him and Odysseus (*Iliad* 23.735–37); close combat against Diomedes, a contest that Achilles stopped and declared a tie, but awarded the prize to Diomedes (*Iliad* 23.822–25); and the weight throw, a decisive victory for Polypoites over Ajax (*Iliad* 23.842–49). These details explain the essay topic assigned to "*Ajax*" in "Night Lessons": "The Dublin Police Sports at Ballsbridge" (*FW* 306.L2, 24–25). There is also a brief allusion to the boxing match (*Iliad* 23.651–99) at the funeral games: "baxingmotch and a myrmidins of psozlers" (*FW* 415.13–14). Confirmation that the context is Homeric comes from the garbled presence of Achilles' troops, the Myrmidon soldiers, at Joycean ringside.

In the second chapter of *Ulysses*, allusive phrases crop up in Mr. Garrett Deasy's letter to the *Evening Telegraph*. In the midst of warning about foot-and-mouth disease, the schoolmaster asks to be "[p]ardoned a classical allusion" (*U* 3.329).[13] A bit later the reference is expanded by its author's comments: "A woman brought sin into the world. For a woman who was no better than she should be, Helen, the runaway wife of Menelaus, ten years the Greeks made war on Troy. A faithless wife first brought strangers to our shore here" (*U* 3.390–93; also see *U* 7.536–37). In his widespread chronological and geographical indictment of women, Deasy neatly summarizes the traditional reason for the war that drives the action of the Homeric epics. When Prince Paris of Troy was asked to judge the divine beauty contest to determine which goddess (Hera, Athena, or Aphrodite) would receive the Golden Apple, each of the Olympian contenders attempted to bribe him. Hera offered power in exchange for his vote; Athena offered wisdom; Aphrodite offered beauty. Paris accepted Aphrodite's tender and was rewarded by being given Helen, the most beautiful mortal woman. Helen, the wife of Menelaus, king of Sparta, ran away—or was forced to sail away—to Troy with Paris. Menelaus's brother, King Agamemnon of Mycenae, then assembled a force of Greek warriors to avenge the insult to his family. Thus it was that a massive fleet sailed to Troy and besieged the city for ten years.

In the Library chapter there is a brief reprise of Paris's judgment and its consequences: "Paris: the wellpleased pleaser" (*U* 9.268). Earlier in the novel, Stephen surveys the racehorse pictures lining the walls of Mr. Deasy's office. Among the images is that of "the duke of Beaufort's *Ceylon, prix de Paris*" (*U* 3.483). I suggest that Helen of Troy, Paris's prize, the woman who caused so many deaths during the war and on the voyages home, lies not far beneath the surface of Stephen's stream of equine reverie.

A rhetorical declamation comparing the beauty of Helen and Penelope was one of the lost works of Antisthenes, who founded the school of Cynic philosophy at Athens in the early fourth century B.C. (see chapter 8). In Antisthenes' opinion, Penelope's virtue and fidelity endowed her with a beauty greater than that of the runaway wife of Menelaus. Joyce memorializes the Cynic's judgment in "Aeolus," when Professor Mac-Hugh reacts to Stephen's parable of the plums:

> SOPHIST WALLOPS HAUGHTY HELEN SQUARE
> ON PROBOSCIS. SPARTANS GNASH MOLARS.
> ITHACANS VOW PEN IS CHAMP.
>   —You remind me of Antistheus, the professor said, a disciple of
> Gorgias, the sophist. It is said of him that none could tell if he were
> bitterer against others or against himself. He was the son of a noble
> and a bondswoman. And he wrote a book in which he took away the
> palm of beauty from Argive Helen and handed it to poor Penelope.
>   (*U* 7.1032–39)

Later, John Eglinton stirs up Stephen's memory of the professor's pronouncement. The sublibrarian avows that he had always thought of Shakespeare's wife "as a Patient Griselda, a Penelope stay-at-home." Stephen reacts and embellishes the prior description of Helen by linking her with events that both started and concluded the war at Troy: "—Antisthenes, pupil of Gorgias, Stephen said, took the palm of beauty from Kyrios [Lord, in Greek] Menelaus' brooddam, Argive Helen, the wooden mare of Troy in whom a score of heroes slept, and handed it to poor Penelope" (*U* 9.620–23).[14]

In the cabmen's shelter in "Eumaeus," the proprietor attacks Parnell's mistress, Kitty O'Shea: "—That bitch, that English whore, did for him. . . ." The town clerk comments: "—Fine lump of a woman all the same. . . . And plenty of her. She loosened many a man's thighs" (*U* 16.1352–55; also note *UNBM* 391:155). That last sentence is almost identical to an imprecation that the loyal Eumaeus delivers in the *Odyssey*. The swineherd has just brought the disguised Odysseus into his forest shelter. Eumaeus tells his guest that his master (Odysseus) has not yet returned from Troy—and is probably dead, "as I would that all the stock of Helen had perished utterly, forasmuch as she hath caused the loosening of many a man's knees" (*Odyssey* 14.68–69). Parnell's mistress, in short, is the last link in the chain of women who are no better than they should be, from Eve to Helen to Devorgilla to Kitty O'Shea. The site of these final comments in

Ulysses (the cabmen's shelter in "Eumaeus") and the venue of Eumaeus's curse in the *Odyssey* rule out the possibility of a coincidental echo here. In the Homeric tradition, Helen did indeed loosen the knees and the thighs of many a man. An archival note, even though its subjects are unspecified, is tangential to my argument here: "lie between Helen's thighs" (VI.C.7.223).

The paucity of the foregoing examples is evidence that the *Iliad,* Homer's poem of unrelenting force, was used very sparingly in the works of James Joyce. Several of the epic's major heroes (like Diomedes) are mentioned in neither archival notes nor the texts. The gallant defender of Troy who participated in so many Iliadic battles is invoked only once: "Hector Protector!" (*FW* 255.16). There are no references to episodes as famous as Helen's survey of the Greek commanders, the farewell of Andromache and Hector, the death of Patroclus, Priam's appeal for the return of his son's corpse, or Hecuba's final lament from the doomed ramparts of Troy. None of the innumerable scenes of bloody warfare and wrangling reappears in mock-epic form in any of the *Wake's* frequent confrontations. The use of Hera's preseduction toilette as a model for ALP's preparations to march forth in "Anna Livia" is a notable exception.

In all of Joyce's fiction there is no substantial scene of violence and very little reference to bloodshed. It stands to reason, then, that the *Iliad* would not serve as a arsenal of allusion. Joyce left an early indication of his comparative judgment of the epic in an entry in the *Pola Notebook:* "Greek culture (Iliad) Barbarian (Bible)."[15] The choice of "Barbarian" to characterize the Hebrew and Christian scriptures is pointedly ironic. The Bible (despite memorable flashes of violence against Egyptians, Philistines, or Benjaminites, and despite bloody passages of dynastic rivalry) is an anthology of law, ethical teaching, song, wisdom, parables of compassion, miraculous cures, and exhortations to love and peace, whereas Homer's epic of the last phase of the Trojan War is a saga of rage, hand-to-hand combat, and mass slaughter. If the *Iliad* is the hallmark of "Greek culture" (as the notebook entry implies), then the people who gloried in the destruction of Troy far more justly deserve to be considered "Barbarian." Comparative culture aside, in the text of the *Wake* there is a hint that Joyce, like the Player in *Hamlet* (2.2.557–60), felt no compulsion to spend literary energy weeping for the loses of Hecuba, queen of Troy: "What's Hiccupper to hem or her to Hagaba?" (*FW* 276.8–9).

5

The *Odyssey*

In a practice sentence that Joyce wrote in Modern Greek, comparing Achilles and Odysseus (see chap. 4), he described the Achaean war leader as the "most fearless" (*aphobotatos*) of the Greeks at Troy, whereas the king of Ithaca had "circled the world" (*kosmogyrismenos*) (VIII.A.1.1). The etymological roots of the second Greek word call for additional comment and contextual illustration.

The Greek noun *kosmos* means order, discipline, ornament; hence the English derivatives *cosmos* (order in the universe) and *cosmetics* (regularity of ornament). Joyce frequently displays his awareness of the correlative force of the word root. In "Circe" Elijah's mission—"to serve that cosmic force. Have we cold feet about the cosmos?" (*U* 15.2196–97)—is balanced by John Eglinton's distinction that "Esthetics and cosmetics are for the boudoir. I am out for truth" (*U* 15.2258–59). In the *Wake* the far-flung potential of the word root is emphatically exploited: "my own most spacious immensity as my ownhouse and microbemost cosm" (*FW* 150.36–151.1); "solarsystemised, seriolcosmically, in a more and more almightily expanding universe" (*FW* 263.23–25); "O.K. Oh Kosmos! Ah Ireland! A.I." (*FW* 456.7); "nikrokosmikon" (*FW* 468.21); and "farbiger pancosmos" (*FW* 613.11–12).

The second element, *gyros*, is the Greek word for ring, or circle. Several changes on that theme are rung in a description of Leopold Bloom's youthful athletic feats: "Though ringweight lifting had been beyond his strength and the full circle gyration beyond his courage" (*U* 17.520–21). In the *Wake* there are a number of multilingual acknowledgments of the word's denotation: "arundgirond" (*FW* 209.18); "Whyfor we go ringing hands in hands in gyrogyrorondo" (*FW* 239.26–27); and "Gyre O, gyre O, gyrotundo!" (*FW* 295.23–24). (One thinks of Yeats.)

The combination of the two elements forms a verb that means "to circle the world," "to travel the globe." In *Ulysses* Leopold Bloom is described as being "a cultured allroundman" (*U* 10.581).[1]

The root meaning and text illustrations here are meant more in the nature of a fantasia on the etymological theme than a historical account of the genesis of Bloom's Homeric epithet. I am not suggesting that Joyce literally sat back and looked over his Greek composition exercise when he was working on *Ulysses*. Rather, in the words he chose to emphasize the difference between Achilles and Odysseus, he prefigured the possibility of a slight expansion in the meaning of the second modifier, *kosmogyrismenos*. In the modern world, the adjective *cosmopolitan* denotes that a person is quite sophisticated, has the manner of a citizen (*politēs* in Greek) of the entire globe. That descriptive term lies behind the contrast between "ruric [from *rus, ruris* in Latin, "the countryside"] or cospolite" (*FW* 309.10; also note VI.B.6.117). Another phrase makes the point explicitly: "ringround as worldwise" (*FW* 314.24–25). Odysseus was not merely a world traveler; he was also well rounded in the ways of the world. In Joyce's epic universe, Leopold Bloom, like his Homeric analogue, is outstanding for his invariable "circumspection" (*U* 17.2115). In one of his verbose internal asides in "Eumaeus," Bloom allows "that Dr Mulligan was a versatile allround man, by no means confined to medicine only" (*U* 16.287–88). The extension of the scope of Mulligan's talent may also contain a Joycean comment on his expanding girth.

Frank Budgen is a witness to the use of the epithet "allround," as he records in describing his first meeting with Joyce in Zürich during the early summer of 1918. Joyce indicated that he was working on a book based on the wanderings of Ulysses and asked whether Budgen knew of "'any complete all-round character presented by any writer?'" The answer that Joyce supplied to his own rhetorical question was, of course, Ulysses. He then expanded his scope with a metaphor based on sculpture: "'He [Ulysses] is both ["three-dimensional" and "ideal"]', said Joyce. 'I see him from all sides, and therefore he is all-round in the sense of your sculptor's figure but he is a complete man as well—a good man. At any rate, that is what I intend that he shall be'."[2]

The phantom presence of the Greek participle *kosmogyrismenos* behind Bloom's most memorable epithet is also morphologically prefigured in a similar grammatical form applied to Stephen Dedalus. In *Portrait* his school companions call him "Bous Stephanoumenos" (*P* 168) and the same term is remembered in *Ulysses* (*U* 9.939).[3] That genuinely Greek phrase means "ox wreathed with a garland." Priests and participants in ancient Greek sacrifices usually wore wreaths or crowns. The bodies of the animals, especially the larger and more expensive beasts to be ritually slaughtered and immolated, were often wreathed with cloth, and their horns were sometimes gilded.[4] In lexical and grammatical terms, the verbal roots of the pair of epithets are almost synonymous: *gyrizō* and the Homeric use of *stephanoō* both denote the act of encircling, and their shared *-menos* ending is that of a middle-passive participle. Thus, Odysseus/Bloom has both "circled the world" and is "a cultured allroundman," and Bous/Stephen has been "circled with a ritual wreath for sacrifice."

There is additional evidence—in an identical Greek grammatical form—that Joyce was aware of the thematic resonance of his choice of exotic terms here. Immediately before the appearance of *"Bous Stephanoumenos"* in the Library chapter of *Ulysses,* Stephen Dedalus includes *"Autontimorumenos"* in his interior attempt to determine his "configuration" (*U* 9.939). That polysyllabic word is Joyce's slightly misrecollected version of *Heautontimoroumenos,* one of Terence's second-century B.C. Roman comedies. The title (lifted directly from its Greek model) means the Self-Tormentor; and again, the grammatical ending *-menos* signals that the form is another middle-passive participle. By selecting two classical terms (both in their ostentatiously transliterated Greek forms) to characterize himself, Stephen signals that his status as a literary sacrifice on the altar of Dublin's neglect is, at least partially, a martyrdom that he has brought on himself. That the first Christian martyr was named Stephen (Acts 7:57–60) reinforces my point. Another example, then, of Joycean grammar in the service of theme is the triple appearance of *-menos* in *Ulysses*—once covertly, in the case of Bloom's pseudo-Homeric epithet as "allroundman"; twice overtly, in the case of Stephen's self-reflective reverie.[5]

The foregoing discussion of the circuitous path of an Odyssean participle into the text of *Ulysses* serves as a programmatic preview of my approach to Joyce and the Greek epic of wandering and return. I aim to determine the impact of documents—primary, archival, and secondary—on the compositional stages and the final form of the novel. Given all that has been written and said about Joyce's use of Homer's *Odyssey,* it would be presumptuous to attempt here either a comprehensive survey of previous work or the discovery of startling new sources. When my conclusions are tentative or the evidence is ambiguous, such limitations are clearly signaled. When I have a new slant on the ancient material, the details are presented for an informed, but Greekless, reader. This chapter, in short, offers a double perspective: a review of the most important works of prior scholarship and my own analysis of the idiosyncratic techniques that comprise Joyce's Homeric matrix for *Ulysses*.

The Greek Text and Odysseus

An important preliminary matter is the question of Joyce's ability to read the original Greek of the *Odyssey*. There is evidence that he briefly tried to work with the Homeric text. His Trieste library included a school edition of book 1 of the epic, complete with copious notes of every sort and a line-by-line translation into grotesquely literal Italian.[6] On several pages of this book Joyce wrote occasional notes, almost all of them involving a mechanical transfer of a vocabulary word from the commentary into the text. For study of Roman authors at Belvedere and University College, Joyce would have used similar texts (without the literal, linear renditions) for study of Roman authors. His mastery of grammar, syntax, and the apparatus of a scholarly commentary for a Latin text would have aided him in addressing the Greek text of Homer. This mechanical process, however, does not mean that Joyce could "read" even a single verse of the original *Odyssey*. Rather, with the appropriate lexical assistance and syntactical clues, he would have been able to decipher the meaning of individual words and to explain how they functioned in the context. All the evidence from this school text of the *Odyssey* indicates that Joyce was following the process I have just described. Such effort, which can sometimes yield sophisticated results for a single word or phrase, falls far short of a claim to be able to "read" the original—and Joyce would be the first to admit that such was the case.

In the same Zürich notebook is another Greek sentence written as a composition exercise but dealing with a Homeric topic. In it Joyce states that Odysseus made a *zylinon alogon* (wooden animal) (VIII.A.1.7). This obvious reference to the Trojan horse uses a somewhat clumsy but entirely correct noun to denote the specific status of the synthetic beast: The Greek prefix *a-* (not) is combined with the noun *logos* (word, speech, idea, reason, and so on) to designate a nonspeaking or nonthinking thing.

In fact, immediately following those two words is a correction or an alternative version, *doureion hippon*. Here the adjective, meaning "made of planks," "of lumber," modifies the standard Greek noun for horse. Almost the same words are used in the *Odyssey* by Homer's hero. While still in disguise at the court of King Alcinous, Odysseus asks the bard Demodocus to change the topic of his banquet song. Instead of the woes of the Achaeans, he requests the tale about the *hippou kosmon . . . dourateou* (the design and construction of the wooden horse) (*Odyssey* 8.492–93; also see 8.512). Here Homer used an adjective from the same root (*dour-*, "beam," "plank")—and note the coincidental epic appearance of the noun *kosmos* (meaning "arrangement" here) that Joyce employed in a previous sentence to characterize Odysseus.

In another notebook, also composed in Zürich at about the same time, there are several incidental references to Odyssean matters. The names for Scylla and Charybdis are written in Greek and followed by two neo-Hellenic nouns for song, *asma* and *tragoudi* (VIII.A.4.14). The latter term, adapted from the ancient word for tragic drama (which involved choral singing and dancing) is used for nondramatic song in Modern Greek. There might be a faint reference to the *Odyssey* here, since its hero and his companions escape the enchanting song of the Sirens and then sail past Scylla and Charybdis in book 12 of Homer's epic.[7] The presence of two other Greek nouns immediately before this cluster of items urges caution, however, in positing a direct reference on such slim lexical evidence. The pair of preceding words, followed by their English equivalents, are "*sphyra* = hammer" and "*akmōn* = anvil" (VIII.A.4.14). While both terms appear in the same line of the *Odyssey* (3.434), the context has nothing at all to do with Odysseus's adventures. If the Greek words for hammer and anvil have any particular literary resonance for Joyce here—which I very much doubt—the effect emerges in Stephen's penultimate diary entry in *Portrait*. There he sets out "to forge in the smithy of [his] soul the uncreated conscience of [his] race" (*P* 253).

There can, however, be no hesitation about the final two examples of Odyssean reference in these Zürich exercise notebooks. In the midst of his basic vocabulary lists, Joyce carefully copied out four verses in Homeric Greek. The first two lines are from the "Telemachia," when gray-eyed (*glaukōpis*) Athena sends a favoring wind over the wine-dark (*oinopa*) sea (*Odyssey* 2.420–21). Although the exact chronology of events cannot be established, the epithet of the goddess-patron of Odysseus may have had a special poignancy for Joyce in the face of his developing eye problems.[8] At any rate, one of Homer's standard epithets for the sea ostentatiously concludes Buck Mulligan's series of vividly original variations on epic usage early in *Ulysses:* "The snot-green sea. The scrotumtightening sea. *Epi oinopa ponton*" (*U* 1.78).

The second set of Homeric lines that Joyce wrote out in Greek are from the narration of Odysseus's encounter with the Cyclops. When the one-eyed monster asks his captive's name, the hero replies: "'Nobody [*Outis*] is my name. My mother and father and all the rest of my comrades always call me 'Nobody' [*Outin*]" (*Odyssey* 9.366–67). Again, the famous ploy of the false name is an incident in Homer's epic that would naturally have attracted Joyce's special attention. And the careful (though not flawless) placement of diacritical marks in the Greek show that Joyce was consulting a printed text here. In the catechetical section of *Ulysses* Leopold Bloom's narrative personality is split into a pair of "universal binomial denominations [that] would be his as entity and nonentity. . . . Everyman or Noman" (*U* 17.2006–8).

In the Homeric world, names are always significant. The hero's young son Telemachus has been left safely at home, far (*tēle-*) from the battle (*machē*); Antinous, the leader of the suitors, clearly has a hostile, or contrary (*anti-*) mind (*nous*). Calypso is literally the "hider." Several explanations are offered for the epic function and force of Odysseus's name. As will be discussed in a few paragraphs, a weird contortion of etymology holds that he was born from Zeus's rain on the road. Joyce himself had an equally farfetched suggestion: The two elements in the name Odysseus come from the alias used to flummox the Cyclops and the name of the chief Olympian god—a phonetic compound of "Outis" and "Zeus."[9] There is also an archival variation on this onomastic theme. In one of the Zürich notebooks Joyce wrote *outis* and *oudeis* (nobody, no one); directly opposite this pair of synonyms he added, also in Greek, the name *Zeus*. Immediately preceding this entry Joyce provided a translation/interpretation of his exercise in etymology: "NO/GOD, *Odys/seus*" (VIII.A.4.30). This atheistic alternative does not appear in *Ulysses,* nor would it be an appropriate explanation of the name of a hero who always respected the gods.

There is, of course, no scientific foundation for these bizarre phonetic collocations. The standard interpretation of the name Odysseus comes directly from Homer's text. Penelope's father, Icarius, told his daughter that, since he himself had caused trouble (*odyssamenos*) to so many men, she should give his grandson that "punning name" (*onom' estō epōnymon*) (*Odyssey* 19.406–9). Thus, Odysseus will be a man "who deals out harsh treatment" to those who stand in his way.[10] Budgen obviously knew about Autolycus's reputation as an impish trickster. In discussing some personal aspects of his time with Joyce in Zürich, he wrote, "On festive occasions and with a suitable stimulus, beribboned and wearing a straw picture hat (Antolycus turned pedant and keeping school, Malvilio snapping up unconsidered trifles) Joyce would execute a fantastic dance . . . that suggested somehow the ritual antics of a comic religion."[11]

Odd pieces of information about the hero of the *Odyssey* were definitely on Joyce's mind in Zürich during early 1918 when he assembled the entries in notebook VIII.A.5. A series of notes, all taken from Roscher's *Lexikon,* summarizes the details of an alternative genealogy for Odysseus. In Homer's epic, Anticleia and Laërtes are the parents of Odysseus, who also inherits a large measure of shrewdness from Autolycus, his maternal grandfather and mythology's master cattle rustler. Joyce also knew a different version, according to which another cunning figure, Sisyphus, is reputed to be the hero's father. Sisyphus (who is most famous for his rock-rolling punishment in Hades) reputedly seduced Anticleia to gain revenge for her father's repeated theft of his royal herd. Some say that Odysseus was born during a rainstorm, when a flash flood cut off the path on which Anticleia was returning home. This bit of obstetrical specificity is designed to offer an outlandish explanation of the child's name: *kata tēn odon ysēn o Zeus* (Zeus poured rain down on the road). In the Underworld book of the *Odyssey,* Anticleia reveals to her son that she died from worry and longing for him (*Odyssey* 11.202–4; also see 15.356–60); in a later version Odysseus's mother commits suicide (also note VIII.A.5.7).

All of these details—including the off-track lunge at meteorological etymology in Greek script—were jotted down by Joyce in his notebook (VIII.A.5.32–33).[12] Although Joyce crossed out in blue crayon a large part of the entry on Anticleia, I cannot point to any obvious redeployment of these mythological minutiae in *Ulysses.* In the novel one finds no information about Leopold Bloom's conception or birth; his father was not in the cattle business and it was he, not Bloom's mother, who was a suicide (*U* 5.197, 6.527–30). Perhaps, however, a wider scope for allusion must be allowed here. For example, just "past ten of the clock" on "Thursday sixteenth June," 1904, it "rained" : "one great stroke with a long thunder and in a brace of shakes all scamper pellmell with a door for the smoking shower" (*U* 14.474–88). The "door" within which all the men seek shelter is that of the National Maternity Hospital, where Mrs. Purefoy is about to give birth to a son. Her husband's occupation is not stated, but he "is to be seen any fair sabbath with a pair of his boys off *Bullock* harbour" (*U* 14.518–19; my emphasis). The chapter of *Ulysses* from which those citations come is, of course, "Oxen of the Sun," with its at-odds emphasis on fertility versus sterility and its omnipresent cattle of every sort. The Homeric analogue to these events involved the theft, slaughter, and eating of the cattle of Helius Hyperion by Odysseus's comrades (*Odyssey* 12.260–425). That crime was avenged—and the episode concluded—by a furious storm sent by Zeus to destroy the ship and drown the crew. Thus, granted Joyce's penchant for quirky transfer of epic energy, we should not entirely discount his covert reuse of the archival Anticleia index, with its crossed entries on a birth "in shower of rain" and a conception caused by "ox strife."[13]

One of Joyce's friends and language students in Zürich, George Borach, recalled some of the author's conversations about the genesis and the ancient Greek background of *Ulysses*. Joyce knew the post-Homeric tale that Odysseus had tried to avoid the Trojan War by pretending to be mad. That ruse was exposed when some comrades placed his two-year-old son just ahead of the plow in a field in which the reluctant hero was working. Odysseus stopped in time to save Telemachus, then marched off to join the Panhellenic expedition.[14] Several entries in a Zürich notebook deal with other traditional tales about the courtship and marriage of Odysseus and Penelope. One crossed note (VIII.A.5.7) reports that Odysseus won his bride in a foot race set up by her father, Icarius. I have not been able to detect where or how Joyce included this post-Homeric incident in *Ulysses*. Leopold Bloom is most definitely not the athletic type—except for his high school mastery of "the half lever movement on the parallel bars" (*U* 17.521–23). On the other hand, a variant on the history of Odysseus and Penelope's marriage bed is both recorded and reused: "ʳbed given by her father" (VIII.A.5.7). Soon after he begins his day in *Ulysses,* Bloom hears "the loose brass quoits of the bedstead" jingle as Molly turns over. He then comments, "All the way from Gibraltar. . . . Wonder what her father gave for it. Old style. Ah yes! Of course. Bought it at the governor's auction" (*U* 4.59–62).

Another episode in the apocryphal life of Odysseus and Penelope is recorded in the following note:

> Ul. = Euippe P. Urges U to kill Eur
> Euryalos whom she cajoled (VIII.A.5.9)

According to Roscher's *Lexikon*, Odysseus consulted the oracle at Epirus after he had killed the suitors. While on this mission, he seduced Princess Euippe, and she bore him a son, Euryalus. When this son matured, he visited the palace at Ithaca so as to be recognized by his father. Penelope, pretending she had learned that Euryalus intended to assassinate Odysseus, persuaded her husband to kill the interloper. This notebook entry is neither crossed nor does it make an appearance in *Ulysses*. Euryalus is not the only natural son of the hero to have entered the tradition. In one of the post-Homeric works that comprise the Epic Cycle, Odysseus meets his death at the hands of Telegonus, his son by Circe.[15] A number of other archival entries indicate that Joyce was aware of the general scope of these fabulous perpetuations of the epic narratives, including this most bizarre detail of all: Telegonus and Penelope produced Italus, the ancestor of the indigenous people of Italy (VIII.A.5.9).

The frontispiece of Ellmann's book *Ulysses on the Liffey* is "[a] 'portrait' of Leopold Bloom by James Joyce, drawn in Myron C. Nutting's Paris studio in 1923 [?]."[16] The sketch features a puckish Bloom sporting a large moustache and bowler hat. Across the top of the sheet Joyce wrote, in Greek—with a minor error in spelling and characteristically skewed accents—the first line of the *Odyssey:* ἄνδρα μόι ἔννεπε μοῦσα πολύτροπον ὡς μάλλα πόλλα (Tell me, Muse, of that man of many turns, who wandered far and wide). At the very start of his homecoming epic, Homer characterized his hero as *polytropos,* a man "of many turns." This epithet is both literally and figuratively appropriate: During the voyage from Troy to Ithaca, shifts in direction were numerous and unexpected, and Odysseus faced these challenges with infinite versatility.[17]

Penelope

Near the end of her soliloquy in *Ulysses,* Joyce's Penelope, Molly Bloom, claims that her husband's sexual ploys are not difficult to unravel: "1 or 2 questions I'll know by the answers when hes like that he cant keep a thing back I know *every turn* in him" (*U* 18.1529–30; my emphasis). Penelope, the heroine of the *Odyssey,* also matched her husband's guile in the way she held suitors at bay. When it seemed likely that Odysseus would never return to Ithaca after the fall of Troy, his wife devised a stratagem: She agreed to marry one of the suitors after she had finished weaving a burial shroud for Laërtes, Odysseus's old father. During the day she toiled at the loom, but at night she undid her work. This ploy was not discovered for almost four years (*Odyssey* 2.85–110).

When Penelope herself told the disguised Odysseus about the trick, her choice of words is significant: *dolous tolypeuō* (I wind up deceptions, I spin out wiles) (*Odyssey* 19.137). The metaphor of her craft is similar to the formulaic phrase *mētin/dolon hyphainein* (to weave a scheme/trick) that is applied to various versatile characters, mortal and immortal, including Penelope herself (for example, *Iliad* 6.187, 7.324; *Odyssey* 4.739, 5.356). Joyce was certainly aware of the association of Penelope with weaving— and aware that the object of her working the loom was deception. There is a puzzling reference in one of the "Penelope" notesheets: "she weaves a deathshroud for / ʳLaertes which is Ulysses' coronation robe" (*UNBM* 496:66–67). The hint of a dual purpose in Penelope's stratagem is intriguing, but I am unaware of any Homeric or post-Homeric legend that makes a connection between the shroud and a royal robe for the son of Laërtes. The second part of the notesheet entry, though crossed out, is not used in *Ulysses;* indeed, Joyce seems not to have transferred any overt aspect of the epic's weaving motif into his novel.[18]

On the other hand, in a February 8, 1922, letter to Harriet Shaw Weaver, Joyce announces that her copy "(no 1)" of the *edition de luxe* of *Ulysses* will arrive in a week or so. He then thanks his patroness for the prompt return of a prepublication version "of the *Penelope* episode (the name of which by another strange coincidence is your own)" (*Letters* I.180; *SL* 289). The typical play on the name referred to in parentheses is Joyce's way of reminding Miss Weaver that the speaker of the monologue in the final chapter of *Ulysses* was also a weaver. There may also be a minor strand of connection between names and weaving in the fictional Molly Bloom's maiden name: "Tweedy" (*U* 6.693). In an earlier letter to Miss Weaver, on August 16, 1920, Joyce mentions a problem with his work on *Ulysses:* "Circe herself had less touble weaving her web than I have with her episode" (*Letters* III.15). At first glance we might suppose that Joyce has confused the Odyssean witch with the Ovidian spider-woman, Arachne; but, in addition to her deceit and magic in the *Odyssey,* Circe is also described as singing sweetly while she worked on her loom (*Odyssey* 10.222–24, 254)—another example of Joyce's remarkable recall of epic detail.

Joyce might also have been aware that Homer, characteristically, invested Penelope with an etymologically significant name, although I can cite no archival evidence to confirm my suggestion. The first element in her name might be derived from the Greek noun *pēnē* (thread on the shuttle, woof of the web on a loom). In fact, some contemporary scholars hypothesize that the second element (-*elopeia*) might derive from the verb *oloptein* (to pluck out). If so, then Odysseus's resourceful wife, Penelope, is both literally and narratively a "Weaver-Unraveller."[19]

In the remainder of the paragraph in the first letter cited here, Joyce indicates that he has "rejected the usual interpretations of her [Penelope] as a human apparition—of the pseudo-Homeric figures." In her comments on "Penelope," Miss Weaver had used the epithet "prehuman" to describe its central character. Joyce agrees with this choice but suggests the addition of a second term, "posthuman." Both epithets are explained by the author's final statement that "[i]n conception and technique I tried to depict the earth which is prehuman and presumably posthuman" (*Letters* I.180; *SL* 289). The ostensibly unflattering equation of Penelope/Molly with "the earth" must be seen in light of the description of Molly, in bed at the end of *Ulysses,* as "Listener: . . . In the attitude of *Gea-Tellus,* fulfilled, recumbent, big with seed" (*U* 17.2312–14; my emphasis). The italicized words are the Greek and Latin terms, respectively, for the earth.[20]

There is another noteworthy aspect of the role of Penelope in ancient mythology. In the Homeric poems and throughout Greco-Roman literature in general, Odysseus's wife stands as the faithful, chaste queen of their palace in Ithaca. She protects his son, Telemachus, respects his father, Laërtes, and resourcefully fends off the suitors, who threaten not only the absent king's bed but all his property. That standard portrait of Penelope was so overwhelmingly prevalent that it naturally generated a minor—though shocking—reaction. A primary example of this type of obscene caricature is *Priapea* 68, an anonymous Latin poem that is a general lampoon on the Homeric epics.[21] The poem argues that all of the action in the *Iliad* and *Odyssey* is motivated by lust; for example, the "revisionist" narrative states that

> Penelope remains so chaste that she soon invited a mob of dinner-
> 　　guests
> and saw that her palace was packed with suitors who had been fucked
> 　　(*fututorum*),
> so that [she] could find out which one was most fit for the job

. . . .

> [since] no man ever used his bow better than Ulysses. (*Priapea*
> 68.29–33)[22]

My translation of the last line is designed to emphasize two memorable Homeric elements that the anonymous Latin poet exploits for a gross laugh: "no man" (*nemo*) is meant to mimic Odysseus's alias stratagem in his encounter with the Cyclops; the Latin noun *nervum* (which I translate as bow) literally means sinew or bowstring, and metaphorically strength or vigor, an obvious reference to Odysseus's sexual prowess as well as to his mastery of the weapon that spelled doom for the suitors upon his return.

An archival note proves that Joyce was aware of the heterodox tradition (Penelope as a foul-mouthed slut) when he was composing *Ulysses:* "Priapea Pen (vetula) sits smutty talking / amg the Freier" (VIII.A.5.10). The parenthetical "vetula" is the Latin word for "[dirty] little old woman" that occurs in line 27 of the priapic Latin poem. "Freier" is the usual German word for suitor; in modern slang *Freier* also means pimp. In *Ulysses,* Molly's "smutty talking" is not aimed at suitors. Rather, near the end of her monologue, Molly—knowing his "every turn"—thinks of Leopold Bloom who lies nearby, and says, "Ill tighten up my bottom well and out a few smutty words" (*U* 18.1530–31).

Joyce's notebook entry, however, does not explicitly establish that he knew the text of *Priapea* 68 firsthand. Rather, Herring has clearly shown that Joyce picked up this bit of scandal sheet gossip about Penelope from a comprehensive German handbook of mythology.[23] In fact, Roscher's *Lexikon* has more information about the alternative, apocryphal tradition of an unfaithful Penelope. Among the data in Roscher's survey is the report that a promiscuous Penelope slept with one of the suitors and was banished by Odysseus; adultery with Amphinomus, later slain by her husband, is also recorded. Finally, Roscher notes two versions of the tale that, during Odysseus's absence, Penelope gave birth to Pan, the shepherd-god, sired either by the leading suitor, Antinous, or by the gods Apollo or Hermes. Joyce scrambles all of these apocryphal details into a series of notes just before the "Priapea" entry in the Zürich notebook:

Pen=Freir / banished by U to Sparta
Pan Antinous

Pen=Amphinomos killed by U
ᵇLB what kind of child can much fucked whore have
Pen=Apollo
Pan (VIII.A.5.9; also see *UNBM* 268:86)

Another archival entry both condenses and expands the foregoing notes on Penelope's extramarital activity: "Pen & Freier=Pan (monster) banished" (*UNBM* 393:9). The parenthetical "monster" undoubtedly refers to a mythological detail, that Pan, whoever his parents were, had the legs and horns of a goat. Despite Pan's numerous amorous adventures and his association with the Satyrs and with Priapus, I have found no allusions to him (at least as bastard son of Penelope) in Joyce's works. At any rate, these archival entries demonstrate that the research for his epic novel of a day's wandering across Dublin took Joyce into remote and murky areas of classical mythology. Nor does lack of specific usage mean that these heterodox slurs on the character of the queen of Ithaca left no traces on the representation of the earthy heroine of *Ulysses:* Joyce's Penelope is not the archetypically faithful wife.

In a brief but densely complex article, Lillian Doherty, a contemporary classicist, has applied some of the insights of feminist Joycean criticism to a reconsideration of Homer's Penelope. As I read her, she draws three primary comparative conclusions. First, an important structural element of the Homeric model kept a full-scale revelation of the wife until the end of the narrative. Thus the heroines of both epics are seen almost exclusively through the eyes of their husbands—and other males. Joyce undercuts the romantic ideal of reunion by having his Penelope speak "not to her husband and the audience simultaneously, as in Homer, but to the audience only." Even so, given the reader's sympathy for Bloom throughout *Ulysses,* some of the details of Molly's monologue might be seen as positive, indeed endearing. Second, the privileged male perspective identifies both heroines primarily in sexual terms, a suspicion of infidelity being the norm. Indeed, her speech of recognition to Odysseus suggests that Penelope is afraid that some mortal stranger might trick her, just as a god stirred Helen to do her shameful deed (*Odyssey* 23.215–24). Doherty interprets Penelope's analogy "as an index of the degree to which she can be seen as having internalized the expectations Helen violated—and with them the self-doubt that negative models like Helen can inspire." Third, society restricts Molly's range: While symbolized as the Earth Mother, the only sphere that she in fact controls is the bedroom. So too, even if she has subliminally recognized her returning husband as the prelude to the archery contest, Penelope is also limited by social pressure: She must admit the possibility of taking another husband. In a footnote Doherty cites another feminist scholar's conclusion that "the *Odyssey* . . . acknowledges the real limitations on human happiness that its own conclusion transcends." Doherty adds her own comment: "While Joyce allows Molly to voice her frustrations, the pain on which he focuses is almost entirely Bloom's. From this perspective, the *Odyssey* may be seen as somewhat more sensitive to the limitations with which its heroine must live."[24] Although couched in tentative terms, those comparative conclusions argue strongly that Joyce's characterization of Molly draws on neglected aspects of Homer's characterization of Penelope.[25]

Nestor and Peisistratus

Stephen Dedalus's first task on Thursday, June 16, 1904, was to teach his class at Mr. Deasy's school, then to collect £3/12 from the headmaster. This chapter of the novel is "Nestor," and Mr. Deasy certainly shares some of the features of the venerable king of Pylos, whom Telemachus visits in book 3 of the *Odyssey*. On the other hand, another element in the "Nestor" chapter reflects action from an earlier section of Homer's four-book *Telemachia*. Just before Deasy pays Stephen, there is a stage direction: "And now his strong-room for the gold" (*U* 2.212). The Homeric analogue occurs *before* Telemachus leaves Ithaca. To secure supplies for his voyage, Odysseus's son "stepped down into the vaulted treasure-chamber for his father, a spacious room, where gold and bronze lay piled" (*Odyssey* 2.337–38; *B-L* 25).[26]

Just as Joyce brought other Homeric elements into "Nestor," so too did he reposition an important Odyssean scene involving King Nestor, inserting it into the third chapter, "Proteus." As Stephen wanders along the tidal beach at Sandymount, he thinks "Am I going to aunt Sara's or not?" (*U* 3.61). His relatives, the Gouldings, live nearby, and in Stephen's imagination, "A bolt drawn back and Walter welcomes me. . . . In his broad bed nuncle Richie, pillowed and blanketed, extends over the hillock of his knees a sturdy forearm." There is an anticipated offer of "[m]alt for Richie and Stephen" and "[t]he rick of a rasher fried with a herring" (*U* 3.74–97). Stephen decides to pass up the call on his relatives. The motif of somewhat tawdry hospitality, however, is clearly meant to be an unrealized reprise of the elaborate welcome of Telemachus to Pylos by the king and Prince Peisistratus: "There was Nestor seated with his sons. . . . Now when they saw the stranger, they went all together, and clasped their hands in welcome. . . . First Peisistratus, son of Nestor, drew nigh and took the hands of each, and made them to sit down at the feast on soft fleeces upon the sands. . . . And he gave them messes of inner meat, and poured wine into a golden cup" (*Odyssey* 3.34–41; *B-L* 30; also note *UNBM* 113:12).

There is a minor, but characteristically Joycean detail in these parallel scenes of seaside hospitality: the names of the two sons who are the first to welcome their respective visitors. In the *Odyssey* Peisistratus plays a broader role than that of mere greeter; after the visit to Pylos he accompanies Telemachus to the palace of Menelaus and Helen. Even though no military action is involved, the royal name of Peisistratus (Urger of the Army) is significant. The name is a combination of *peisi-*, from the verbal root *peith/peis* (to persuade, to win over), and the noun *stratos* (army, soldier). I suggest that this onomastic datum from the *Odyssey* is the reason why Joyce gave the Christian name Walter to Nuncle Richie's son (who occurs nowhere else in *Ulysses*). In Old High German the heroic name Walthari means commander, ruler of the army.

In *Finnegans Wake* there is another reprise of the accepted Odyssean and the deferred Ulyssean receptions of Nestor's hospitality. The aged king of Pylos spends much of book 3 of Homer's epic making sure that Prince Telemachus is received in a manner befitting his rank and lineage. After the seaside welcome there is a glorious feast, followed by a sacrifice to Poseidon before retiring. Telemachus and Mentor then begin to head to the beach, but Nestor protests that no guest of his will "lay him down upon the ship's deck, while as yet I am alive, and my children after me are left in my hall to entertain strangers" (*Odyssey* 3.353–55; *B-L* 39–40). The next morning there is another elaborate ritual, then Nestor sends his guests away on their mission in a royal chariot, with plenty of food and wine and his son Peisistratus as a guide. In the "Night Lessons" section of the *Wake* the name *Nestor* is keyed to the essay topic "Hengler's Circus Entertainment" (*FW* 307.L and 8). I suggest that the "Entertainment" in that phrase was recalled directly from the *Odyssey*—and used to complete an HCE acrostic. There is also the possibility that Hengler's Circus featured memorable equestrian acts, which would resonate to two of Nestor's primary Homeric epithets, "tamer of horses" (*Odyssey* 3.17; *B-L* 29) and "horseman" (*Odyssey* 3.68 and frequently elsewhere; translated as "lord of chariots" in *B-L* 31).[27]

Eumaeus

A cryptic archival note plays another minor but thematically appropriate part in the novel. After a brief reference to the loyal swineherd, Eumaeus, Joyce wrote "[b]shoes—oxhide shoes [r](pampootis)" (VIII.A.5.7). The Homeric source (mediated through Roscher) of this epic fashion item is the report that Eumaeus "was fitting sandals to his feet, cutting a good brown oxhide" (*Odyssey* 14.23–24; *B-L* 209). In *Ulysses* Joyce transferred this bit of rustic realism to the heady literary atmosphere of the National Library. There Buck Mulligan bends down to warn Stephen:

"—The tramper Synge is looking for you, he said, to murder you. He heard you pissed on his halldoor in Glasthule. He's out in *pampooties* to murder you" (*U* 9.509–71; my emphasis). The link between the archival note, the *Odyssey*, and the novel is "pampooties." In his 1912 article "The Mirage of the Fisherman of Aran," Joyce himself includes some local color with the following description: "The fisherman of Aran has sure feet. He wears a rough sandal of untanned cowhide, without heel, open at the arch, and tied with rawhide laces" (*CW* 236). In *Ulysses* this insular footwear (called pampooties) is assigned by Mulligan to Synge as an oblique send-up of the playwright's frequent visits to the Aran Islands to prepare to write about Irish peasant life. Synge's record of his trips, *The Aran Islands,* did not appear until 1907. Nevertheless, Mulligan's mockery of affected folkloristic attitudes of the leading lights of the Irish Revival is best regarded as Celtic poetic license rather than as a post–Bloom's Day anachronism.

The Cyclops

The encounter with Polyphemus the Cyclops is usually regarded as the most exciting and tightly constructed episode on Odysseus's long voyage home. Following Joyce's hints in the schemata, readers and commentators have found numerous parallels between book 9 in the *Odyssey* and the "Cyclops" chapter of *Ulysses*. Gilbert, for example, points out that Joyce's monstrous Citizen excels "in the eminently volcanic sport of 'putting the [sixteen pound] shot'" (*U* 12.881–83).[28] That skill prepares him—and the reader—for his seismic heave of a biscuit box at the conclusion of the chapter (*U* 12.1812–96). The Homeric analogue to this is the pair of boulders thrown at Odysseus by the blinded Cyclops when he learns the real name of his tormentor (*Odyssey* 9.500–542). The evidence for Bloom's affirmation of his Jewishness (*U* 12.1804–9) as the novel's equivalent of Odysseus's ringing renunciation of the false name Outis is cogently laid out by Ellmann.[29] Joyce picks up on this crucial example of Homeric "nomanclatter" (*FW* 147.21) in the *Wake* when he uses a Latin phrase to both name and describe the trick: "*simplex mendaciis,* by which our Outis cuts his truth" (*FW* 493.24).[30] Both Homeric protagonists are present in "nobodyatall with Wholyphamous" (*FW* 73.9), and the Cyclops's rage-propelled boulders are piled up all over the same page of the text: "rocks," "rochelly," "cairns," "eolithostroton [*lithos* in Greek means stone]," "rocks," and "skatterlings of a stone" (*FW* 73.9, 23, 29, 30, 33, 34).

After Odysseus has hoodwinked Polyphemus and then poked out his eye, the monster calls his fellow Cyclopses for aid. They crowd around his sealed cave and react: "Surely nobody is killing you by trickery or force (*dolō ēe biēphin*)?" Polyphemus replies, "My friends, Noman is killing me by trickery not force (*dolō oude biēphin*)" (*Odyssey* 9.406, 408). The verbal byplay here involves Odysseus's cunning, the various interpretations (and misinterpretations) of the fake name, and the blinded victim's unwitting admission that he has been outwitted, yet again.[31] I suggest that Joyce incorporated an echo of two key Homeric terms from this exchange into his play *Exiles.* Near the start of the second act, Robert Hand reveals his love for Richard Rowan's woman and says he will take her away with him. Rowan replies: "That is language I have heard often and never believed in. Do you mean by stealth or by violence? Steal you could not in my house because the doors were open: nor take by violence if there were no resistance" (*E* 62). The Greek nouns used by Homer are *dolos* and *biē;* the former can be translated as guile, trickery, stealth; the latter as force, might, violence. In their version Butcher and Lang opt for "force or craft" and "guile, nor at all by force" (*B-L* 138). As is epically demonstrated by the robust wine, the trick name, and the twisted stake, Odysseus overcame the Cyclops by both stealth *and* violence.

In his discussion of the "Cyclops" chapter, Gilbert nicely explicates the reason why the Citizen's biscuit box misses Bloom: "Mercy of God the sun was in his eyes" [*U* 12.1853–54]. (In cant jargon a person who is drunk is said to have "the sun in his eyes.")[32] I suspect that Gilbert learned about that interpretive twist from his most consistent and authoritative source, Joyce himself. The basis for my suggestion is another crossed entry in the Zürich notebook: "ʳElpenor—face of light" (VIII.A.5.17). Elpenor was the youngest member of Odysseus's crew. He was drunk on Circe's roof, forgot to use the ladder down, and broke his neck when he fell. In the Underworld, the soul of this improvident sailor is the first to approach his captain and tell how he met his death (*Odyssey* 10.552–60). In the "Hades" chapter of *Ulysses*, several of the mourners discuss the cause of Paddy Dignam's sudden death: "Blazing face: redhot. Too much John Barley-corn" (*U* 6.307). The three similar phrases ("sun in his eyes," "face of light," "blazing face") are all applied by Joyce to men presented as epic drinkers. In the cases of Elpenor and Paddy Dignam the overconsumption was fatal. The Cyclops (who got drunk on Odysseus's superpotent wine) and the Citizen (who had been liberally sampling the "Wine of the Country" [*U* 12.144]) merely missed their targets, the former with a brace of boulders, the latter with a biscuit box.

Shirley C. Scott has compiled an accessible and up-to-date survey of the Cyclops tale, from Homer to Joyce with prominent intermediate stops at Euripides, Vergil, Ovid, Petronius, and Eliot.[33] The Ulysses section starts out well with a minicatalog of "monocular" preachers who bob onto stage during the "Cyclops" chapter: "Balor of the Evil Eye" (*U* 12.197–98), an English welterweight "whose right eye was nearly closed" (*U* 12.973), "flash toffs with a swank glass in their eye" (*U* 12.1224), "old Mrs Verschole with the turnedin eye" (*U* 12.1497), "a loafer with a patch over his eye" (*U* 12.1800), and so on. There are no new critical insights in Scott's review of the Joycean material; at the same time, the documentation throughout the article is exhaustive, and future students of "Cyclops" would be foolish to put a "blind eye to the telescope" (*U* 12.1194) in scanning her bibliographical footnotes.

The Enchanted Island of Brissago

From mid-October 1917 to early January 1918, the entire Joyce family enjoyed the milder climate in Lucarno, a Swiss resort town at the northern end of Lago Maggiore (*JJII* 417–21). While on that visit they met the Baroness Antonietta St. Leger and probably were invited to her villa on what is now called Isola di Brissago. The "Baroness" was the estranged wife of Richard Flemyng St. Leger, a wealthy Anglo-Irishman from

County Cork. Although St. Leger was indeed a member of the distinguished ascendancy family whose head holds the title Viscount Doneraile, he himself was neither a viscount (as local tradition has it) nor in line for that title.[34] The lineage of St. Leger's wife is not entirely clear, but rumor has her the illegitimate daughter of Czar Alexander II, born in either Malmö, St. Petersburg, or Tilsit. She also seems to have been married several times before becoming St. Leger's wife.[35] It is a fact that the couple purchased two small islands in the lake in 1885 and built a villa there. The two-story mansion was packed with paintings, sculpture, and books of every sort; the grounds were planted with exotic trees, plants, and flowers from all over the world.

From my perspective the most significant aspect of the baroness's tenure on the island was her local reputation as a latter-day reincarnation of Homer's witch-goddess. Budgen wrote that "[a]long the mainland she was called Circe and many farfetched stories went to make up her Circean legend."[36] Reinforcing this image were the ferocious dogs that guarded her island estate. Gossip had it that she customarily wore a necklace to which each of her seven husbands had contributed a gem or a pearl. This was supposedly the practice of a primitive African tribe that attributed wonder-working powers to such amulets. Also adorning this necklace was a miniature gold replica of a human phallus—most significant in Circean light.

Behind the web of malignant gossip may lie a chunk of archaeological misinformation. Not long before the St. Legers purchased the property, a Roman gravestone was discovered in a ruined church on the island. An expanded transcription of the inscription on the stone:

> D (*is*) [M (*manibus*)] [M(*atri*) *car* (*issimae*] /
> [*Th*] AI. ET A / PHRODITE / SOR(*ori*).
> P [*etr*] / ONIA F[*il*(*ia*)] / TYC [*he*].
> (To the departed spirits of her dearest Mother,
> Thais, and her sister Aphrodite,
> the daughter Petronia wishes good fortune.)[37]

Until this correct reading and interpretation of the inscription was proposed in 1946, it was believed that the gravestone was a Roman altar. The presence of the complete name "APHRODITE" in the dedication led early investigators to suggest that the stone had originally been placed before a temple of Aphrodite/Venus, the Greco-Roman goddess of sexual rapture. That epigraphical error naturally helped to establish an aura of antique eroticism that loomed over the baroness and her enchanted island.

In May 1919, a year and a half after the family's visit to Lucarno, Joyce and Budgen spent two weeks at the lakeside resort. They were invited to Isola Saint-Leger by the baroness. Budgen concluded his report of the visit to the villa with this bit of archival information: "Before we left she [the baroness] entrusted to Joyce a packet of letters and a valise of books on the theme of erotic perversions, remarking that he might find the contents useful as documentation for his writing. She was afraid too that in the event of sudden death these might be found and give rise to misunderstandings. All this material was no doubt useful enough to Joyce when a month or two later he began the composition of *Circe.*"[38] A May 15, 1919, note from the baroness to Joyce at his *pensióne* in Lucarno confirms the dispatch of "the boatman with 2 parcels: one wrapped up in paper & containing 2 books; the other wrapped up in linen & containing 2 books, 1 paper parcel & 1 box." Nothing else in any of the four surviving letters from the Baroness St. Leger to Joyce even hints at anything the least bit salacious, not to mention Circean. Indeed, the only specifically Homeric aspect of her island estate was the walls of the salon "hung with oil colours drawings depicting scenes from the *Odyssey.*"[39]

A year later Joyce consulted the Baroness St. Leger to see if she had any botanical suggestions about Homer's *moly.* In her reply she indicated that the plant that Hermes gave to Odysseus to make him immune to Circe's charms might have been a form of garlic, *allium niger* [*sic*]: "it is equally known also as a strong aphrodisiac and used as such as late as the XVIth Century (Matthiolo 1563) as well as a preservative from every kind of poison and witchcraft."[40] Although Odysseus hardly needed an aphrodisiac for his encounter with Circe, nevertheless the prophylactic properties described would have been appropriate. The scientific tone and detail of the baroness's reply fit well with what is most likely a more valid view of her interests than that of an insular enchantress. In 1913 she published an article, "The Vegetation of the Island of St. Léger in Lago Maggiore," in the *Journal of the Royal Horticultural Society* (London).[41] The lavish formal gardens on the estate continue to attract boatloads of tourists today.

The flora and fauna of the baroness's island do not seem to have left much of an impression on the "Circe" chapter in *Ulysses.* The only garlic present in that episode is not specified as a prophylactic for Bloom but is transferred to his would-be seductress. Even Bloom's *"hard black shrivelled potato"* is surrendered to Zoe for most of the episode (*U* 15.1309–15); shortly thereafter the whore bites Bloom's ear, *"sending on him a cloying breath of stale garlic"* (*U* 15.1339–40).

Structure and Narrative Parallels

Certainly the most influential—and intermittently the most maligned—of the early commentators on *Ulysses* was Stuart Gilbert.[42] His *Study,* published in 1930 and revised in 1952, includes many "ideas, interpretations, and explanations endorsed by Joyce himself."[43] A number of critics have concluded that Gilbert was too quick in accepting as authentic some of "the hints thrown out quite casually (this was Joyce's inevitable way) as to the sources of *Ulysses*" (*Study* vii). Archival notes support the authenticity in his presentation of the repeated references to Bérard's book, as well as to Joyce's serious research in classical mythology. Moreover, Gilbert, who read "Greats" (classics) at Oxford, checked out suggested citations in Latin and Greek. Although he found his "knowledge of the Early Ionic sadly rusty after many years' obsolescence," he prepared for his task by "re-reading the Odyssey . . . the greatest of all epics" (*Study* vii). I very much doubt that any other critic of *Ulysses*—except for W. B. Stanford, Regius Professor of Greek at Trinity College—could make that claim.[44]

Gilbert's *Study* was the first major work of criticism for which Joyce permitted explicit use of his schema (*Study* 30). In it each chapter is given a corresponding title from an episode in the *Odyssey.* These now familiar Homeric titles are repeated as the headings for Gilbert's discussion of the eighteen chapters.[45] In the course of his explanations and interpretations, Gilbert cites the *Odyssey,* in Greek, six times and the *Iliad* once—as well as several incidental passages from the original texts of Herodotus and Strabo. (The vernacular quotations from such exotica as *The Smaragdine Tablet* of Hermes Trismegistus and *The Cave of the Nymphs* by Porphyry [*Study* 44–45, 297] are most probably secondhand, lifted from contemporary occult literature.) Numerous excepts from Latin and French are left untranslated. That is the linguistic world in which Joyce and Gilbert moved.[46] At other times and in other places, such display of learning might be regarded as parodically professorial. In fact, in the preface to the revised edition of his work, Gilbert writes, "I have not tried to alleviate the rather pedantic tone of much of the writing in this Study. For one thing, Joyce approved of it." Immediately after that remark, he stresses his admiration of *Ulysses* "for its structural, enduring qualities" (*Study* ix). Paramount among Joyce's structural devices, at least during the evolving process of composition, were the episodic "frames" and the numerous narrative parallels to the *Odyssey*. Joyce and his notes also repeatedly testify to the importance of Bérard's general thesis and his cascade of geographical and etymological detail. The presence and the impact of these sources and the extent of the Homeric matrix—now commonplaces to be acknowledged, then dismissed as irrelevant—were brought to the fore by Gilbert. His informed, learned, and often witty study was the first of such scope. As such, it has the defects of a pioneering effort, most notably the exaggeration of the value of this recherché material to the normal reader of *Ulysses*. For example, no reader really needs to know that the fierce descent of Stephen and Simon Dedalus on the scene in "Circe" is probably meant to recall the simile of the vultures used by Homer in the slaughter of the suitors by Odysseus and Telemachus (*Odyssey* 22.302–6). But Joyce's *"vulture talons sharpened"* and *"wheeling . . . buzzard wings"* (*U* 15.3940–46) came from somewhere, and Gilbert was quick enough to catch the fleeting allusion (*Study* 288.)

It is possible that Joyce occasionally pulled Gilbert's pedantic leg with classical misinformation, although I would not like to be called upon to identify such instances in his book. What I do recommend, however, is that readers who are perplexed by Gilbert's footnotes and the apparatus of his structural parallels take a look at the balanced and sympathetic evaluation of the work by Patrick McCarthy. The concluding paragraph of his review praises the *Study* for revealing and emphasizing the origins of *Ulysses*, which "Joyce was at pains to demonstrate . . . 'It's Greek: from the Greek'" (*U* 4.341).[47]

If there is a single scholarly work that is equally well known to both Joyceans and classicists, it is W. B. Stanford's *The Ulysses Theme: A Study in the Adaptability of a Traditional Hero*. Its three sections trace Odysseus/ Ulysses as an epic hero; as a figure of controversy in the Greek dramatists, Vergil, Ovid, and the revisionists of late antiquity; and as a subject of modern variations on the classical themes. Six appendices on more specialized topics complement the extraordinary range of documentation. Stanford's work, in short, is a model of cross-cultural literary criticism, still regarded as *the* primary source for information about the afterlife of

Homer's wanderer. One chapter, "The Re-Integrated Hero," is devoted to Joyce's *Ulysses* and Nikos Kazantzakis's *Odyssey*. Stanford's summary of the day-long adventures of Leopold Bloom is concise, and bristling with insights informed by a command of the tradition.

Individual Episodes

"Ithaca"

An article by Constance Tagopoulos examines the links between Homer's narrative of the homecoming of Odysseus and Joyce's "Ithaca" chapter in *Ulysses*. Disguise, recognition, and hospitality (*xenia*) are the primary motifs.[48] In the study are several missed opportunities through which the author could have bolstered her comparative points with more concrete detail from the two texts. It is absolutely correct that Bloom's insertion of the key into the lock at 7 Eccles Street is "sexually suggestive." And his action does echo Penelope's opening of the storeroom to remove Odysseus's bow for the archery contest in the *Odyssey*. Tagopoulos's parenthetical notice that Joyce's key passage, "(characteristically featuring a bow)," forebodes a new birth does not do justice to either Homer or Joyce. In the Greek epic, similar participial forms, *tityskomenē/-os*, are used for Penelope's action ("and with a straight aim shot back the bolts" [*Odyssey* 21.47]) and, later in the same episode, for Odysseus's action ("and with a straight aim shot the shaft" [*Odyssey* 21.421]). That Homeric repetition of the same word, in the same emphatic position at the start of a hexameter line, is the reason for Joyce's insertion of Odysseus's weapon ("obtaining a purchase on the bow of the key" [*U* 17.1216]) into his description of the procedure whereby Leopold Bloom characteristically appropriates the action of both the epic hero and his equally adaptable wife.

Tagopoulos also calls attention to Homer's specification that Odysseus returned to Ithaca at *lykabas*, "when the old moon [month] wanes and the new [moon-month] is born" (*Odyssey* 14.161–62, 19.306–7). Following Austin, Tagopoulos associates this moment with the beginning of spring and a symbolic rebirth of the returning hero.[49] The emphasis on a "new birth" here is, in my judgment, misplaced. Joyce was an astute student of Greek vocabulary and menstruation; and he was certainly aware that the Homeric noun *mēn, mēnos* (lunar month) supplies the root for the term for the female physiological phenomenon. In *Ulysses* both Leopold and Molly Bloom directly relate menstruation to its cyclic period of recurrence. The husband waxes universal and particular on the topic: "Near her [Gerty MacDowell's] monthlies I expect, makes them feel ticklish. . . . That's the moon. But then why don't all women menstruate at the same time with the same moon, I mean? Depends on the time they were born, I suppose" (*U* 13.777–84). Of far greater significance for a narrative and thematic link between the two epic heroes is Molly's realization, in the last chapter of *Ulysses*, that she has begun to menstruate: "O Jesus wait, yes that thing has come on me yes . . . there's always something wrong with us 5 day every 3 or 4 weeks usual monthly auction" (*U* 18.1104–9). In both the *Odyssey* and *Ulysses*, the true husband returns home at the time of a new month.[50]

"Cicones"

Lynn Childress neatly reviews the reasons why *Ulysses* lacks an analogue to the "Cicones" episode in the *Odyssey*. In the Homeric epic, that incident serves as a transition from the *Iliad* to the tale of Odysseus's return from Troy. When they and their commander sack the city of Ismarus, the Achaeans are still a formidable fighting unit; their last-minute defeat and loss of life there mark the beginning of the disintegration of Odysseus's fleet (*Odyssey* 9.39–61). Joyce did not need a comparable scene in *Ulysses*. Moreover, the "Cicones" episode in Bérard's discussion of Homeric background is submerged by his digression on the role of piracy in the early Mediterranean world. Thus, even though Joyce took notes on some of Bérard's remarks, he uniquely omitted this Homeric episode in his adaptation of epic material, primarily because an initial episode with "a picture of a heroic (and aggressive) Bloom would not be in keeping with the character that he sought to create."[51]

Childress's treatment of this topic is so clear and succinct that I hesitate to add a comment. There might, however, be an apparently inconsequential aspect of the sack of the city of the Cicones that Joyce did indeed use in *Ulysses*. Childress records that one of Joyce's notes from Bérard indicates that Odysseus's raiders spared priests from their slaughter: "ʳHands off priests (Ulysses)" (VIII.A.5.1). The fact that this entry is crossed out in red is a sign (though not an infallible one) that Joyce used it somewhere in his work. A search for its insertion is worth some textual speculation. The Homeric locus for the sparing of at least one of the Ciconian priests is found not in that episode but later in the same book of the *Odyssey*, when Odysseus tells what happened in the cave of the Cyclops. The Achaean leader had with him "a goat-skin of the dark wine and sweet, which Mason, son of Euanthes, had given me, the priest of Apollo. . . . And he gave it, for that we had protected him with his wife and child reverently" (*Odyssey* 9.196–200; *B-L* 131–32). This is the ultrastrong, unmixed wine that Odysseus serves to the Cyclops to get him drunk. Joyce's chapter entitled "Cyclops" takes place in a bar, but Leopold Bloom does not buy a drink there for the Citizen—that's part of the problem, since it is firmly held that he "had a few bob on *Throwaway* and he's gone to gather in the shekels" (*U* 12.1550–51). On the other hand, the Citizen and his cronies, without Bloom's help, have been imbibing deeply in the "Wine of the country" (*U* 12.144). Thus, since Odysseus/Bloom was not called upon to serve wine in "Cyclops," I suggest that Joyce incorporated the epic gift elsewhere in his novel, in one of the fantastic interludes of the "Circe" chapter. There the drink—but with no mention of its priestly source or circumstance—is offered to Bloom by Bello: "I can give you a rare old wine that'll send you skipping to hell and back" (*U* 15.3205–6).

"Circe"

There are a number of direct verbal parallels between the Butcher and Lang translation of the *Odyssey* and Joyce's "Circe" chapter in *Ulysses* (see later section of this chapter). There are also some narrative links between that episode in the novel and Homer's tale of the enchanted island. Hermes provides Odysseus with *moly,* the supranatural herb that will prevent the witch-goddess from transforming him, like many of his crew, into a swine. The hero is also warned to make Circe swear a mighty oath that she will not "unman" him when they lie in the bed of love. At the Ulyssean brothel in the novel, Bloom temporarily loses his talisman-potato and is the victim of a humiliating transformation. The madam changes into a dominating male, while Bloom creeps on all fours and yaps "Truffles!" (*U* 15.2851). Bello also threatens to slaughter Bloom and to serve him "baked like a suckling pig with rice and lemon or currant sauce" (*U* 15.2900–2901). Later, when Bloom confesses his many sins, he admits, "O I have been a perfect pig" (*U* 15.3397).

Bloom's porcine metamorphosis must also be seen in the context of an earlier scene in "Circe" in which several "medicals" testify about his ambivalent gender. Dr. Mulligan claims that Bloom is not merely "bisexually abnormal," he is also *"virgo intacta."* By the end of this episode the transformation is complete, and Bloom gives birth to *"eight male yellow and white children"* (*U* 15.1776–1822). In the midst of the proceedings Dr. Dixon declares that Bloom "is a finished example of the new womanly man" (*U* 15.1778–79). An ingenious note by Scott Klein suggests that Bloom's Circean androgyny has an epic parallel in two distinctive Homeric similes that characterize Odysseus. In the *Odyssey*, after the Phaeacian bard has sung about the hero's exploits at Troy, Odysseus weeps, just as a woman cries when her husband has been slain defending his home (*Odyssey* 8.521–31; *B-L* 123–24). The second example occurs when Odysseus rejoins his shipmates after his first encounter with Circe. The crew reacts to his safe return at the same time as a pack of calves flocks around the cows that have come back to the fold from the pastures (*Odyssey* 10.408–15; *B-L* 157). Homeric similes with feminine analogues are rare, and it is not unlikely that Joyce, "with his sensitivity to figurative language . . . noticed these intimations of Homeric androgyny and integrated them into his own 'heroic' characterization [of Bloom as a womanly man]."[52]

It is also possible that Joyce knew that the Greek words *sus* (swine, sow) and *choiros* (piglet) were frequently used in an obscene sense for female genitalia.[53] In *Ulysses* that Aristophanic denotation is grossly exemplified in Bella Cohen's mockery of Bloom's sexual inadequacy: "You're not game, in fact. (Her *sowcunt barks*) Fbhracht!" (*U* 15.3489–90). The case for thematic intentionality here is strengthened by Joyce's comment in a 1920 letter to Budgen, while he was in the midst of composing "Circe": "*Moly* is a nut to crack. My latest is this. Moly is the gift of Hermes . . . which saves in case by accident. This would cover immunity from syphilis (σύ φιλις = swine love?)" (*Letters* I.147).[54] The scientific etymology of syphilis is disputed, but the derivation Joyce hesitantly proposed was once widely accepted. Thus, in his re-creative imagination there was a series of links between various sources for and elements in the "Circe" chapter:

Hermes as Odysseus's protector;
Moly as a charm against being transformed and unmanned;
Moly as a prophylactic against syphilis;
Bloom's loss of his talisman-potato;
Bello's transformation of Bloom into both a woman and a pig;
Greek words for pig and piglet as obscene terms for female sex organs;
Bella's *"sowcunt,"* which scorns Bloom's sexual inadequacy.

Two other philological items can be added at either end of the lexico-
logical catena just forged. In a Zürich notebook compiled while Joyce was
working on the later chapters of *Ulysses,* the word *choiros* (piglet) appears
in a list of Greek terms (VIII.A.4.32). There is no hint that Joyce was interested in the obscene use of this word (which he defines as "= pig"); rather,
it appears with five other words that begin with the letter chi (*ch*). At the
same time, one of his native-speaking Greek informants might have
alluded to its crude sexual connotation. That type of lexical extension
certainly would not have shocked Joyce.

In *Finnegans Wake* there is an incontrovertible example of Joyce's use of
the extended sexual meaning of another Greek word: "Totumvir and
esquimeena, who so shall separate fetters to new desire, repeals an act of
union to unite in bonds of *schismacy.* O yes! O yes! Withdraw your
member! Closure. This chamber stands adjourned" (*FW* 585.24–27; my
emphasis). The male (totally, totemically virile) and the female (a cute
little quim) mock the evangelical injunction, "What therefore God hath
joined together, let not man put asunder" (Matthew 19:6). Their union in
one flesh is, at least temporarily, about to be broken, and the courtroom
terms hint at some legal or parliamentary action. The move to quash the
proceedings is, however, momentarily interrupted by an appeal to Molly
Bloom's ecstatic affirmation of delight. The emphasized term, "*schismacy,*"
is ostensibly meant to stand in contrast to "an act of union"; but there is
more than ecclesiastical paradox at play here. The Greek word *schisma*
means cleft, split, as in the schism between the Roman Catholic and Eastern Orthodox churches. It is also used, obscenely and graphically, for the
vulva.[55]

Adventures with Lamb

Although there can be no doubt about Joyce's abiding dedication to
etymological oddities and snippets from scholarly compendia (including
an occasional bit of ancient erotica), his initial encounter with the Homeric tales involved far less recherché media. One of Joyce's Zürich friends
reports that the author told him that he "was twelve years old when we
dealt with the Trojan War at school; only the *Odyssey* stuck in my
memory."[56] During his first year at Belvedere College, Joyce answered
"Ulysses" to a teacher's question, "Who is your favorite hero?"[57] Charles
Lamb's popular *Adventures of Ulysses* was the book in which Joyce first read

about the challenges that faced Homer's hero as he made his way back from Troy to Ithaca. He did not forget that book.[58] In a November 10, 1922, letter, he wrote the following advice to his Aunt Josephine, who reported that she did not understand a lot in her nephew's recently published novel: "buy at once the *Adventures of Ulysses* (which is Homer's story told in simple English much abbreviated by Charles Lamb)" (*Letters* I.193; *SL* 293–94). Another friend reports a touching scene from the end of Joyce's life. When he finally arrived safely in Zürich in mid-December 1940, one his first tasks was to go "to the French bookstore near the lake in order to buy a French edition of the Greek epics for his grandson. The boy was just the age Joyce had been when the *Odyssey* made its first strong impression on him."[59]

Epic Apocrypha

Joyce himself called attention to a theory that some episodes of Homer's original epic have not survived. The source of his information was not the research of a classical scholar but the reputed speculation of a writer of romances. The following incident is reported in Ellmann's biography:

> One night when [Tristan] Rawson had accompanied him home, Joyce steered the conversation round to the Odyssey. "Do you know the Rider Haggard theory about the Odyssey?" Rawson did not. "He thinks that two books of the Odyssey have been lost, and that they fulfilled two prophecies by Tiresias—one about Odysseus wanting another son, the other about a country without salt. Haggard thinks these are not fulfilled. But I don't agree at all. I maintain that the two prophecies are fulfilled; but that the Odyssey has been mistranslated. One of these days I am going to trump up a Joyce theory." His [Joyce's] mind was playing with Bloom's desire for another son, and perhaps with the idea that the saltless country would be Ireland in his book. (*JJII* 426)

That conversation between Rawson and Joyce took place in April 1918, after one of the rehearsals for the performance of *The Importance of Being Earnest* by the English Players in Zürich. Ellmann's interview with Rawson took place in 1954, thirty-six years after the event. Perhaps Rawson's memory confused some of the details; perhaps Joyce's original report of Haggard's "theory" was itself not crisply accurate. Several of my previous citations of archival notes have called attention to other incidents in the post-Homeric mythological tradition about Odysseus and his family. It must be remembered that the process of composing apocryphal sequels to the original epic began with Eugammon in the sixth century B.C. The outstanding modern scholar of this tradition, Stanford, writes that primary impetus to such ancient and modern speculation was Tiresias's vague description of Odysseus's propitiatory pilgrimage to the unnamed inland region. That Homer left this episode to be fulfilled served as a challenge to the ingenuity of many poets and novelists.[60]

Be that as it may, I know of no place in Haggard's massive oeuvre— over thirty adventure novels alone from 1882 to 1925—that would support Joyce's claim that the author or one of his characters refers to "two lost books" of the *Odyssey*.[61] On the other hand, Rawson's recall of the specifics (the prophecy about a son and salt) of the conversation distinctly suggests a definite source for Joyce's assertion. Here I can come up with a likely candidate, *The World's Desire*, a novel that Haggard published in 1890. His coauthor was Andrew Lang, an equally prolific poet, author of fairy tales, essayist, anthropologist, and Homeric scholar. Lang collaborated with S. H. Butcher to produce the version of the *Odyssey* (1879) that Joyce used while working on *Ulysses*. He also wrote three books on the current state of the Homeric question, each staunchly arguing for the unity of the epics. Nowhere in these volumes does Lang propose that two books are missing from the ancient tale of Odysseus's return.[62]

There is some fictional evidence on the topic embedded in *The World's Desire*. In that novel's opening chapter, Odysseus, having punished the suitors and reestablished himself in Ithaca, sets out to fulfill the tasks imposed on him as a curse by Tiresias in the Underworld: "He must wander again till he reached the land of men who had never tasted salt, nor even heard of the salt sea."[63] There the Wanderer must plant his oar in the ground and sacrifice to Poseidon. Odysseus scrupulously follows these instructions, but on his return to the palace he discovers that a pestilence has killed Penelope and Telemachus. In the third chapter of the novel, he learns from the goddess Aphrodite that he must "lift [his] head and look on The World's Desire!" (*WD* 23). That capitalized term is Haggard and Lang's way of referring to Helen, whom Odysseus has desired since he first saw her on a youthful mission to her father's court. Aphrodite tells him to set out to find the golden Helen, who still lives, in Egypt.

To make a long story short—and in the case of *The World's Desire* that procedure is absolutely necessary—the Wanderer is kidnapped by Sidon-ian merchant-slavers, but winds up free in the land of Khem. There he encounters Pharaoh, the witch-queen Meriamun, a bard-priest, the Hebrew prophets Moses and Aaron, and The Strange Hathor. That last threat is a divinely beautiful goddess, who turns out to be Helen. After a furious battle *against* some invading Achaeans, the hero dies in Helen's arms, his body pierced by an arrow shot by Telegonus, the son of Circe and Odysseus. This is the death "from the water as the Ghost [of Tiresias] fore-told" (*WD* 219).

I offer several hypotheses about Rawson's report of Joyce's comments on Haggard's *Odyssey* theory. Perhaps Joyce did not remember the intri-cate plot of *The World's Desire* (assuming that he had read it). Or maybe Rawson confused some of the details in Joyce's original statement, since it is entirely possible that they had stopped for a glass or two of wine after the rehearsal of the play. At any rate, Haggard and Lang do *not* specifically refer to two "lost" books of the *Odyssey,* nor did Tiresias prophesy that the hero would sire another son. The tale of Telegonus, Circe's son by Odysseus, is part of the post-Homeric legend, and there is a stand-ing philological debate on how to translate the Homeric phrase that Odysseus's death shall come *ek halos* (*Odyssey* 11.134): *either* "from/out of the sea" *or* "away from the sea." When all is said and done, Stanford's comment on this prepositional crux is right on the mark here; it autho-rizes a Joycean attempt to trump up his own theory: "Where scholars cannot reach agreement creative writers are likely to produce some surprising interpretations. From this one phrase in Homer an astonishing wealth of imaginative detail evolved in the later tradition."[64]

Phoenician Dimensions

During the composition of *Ulysses,* by far the most important work of Homeric scholarship that Joyce consulted—and conspicuously called attention to—was Victor Bérard's study of the Phoenicians and the *Odyssey* (1902–5). Bérard spent several postgraduate years (1887–91) at the French School in Athens and traveled widely throughout Greece and Albania; later voyages took him to almost every shore of the Mediter-ranean. In addition to his primary scholarship in ancient geography, he published several volumes on British and Russian imperialism, and later on Franco-Swiss relations. He was elected a senator from the department of Jura in 1920 and held that office until his death in 1931. Like Joyce, Bérard had an early interest in motion pictures and sought ways to use the cinema as a medium of social education. An appointment as director of the division of ancient geography at l'Ecole Supérieure des Hautes Etudes crowned his academic career.[65]

Bérard's primary topic in classical scholarship was Homer's *Odyssey*, especially the process of its cross-cultural and trans-Mediterranean formation. In addition to his early book on the Phoenician background of Homer's tale, he also produced a Greek text, commentary, and a French translation of the *Odyssey*. His research culminated in the four-volume *Les navigations d'Ulysse* (1927–29). The latter work, like his others, is punctuated with extracts from his own travel diaries:

> 29 April 1901—From Sainte Maure, a small Greek steamer, the *Pylaros*, took us toward Ithaca.
> 2 May 1908—Coming from Gibraltar, I have at last put my foot on [the islet of] Perejil [and grotto of Calypso].
> 7–10 November 1912—Milazzo, Palermo [Sicily], Tunis, following the route of the Rocks towards Utica and Carthage.
> 24–26 October 1912—We have been able to get to the village of Diocles Aliphera, Pheses of Alpheus—the journey of Telemachus [*Odyssey* 3.488].

The overriding thesis of Bérard's work on the prehistory of the Homeric *Odyssey* was its Semitic matrix: Behind the consolidated tale of the wanderings of a Greek hero on his way home from the Trojan War lie centuries of *periploi* (sailing routes, navigation guides) compiled and used by ancient Phoenician merchants for their voyages all over the known world. The following excerpts summarize the fundamental arguments and outline the basic methodology of Bérard's work:

> The *Odyssey* [is] a Greek poem with a Semitic intelligence behind it: "The poet—Homer, if one wishes—is Greek; the mariner—Ulysses, to give him a name—is Phoenician." Geographical facts, faraway places, and local mappings, at times anthropomorphic in detail, at times buried under layers of etymological clues, fill the *Odyssey*. The poem's geology or "topology" of place names (Egyptian, Semitic, and Greek) mark the appearance of an easterner in western waters.[66]
>
> The *Odyssey* which we have today is an artificial and recent construct, in which the Homeric poet brought together three originally indepen-

dent poems: *The Voyage of Telemachus, The Tales at the Court of King Alki-noos, The Vengeance of Odysseus.*[67]

For those who want a more detailed overview of Bérard's research— and a thorough application of its methods to *Ulysses*—Michael Seidel's *Epic Geography* is the place to go. As his title indicates, the author's critical orientation is resolutely geographical, and that on a grand scale. Seidel's work is packed with charts and maps, ranging from an Egyptian scheme of the world recorded in one of Joyce's Zürich notebooks to twenty-three pages of detailed graphic comparisons of the wanderings in *Ulysses* and the *Odyssey.*[68] Supporting these diagrams are numerous citations from the works of Bérard, Joyce, and other literary navigators. The result is a mixture of occasional insight and irrelevant marginalia. In his analysis of "Sirens," for example, Seidel notes Bérard's indication that the name of the Homeric enchanters may be derived from a Semitic root for binders, or shacklers. That etymology works well for both the Sirens' threat and Odysseus's stratagem in Homer's epic; but I am not convinced that a major factor in the analogous episode in *Ulysses* is the alleged motif that Bloom is *"tied* to Richie Goulding" or *"bound* by circumstances" in the grill of the Ormond Hotel.[69]

The comparative maps are the central exhibit in Seidel's exercise in epic geography. A glance at most of them is enough to convince a reader that neither the grand axes nor most of the individual diagrams for the later books are anything more than coincidentally parallel. Sometimes, even that factor is forced to the outer margins of probability. Prompted by Joyce's own diagrams of Egyptian and Greek directions (VIII.A.5.16), Seidel makes much of Odysseus's statement that his home island, "Ithaca, lies low, farthest out in the sea, towards the dusk" (*Odyssey* 9.25–26). The Greek word for dusk, or gloom, is *zophos;*[70] its most memorable epic application is to the gloom of the Underworld (see *Iliad* 15.191, 21.191; *Odyssey* 11.57, 155). In Dublin, both 7 Eccles Street and Glasnevin Ceme-tery are in the northern quadrant, with no more than a minor tilt to the west side of town. Seidel's discussion of the west-northwest orientation of Ithaca and Bloom's residence ("Zophos: Toward the Gloom") and his trac-ing of the epic heroes' parallel trips to Hades twist the geographical evidence away from its original frame.[71] Although it is certain that the author of *Ulysses* took frequent and special note of Bérard's claims of a Phoenician matrix for the *Odyssey,* Joyce did not literally superimpose a chart of Odysseus's wandering onto a map of Dublin. In short, despite its chartographic ingenuity, Seidel's Ulyssean *periplous* can lead a reader of the novel seriously astray.

It is doubly ironic that Seidel's 1976 book has enjoyed more or less the same reception at the hands of Joyceans as Bérard's earlier research has received from contemporary Homeric scholars. Both groups largely ignore their findings. In his section on geography, Stanford, the editor of the standard annotated text of the epic, mentions Bérard's "extreme literal views"[72] and rarely cites them in his notes. Bérard's name does not appear in the index of the most recent scholarly commentary on the *Odyssey;* none of his books is listed in the extensive bibliography.[73] Seidel's book, remarkable mainly for its complex maps, has not convinced Joyceans of their critical applicability to *Ulysses.*[74] In short, neither cartography nor toponymic etymology has left a permanent mark on the central scholarship of the Ulysses tradition.

The field of epic geography is the purported area of another contemporary work on Joyce. Its subtitle signals a topical—indeed, a topographical—affinity to the approaches of Bérard and Seidel. Jackson Cope's *Joyce's Cities: Archeologies of the Soul* has, in fact, nothing in common with either. The only genuinely archaeological aspect of Cope's book is its citation of Heinrich Schliemann, the pioneer excavator of Mycenae and Troy, and Sir Arthur Evans, the father of Cretan archaeology. Those references, however, are far more concerned with D'Annunzio and futurism than with Bronze Age Greek or Minoan sites. A circuitous anecdotal link between Tutankhamen's tomb and Joyce's interest in ancient Egyptian religion is about as deep into the discipline of urban archaeology as this study delves.[75]

The current status of Bérard's research on Homer's epic has, of course, no bearing on Joyce's use of his study of the Phoenician background to the *Odyssey.* As previously noted, Joyce came upon a reference to Bérard in a book on the Homeric geography of Troy. He then consulted the texts themselves in Zürich's Zentralbibliothek in early 1918.[76] The *Ulysses* notebook VIII.A.5, cited so frequently here, is the primary repository of these annotations. They total almost two hundred separate items, most from Bérard's second volume, which deals with "Homeric" sites in the Red Sea and Mediterranean. Joyce later transferred a number of these entries to various notesheets keyed to individual chapters of the novel;[77] but there is no archival evidence to suggest that he continued to take notes from Bérard's work during 1919–21, when he was completing *Ulysses* in Paris.

It is certain, however, that Joyce regarded *Les Phéniciens et l'Odyssée* as an essential text for understanding his novel. In 1928 Stuart Gilbert told Joyce that he was reading the *Odyssey* in Greek to help him better to understand *Ulysses*. Joyce asked, in return, if he had read Bérard's book.[78] Shortly after that suggestion, Joyce wrote to Miss Weaver: "Mr. Victor Bérard, author of *The Phoenicians and the Odyssey*, has expressed a great desire to see me, having been attracted by the *Protée* article in the N.R.F.[79] He is a man of great erudition and he will never recover from his disappointment when he does meet me" (*Letters* I.272).

Mary and Padraic Colum record Joyce's long-term admiration for Bérard's work and report that he attended the scholar's funeral in mid-November 1931. That was shortly after the Joyces had returned from a six-month visit to England, during which James and Nora legalized their marriage. Joyce also was accustomed to giving copies of Bérard's translation of the *Odyssey* as gifts to friends.[80] A final reference to Bérard is found in Joyce's September 8, 1938, letter to Louis Gillet: "Another strange parallel to the Ulysses–Victor Bérard incident. His Homeric research served to confirm my theory about the Semitic aspect of the *Odyssey* when I had already written three-fourths of the book. Suddenly I find out that my theory about the Scandinavian aspects of my hero Finn MacCool . . . are confirmed by the research of a German scholar, Zimmer, whose works I know nothing about" (*Letters* I.410).

As for the nature of Joyce's use of material from Bérard in *Ulysses*, it is enough to point to the similar process involving entries from Roscher's *Lexikon* cited previously in this chapter. As they are deployed in Joyce's text, most of these items are ornamental; that is, they contribute to the verbal complexity and texture of a passage, rather than acting as narrative guides or thematic props. Many of the notes from Bérard that were placed in *Ulysses* seem to be little more than Joyce's pedantic archival and linguistic jokes. For example, without Herring's commentary, who would guess that the notebook phrase "¹unwooded isles now (cf. Ireland)" (VIII.A.5.5) came from Bérard's work (II.491)? Who would imagine that that documentary source lies behind the local ecological concern in Barney Kiernan's bar: "—As treeless as Portugal we'll be soon, says John Wyse. . . . Save the trees of Ireland [says the Citizen] for the future men of Ireland" (*U* 12.1258–64)? More to the point, even though the archival item is appropriate to the plot and tone of the scene, who would care to know what the source was? On the other hand, before we dismiss the value of tracing the Bérard notes *tout court,* it may help to repeat some consolatory advice from their principal editor: "If on subsequent readings the enthusiast with a taste for acrostics wishes to unveil the mythic [or the Punic or the genetic] level, he may puzzle it out as he pleases. Perhaps Joyce misjudged his audience."[81] I, for one, can relate to that.

In addition to catering to Joyce's obsession for scribbling notes and his apparent need for extravagantly elaborate structural scaffolds, there is a far more significant justification for his dedication to *Les Phéniciens et l'Odyssée.* Bérard's research demonstrated that it was possible to impose a pre-Homeric template on the *Odyssey.* The esoteric nature and transcultural scope of this material provided Joyce with an allusive perspective that was more expansive and flexible than the naive moralization of Lamb's Homeric tales. The topographical specificity, the citation of numerous place names in various languages and scripts, the conflation of circum-Mediterranean trade routes and the track of Odysseus's epic voyage, and the transfer of elements of Semito-Homeric geography into Dublin—all of these procedures are compositional strategies that appealed to Joyce throughout his career. The epigraph to Seidel's book is a marvelously apt statement made by John Joyce when his son was seven years old: "If that fellow was dropped in the middle of the Sahara, he'd sit, be God, and make a map of it" (*JJII* 28). Referring to the work-in-progress years, Budgen wrote, "Rathfarnham, Finglas, Howth Head and Lucan: the stage is small, yet big enough. Roman history can be enacted in the courtyard of an inn."[82] That is precisely the creative impulse that drove Joyce to his Punic notes: not merely the exotic local color but also the cumulative levels, languages, and venues of the narrative. Bérard believed that the background of the *Odyssey* could be reconstructed from an examination of Phoenician *periploi.* Joyce dreamed that Homer's epic could be deconstructed in the streets of Dublin.

Among more recent work on Joyce and Bérard is a short piece by Lynn Childress that closely examines Joyce's Zürich notes as a source for the "Lestrygonians" chapter of *Ulysses.*[83] She emphasizes the anthropomorphic slant of the French scholar's analysis of the Homeric epic: In shaping the practical data of his Semitic "sources" into an epic poem, the Greek composer of the *nostos* (homecoming tale) humanized the natural forces and geographical details of the merchant mariners' sailing guides. The radical thrust of that re-formation is convincingly illustrated by a long extract from Bérard's own translation of the Lestrygonian episode in the

Odyssey and is followed by a close analysis of the long index of the notes (VIII A.5.11–14) that Joyce drew from approximately seventy-five pages of *Les Phéniciens et l'Odyssée.* In the choice and deployment of these data, Childress detects the roots of the major motif of hunger in "Lestrygonians" and the pronounced thematic link between that episode and "Oxen of the Sun" (*U* 18.442–44).

Homeric Immanence

The third chapter in Hugh Kenner's general introduction to *Ulysses* is entitled "Uses of Homer." As always, the distinguished critic is clear, insightful, and clever. After stating that "minor correspondences abound, most of them mocking mirrors," Kenner offers a half dozen of his own examples, several of them not very convincing. It is not surprising, then, that he winds down his discussion on a somewhat low note. The large pattern is "at bottom no mystery. . . . [S]ome [of the lesser correspondences], if we chance to know them, lend definition, some contrast. . . . Their dubious immanence adds fun to our endless exploration of [Joyce's] book."[84]

In my judgment, Walton Litz strikes closer to the truth in his study of the method of Joyce's two major works. His opening chapter, "The Design of *Ulysses*" acknowledges that "the 'epic' proportions of *Ulysses* are absolutely dependent on the major Homeric analogues." Litz immediately calls attention to several qualifying factors: "Joyce's increasing preoccupation with linguistic experimentation" and the recognition that many of the Homeric entries on the *Ulysses* notesheets were "more useful to Joyce during the process of composition" than they are to his readers. Support for these distinctions is given in a brilliant summary of the function of the "*Moly*" entries on six different "Circe" notesheets, with reference to a 1920 letter from Joyce to Frank Budgen. Multiple functions were assigned to the "many leaves" of the prophylactic plants that Odysseus and Bloom carried to counteract Circe's magic.[85]

In an introductory essay to the "Eumaeus" section of his edition of the *Ulysses* notesheets, Phillip Herring reviews Joyce's sources for the Homeric material found in those archival documents.[86] His examples of how the notes contributed to the final text are significant and enlightening. He also discusses a number of cases in which Joyce merges the identities of Homeric and Ulyssean characters (Telemachus, Odysseus, Theoclymenus, the Pseudangelos/Stephen, Bloom, the Sailor, M'Intosh). His sharp eye and ear detect puns on names involving several languages: Antinous (*UNBM* 965:95) and Irus (*UNBM* 465:101). I suspect that most readers of *Ulysses* would not connect Bloom's sleek cat *(U* 4.16–48) with Odysseus's neglected dog (*Odyssey* 17.290–325). A crossed note confirms the connection: "ᵍthe cat = Argos" (*UNBM* 416:23). Herring also points out the "distinction between the *function* of the myths and literary parallels in Joyce's creative process . . . and their *effect,* or the extent to which the meaning of *Ulysses* is dependent upon them."[87] The habit of allusive overkill, he concludes, provided Joyce (and symbol hunters) some comic relief; indeed, he visualizes Joyce secretly smiling at a reader lost in the novel's mythic labyrinth. Nonetheless, his painstaking transcription of the notesheets, his identification of documentary sources, and his context-setting essays mark Herring as a master of careful genetic research and a pioneer in the movement away from unrestrained speculation and back to Joyce's texts and their origins.

The term *epiphany* is familiar to all students of Joyce's works. It has also been used, from an analogous perspective, by a contemporary classics scholar. In his riveting study of some major poetic problems in the "formulaic" interpretation of Homer's *Odyssey,* Norman Austin writes, "A fundamental law of epiphanology is that epiphanies come only to those who can see, which is to say only to those who seek."[88] The validity of that law seems to be upheld by critics who seek to demonstrate this fundamental presence of Homeric parallels in Joyce's *Ulysses.* While emphasizing reasonable distinctions between raw notes, structural outlines, evolving drafts, and the final text, scholars continue to display considerable ingenuity in detecting and applying epic analogues. Even those who are most suspicious of the "dubious immanence" of Joyce's Homer do not disdain the search. Kenner, for example, ends his basically skeptical chapter on Homeric correspondences with the playful warning that "it would be a pity not to let that heroic arc [Bloom's schoolboy urination] remind us of Odysseus's power manifested in his great bow."[89]

Verbal "Recalls"

The standard commentaries on Joyce's work do not mention Joseph Prescott's eighteen-page article published over a half-century ago on correspondences between the *Odyssey* and *Ulysses.*[90] After a brief overview of structural matters, this piece is a chapter-by-chapter presentation of mainly verbal "recalls." Several instances involve a reversal of Homer's intent. Odysseus, for example, is warned by Hermes to make Circe swear an oath not to enchant him and leave him "unmanned" (*anenora* [*Odyssey* 10.30, 343]). In Joyce's brothel episode, Bloom confesses that he was "unmanned" by the "artless blush" of the young woman at the zoo (*U* 15.1188–90). Later Bello declares, "What you longed for has come to pass. Henceforth you are unmanned and mine in earnest, a thing under the yoke" (*U* 15.2964–66). Throughout Prescott's discussion of these examples, the Homeric medium of his comparison of the two texts is the Butcher and Lang translation of the *Odyssey,* which he uses, without comment, as Joyce's reference.

In this day of hypersophisticated theories about the ins and outs of intertextuality, some readers would not agree with many of the "recalls" educed by Prescott. Nevertheless, after Stuart Gilbert's *Study* (which side-steps the issue of the English translation used by Joyce), Prescott's article was the first to subject *Ulysses* to such microscopic scrutiny. The verbal parallels prove that Joyce's use of Homeric material extended to compositional elements that are far less overt than the thematic schemata or transcendent archetypes. Without Gilbert's footnote to Porphyry's *Cave of the Nymphs,* no reader would have dreamed of a link between the priestesses of Ceres, Taurus, ox-begotten bees, and the bumblebee that stung Leopold Bloom on May 23, 1904.[91] So, too, would the same reader have passed right over most of the instances of direct echoes from Butcher and Lang's version of the *Odyssey* that Joyce worked into the text of *Ulysses.* An awareness of this type of intertextual finesse is not, it must immediately be emphasized, necessary for or even conducive to an appreciation of the novel at any level. The Homeric correspondences were, however, liberally deployed in the narrative by Joyce. Their detection is thus an important and legitimate contribution to tracing some of the individual steps in the composition of *Ulysses* and to revealing the multiple layers of allusion in that process.

Those judgments, which represent a belated nod to Prescott's initial study, are also a prefatory rationale for an additional series of "recalls" in what might seem to be the least Homeric chapter in *Ulysses.* The dramatic setting, hallucinatory action, and sexually explicit language of "Circe" are far removed from Homer's tale of the enchanted island of the goddess. Indeed, Joyce's radically innovative form in this episode makes it an unlikely matrix for the distinctly archaicizing diction of the Butcher and Lang version of the epic. It is therefore a surprise to find in Joyce's text a number of direct verbal echoes of that once standard translation. Most of the following recalls from—and around—"Circe" have not been cited before.

- *Odyssey* 10.158. While exploring Circe's island, Odysseus kills a "tall antlered stag" (*B-L* 149): In the fantasy encounter between Blazes Boylan and Bloom, the former *"hangs his hat smartly on a peg of Bloom's antlered head"* (*U* 15.3763–64).

- *Odyssey* 10.212–13. Odysseus comes to Circe's forest house, which is surrounded by lions and wolves that the goddess had "bewitched" *(B-L* 150): Signor Maffei brings a man-eating Libyan lion and a hyena to heel. "The glint of my eye does it with these beast sparklers (*with a bewitching smile*)" (*U* 15.711–15).

- *Odyssey* 10.224. Odysseus's most valued friend in the crew, Polites (the Greek word for citizen), tells his comrades that they should call Circe out of her house (*B-L* 151): After Bloom has been declared Leopold the First and has promised the new Bloomusalem, one of the first commoners to hail him is his former nemesis, the Irish nationalist at Barney Kiernan's bar: "THE CITIZEN (*choked with emotion, brushes aside a tear with his emerald muffler*) May the good God bless him!" (*U* 15.1616–18).

- *Odyssey* 10.277, 331: Hermes appears to Odysseus to warn him about the dangers that Circe poses; one of his Homeric epithets is the god of the "gold wand" (*B-L* 152, 154): On their way to Nighttown, when Stephen asks Lynch to hold his stick, Lynch replies, "Damn your yellow stick" (*U* 15.120). Later, at Bloom's coronation, among the attendants at the ceremony are *"gentlemen of the bedchamber, Black Rod, Deputy Ganter, Gold Stick"* (*U* 15.1436–37).

- *Odyssey* 10.394. After Odysseus has mollified Circe, she restores the crew to human shape with an antidote to her "venom" (*B-L* 156): When the revelers pass a bawd, she *"spits in their trail her jet of venom* (*U* 15.86).

- *Odyssey* 10.545. When Circe dresses to send Odysseus and his crew on their way, she puts on a "veil" (*B-L* 161): Throughout "Circe" there appear a number of vaguely threatening women, only one of whom would seem to have a natural reason for wearing a veil: Mrs. Breen, *"in . . . white velour hat and a spider veil"* (*U* 15.543); Martha Clifford, *"sobbing behind her veil"* (*U* 15.765); "THE VEILED SIBYL" (*U* 15.1735); the specter of Stephen's dead mother, *"with a wreath of faded orangeblossoms and a torn bridal veil"* (*U* 15.4158).

- *Odyssey* 10.121–32. Just before Odysseus and his crew arrive on Circe's island, they barely escape the destruction of the rest of their fleet by the Lestrygonians (*B-L* 147–48): In "Circe" Leopold Bloom is hauled before a court on the charge of assaulting Mary Driscoll "in the rere of the premises" (*U* 15.885). The defendant's barrister cites mitigating circumstances, "There have been cases of shipwreck and sonambulism in my client's family" (*U* 15.930–31).

- *Odyssey* 10.490–91 and 519. Circe tells Odysseus that he must complete "a journey to Hades" (*B-L* 159–60); she instructs him to pour a propitiatory offering of "sweet wine" (*B-L* 160) to all the dead: Bella Cohen berates Leopold Bloom for his irresponsibility, "Die and be damned to you if you have any sense of decency or grace about you. I can give you a rare old wine that'll send you skipping to hell and back" (*U* 15.3205–7).

- *Odyssey* 11.128. When Odysseus arrives in Hades after leaving Circe's island, the prophet Tiresias tells him how he must placate Poseidon. After he has taken care of matters in Ithaca, Odysseus must walk inland so far away from the sea that a wayfarer will mistake the oar he carries for a "winnowing fan" (*B-L* 166); there Odysseus is to offer a final sacrifice to the Lord of the Sea: In the midst of "Circe," Bella Cohen arrives on the scene, in "all of a mucksweat." She notices Bloom; then "[h]*er large fan winnows wind towards her heated faceneck and embonpoint*" (*U* 15.2750–53).

- *Odyssey* 11.152–224. After Odysseus has received the prophetic instructions of Tiresias in Hades, he speaks with the shade of his mother, Anticleia (*B-L* 166–68): In Bella's brothel in "Circe," the wildly intoxicated Stephen Dedalus is admonished to think of his mother's people. He requests that the pianola play the "Dance of Death." At that, *"Stephen's mother, emaciated, rises stark through the floor"*; she begs him to repent; he resists (*U* 15.4137–242).

- *Odyssey* 22.481–82. After he has slain the suitors, Odysseus instructs his faithful old nurse to "bring sulphur" (*B-L* 352–53) and brimstone, so that he can purify the great hall of every trace of the bloody slaughter: In "Circe" Joyce twists this detail topsy-turvy. When the young whore Zoe leads Stephen and Bloom into the brothel, the Male Brutes roar their approval, "*exhaling sulphur of rut and dung*" (*U* 15.2018–20). In her final monologue Molly Bloom remembers the night when Leopold ran "into off with the Albion milk and sulphur soap I used to use"(*U* 18.1193–94).

These recalls, most of them clustered around the events in a single chapter in Ulysses, are conclusive evidence for Joyce's reliance on the Butcher and Lang translation of the *Odyssey*. The presentations of several participants at the 1995 Zürich Summer Workshop, "Homer/Joyce/ Homer," provided additional examples. My emphasis on the unacknowledged presence of Butcher and Lang in the novel is necessary, since a discursive essay by the influential Hugh Kenner points to the primary influence of another translation.[92]

Kenner allows that Joyce may be parodying the self-consciously archaic diction and style of the Butcher and Lang version in the following excerpt from his "Cyclops" chapter: "And lo, as they quaffed their cup of joy, a godlike messenger came swiftly in, radiant as the eye of heaven, a comely youth and behind him there passed an elder of noble gait and countenance" (*U* 12.244–46). That may in fact be a parody. On the other hand, that chapter of *Ulysses* is packed with irreverent allusions and burlesques, not merely of the Homeric epic but of all sorts of recently revived local legend and Celtic myth. Nineteenth-century translations from Irish sources—except for the proper names—would have been replete with the same verbal paraphernalia as is the Butcher and Lang rendition of the Odyssey.

Lacking definitive internal evidence, Kenner went to Stanford's study of the Ulysses tradition. There he discovered that the distinguished Irish classicist had asked Stanislaus Joyce what books on Homer did his brother use. Stanislaus's reply included Samuel Butler's *The Authoress of the "Odyssey,"* Bérard's work, "and the translations by Butler and Cowper."[93] I am not convinced that that bibliographical information, despite its fraternal source, can be trusted. After all, Joyce was not in Trieste with Stanislaus during the most intense work on *Ulysses;* that took place first in Zürich, then in Paris. Second, neither Butler's nor Cowper's version of the *Odyssey* has left any trace whatsoever in Joyce's notesheets or the text. (Joyce did in fact buy Cowper's translation of the *Odyssey* in Zürich in August 1915, and it remained, among the other volumes, in the Trieste library left with Stanislaus.[94] The same lack of textual traces is true of Butler's *Authoress of the "Odyssey,"* which is not in the Trieste library. Stanislaus did not mention Butler's *The Humor of Homer and Other Essays,* which is in Joyce's collection.)[95] Finally, there is direct testimony from Frank Budgen, a friend and confidant who was with Joyce during the crucial period of composition in Zürich. Budgen discusses Joyce's association with Greeks in that wartime city and his nonacademic background in Modern Greek. Then he explicitly states: "As a work of reference for his *Ulysses* he used the Butcher and Lang translation of the *Odyssey.*"[96] Kenner (along with Stanislaus and Stanford) is incorrect; Joyce's use of Butcher and Lang was more than just a "high-falutin' Mediterranean" exercise in parodic prose or one of his overly schematic structural props. That translation, however mannered and archaic it sounds to us, *was* the primary text through which Joyce contemplated Homer's *Odyssey.* I see a belated reverse recognition of his debt to Butcher and Lang in the essay topic assigned to "*Homer*" in the "Night Lessons" of the *Wake:* "Describe in Homely Anglian Monosyllables the Wreck of the Hesperus" (*FW* 306.L3 and 25–27).

The Oral Theory

During the past century the primary topic of professional scholarship on the epics of ancient Greece has been the Homeric Question. The "unitarians" (mainly English) held that the poems, with few exceptions, were the products of a single creative imagination; the "analysists" (mainly German) distinguished, without any consensus in detail, various layers and stages of production that were then imperfectly combined. During the last fifty years, problems involving the unity of the epics (and whether the *Iliad* and the *Odyssey* were produced by the same poet) have largely been subsumed by debate on *how* the poems were composed: Were they oral compositions in which the traditional formulaic phrase was the essential verbal/metrical factor in an ad hoc production? Or were they written compositions for which the considered choice of words and rhythm was the primary creative determinant?[97]

The theory of oral poetry proposed by Milman Parry and developed by his followers (mainly Anglo-American) is now the dominant, but not exclusive, position. Parry's first two works were published, in French, in Paris six years after the publication of *Ulysses*. There is no indication that Joyce ever heard of Parry or his groundbreaking work on "name-epithet" phrases ("swift-footed Achilles," "Odysseus sacker of cities"). There were, however, several prior works that had decisive influence on Parry's theories—and there is evidence that Joyce was familiar with at least the basic elements of these hypotheses. In his *Prolegomena ad Homerum* (Introduction to Homer) (1795), Friedrich Wolf proposed that, since writing was unknown to Homer, the epics attributed to him must be collections of originally oral songs transmitted for generations by rhapsodists and imperfectly joined together to form what we know as the *Iliad* and the *Odyssey*. In one of Joyce's *Finnegans Wake* Notebooks, compiled in the spring and early summer of 1926, the following item occurs: "Wolf's Theory / of Homer" (VI.B.20.33). There is nothing in the context of this entry that would indicate either a source or its application to the work in progress. An entry in an earlier Notebook (1924) refers to the ceremonial occasion at which, in historical times, the epics were publicly performed by rhapsodists. The annual festival of the city's goddess-patroness at Athens was the Panathenaea; it involved an elaborate procession to the Acropolis, sacrifices, athletic competition, and, by law, the recitation of the Homeric poems. Joyce indicates his awareness of this custom in "Homer sung at Panathenae" (VI.B.14.213).[98]

In 1924 Père Marcel Jousse published a study of the differences between the style of oral verse, with its mnemonic devices, and modern literary poetry. This work greatly influenced Parry's thesis of an oral-formulaic Homer. Friends report that Joyce had more than a passing awareness of Jousse's work. Mary and Padraic Colum describe his interest in the French priest's suggestion that language grew out of gesture.[99] Gillet says that Joyce attended one of Jousse's Sorbonne lectures on comparative phonetics and linguistics.[100] Others have discussed how much Joyce was inspired or informed by these academic theories.[101] He left explicit proof, for example, that he was delighted by the resonant title of Jousse's most influential work: "a famous phrase has been restructured out of oral style into the verbal for all time with ritual rhythmics" (*FW* 36.8–10) is clearly a send-up of *Les style oral rythmique et mnémotechnique chez les verbo-moteurs*. Two other Wakean passages paraphrase the nub of the theories and credit their author: "Exquisite Game of inspiration! . . .

without the scrape of a pen. Ohr for oral" (*FW* 302.19–22) and "In the beginning was the gest he jousstly says" (*FW* 468.5). For Joyce, serious linguistic scholarship never got in the way of studied verbal humor.

The Oracle at Zürich

In Homeric times, when people needed answers to crucial questions, they went to the oracle of Zeus at Dodona (*Odyssey* 14.327–30; also note VIII.A.5.5) or consulted a seer of Apollo (*Iliad* 1.69–72). Nowadays, the best way for Joycean scholars to get precise information is to send an e-mail to Fritz Senn in Zürich. There, on the third floor of a restored medieval building on Augustinergasse, are the offices and library of the Zürich James Joyce Foundation. Its collection, continually and profession-ally augmented, is composed of books, journals, pamphlets, documents, letters, realia, recordings, photographs, posters, programs from countless symposiums, conferences, workshops, snapshot albums, annotated re-marks of visitors, and other pertinent material for scholarly research. But Senn, the driving force behind this operation, is anything but a sedentary academic curator of the world's best collection of Joyceana. He is an aston-ishingly prolific scholar on every aspect of Joyce's works.[102] There is, however, no research topic in which Senn takes more pride than in his discussions of the interaction between Homer's epic verses and the text of *Ulysses.*

The best known of Senn's Greek essays is his "Book of Many Turns," a close analysis of the structure of several episodes in *Ulysses.* He convinc-ingly demonstrates that Joyce's narrative is genuinely *polytropos,* that it shares Odysseus's foremost Homeric epithet by constantly finding new ways to shift and turn to avoid repetition.[103] "Remodeling Homer" is even more closely tied to the original text of the *Odyssey.* Notice of the adverbial means of asserting and subverting the epic's theme of "benevolent dissemblance" and the "clash of two *lekto*-forms" in the Proteus episode are a close reading of small but significant points. On a greater scale is Senn's detection of a connection between the Cyclops's barbaric prepara-tion of a *[pymaton] dorpon* (last supper) from two of Odysseus's crew (*Odyssey* 9.344), his promise to eat Odysseus last (*pymaton*) as a "guest-gift" (*Odyssey* 9.369–70), and the hero's announcement, in the great hall of his palace before he takes up his bow, that it is time to prepare *dorpon* (supper) for the suitors (*Odyssey* 21.420)—it will be their last. That concatenation of thematic words is a discovery that any classical scholar would have been proud to point out. Equally ingenious is Senn's suggestion of a phonetic link between *oúlēn* (woolen [cloak]) that Odysseus is reported to be wearing, and *oulḗn* (scar) that is the result of a boar's gash in Odysseus's thigh (*Odyssey* 19.225, 391). To the best of my knowledge, no professional Homerist has noticed the similarity of sound (but not accent) in those two words in adjacent scenes that "identify" the returning hero.[104]

Another foray into comparative philology is Senn's brief, but dead-center, discussion of things that "miss the mark" in Homer and Joyce. The evidence ranges from Diomedes' spear (*Iliad* 5.287) to Bloom's purchase of a racy book for Molly, "*Sweets of Sin*" (*U* 10.606–42). In both works, thrown objects—rocks, an ox-hoof, an empty biscuit tin, the ball Bloom tosses to Cissey Caffrey (*U* 13.350–58), the ball thrown to Nausicaa on the beach (*Odyssey* 6.115–17)—fail to hit their targets. At the crucial moment, however, Odysseus does not miss his marks: the aligned holes in the oxheads—and the suitors. The philological connection here is the Greek noun *hamartē/harmartia* (miss, mistake, error, fault, or—as a Christian term—sin) and the cognate verb *harmartanō*. Senn deftly exemplifies and discusses every sort of missed mark as a literary motif, plot device, and character trait. He concludes: "Missing one's aim is part of the human condition, one recognized by Homer and profusely modulated by Joyce, who may differ from most of his predecessors by not concentrating on reports of success, without, however, making failure necessarily tragic."[105] Senn's article is a typical example of his command of various languages, his close attention to the nuances of the text, and his genuinely humanistic perspective.

The most recent of his essays on *Ulysses* is a detailed examination of catachetical catalogs and their Homeric analogues, especially the climactic "recount" of his adventures by the hero to Penelope (*Odyssey* 23.309). Senn begins by noting the force of the Greek verb *katalegein* (to enumerate, to list), then discusses the application of this epic technique to the narrative mode of "Ithaca." As usual, the analysis is undulating, limpid, and informative.[106]

The *Odyssey* in Art

One of the many stages of mediation between Homer's *Odyssey* and Joyce's *Ulysses* was the large number of Victorian paintings inspired by the ancient epic.[107] Joseph Kestner has discussed, with thirty illustrations of typical examples, many of the artists who exhibited their works in major London galleries. Calypso, Circe, Nausicaa, the Sirens were subjects that afforded the painters ample and repeated opportunities to display their mastery of human anatomy, with and without period costume. Although he does not cite any examples of definite influence, Kestner concludes, "The 'mythical method' of these nineteenth-century artists—the incorporation of myth into contemporary history through classicizing iconography—is the crucial element in cultural poetics that established this practice and prepared for both the creation of and the reception of *Ulysses*."[108] When Frank Budgen first met Joyce in Zürich in the early summer of 1918, the writer mentioned that he was working on a book based on the wanderings of Ulysses. A painter himself, Budgen's first reaction was to think of the original work in these terms: "The *Odyssey* for me was just a long poem that might at any moment be illustrated by some Royal Academician. I could use his water-colour Greek heroes, book-opened, in an Oxford Street bookshop window."[109]

During a slightly later period Joyce himself commented on the Odyssean aura of the French capital. In a July 20, 1920, letter to Stanislaus he wrote that recent productions in Paris had included Gabriel Fauré's opera *Pénélope* and Guillaume Apollinaire's surreal verse drama *Les Mamelles de Tirésias* (Letters III.10).[110] There was also a personal artifact in a different artistic medium: On a wall of one of Joyce's apartments in Zürich "was pinned a photograph of a Greek statue of Penelope. It represented a woman, draped, seated, looked at her upheld forefinger."[111] That statue has been on display for decades in the Gallery of Statues (exhibit no. 754) of the Vatican Museum. Joyce might well have seen it during his seven-month stay in Rome (1906–7); in any case, inexpensive photographic reproductions were widely available. The sculpture looks exactly as described by Budgen—except that scholars have determined that the head of "Penelope" originally belonged to another statue, and the upraised right hand (and its pensive pose) is a modern replacement.[112]

The *Odyssey* in the *Wake*

In the midst of the "mime of Mick, Nick and the Maggies," Glugg/ Shem establishes his credentials as an author. One of the works that he is planning to produce has episodes that are clearly intended to recall parallel scenes in the *Odyssey* and *Ulysses:*

> Ukalepe [both the title *Ulysses* and "Calypso"]. Loathers' leave ["Lotus Eaters," in which those who consume the plant are reluctant to leave the island]. Had Day ["Hades," the realm in which one's days in the sun are in the past]. Nemo in Patia ["Cyclops," whose homeland (*patria* in Latin) the hero escapes through the name-ploy of "Nobody" (*nemo* in Latin)]. The Luncher Out ["Lestrygonians," the cannibals in Homer's epic, lend their name to the episode in which Bloom has lunch at Davy Byrnes's pub]. Skilly and Carubdish [Scylla and Charybdis]. A Wandering Wreck ["Wandering Rocks"]. From the Mermaids' Tavern ["Sirens," the Ulyssean locus of which is the Concert Room, the bar at the Ormond Hotel]. Bullyfamous ["Cyclops," the one-eyed monster in the *Odyssey* whose name is Polyphemus (Much Famed, in Greek)]. Naughtsycalves ["Nausicaa," in which the princess does not see Odysseus's naked calves, but Bloom does get an eyeful of Gerty's thighs]. Mother of Mercy ["Oxen of the Sun," which in the *Odyssey* do not reproduce, whereas in *Ulysses* the scene is set at the National Maternity Hospital (not Mater Misericordiae [Mother of Mercy, in Latin])]. Walpurgas Nackt ["Circe," in which the turbulent action is similar to the *Walpurgis Nacht* episode in Goethe's *Faust*]. (*FW* 229.13–16)

A second catalog of Odyssean material, but in this instance based on plot-themes, is recorded in the *Scribbledehobble* Notebook:

> correspondences (fishisle = Eolus: fucking sea stallion = Oxen of Sun: black ogre = Cyclops: cannibals = Lestrygonians: bhang = Lotuseaters: vivisepultre = Hades: slaughter of the roc: Oxen of sun: old man of sea = Proteus: good king = Alkinoos); whilst preceeding [*sic*] home: know that [what?] he's talking about: obliging beauty: ingenious attendant: the unwritten law: carried his bat: wholesale murder: a glass of drink: her head would pay off: have experienced pain: bakes all the confectionery: back he went: perfectly dreadful: familiarity took place: intercepted a glance. (*Scribbledehobble* 153–54 [803])

In that list the initial parenthetical summaries of selected episodes of the Odyssey require no comment. Some of the subsequent phrases are a bit more cryptic. The "obliging beauty" is Calypso; the "ingenious attendant" Eumaeus. Penelope's resourcefulness ("head") in setting up Odysseus's final identification of their marvelous marriage bed is rightfully praised. The reference to "familiarity" probably summarizes the dishonorable conduct of the serving women with the suitors. The "confectionery" may allude to the clever camouflage of the bustle of the postslaughter cleansing of the great hall at Ithaca: Odysseus tells the servants to "say that it is a wedding feast" (*Odyssey* 22.419–73; *B-L* 358). At any rate, although Joyce did not forget the details of Homer's poem after the completion of *Ulysses*, only one of these pre-text phrases was inserted into the *Wake*. The crossed "ᵍcarried the bat" reappears in a paragraph that describes—with heavy use of cricket terms—the early morning sexual intercourse of HCE and ALP. At the end of those epic innings in their bed in Chapelizod, the hero has not yet been declared out: "(how's that? Noball, he carried his bat!)" (*FW* 584.23).[113]

My preceding discussion of Bérard's Phoenician-Homeric studies cited the term *periplous* (sailing guide) several times. Joyce remembered this item of ancient navigational terminology and inserted several variations of it into the *Wake*. The most direct reference is "the littleknown periplic bestteller . . . of the wretched mariner . . . a Punic admiralty report . . . saucily republished as a dodecanesian baedeker of the every-tale-a-treat-in-itself variety" (*FW* 123.22–28). Here one can trace the evolution of the Homeric *Odyssey* from an obscure chartbook for Punic (Phoenician) sailors to an exciting series of adventure stories set in the Greek isles, an accurate synopsis of Bérard's thesis. It was "Hanno" who produced the "original document" in his "unbrookable script" (*FW* 123.32–33; see *FW* 182.20). The only extant fragment of a Punic *periplous* is taken from an inscription on a bronze plaque set up in the ancient Phoenician colony of Carthage in North Africa by King Hanno. Excerpts (surviving only in a Greek translation) describe a fifth-century B.C. voyage beyond the Pillars of Heracles (Gibraltar) down the west coast of Africa.[114] In the *Wake* episode featuring the Norwegian ship captain, that northern mariner is called a "peripulator" (*FW* 313.33–34).

The next example of an Odyssean influence on the *Wake* is quite straightforward. When Poseidon spots Odysseus on his raft sailing away from Calypso's island, he rouses all the winds of the heavens to drive him off course: "the East Wind [*Euros*] and the South Wind [*Notos*] clashed, and the stormy West [*Zephyros*] and the North [*Boreēs*]" (*Odyssey* 5.295–96; *B-L* 79–80).[115] In Joyce's re-creation the winds become "borus pew notus pew eurus pew zipher" (*FW* 283.3–4). The Homeric order is rearranged, but the repeated "pew" is a close phonetic echo of the Greek root *pneu-* (wind, breath, blowing).

My last suggestion stretches the claim for allusion to the outer limits, which is almost never rash in the case of the *Wake*. In the midst of the rivers in "Anna Livia," a group known as the "pollynooties" (*FW* 209.31) surfaces. O Hehir and Dillon gloss this with *polynautes* (Greek for "involving many sailors"). That makes some sense, since it takes many sailors to ply their trade on the hundreds of rivers in that section of the text. There was also a famous mid-fifth-century B.C. Greek artist named Polygnotus, best known for his wall paintings at Delphi. One of these depicts the fall of Troy and the departure of the Greek fleet. Odysseus is shown near the Wooden Horse. Another section of the mural depicts Odysseus's descent into Hades, with many of the details from book 11 of the *Odyssey*. All of the information about these now-lost paintings comes from Pausanius's *Description of Greece*, in which twenty pages in the section on Delphi are devoted to Polygnotus's work.[116] Although I have not discovered any archival entries that cite this artist or his heroic paintings, it is possible that Joyce came across Polygnotus in his research and transferred the reference, appropriately disguised, into the *Wake*.

Archival Trivia

Throughout this book I locate and cite relevant material from Joyce's pre-textual notes. In the case of *Ulysses*, that meant combing the entries in the Zürich notebooks and the notesheets deposited in the British Museum. For *Finnegans Wake*, the Buffalo Notebooks are the repository of occasional Homeric items. Most of these entries show that Joyce looked back on *Ulysses* and its characters with a smile; a couple refer to literary work in progress; only a few deserve citation and learned commentary:

- "¹Occulina the hider" (VIII.A.5.5). This crossed note comes from Roscher's *Lexikon* and refers to a minor Roman goddess who hides people and things. Linguistically, her name in Latin (from *occulo*, to hide, to cover) is parallel to that of the immortal nymph Calypso in the *Odyssey;* she hides (*kalyp/psō* in Greek) the hero for nine years by keeping him under cover on her out-of-the-way island. Joyce converted the proper name into an abstract noun for inclusion in the "Ithaca" chapter of the novel. The context is a hypothetical "public advertisement" designed to "divulge the occulation" of the missing Leopold Bloom (*U* 17.2000). Shortly thereafter it is revealed that one of the departed husband's honors or "tributes" was "A nymph immortal, beauty, the bride of Noman" (*U* 17.2009–11).

- "ᵇ12 unchaste virgins swab up and are killed hanged all in a row" (*UNBM* 464:62). This note is a reference to the unfaithful servant women in Odysseus's palace. Joyce's paradoxical "unchaste virgins" may have been inspired by the fact that the Butcher and Lang translation sometimes calls them "maidens"; in neither Homer's text nor the translation is their number given as a dozen. They were, however, all memorably strung up: "The women held their heads *all in a row,* and about all their necks nooses were cast, that they might die by the most pitiful death. And they writhed with their feet for a little space but for no long while" (*Odyssey* 22.471–73; *B-L* 352). Even though the entry is crossed, it stretches intertextuality pretty thin to claim an echo in Molly's thought that she should have "kicked up a row" (*U* 18.442–44) over some defective stockings.

- "No man's land / = Cyclops" (VI.B.1.26). Here Joyce combines a term from the trench warfare of World War I with the famous wordplay on his name that Odysseus used to outwit the one-eyed monster.

- "Ul not a Homer" (VI.B.3.122). The hero of the Greek homecoming epic, in fact, spent most of that tale (and all of the *Iliad*) far away from his palace and family in Ithaca.

- "Ulysses rex in partibus / goes away to test" (VI.B.10.40): The Latin phrase that modifies Homer's hero is properly applied to Roman Catholic prelates who are honorarily assigned to a diocese that is no longer part of the Christian world. Another archival entry, in the midst of some material about Gibraltar prepared for *Ulysses*, makes this application specific: "bishop in partibus" (VI.C.7.250). Thus, in Joyce's youth there was an auxiliary bishop in Dublin whose titular see was the diocese of Canea in Crete.[117] When that area was conquered by Muslims, its bishop's chair fell vacant and only the title remained—and remained to be assigned by the pope to a priest with the duties of episcopal rank but no actual diocese of his own. The full technical term for such a "titular" diocese is *in partibus infidelium* (in the territory of nonbelievers). Joyce's note seems to imply that King Odysseus left his throne in Ithaca by design, and that he traveled to far-flung regions in order to test the fidelity of his wife and subjects. If this interpretation of the phrase is correct, then Joyce should be credited with inventing a new twist on the age-old tale.[118] None of the post-Homeric legends suggest this motive. At any rate, this hallowed custom of episcopal nomenclature was incorporated into the *Wake:* "The most eminent bishop titular of Dubloonik to all his purtybusses in Dellabelliney" (*FW* 432.19–21).

- "Ulysses / this ad man out" (VI.B.36.100). Joyce alludes to the fiction that the hero of his novel earned his living by canvassing for advertisements. That occupation kept him away from home on June 16, 1904, so that he became the victim of betrayal; but there can be no question here of a direct allusion to Frederick L. Green's novel, *Odd Man Out,* or to the movie made from it. The book was written in 1945; the movie was produced in 1947.

- "HCE hides in sand" (VI.B.11.53). Here the hero of the *Wake* follows the lead of Menelaus. In the *Odyssey* the king of Sparta tells Telemachus how Proteus's daughter "scooped out lairs in the sea-sand" and covered Achaean warriors with seal skins so they could ambush her father (*Odyssey* 4.437–55; *B-L* 58). Although HCE needs all the help he can get to escape those who seek to do him evil, this Homeric ploy was not transferred into the action of the *Wake.*

- "πομπαθειν Od 4 413" (VI.C. back leaf verso): This entry, ostensibly a citation of a word from the Greek text of the *Odyssey,* requires special comment. First, it comes from one of the secondary Notebooks transcribed by Madame Raphael from the primary VI.B. series during 1933–36. Second, in this case the original VI.B Notebook has been lost. Third, there is no such word as *pompathein* (or anything like it) in all of Homer, much less at *Odyssey* 4.413. In light of those facts, I offer the following suggestions. First, since Madame Raphael frequently misread Joyce's handwriting in English (and other languages that use the Latin alphabet), her transcription of an entry in his Greek script (as well as the notation of its Homeric source) is probably garbled. Second, κοιμηθείη (*koimētheiē*) from *Odyssey* 4.443 (not 413) might be the original, mistranscribed entry. Its length and the form of its letters are—to the Greekless eye reading Joyce's difficult handwriting—not entirely dissimilar to πομπαθειν. The Homeric context is Menelaus's recitation to Telemachus of his homeward-bound adventures in Egypt. He remembers the terrible stench of the seal pelts when the Greeks hid on the beach. Menelaus then comments, "[N]ay, who would lay him down [*koimētheīē*] by a beast of the sea?" (*Odyssey* 4.443; *B-L* 58). The camouflage tactic of this ambush would have appealed to Joyce's Ulyssean sense of cunning.[119]

- "ᵇblepharospasm" (VI.B.20.73). The Greek word *blepharon* means eyelid; blepharospasm is a medical term for a tic of the eyelid. This note was used in the *Wake* when the Four Old Men accuse Yawn of trying to "sublimate your blepharospasmockical suppressions" (*FW* 515.16–17). There is, of course, an epic eyelid in Homer. When Odysseus and his comrades plunge the red-hot stake into the eye of the Cyclops, "the breath of the flame singed his eyelids [*blephar'*] and brows all about" (*Odyssey* 9.389; *B-L* 137).

- "Lypogrammatic / Tryphidoros [*sic*] / Odyssey B.1 no α" (VI.B.21.10). This entry also requires minor correction and major explanation. The first term, correctly spelled lipogrammatic, refers to a work in which a letter of the alphabet (*gramma* in Greek) is rigorously left out (the initial element in the word is derived from the verbal root *leip/lip*). Thus, there was a retelling of the Odysseus tale in which the consecutive books (1–24/α–ω) *left out* the *letter* that was their ordinal marker: Book 1 had *no* words containing an α (*alpha*), the first letter of the Greek alphabet; book 2 had no words with a β (*beta*), the second letter; and so on down to book 24/ω (*omega*). As fantastic as this exercise may seem, it was undertaken by Tryphiodorus, an otherwise totally unknown sixth-century A.D. poet from Egypt. Since the first word, *andra* (man), of the first line of the first book of the *Odyssey* has an α as its first and last letters, it would be instructive to see how that versatile epicist coped with his self-imposed challenge. Unfortunately, my philological curiosity will not be satisfied unless there is a momentous new papyrus find: None of Tryphiodorus's lipogrammatic masterpiece survives. That example of the Ulysses tradition manqué concludes my parade of archival trivia.

An appropriate flourish with which to summarize this long and diverse chapter comes from the stately (and occasionally plump) *James Joyce Quarterly.* Some of the recent issues of that periodical have featured a cartoon comment, enigmatically styled a "Dazibao," by Simon Loekle. An example, entitled "Homer Alone!," has the following message in one of its panels:

> PARALLELS !
> "The danger," we sometimes wish someone had said to Mr. [Stuart] Gilbert, "is in the neatness of identifications." Still, the discovery of Homeric overtones is always a delight.[120]

At the bottom center of the entire page on which the "Dazibao" appears, a cat, seated with its back to the viewer, is thinking, "God Bless Homerica!" Absolutely, I say, from the Ulyssean mountains to the Wakean "wet prairie[s]" (FW 19.14) white with foam.[121]

6

Plato and Neoplatonism

The name of Plato looms large in any history of Western thought. As if to underscore the vital and universal importance of his teaching—and that of his mentor, Socrates—the Athenian philosopher maintained that the unexamined life was not worth living (*Apology* 38a).[1] Centuries later, Alfred North Whitehead wrote that subsequent European philosophy was "a series of footnotes to Plato."[2] In the face of that portentous reputation, an overview of the intellectual and aesthetic life of James Joyce would seem to relegate Plato to little more than a few footnotes in commentaries on his fiction. That judgment is a hasty overexaggeration, even though it can be supported by several sharp quotations. In *A Portrait of the Artist as a Young Man*, for example, Stephen Dedalus claims that "Plato, I believe, said that beauty is the splendour of truth. I don't think that it has meaning but the true and the beautiful are akin" (*P* 208).[3] In *Ulysses* Stephen asserts that "[t]hat model schoolboy [Aristotle] . . . would find Hamlet's musings about the afterlife of his princely soul . . . as shallow as Plato's" (*U* 9.76–78). When John Eglinton counters that any comparison of the two ancient Greek philosophers makes his blood boil, Stephen asks, "Which . . . would have banished me from his commonwealth?" (*U* 9.80–83). That question refers to the section of Plato's *Republic)* in which Socrates argues that dramatic poetry, tragic or comic, has a most formidable power of corrupting even men of high character. Thus, it stands to reason that such a dangerous influence must be banished from the ideal state, which is the topic of that long dialogue (*Republic* 605c–608a). In this chapter I attempt to present a more even-handed review of the influence of Plato and Neoplatonism on Joyce's thought and fiction.

Almost all of the Ulyssean allusions to Plato come from the "Scylla and

Charybdis" chapter, set in Mr. Lyster's office at the National Library. There Stephen presents his radical views on *Hamlet* as a refraction of Shakespeare's life. In this disquisition aesthetics is as important as biographical detail. Stephen's audience includes George William Russell (known as AE), who, like Yeats and other Dublin literati, was deeply involved in the mysticism of the Hermetic movement. AE's first contribution to the topic, supported by John Eglinton, emphasizes that perspective: "Art has to reveal to us ideas, formless spiritual essences . . . Plato's world of ideas" (*U* 9.48–53). The ancient Greek philosopher would not have approved of the appropriation of his name and several key terms to bolster this line of argument. In Plato's system it was the task of philosophy—not art—to explore and express the world of ideas. Joyce captures Stephen's reaction to the comments of Russell and Eglinton in three paragraphs of interior monologue packed with mockery of their pseudo-Platonic and Theosophical catchphrases: "Hiesos Kristos, magician of the beautiful. . . . repentant sophia, departed to the plane of buddhi. . . . Mrs. Cooper Oakley once glimpsed our very illustrious sister H.P.B.'s elemental. . . . You naughtn't to look, missus, so you naughtn't when a lady's ashowing her elemental" (*U* 9.61–73).

Shortly thereafter, Stephen silently instructs himself: "Unsheathe your dagger definitions. Horseness is the whatness of allhorse. Streams of tendency and eons they worship. God: noise in the street: very peripatetic" (*U* 9.84–85). The first two sentences in that citation refer to typical Aristotelian procedures: precise definitions derived inductively from a number of specific manifestations of the phenomenon. The third and fourth elements are meant to contrast the fluid "theology" of Neoplatonism with the fact-bound skepticism of Aristotle's peripatetic school. For Stephen, the data of Shakespeare's life are the basis of his theory of the meaning of Hamlet. AE dismisses mundane biographical matters as having no bearing on art: "—All these questions are purely academic, Russell oracled out of his shadow. I mean, whether Hamlet is Shakespeare or James I or Essex" (*U* 9.46–47). I strongly suspect that Joyce's choice of an adjective here is meant to be picked up as a self-pronounced refutation of AE's position. The disciples of Plato were called members of the "academic" school because they met and argued their philosophy at the Academy, a grove and gymnasium near Athens—just as Aristotle's followers formed the "peripatetic" school, since they learned from the master while "walking around" (*peripatein*) the shady paths near the

Lyceum, another Athenian gymnasium. Thus, if Russell's phase "purely academic" were to be taken literally, he would be assigning the approbation of Platonic authority to the very method that he rejects with scorn.

Critics have made much of the opposition of Platonic and Aristotelian aesthetics in this chapter.[4] The excerpts previously cited present some evidence for that distinction. The primary reason that critics have stressed the Academic-Peripatetic opposition, however, is the schemata prepared by Joyce himself. The author worked out these detailed plans to assist early commentators in identifying all the elements, including the Homeric parallels, that contribute to each of the chapters of *Ulysses*. In both the Linati and the Gorman-Gilbert versions of the schema for "Scylla and Charybdis," the "Symbols" include "Hamlet, Shakespeare; Christ, Socrates; Scholasticism and Mysticism; Plato and Aristotle." The Gorman-Gilbert scheme adds the following "Correspondences": "The Rock— Aristotle, Dogma . . . The Whirlpool—Plato, Mysticism."[5]

Some commentators on "Scylla and Charybdis" have noted that the chapter is modeled on the form of a Platonic dialogue. Perhaps so, but even in the original works, Socrates frequently does most of the arguing, and the other disputants sometimes contribute little more than affirming, "That seems true," or asking, "How is that so?" While AE, Eglinton, and the others smugly assert their positions in clipped phrases, Stephen Dedalus has the floor during most of the library discussion. His theories are presented in a form that is more lecture than dialogue. In fact as opposed to fiction, according to a lifelong friend, James Joyce's personal style of argument seems to have been quite a bit like that of AE in this episode of *Ulysses:* "Joyce's conclusions were oracular, cryptic, and admitted little debate."[6]

There can be no doubt then that one of the factors contributing to the dialectic in this chapter is the distinction between Platonic idealism (and its exaggerated extremes in Neoplatonism) and Aristotelian realism. On the other hand, the primary purpose of "Scylla and Charybdis" is not a debate on aesthetics carried on by Irish proxies for two ancient Greek philosophers. Stephen's genealogical paradoxes ("the father of his own grandfather, the father of his unborn grandson" [*U* 9.869]), Mulligan's obscene parodies ("—*Everyman His Own Wife / or / A Honeymoon in the Hand*" [*U* 9.1171–73), and Joyce's pervasive deployment of allusions to Shakespeare's works ("He came a step a sinkapace forward on neatsleather creaking. . . . Twicereakinly analysis he corantoed off"

[*U* 9.5–12]) are of greater importance, structurally and thematically, in the discussion. What is more, they are funny. This factor, in my judgment, should not be overlooked: Joyce's sense of the comic is more significant in *Ulysses* than his display of Hellenic aesthetic theory. There are other hints that Joyce was covertly playing games with Greek philosophy in the early portion of this episode.

In a weird enthymeme that leaps from the "visions in a peasant's heart on the hillside" to "the finest flower of corruption in Mallarmé" to "Homer's Phaeacians," Mr. Best reminds Stephen Dedalus that Mallarmé wrote "those wonderful prose poems Stephen MacKenna used to read to me in Paris" (*U* 9.105–13). One of those recited poems describes a provincial production of *Hamlet*. The flyers advertising the play read: "*Hamlet / ou / Le Distrait / Pièce de Shakespeare.*" Stephen's irreverent translation of the unauthorized subtitle, "—The absentminded beggar," is meant to trigger a minor laugh at the expense of some unnamed French town and the "French point of view" (*U* 9.118–25).

It is important to note that Best cites his source of information about Mallarmé's "Hamlet et Fortinbras": Stephen MacKenna. In 1908 MacKenna resigned from his position as chief reporter for the *New York World* in Paris and settled in Dublin. He devoted the rest of his life to the translation of the Greek text of Plotinus's *Enneads* into English. This difficult task was completed in stages; the first of five volumes appeared in 1917, the last in 1930. MacKenna's version was universally hailed as a work of genius. A review of the complete edition called it "one of the great translations of the century. . . . A crabbed and difficult text is made to read like the work of a stylist; and abstract ideas are amazingly clarified."[7] On the first Bloomsday, it would have been possible for the Dublin Hermetists to have referred only to inaccurate (and often incomprehensible) selections from the *Enneads*. In addition to garbled versions of Plotinus, the translations and editions of various other Gnostic, eastern, and Theosophical texts were equally inadequate and abstruse. This situation, of course, did not prevent members of the movement from using such material, or from larding their arguments with inscrutable jargon of these documents, all of which they considered vaguely Platonic.

Although there is no direct reference to the fact, Joyce and MacKenna must have met during this period during the former's second trip to Paris. Two letters give indirect testimony to their introduction. One letter was sent on June 8, 1910, by Joyce to Theodore Spicer-Simson in Paris; it recalls a previous meeting, which Ellmann notes was arranged by MacKenna in 1903 (*Letters* II.284–85). The second letter (June 5, 1933) was written to Joyce by E. R. Dodds, who would become Regius Professor of Greek at Oxford. In that note Dodds requests, for the memoir he was preparing, any information about MacKenna's introduction of Spicer-Simson to Joyce.[8] There is no record of Joyce's reply to Dodds's inquiry. From that evidence one can infer that, when he was composing *Ulysses,* Joyce was aware that MacKenna was on the scene in Paris in 1903. It is also possible that, on one of his two return trips to Dublin in 1909, Joyce ran into MacKenna again. By that time he was beginning to work on the text of Plotinus and had become part of the Russell-Eglinton-Best intellectual coterie.[9]

Whatever the circumstances of their actual meeting, I strongly suspect that the primary reason why Stephen MacKenna is assigned a cameo role early in "Scylla and Charybdis" is not his extended residence in Paris or his recitation of Mallarmé to Richard Best. These factors merely conform to the realistic time frame of *Ulysses,* since on June 16, 1904, MacKenna himself cannot be placed in the National Library nor can he yet be acknowledged as an expert in Neoplatonism. Rather, it is his later dedication to Plotinus, projected into the past, that is the real purpose for MacKenna's inclusion in the narrative: he is one more anti-Aristotelian, as it were, in the phalanx lined up against Stephen's insistence on facts and induction.[10] This type of unobtrusively accurate casting is characteristic of Joyce's attention to writerly minutiae in *Ulysses.* AE's oracular dismissal of autobiographical considerations in art is part of the same process, a bit of terminological irony that Socrates would have relished to turn against an opponent in one of the dialogues. MacKenna's alleged quotation from Mallarmé ("*reading the book of himself*") can also be taken as a summary-parody of Stephen Dedalus's biographical line of argument in the disputation that follows.

The foregoing discussion of several textual details is meant to demonstrate that, whatever the schemata seem to imply, Joyce is an artist, not an aesthetician. A corollary to that deduction is the proposition that the participants in the fiction of *Ulysses* are presented with more attention to their comic potential than to any standard of philosophical consistency or historical verisimilitude.

A minor but characteristic measure of support for my emphasis on Joyce's sense of humor as an important factor in this episode is found in his treatment of Russell's pseudonym, AE. In the Gnostic-Hermetic tradition the Greek noun *aion,* sometimes transliterated as "aeon," is a frequently repeated term. It means age, space of time, eon, eternity, and is often personified and applied as a title to various divine beings. When Stephen Dedalus unsheaths his definitions to slash at the "eons they worship" (*U* 9.85), the "they" are his "Platonic" opponents in the *Hamlet* debate. Later in the same episode he mocks the "Cypherjugglers. . . . Mummed in names: A.E., eon" (*U* 9.411–12). Earlier Stephen recalls that he has not repaid Russell for the loan of a pound. His internal deliberation on the means and time of settling that debt concludes with an elegant formula: "A.E.I.O.U." (*U* 9.213).

An important factor in Stephen's analysis of Shakespeare's unhappy married life is the bard's legacy to his wife of his "Secondbest Bed" (*U* 9.698–99). One of the participants in the discussion has a comment: "—Antiquity mentions famous beds, Second eglinton puckered, bedsmiling. Let me think" (*U* 9.718–19). Indeed antiquity does so—and Mr. Eglinton's memory needs some prodding. The most famous such bed is surely the marriage bed of Odysseus and Penelope. Its headboard had been carved into the trunk of a living olive tree by Odysseus, a fact known only to the bride and groom. When the wanderer returned to his palace in Ithaca, the secret of the bed was the ultimate test of revelation/ recognition for the reunited royal pair (*Odyssey* 23.181–206). Although Eglinton was not aware at the time that he had been assigned a minor role in Joyce's re-creation of Homer's *Odyssey,* his recollection of that epic bed should not have required much thought.

Another famous bed in antiquity is even more appropriate for Eglinton to recall in the novel's narrative context. In his argument against the presence of the poets in his utopia, Plato claims that the products of their imagination are three steps removed from reality—imitations of imitations of ideal Forms. The philosopher offers an analogy: The painter who portrays a bed is such an imitator. The reality is the Idea of "bedhood" that the divine creator makes; one step from that is the carpenter's product, based on the ideal design; finally, the artist reproduces, in his medium, the craftsman's imitation of the real Form (*Republic* 597a–598c). *That* is an unforgettable bed from antiquity. Joyce's mention of Eglinton's puckered thought is meant to mock, on Platonic and Homeric grounds, the sublibrarian's hesitant classical learning.

Socrates, Plato's mentor and the spokesman of the *Dialogues,* makes several brief appearances in "Scylla and Charybdis." The first is in Stephen's argument that Ann Hathaway had an essential impact on Shakespeare's life and works (*U* 9.214–67). Eglinton claims that their marriage was a mistake. Stephen counters that a genius makes no mistakes and that his errors are "the portals of discovery." The librarian then asks, "What useful discovery did Socrates learn from Xanthippe?" Stephen's one-word reply ("Dialectic") requires some comment. The role that Socrates' wife, Xanthippe, plays in the classical tradition is that of an archetypal shrew (note "henpecked Socrates" [*U* 15.111]). Biographical information from antiquity is sparse and unreliable, but the tone of the following citation fills the gap. It is from the *Phaedo,* Plato's dialogue about the final days of Socrates' life. The Athenian commissioners have just announced that this is the day on which he must drink the hemlock. His disciples enter the prison. There they find "Socrates just released from his chains, and Xanthippe—you know her!—sitting by him with their little boy on her knee. As soon as Xanthippe saw us she broke out into the sort of remark you would expect from a woman" (*Phaedo* 60a).[11] In this context Joyce's choice of "dialectic" to epitomize the discovery Socrates made in Xanthippe becomes clear. From his wife he learned the techniques of sharp verbal argument for which he was so famous. There is an archival note on this general topic: "ʳidea of Socrates, husb of Xanth., master of Plato" (V.A.2.28:32). In the same section of *Ulysses,* Stephen also asserts that from his midwife mother Socrates learned "how to bring thoughts into the world." The lessons derived from his other "wife," Myrto (*U* 9.235–37)—and the obscene connotation of her name—are discussed in chapter 10, on Aristophanes and the techniques of personal abuse in ancient Greek comedy.

Another Ulyssean allusion to Plato's *Phaedo* occurs near the end of the same episode in the National Library. Stephen and Mulligan have left the office and are walking through the readers' room on their way out of the building. Stephen seems to have thought of another point to bolster his argument: "Afterwit. Go back." That reflection is followed by "The dour recluse still there (he has his cake) and the douce youngling, minion of pleasure, Phedo's toyable fair hair" (*U* 9.1137–39).[12] The "recluse" is Thomas William Lyster, "the quaker librarian" (*U* 9.1); his assistant, John Eglinton, is the youngling. The phrase from Shakespeare's *Sonnet* 126.9, "minion of pleasure," is Stephen's imputation of a homosexual relationship between the two. The implication is reinforced by the coyness of

"Phedo's toyable fair hair."[13] That phrase has been distilled from a passage in Plato's *Phaedo*. Phaedo is telling a friend what happened during Socrates' final days. There was a general discussion about the immortality of the soul, during which Socrates buoyed Phaedo's spirits, downcast in the face of his teacher's imminent death: "'So he [Socrates] laid his hand on my head and gathered up the curls on my neck—he never missed a chance of teasing me about my curls—and said, "Tomorrow, I suppose, Phaedo, you will cut off this beautiful hair?"'" (*Phaedo* 89b). In the Platonic passage itself there is no hint of homosexuality. Rather, Socrates asks his young student if he intends to cut his hair to show that he is in mourning for a friend. When Phaedo indicates that he will follow that custom after Socrates' death, the master informs him that they *both* should cut their hair, *today,* if they permit their side of the argument to flee their grasp (*Phaedo* 89c). Socrates' question, then, is loaded with characteristic irony. Its intent is to induce a smile on a dark day and to remind a pupil of his obligation to the master's lessons, not to his person. Only when twisted entirely out of context can Phaedo's "toyable" curls serve the purpose that Joyce allusively intends.

A second reference to the *Phaedo* in *Ulysses* occurs in "Hades." Here Joyce perfectly captures Plato's intent and cleverly re-creates the original context. In the final section of the dialogue, after he has drunk the hemlock, Socrates gradually loses feeling in his limbs. Suddenly he pushes away the sheet that covers him and speaks: "'Crito, we ought to sacrifice a cock to Asclepius. Take care of this obligation and don't forget'. These were his last words" (*Phaedo* 118). And those last words were playful. Ancient Greeks with serious diseases sometimes went to the shrine of Asclepius at Epidaurus to seek help. After offering the required gift (a rooster), the invalids would spend the night in the temple of the god of healing, hoping to awake cured. Thus, in his final moments, Socrates tries to cheer his disciples with a bit of black humor—perhaps the god could counteract the poison, or the poison may be seen as the cure of all Socrates' mortal ills.

The traditional method of Athenian execution appears twice in Joyce's works: once in a mixture of Greek and Irish settings, "the archers of Sinn Fein and their naggin of hemlock" (*U* 9.239–40); and again in an alliterative burst of deadly drinks, "Lethals lurk heimlocked in logans. Loathe laburnums. Dash the gaudy deathcup! Bryony O'Bryony, thy name is Belladama!" (*FW* 450.30–32). In *Ulysses* Joyce transfers the scene from a prison to the mortuary chapel in which the coffin of Paddy Dignam lies on its bier. Leopold Bloom stands behind Dignam's young son, and thinks: "Poor boy! Was he there when the father? Both unconscious. Lighten up at the last moment and recognize for the last time. All he might have done. *I owe three shillings to O'Grady.* Would he understand?" (*U* 6.576–79; my emphasis). The italicized words are, at least partially, Joyce's localized translation of Socrates' last words from the *Phaedo.*[14] Latter-day descendants of the ancient Greek healer-Hero, to whom the gift rooster was owed, also appear in the *Wake* as "esculapuloids" (*FW* 540.33).

There is a puzzling reference to Socrates' final moments in the "Night Lessons" section of the *Wake*. There the marginal "*Socrates*" is keyed to the essay topic "Devotion to the Feast of the Indulgence of Portiuncula" (*FW* 306.L and 23–24). The phrase may refer to the small portion (*portiuncula* in Italian) of hemlock that was sufficient to cause the philosopher's death. There is, however, an authentic "Feast of the Indulgence of Portiuncula," August 2, which commemorates the day in 1216 when Pope Honorius III granted remission of the punishment for sin (an indulgence) to each visitor to St. Francis's newly restored chapel at Portiuncula near Assisi. Both St. Francis and Socrates obeyed the commands of supranatural voices; each was dedicated to teaching, by personal example, that riches and position mean nothing to the truly wise man.

My thesis that Joyce was primarily interested in "lightening up" Plato gains some support, paradoxically, from the traditional source of scholarship, Jacques Aubert. His book, *The Aesthetics of James Joyce,* is a thorough study of the philosophical foundations of Joyce's statements on art. Aubert's primary emphases fall on the explicitly aesthetic pronouncements in several essays collected in *Critical Writings* and in well-known sections of *Stephen Hero* and *A Portrait of the Artist As a Young Man.* The evidence demonstrates the unexpected influence of a "Neoplatonic strain in young Joyce's theorizing perceptible in his specific use of Aquinas."[15] This is not to claim that Joyce was a student of the works of Plotinus or Proclus. Far from it, since Aubert shows how closely Joyce followed a standard and frequently reprinted text, Bernard Bosanquet's *A History of Aesthetic.* For *Ulysses* and *Finnegans Wake* this characteristic reliance on predigested source material is philosophically irrelevant. By that stage in his fiction, Joyce habitually appropriated Plato, the Neoplatonists, Aristotle, and other ancient thinkers, not for logical or exemplary support in debates on aesthetic matters, but for narrative and largely comic impact.[16]

Even so, during the early days of work in progress for the *Wake*, Joyce did not entirely forget the original context of his early use of Greek philosophy. In an October 31, 1925, letter to Dámaso Alonso, who was translating *Portrait* into Spanish, Joyce offered the following advice: "A reference [at *P* 212–13] to Plato's theory of ideas, or more strictly speaking to Neo-Platonism, two philosophical tendencies with which the speaker at that moment is not in sympathy" (*Letters* III. 130).

A classical scholar has suggested that Plato also plays an overarching role in the literary parodies in "Oxen of the Sun." June W. Allison reconstructs the boozy discussion at the Maternity Hospital into a burlesque reenactment of Plato's *Symposium* (The Drinking Party).[17] Her arguments and parallels are ingenious: Both works repeatedly emphasize seating arrangements ("at the head of the board was the young poet who found a refuge from his labours of pedagogy and metaphysical inquisition in the convivial atmosphere of Socratic discussion" [*U* 14.1213–15]); the topics of the two "debates" (*Eros* and procreation) are not unrelated; the individual styles of the disputants are distinctive; there are direct and to-the-point allusions to "Venus Pandemos" (*U* 14.1494 and *Symposium* 180d–185c); Mulligan plays the role of the late-arriving Alcibiades. Allison is scrupulous in her analysis and conclusion; the title of her article, "A Literary Coincidence? Joyce and Plato," is remarkably forthright. Like her, I wish there were some archival hints in notesheets, letters, or suggestions to Stuart Gilbert. In the absence of that sort of authorial patent, it would be rash to claim certainty here. But, if the *Symposium* is part of the process in "Oxen of the Sun," then its presence is, at one and the same time, unique and typical. To accomplish what Allison suggests, Joyce would have had to go over the text of Plato's dialogue (in English translation, of course) with great care to select unobtrusively transferable material from its structure, setting, technique, and argument.[18] This was not his regular procedure with even the most accessible works of ancient philosophers, where exploitation of a few phrases or a spot passage is the rule. The comic, even ribald result of the suggested adaptation of a classical text, however, is both typical of Joyce's technique and effective in execution.

With the possible exception of his wholesale reworking of the *Symposium*, Joyce's use of Plato was generally secondhand. His reliance on Bosanquet's *A History of Aesthetic* for theories and formulas in the early critical essays and in *Portrait* is a fair example of this type of intellectual appropriation.[19] In a few instances, the presence of the intermediate source is acknowledged, as is the case near the end of the *Hamlet* discussion: "He [Shakespeare] found in the world without as actual what was in his world within as possible. Maeterlinck says: *If Socrates leave his house today he will find the sage seated on his doorstep"* (*U* 9.1041–43; Joyce's emphasis). In a March 1922 letter to Robert McAlmon, Joyce wrote, "Don't throw *Ulysses* out the window as you threaten. Pyrrhus was killed in Argos like that. Also Socrates might be passing in the street" (*Letters* I.182). I discuss Pyrrhus's death elsewhere;[20] all that I can venture to explain about the reference to Socrates is a line from Aristophanes' *The Clouds.* In that comedy a character visits Socrates' think tank and registers his pleasure at an accident that befalls the philosopher as he wanders around contemplating the heavens: "I got a big kick when the lizard down-loaded on Socrates" (*Clouds* 174). My translation emphasizes the prefix *kata-* (down, from above) in the key Greek word; I visualize a lizard perched on the eave of a house and bespattering Socrates as he passed by. If this suggestion of historical-cultural analogues is correct, then Joyce is humorously warning against an urge to defenestrate *Ulysses:* tossing it out could have unforeseen consequences, as did the roof tile at Argos (Pyrrhus) and the Athenian lizard shit (Socrates).

In *Finnegans Wake* there is a single direct reference to Plato, several covert allusions, and a rare acknowledged example of an intermediate source. In the "Night Lessons" catalog of famous classical and Old Testament figures, a marginal *"Plato"* is keyed to the shortest of the suggested essay topics, "Clubs" (*FW* 307.L1 and 1). The link must be Plato's record of the after-dinner talk of some of Athens's renowned citizens in the *Symposium* as an ancient precursor echoed by similar sessions, over brandy or port, at a Dublin gentlemen's club. Although its topic is universal in human discourse, the following archival item might be read as a reference to the matters under discussion in Plato's *Symposium:* "Finn asks O what then is love" (VI.B.18.103).

Another allusion to that dialogue certainly lies behind the following passage from the same section of the *Wake* as the previous citation: "Plutonic loveliaks twinnt Platonic yearlings—you must, how, in undividual reawlity draw the line somewhare" (*FW* 292.30–32). In the *Symposium* Plato has the comic poet Aristophanes speak, in character, about Eros. His pseudomythic explanation of the origins of sexual passion involves some bizarre biology. Once upon a time, Aristophanes claims, all human beings had four legs, four arms, two faces, two sets of sexual organs, and so on. These weirdly compounded creatures attempted to assault the heights of Olympus. Zeus punished them by splitting each person in two, the way we might "slice an egg with a hair. . . . The puckers around the belly and the navel remind us of what we suffered long ago" (*Symposium* 190c–191a). Since that primeval division, humans desire to be reunited with their separated half. Those whose original sex was male-female are heterosexual lovers; those who were once male-male or female-female are homosexual lovers. Joyce's twins, Shem and Shaun, are seeking to uncover the mystery of sexuality and gender in this section of the *Wake*. The urge to knowledge has led them, via Euclid's First Proposition, to the imminent completion of a linear and curved figure that will reveal everything. A Platonic element in the boys' academic curiosity contributes to their surprise at what they see in the completed diagram: "As round as the calf of an egg! O, dear me! O dear *me now*! (*FW* 294.11–12; my emphasis). Plato's *Meno* is a dialogue devoted to the question "Can virtue be taught?" A significant section of the argument pivots around an analogy from and exercise in geometry (*Meno* 82a–86c). In short, those citations demonstrate that the philosophical-geometric learning process influenced the text's "loveliaks twinnt Platonic yearlings . . . in undivided reawlity" (*FW* 292.30–31).

But there is far more going on here—all of it with some bearing on Plato's method of instruction and the interpretation of his teachings. One of the most memorable passages in the *Republic* is the use of the figure of the "Divided Line" to explain the different orders of the visible and the intelligible order. Socrates asks Glaucon to represent these distinctions by a line divided into two unequal sections, each section of which is cut in the same ratio:

A / B // C /   D

In the first section (A) are shadows and reflections; in (B) all the objects in the visible world. In (C) are the results of the intellect as it rises above the visible by means of geometry and similar techniques; in the longest section (D), reason grasps, by dialectic, the realm of Forms. These four divisions may also be expressed in terms of the process involved: D intellect or reason, C understanding, B belief, and A conjecture (*Republic* 510d–513e).

Immediately following the analogy of the Divided Line, Socrates tells the "Myth of the Cave," another famous device to illustrate the stages of apprehension and knowledge culminating in the task of the philosopher: the guided ascent of the soul from darkness into light to contemplate the essential forms (*Republic* 514a–521b). These two analogies, the "Divided Line" and the "Myth of the Cave," are the essential statements of Platonic theory of knowledge. Indeed, for Plato epistemology recapitulates ontology: The only genuine life of reality is that in the realm of the Forms, the eternal Ideas.

My line of argument now returns from the anagogical realm of Plato's Ideas to the hard reality of the text of *Finnegans Wake.* The philosophical excursus was necessary to indicate how both the "Divided Line" and the "Myth of the Cave" have some bearing on the education of Shem and Shaun. A final comment on the immediate source of that phrase is drawn directly from McHugh. He points out that, in his monument to Theosophical mysticism, *A Vision,* Yeats calculates the duration of the great Platonic year. That cyclic period definitely influenced Joyce's phrase "twinnt Platonic yearlings" (*FW* 292.30–31). Certainty in the matter of a direct Yeatsian source is confirmed by another sentence from *A Vision* that Joyce appropriated in the passage quoted here: "Nicholas of Cusa's *undivided reality* which human experience divides into opposites" (my emphasis).[21]

In half a dozen pages of his study of the *Wake,* Clive Hart discusses the influence of Plato's *Timaeus* on Joyce's work.[22] That dialogue, one of the most difficult of the entire Platonic corpus, is an explanation of the creation of the universe. In the course of this exercise, physics, astronomy, and biology give way to mysticism, and the emphasis on temporal creation shifts to a contemplation of the timeless Creator. The central Joycean motif derived from the *Timaeus* is that of the polarity of the two circles of World-Soul: "The exterior motion he [the Creator] named the motion of the Same, the interior that of the Other. And the circle of the Same he made revolve to the right by way of the side, that of the Other to the left by way of the diagonal" (*Timaeus* 36c). The twins Shaun and Shem (and their dopplegängers Mutt and Jeff, Muta and Juva, et al.) are the Wakean manifestations of this polarity. Hart neatly traces the appearances of the motif, including the two circles in the geometric figure at *FW* 293. A bit later in the text the twins are specifically referred to as the "Other" and the "Same" (*FW* 300.20–22). In similarly obscure terminology, a creation-and-fall context is injected into HCE's justification of his oscillating behavior: "the farst wriggle from the ubivence whereom is man, that old offender, n*other* man, wheile he is a*same*" (*FW* 356.12–14; my emphases).

Hart reasonably suggests that Joyce came upon these motifs from the *Timaeus* secondhand, through the medium of Yeats's *A Vision*. That work was the certain source for the statement from Nicholas of Cusa cited here. In adapting the medieval formula to his purposes in the *Wake*, Joyce gives its axis a typical—in his case, a semi-Platonic—tilt. Several lines before the "nother . . . asame" passage cited, Joyce provides an uncharacteristic hint of a source when he has HCE ask "*how* comes *ever* a body in our *taylorized* world to selve out thishis" (*FW* 356.10–11; my emphases). The first set of italics highlights an HCE acrostic; the second calls attention to the name of Thomas Taylor, a prolific eighteenth- and nineteenth-century translator of the works of Plato and the Neoplatonists. The conversion of his name into a verb is particularly appropriate here, since Joyce is discussing creation, which in Platonic terms is a division and shaping of preexistent matter to form an orderly universe. In *A Vision* Yeats specifically cites Taylor's discussion of the length of the Great Platonic Year in his version of the *Timaeus*.[23] Since some of Taylor's translations were extraordinarily obscure, it is also fitting that Joyce places his name in the midst of a passage so imbued with Yeatsian "Messafissi" (*FW* 356.9) that it is a challenge to any commentator and all readers.

In several of his dialogues Plato reported the discussions at some distance from the actual event. In the *Symposium,* for example, the author tells how Apollodorus tells an anonymous friend that Glaucon had asked, only the day before yesterday, about what had happened, when both of them were infants, at Agathon's drinking party. Aristodemus, one of the original participants, had told Apollodorus about the celebration and the discussion of *eros*. The friend asks Apollodorus to tell him what he told to Glaucon about what Aristodemus told to him (*Symposium* 172a-174a). There is nothing quite so convoluted—at least not as *overtly* convoluted— in *Ulysses* or *Finnegans Wake*. At the same time, there are a number of complex ways and means by which Joyce works Plato into the narrative. Although not acknowledged, Bosanquet's *Aesthetic* is the source for much of what is reported about ancient thought on this topic in the early writings. Maeterlinck is cited by Stephen as the source of an aphorism that Socrates cannot help being himself. A passage from the *Timaeus* is filtered through Thomas Taylor's translation as cited by Yeats.

In one of his Wakean fables Joyce presents the Ondt "sated before his comfortumble phullupsuppy of a plate o'monkynous" (*FW* 417.14–15). In a March 26, 1928, letter to Miss Weaver, the author pointed out that "monkynous = monkeynuts also the 'nous' rational intelligence" (*SL* 331). The interpretation of the Greek noun (*nous*) is only one of several classical glosses that help to clarify the philological aspect of the citation. The Greek adjective *platys* (wide, broad, flat) probably lies behind the name Plato (broad-shouldered) and is certainly the root of the English word *plate*, a broad, flat serving dish.[24] Neither Skeat nor the *OED* finds any etymological connection between a "monk" and a "monkey"; but Joyce must have linked the two, since he includes "cf monasticism" at the end of his explanation of the primary term in the letter to Miss Weaver. Finally, for those students of Plato who might wonder what is on the plate that Joyce's philosophical Ondt finds so satifying, a monkeynut is better known as a peanut.

At the conclusion of the *Hamlet* discussion in *Ulysses*, Mr. Best makes the following suggestions to Stephen Dedalus about the theory he has expounded: "—Are you going to write it? . . . You ought to make it a dialogue, don't you know, like the Platonic dialogues Wilde wrote" (*U* 9.1068–69). It is likely that Mr. Best was thinking of Wilde's "The Portrait of Mr. W.H.," published in 1889. This thirty-page piece explores a theory that Shakespeare wrote his sonnets to a boy actor, Willie Hughes. Wilde's story is not, strictly speaking, a dialogue, but its bold thesis marks it as a natural analogue to Joyce's arguments about Shakespeare and *Hamlet* in *Ulysses*.[25] As a matter of fact, Plato and Wilde are frequently linked in Joyce's imagination. In his 1909 essay on "The Poet of Salomé," Joyce writes that Wilde "was to meet his public death as he sat at table, crowned with false vine leaves and discussing Plato" *(CW* 201; note "Platonic garlens" [*FW* 622.36]). If there is an actual event that inspired this description, it occurred during the period in early 1893 when Wilde, his lover "Bosie" Douglas, and the latter's Oxford tutor were ensconced at Babbcome Cliff. The following is an excerpt from a letter written by the tutor to a friend: "Our life is lazy and luxurious; our moral principles are lax. We argue for hours in favour of different interpretations of Platonism. . . . Bosie is beautiful and fascinating, but quite wicked. He is enchanted with Plato's sketch of democratic man, and no arguments of mine will induce him to belief in any absolute standards of ethics or of anything else."[26] Immediately after this idyll, Wilde and Douglas went to

London. There the pair were conspicuously together at the Savoy Hotel.
The visit to Babbcome and its public aftermath in London were fatal to
Wilde.[27]

Joyce makes an obvious connection between Plato and homosexuality:
"Plutonic loveliaks twinnt Platonic yearlings" (*FW* 292.30–31). The presence of the Lord of the Underworld, Pluto, close to Plato, casts the aura of
doom and danger that the Victorian and Edwardian worlds perceived to
hover over love between two men. Another passage reinforces this association: "as I now with *platoonic leave* recoil . . . all them old boyars that's
now boomaringing in *waulhollar*" (*FW* 348.8–10; my emphases). Here,
however, the deceased have been gathered in the great hall of immortality, Valhalla, that is reserved for warriors slain heroically in battle. The
shift in venue would have been approved by Phaedrus, one of the participants in Plato's *Symposium*. In his speech on *eros* at that gathering, Phaedrus reminded his drinking companions of the fate of Achilles, the hero of
the *Iliad:* "He made the braver choice and went to rescue his lover Patroclus, avenged his death, and so died, not only *for* his friend, but to be with
his friend in death. And it was because his lover had been so precious to
him that he was honored so signally by the gods" (*Symposium* 179e).

Probably the most memorable mention of Plato in all of Joyce's works
is the one cited at the start of this chapter: "Plato, I believe, said that
beauty is the splendour of truth" (*P* 208). Several variations on this statement occur elsewhere (*CW* 83, 146–47; *SH* 80), and the emphatic repetition raises the question of its genesis. Ellmann first suggested a possible
source for this "Platonic" formula.[28] In a March 18, 1857, letter to Mlle.
Leroyer de Chantepie, Gustave Flaubert wrote that *Madame Bovary* was a
totally invented story, impersonal; his primary problem was style, form:
"le Beau indéfinissable *résultant de la conception* même et est la splendeur
du Vrai, comme disait Platon."[29] During his studies (which included a
heavy ration of Greek), Flaubert was greatly influenced by the philosophical works of Victor Cousin, one of the premier and most prolific French
thinkers of the first half of the nineteenth century.[30] In fact, in a September 22, 1846, letter to Louise Colet, Flaubert writes that he has read a
letter from Cousin; he has deduced from it that the philosopher's "vie est
triste et rien n'y rayonne."[31] What is important here is that Flaubert gives
Cousin the honorary name "Plato," an ironic tribute to a learned mentor
whose life has lost its splendor. I suspect that the citation in the 1857
letter, attributed to the ancient Plato and so accepted by scholars of both

Flaubert and Joyce, is in fact a paraphrase of an aesthetic statement made by the contemporary French "Plato," Maître Victor Cousin.[32]

My suggestion gains some support from the fact that the key phrase ("beauty is the splendour of truth"), which Joyce quoted in *Portrait* (208) and elsewhere, cannot be found anywhere in Plato's extant works. I do not think that Joyce was knowingly perpetuating Flaubert's verbal sleight of hand here. Rather, Stephen Dedalus's modest qualification ("Plato, I believe, said . . .") seems more like a signal of documentary hesitation than of genetic coyness. At any rate, in the most studied statement of the phrase in *Portrait,* Stephen immediately dismisses (Plato's? Cousin's? Flaubert's?) connection between the true and the beautiful. As the last link in this long chain of documentary evidence, Joyce was certainly aware of Victor Cousin's French translation of Aristotle's *Metaphysics,* from which he quotes in his *Paris Notebook.*[33]

Neoplatonism

Plotinus (A.D. 205–70) was the founder and the leading exponent of the Neoplatonist school of philosophy. The geography of Plotinus's career is in itself a commentary on the spread of Greek culture and thought in a Mediterranean world dominated by Rome. He was born in Lycopolis (today Asyut), a city on the Nile on the northern edge of Upper Egypt. He studied at Alexandria, traveled to Antioch, then went to Rome. After teaching in the imperial capital with great success, he planned to found a utopian community, Platonopolis (Platoville), in Campania. When the venture did not work out he retired, and he died at Puteoli on the Bay of Naples.

Neoplatonism is a religio-philosophical system based on a fusion of elements from several classical schools, with the addition of Egyptian and Middle Eastern mysticism. Its highest good was to elevate the soul above sense and reason to a state of ecstasy where it can behold and unite with the One Good. Plotinus's teachings were preserved and published, after his death, by his disciple, Porphyry. These six *Enneads* (each a set of nine treatises) display occasional moments of insight and power, but they are on the whole extremely difficult and diffuse. In the hands of its later adherents, Neoplatonism became associated with every conceivable form of superstition, especially in its Hermetic forms, ancient and modern.[34]

In *Portrait* Stephen Dedalus pontificates: "The mind in that mysterious instant Shelley likened beautifully to a fading coal. The instant wherein that supreme quality of beauty, the clear radiance of the esthetic image, is apprehended luminously" (*P* 213). A bit later in the same discussion, Stephen goes on in a similar vein, "The mystery of the esthetic like that of material creation is accomplished. The artist, like the God of the creation, remains within or behind or beyond or above his handiwork" (*P* 215). Despite the stated presence of Shelley (and the unacknowledged influence of Pater, Wilde, Yeats, and others), those formulations could pass as decent imitations of Neoplatonic thought. It would be rash, of course, to attempt to set rigid scholastic parameters here—Joyce was a writer, not an academic aesthetician; but the label "Neoplatonic" is plastic enough to attach to this sort of argument and imagery. Some of the same diction and views punctuated Joyce's 1909 lecture "James Clarence Mangan" (*CW* 73–83), delivered to the Literary and Historical Society of University College. One of Joyce's fellow students duly noted his words on that occasion concerning "death, the most beautiful form of life" (*CW* 83). The proposition became the basis of a burlesque in a feature column in the college magazine: "Tho, as Plotinus was fain to utter, absence is the highest form of presence."[35] The collegiate author's choice of the ancient founder of the philosophical school as a proper parodic source in his send-up of Joyce was no accident. Neoplatonism (especially the Hermetic tradition) is riddled with similar paradoxes. In fact, Joyce himself gave into the temptation to recycle his own collegiate rhetoric in *Ulysses*. In "Circe" THE CAP exclaims "(*with saturnine spleen*) Ba! It is because it is. Woman's reason. Jewgreek is greekjew. Extremes meet. Death is the highest form of life. Ba!" (*U* 15.2096–98).

An exotic passage in the *Wake* combines elements from the Old Testament (Ecclesiasticus 24:13–15), the Maronite (Lebanese Catholic) Liturgy for Good Friday, and invocations of the ancient Egyptian goddess Isis (see *Letters* I.263–64). In the midst of this multicultural litany, the name of Plotinus crops up twice: "Oisis, *plantainous* dewstruckacqmirage *playtennis*!" (*FW* 470.20; my emphases). At the forefront of Plotinus's enormously complex system is the transcendent first principle. It is sometimes called The Good, or Father, rarely God; but the primary name for this elemental absolute of unity is "The One," in Greek τὸ ἕν (*to hen*).[36] The hen of primary significance in *Finnegans Wake* is the fowl whose scratching in the midden first uncovers the all-important letter. She is "that original hen" (*FW* 110.22).

Some vaguely Neoplatonic terminology certainly underlies Stephen's unvoiced comments as he compares Aristotle with Plato in the National Library: "Streams of tendency and eons they worship" (*U* 9.85). Later in the same chapter, Stephen contemplates the propriety of assumed names: "A.E., eon" (*U* 9.412). The latter term, from the Greek αἰών (ever-being, eternal), although it occurs in Plotinus, is a catchword in all sorts of texts loaded with Gnostic-Hermetic speculation. Its application to AE, the pen name of the poet George Russell, is an indication that Joyce intended the word to be understood as the mark of pseudoantique mumbo-jumbo. The astute J. J. O'Molloy is right on the mark when he asks Stephen, "What do you think really of that hermetic crowd, the opal poets: A.E. the mastermystic?" (*U* 7.783–84). A similar slur is intended by Mulligan in "Oxen of the Sun": "Any object, intensely regarded, may be a gate of access to the incorruptible eon of the god. Do you not think it, Stephen? Theosophos told me so, Stephen answered" (*U* 14.1166–68). In the *Wake* the following invocation of Holy Wisdom (*Hagia Sophia*) occurs: "descent from above on us, Hagiasofia of Astralia, our orisons thy nave and absedes, our *aeone tone aeones* thy studvaast vault" (*FW* 552.6–8; my emphasis). The italicized words are meant to echo the Christian Greek liturgical phrase "for ages of ages." Extended discussion of the sort of theosophical mysticism associated with and practiced by AE, Yeats, and other Dublin adepts of theosophy would take this chapter at least one step beyond even the extended limits of ancient philosophy.[37]

It is possible, however, to find Joycean adaptations of several catchwords from one of the movements lying on the other side of the threshold of classical Neoplatonic philosophy, the Hermetic tradition. The name Hermes Trismegistus (Greek for Thrice Great) was given by devotees of the occult and alchemy to the Egyptian god Thoth. This divinity was more or less identified with the Greek Hermes, and a body of mystical writings (perhaps dating from the third century A.D.) were attributed to him. One such collection of *Hermetica* was entitled the *Poimandres*. Most commentaries state that the derivation and meaning of this title are uncertain. There is an obvious solution: A late Greek noun for shepherd, or guide, is *poimant/dēr* (in the plural, *poimant/dres*); the metaphorical application of that pastoral term to the field of mystical philosophy would be a natural transfer.[38] Moreover, it is certain not only that Joyce was aware of the Hermetic use of *poimandēr* (transliterated as *pimander*, as it would be pronounced in Modern Greek), but also that he had figured out its etymological force: "AE, pimander, good shepherd of men" (*U* 3.227–28). Later in *Ulysses,* Joyce has AE appear on stage in "Circe" as a character from one of his own blatantly "Celtic" plays; near the start of a paragraph of verbose nonsense, Mananaun Machir intones "Occult pimander of Hermes Trismegistos" (*U* 15.2269).

In "Night Lessons" an alchemical passage reveals that "[t]he tasks above are as the flasks below, saith the emerald canticle of Hermes" (*FW* 263.21–22). Atherton shows that Joyce quoted this reference to the *Smaragdine* ["emerald" in Greek] *Tablet* of Hermes from Arthur Symons's book *The Symbolist Movement in Literature.*[39] Atherton also suggests the presence of undetected sources for other alchemical phrases in the *Wake,* notably "mehrkurious than saltz of sulphurs" (*FW* 261.25–26). In mystical chemo-theology the elements of mercury, salt, and sulphur were equated with the Trinity—as the Greek *kyrios* (lord) is designed to point out. But additional discussion of this wild perversion of classical concepts is futile, even though the "faithful hermetists await the light" (*U* 9.282).

Two additional figures must be considered medieval footnotes to Joyce's manipulation of the Platonic tradition. During the ninth century, just after Viking raiders had begun to ravage the Irish coast, Johannes Erigena left the island to become a member of the foremost intellectual community in western Europe, at the Carolingian court at Aachen. His cognomen means Irish-born; a more familiar designation is "Scotus." Joyce used the latter ethnic designation to lend a patent of learning to a 1903 review of a life of Giordano Bruno, whose legend was "more sanctified, and more ingeneous than that of Averroes or of Scotus Erigena" (*CW* 134; also note "erigenus scotto gene" [VI.B.17.17]). Johannes was reported to have mastered Greek before his exile from the Emerald Isle, and he was regarded as one of the two most competent scholars of his time in western Europe. An archival note records Joyce's awareness of medieval Irish scholarship: "ʳthey knew Greek / used Gr words in / their Latin with / verses in Greek / (Scotus Erigena)" (VI.B.3.95). In the *Wake* a touch of sartorial elegance is added to the allusion to this intellectual accomplishment: "their half a Roman hat, with an ancient Greek gloss on it" (*FW* 390. 17–18; also note "ʳgloss" [VI.B.1.119]).

Although Erigena's primary philosophical work, *De Divisione Naturae* (On the divisions of nature) was composed in Latin, its models and points of view were resolutely Greek. In this treatise, he classified physical phenomena into four divisions on the basis of their status as beings that create or are created. His purpose was to construct a "new synthesis of Christian and Neoplatonic thought into an immense metaphysical and theological epic."[40] The unorthodox theological views and obscure style of this work prevented it from becoming widely influential. Joyce links the philosopher's name with the Irish-born Pelegian heretic, Celestius, in a passage that describes the rise of HCE: "erigenating from next to nothing and celescalating the himals and all" (FW 4.36–5.1). Two other probable references are "But Erigureen is ever" (FW 279.3) and "the mainstay of our erigenal house" (FW 431.35). It is also tempting to read the following passage as a parody in summarizing Erigena's fourfold division of nature: "Creator he has created for his creatured ones a creation" (FW 29.14–15). That sentence occurs in the midst of a cluster of cabalistic terms, but the concept and wordplay on active-passive cognates cannot be tied to a specific model.

Another Christian Neoplatonic work is associated with Johannes Erigena. The Acts of the Apostles mention Dionysius, an Athenian who listened to Paul preach on the Areopagus (Acts 17:34). Tradition wrongly attributes to Dionysius a number of heterogeneous works that were deeply influenced by Neoplatonism and other schools of eastern mysticism. (They were in fact composed much later, but before the fifth century A.D.) These syncretistic treatises had significant impact on medieval theology and art. That influence was greatly facilitated by the translation of the difficult Greek works into Latin by Johannes Erigena sometime around A.D. 860. Joyce recorded that event in the history of philosophy in an pre-Wake note: "JSE translated Dionysius Areopagus" (VI.B.3.95).[41] Two of the most important documents in the pseudo-Dionysius corpus are the treatises Concerning the Celestial Hierarchy and Concerning the Ecclesiastical Hierarchy. A combined edition of these works appears in the margin of "Night Lessons": "Ecclesiastical and Celestial Hierarchies. The Ascending. The Descending" (FW 298.L2; also see FW 4.36–5.1 cited in the previous paragraph).

This chapter on Plato and Joyce has frequently meandered far from the grove outside Athens where the philosopher's mentor, Socrates, and his disciples discussed the world of the Forms. In Joyce's latter-day universe, strange, non-Greek names like John Eglinton, "my jo, John" (U 9.1126), Stephen MacKenna, George William Russell, and Oscar Wilde constituted some of the participants in the philosophical discourse. The most frequently cited scene of a Joycean dialogue is Thomas William Lyster's office at the National Library of Ireland. There Stephen Dedalus, with increasing passion, expounds his heterodox dogma on Shakespeare and *Hamlet.* Schemata statements about the opposition between Plato and Aristotle in "Scylla and Charybdis" must not be seen as an indicator of their author's deep scholarship into Plato's dialogues—except, of course, to mock Eglinton's inability to recall several antique best beds. Rather, as in his early essays, in *Stephen Hero,* and in *Portrait,* Joyce poached judiciously from intermediate sources such as Bosanquet, AE, Yeats—and perhaps Victor Cousin. A parody of the *Symposium* in "Oxen in the Sun" may be an exception to this rule; but apart from the early comments on aesthetics (which are more precisely Neoplatonic than Platonic), almost all of Joyce's references to Plato are designed to trigger not philosophical contemplation of the Ideal world, but comic appreciation of the actual text. In wrapping up this chapter, the series of Neoplatonic allusions— from Plotinus to pseudo-Dionysius the Areopagite—are intended to highlight my focus, especially in *Ulysses* and the *Wake,* on the humorous as opposed to the metaphysical dimension of references to ancient philosophy. In the criticism of Joyce's fiction, that distinction, in the immortal words of AE, is a matter of more than purely academic significance.

7

Aristotle

At the very beginning of the debate on *Hamlet* in the National Library, George Russell (AE) claims that art reveals "formless spiritual essences. . . . Plato's world of ideas. All the rest is speculation of schoolboys for schoolboys." Stephen replies "—The schoolmen were schoolboys first. . . . Aristotle was once Plato's schoolboy" (*U* 9.49–57). This retort, delivered "super-politely," is an indicator of Stephen's decided preference in matters philosophical: Aristotle (and the schoolman Aquinas) over Plato.[1] James Joyce's personal preferences coincide with those of Stephen Dedalus. There is clear evidence that Joyce studied Aristotle seriously. He took systematic notes on several works and applied this research to effect in *Ulysses*. Moreover, when the master of the Peripatetic school is cited by Joyce's fictional characters, the reference bolsters, rather than ironically undercuts, their case. This does not mean that the covert humor that so often marks the presence of Plato in his fiction is entirely lacking in Joyce's allusions to Aristotle. In general, however, the references are deployed in serious and appropriately philosophical contexts. Nevertheless, like "henpecked Socrates," being a philosopher does not prevent Aristotle from incidental comic entrapment in that most ineluctably universal of all human categories: "Even the allwisest Stagyrite was bitted, bridled and mounted by a light of love" (*U* 15.111–12).

Two pertinent but quite different books have addressed aspects of Joyce's use of Aristotle in his works. The first chapter of Theoharis Theoharis's monograph is a sensitive essay on the influence of *De Anima* (Psychology) on the narrative of *Ulysses*.[2] In the last section of Jacques Aubert's meticulous analysis of Joyce's aesthetics, Aristotle is the most frequently cited ancient source.[3] A recent lengthy article by Sidney Feshbach thoroughly investigates the Aristotelian tradition in *A Portrait of the*

Artist as a Young Man.[4] By design the last two studies mentioned are focused almost exclusively on the early, explicitly theoretical essays and their adaptations in the evolution of Joyce's first long work of fiction. The purpose of this chapter is to present a synthesis, with as much illustrative concrete detail as possible, of the entire range of Aristotelian influence and allusion in all of Joyce's works.

Aristotle was born at Stagira in northeast Greece in 384 B.C.; when he was eighteen he began his studies at the Academy at Athens and remained there until Plato's death. For several years he served as the personal tutor to young Prince Alexander, son of the king of Macedon. In 335 B.C. Aristotle founded his own school of philosophy, the Lyceum. There he wrote, lectured, and conducted scientific experiments until, after the death of Alexander the Great, anti-Macedonian feeling forced him to retire. He died in 322 B.C. None of Aristotle's early, general dialogues survive; the extant works are probably lecture outlines or even student notes that have been patched together. The large number of treatises ascribed to Aristotle include works on psychology, biology, physics, metaphysics, ethics, logic, and poetics-rhetoric.[5] Joyce was primarily interested in material from the first and last of these categories; hence his frequent direct citation from Aristotle's *De Anima* and the *Poetics.*

Joyce's university education did not include the formal courses in philosophy per se, be it ancient, scholastic, or modern. There were, however, numerous occasions on which his teachers discussed philosophical matters. Two of Joyce's fellow students provide relevant testimony:

> Dublin at that time could well have been described as a city of peripatetic discourse. . . . The aesthetic discussion with Father Darlington [*P* 185–90] may be an idealised or a synthetic version of many such talks but it conveys the essence of the spirit of reference to Aristotle, which was the salient characteristic of Father Darlington's interventions in the discussions [of various collegiate societies].

> It was my first lecture [at UCD]; the class was English Literature; the lecturer was Father Darlington, and his first words were from Aristotle's *Poetics.*[6]

Stanislaus Joyce also reports that his brother displayed an "exalted opinion of philosophy. He upholds Aristotle against his friends, and boasts himself an Aristotelian."[7]

In a highly autobiographical section (Va) of *Portrait,* Stephen Dedalus confirms that he was not a deep student of ancient or scholastic philosophy during his university years. He often turned "to the dainty songs of the Elizabethans" when his mind "wearied of its search for the essence of beauty amid the spectral words of Aristotle or Aquinas." Almost immediately, however, there is an admission of the thinness of the basis for his search: "The love which he was believed to pass his days brooding upon so that it had rapt him from the companionships of youth was only a garner of slender sentences from Aristotle's poetics and psychology and a *Synopsis Philosophiae Scholasticae ad mentem divi Thomae* [A synopsis of scholastic philosophy according to the thought of St. Thomas]" (*P* 176–77).

A bit later in the same episode, Stephen realizes that he has missed his English lecture: "He saw the heads of his classmates . . . as they wrote in their notebooks . . . nominal definitions, essential definitions and examples or dates . . . chief works . . ." (*P* 178). There is a minor Peripatetic element in this description of the study habits of University College students: Nominal and essential definitions—and the distinction between them—are key terms in Aristotle's logic. While it is highly unlikely that Joyce actually traced these terms to their ultimate source (*Posterior Analytics* 2.7.92a34–92b38), he does know how to inject a bit of locally classical color into his mind-numbing catalog of Jesuit literary criticism in action.

In *Stephen Hero* and *Portrait* there are several other minor but specific examples of Aristotelian influence on Stephen Dedalus's theories of art and literature. The details of that process have been carefully examined in an article by David E. Jones, "The Essence of Beauty in James Joyce's Aesthetics."[8] That study also traces the interaction between the works of Aristotle and Thomas Aquinas on this topic. Although I do not agree with Jones's implication that actual study of Aquinas's work on Aristotle, *Commentary on "De Anima,"* played a role in Joyce's aesthetics, that medieval work is mentioned as part of the heritage of the Catholic Church in *Stephen Hero* (143). For Joyce, casual citation of an impressive title was one thing; detailed analysis of the work itself was another. Without archival notes or direct verbal echoes, like those that exist for some of the other treatises, I hesitate to certify Joyce's study or direct use of this fairly abstruse commentary by Aquinas.[9]

At the completion of his university studies in Dublin, Joyce went to

Paris in December 1902; after a brief trip home for Christmas, he returned until called back in April 1903 by the telegram announcing that his mother was dying. Two letters to Stanislaus from that period refer directly to his current study of Aristotle (*Letters* II.28, 35). During February and March 1903 he compiled the so-called *Paris Notebook,* which contains a number of direct quotations or close paraphrases from several of Aristotle's works.[10] These excerpts were undoubtedly the ones that Joyce has Stephen Dedalus recall early in *Ulysses:* "Aristotle's phrase formed itself . . . and floated out into the studious silence of the library of Saint Genevieve where he had read, sheltered from the sin of Paris, night by night" (*U* 2.68–70). A year and a half later, after he had left Ireland with Nora, Joyce reported that he was keeping up his work in ancient philosophy. In a November 19, 1904, letter from Pola he writes to Stanislaus, "I think that after a short course in Aristotle I will shut up the books and examine for myself in a cafe" (*Letters* II.71).

It is clear that, in his choice of Aristotelian passages and from the angle of his comments on them, Joyce followed the directions laid down in well-known books by two scholars. Aubert has demonstrated Joyce's use, as early as his 1898–99 essay "The Study of Language," of Bernard Bosanquet's *A History of Aesthetic* (1892).[11] The fourth edition (1907) of Samuel H. Butcher's critical edition of Aristotle's *Poetics,* with a thorough discussion of the Greek philosopher's theory of art, was in Joyce's Trieste library.[12] Aubert suggests, in an appendix to his book, that Joyce also consulted the most recent French edition of the *Poetics,* by Hatzfeld and Dufour (1899). That work continually refers readers to other works of Aristotle, and a large part of its introduction seeks to reconstruct a theory of comedy parallel to the extant text's anatomy of tragedy. A second appendix to Aubert's book presents the actual passages (from the French translations of Aristotle's psychological treatises and the *Metaphysics*) that Joyce used as the bases for the entries into his *Paris Notebook.*[13]

The foregoing background and documentation set the stage for an analysis of where, how, and why Joyce refers to Aristotle in his *fiction.* I stress that term because Aubert's book quite adequately covers the aesthetic dimension of Joyce's early essays. Moreover, the French scholar's discussion of Aristotle and "applied Aquinas" in *Portrait* and his general conclusions on Joycean aesthetics will certainly satisfy those readers whose primary interest is theoretical or fundamentally philosophical. It should be apparent that my critical inclinations do not bend in that direction. To deflect censure for that confession, I make pious reference to two brief but complete lines that Joyce embedded deep in "Scylla and Charybdis," the most philosophical of the chapters in *Ulysses:*

> —Saint Thomas, Stephen began . . .
>
> —*Ora pro nobis,* Monk Mulligan groaned, sinking into a chair. (*U* 9.772–73)

The ellipsis in the first line is Joyce's. He allows Mulligan's immediate invocation of a formula from the Litany of the Saints to squelch any scholastic discourse at its inception. I have always appreciated that authorial act of grace. As a matter of narrative fact, Buck Mulligan had already deflected a potential disquisition on Thomistic topics in the Martello tower: "—No, no , [he] shouted in pain. I'm not equal to Thomas Aquinas and the fiftyfive reasons he has made out to prop it up. Wait till I have a few pints in me first" (*U* 1.546–48). A note on that passage in Gifford and Seidman refers to the assertion in Aristotle's *Metaphysics* (12.8.1074a12) that the universe consists of fifty-nine concentric spheres.

Before I turn to the Aristotelian aspects of *Ulysses*, observe, briefly, a younger Stephen Dedalus invoking the authority of the Stagyrite. In the midst of his discussion of aesthetics with Lynch in *Portrait,* Stephen outlines the basic details of his theory about the relationship between truth and beauty: "The first step in the direction of truth is to understand the frame and scope of the intellect itself, to comprehend the act itself of intellection. Aristotle's entire system of philosophy rests on his book of psychology and that, I think, rests on his statement that the same attribute cannot at the same time and in the same connection belong to and not belong to the same subject" (*P* 208). The "book of psychology" is Aristotle's *De Anima,* which is frequently referred to as his treatise "on psychology" in English, since neither "mind" nor "spirit" nor "soul" as translations of the *anima* in the traditional Latin title does justice to the scope of the Greek philosopher's method or topic. Joyce's primary point in the *Portrait* citation is highlighted by the following entry (taken directly from a French translation of Aristotle) in his *Paris Notebook:* "The same attribute cannot at the same time and in the same connection belong and not belong to the same subject."[14] This famous statement of the principle of noncontradiction is the basis of Aristotelian logic—and of all subsequent Western science. One is not two, nor can an object be simultaneously hot and cold on the same scale of temperature. Joyce elegantly applies this axiom to his comments on the time-space, "dime-cash" problem in the *Wake:* "I mean the system means . . . that I cannot now have or nothave a piece of cheeps in your pocket at the same time and with the same manners as you can now have nothalf or half the cheek piece I've in mind unless Burrus and Caseous have not or have seemaultaneously sysentangled themselves" (*FW* 161.8–13). Joyce's immediate source for the excerpt in his notebook was not the *De Anima,* but Aristotle's *Metaphysics.* So fundamental is this proposition that Aristotle concludes his discussion of its force by stating, "This, then is the most certain of all principles. . . . this is naturally the starting-point even for all the other axioms" (4.3.1005b19–34; McKeon 736–37).[15] (Other incidental Aristotelian allusions in *Portrait* are treated later, when this chapter examines Joyce's manipulation of some of the central concepts and formulas from the *Poetics.*)

The next examples of Joyce's deployment of Aristotelian material in *Ulysses* are based, more or less, on Theoharis's discussion, with added reference to Aubert's identification of specific sources. With a few exceptions, these passages illustrate the serious, personally pertinent context of the allusions to Peripatetic teachings.

Early in "Nestor," Stephen's thoughts are presented as a silent commentary on a recitation of Milton's "Lycidas" by one of the students: "It must be a movement then, an actuality of the possible as possible. Aristotle's phrase formed itself within the gabbled verses. . . . Thought is the thought of thought. Tranquil brightness. The soul is in a manner all that is: the soul is the form of forms. Tranquility sudden, vast, candescent: form of forms" (*U* 2.67–76; my ellipsis). Joyce lifted the initial sentence almost directly from an entry in his *Paris Notebook:* "Movement is the actuality of the possible as possible." Aubert identifies the ultimate source as Aristotle's *Physics* (3.1201a10–11), which Joyce read in French translation; the source of "Thought is the thought of thought" is the philosopher's *Metaphysics* (12.7.1072b20; McKeon 880). Earlier entries in the *Notebook* are "The intellectual soul is the form of forms" (*De Anima* 3.8.432a2; McKeon 595) and "The soul is in a manner all that is" (*De Anima* 3.8.431.b21; McKeon 595). In the silent commentary in "Nestor," Joyce combines key formulas from Aristotle with phrases flashing with the language of mysticism ("Tranquil brightness . . . candescent"). His purpose in creating this mélange of recalled terminology is to contrast Stephen's current status (part-time teacher in a run-of-the-mill boys' school) with the fierce literary ambition and the urge for artistic freedom that sent him to the venerable libraries of Paris. Like the angel of "Lycidas" he has been forced to look homeward, where he sees neither movement nor light.

The opening paragraph of "Proteus" records Stephen's interior monologue as he walks across the tidal beach at Sandymount. The movement from sensory perception to abstract generalization is circular, not linear. "Ineluctable modality of the visible" precedes "Snotgreen, bluesilver, rust" and is followed by "Limits of the diaphane. But he adds: in bodies. Then he was aware of them bodies before of them coloured. How?" (*U* 3.1–5). Again, interwoven tag lines from Aristotle's psychology are the clues to Stephen's elliptical thought process. "Color is the limit of the diaphane in any determined body" appears in the *Paris Notebook;* its classical source is *On Sense and Sensible Objects* (3.349b11; not in McKeon). In that treatise Aristotle is concerned with an analysis of sensation, the fundamental stimulus of the mental images without which no thought can occur. Theoharis demonstrates with great skill how Joyce mixes Jacob Boehme, Bishop Berkeley, and Samuel Johnson into this paragraph,[16] but at the center of Stephen's seaside ruminations in this paragraph is Aristotle.

The primary but certainly esoteric indicator of allusion here is the term "diaphane," which is repeated (and negated) four lines later in "Diaphane, adiaphane" (*U* 3.8). In both *De Anima* (2.7.418a27–418b24) and *On Sense and Sensible Objects,* Aristotle defines "diaphane" as that which owes its visibility to the color of something else—in other words, as the translucent medium that color has the power to set in motion. That formulation leads Stephen to recall not merely Berkeley's English phrase "coloured signs" but also Dante's description of Aristotle in the *Inferno* 4:131: "*maestro di color che sanno* [master of those who know]" (*U* 3.6–7). The connection between these phrases is not merely honorific or epistemological;[17] rather, Stephen (and Joyce) are playing a linguistic trick. Dante's Italian word *color* (*colóro* in modern Italian) means "those people"; it is pronounced like the English noun *color*. To a student of the language—and both Joyce and Stephen Dedalus knew Italian well—another link between the Aristotelian theory of sense perception and the mood-setting topic of the paragraph is the semantically translucent plural pronoun, "*color.*"[18]

That sense of topically appropriate humor is also evident from another, closely related incident in the "Proteus" chapter. Stephen has trouble bringing a match to the tip of his cigarette: "Distance. The eye sees all flat. (*He draws the match away. It goes out.*) Brain thinks. Near: far. Ineluctable modality of the visible"(*U* 15.3629–31). Here the distinction between "flat" sensory perception and the mental judgment of "distance" is from Bishop Berkeley's *Essay towards a New Theory of Vision*. Nonetheless, the self-conscious attempt to move from sensed examples to a psychological process to general theory of perception is typical of Aristotle's method in *De Anima* and *On Sense and Sensible Objects*. In fact, throughout the entire "Proteus" chapter of *Ulysses* there are frequent and emphatic references to the five senses and various processes and media though which humans perceive sensory data.[19] The most conspicuous examples:

Sight: "Darkly they [stars] are there behind this light, darkness shining in the brightness, delta of Cassiopeia" (*U* 3.409–410).

Sounds: "His tune whistle sounds again, finely shaded, with rushes of the air, his fists bigdrumming on his padded knees" (*U* 3.102–3).

Taste: "Damn your lithia water. It lowers. Whusky!" (*U* 3.90).

Touch: "Touch me. Soft eyes. Soft soft soft hand. I am lonely he. O, touch me soon, now" (*U* 3.434–35).

Smell: "A shefiend's whiteness under her rancid rags. Fumbally's lane that night: the tanyard smells" (*U* 3.378–80).

A further note about the Dantean verse in the opening paragraph of "Proteus," which is introduced by a phrase that refers to Aristotle: "Bald he was and a millionaire, *maestro di color*" (*U* 3.6–7). The ancient life of Aristotle says nothing about his baldness; in fact, a rare bit of personal information reports that "he was conspicuous for his dress, his rings, and the way he wore his hair."[20] Nor is there any ancient report on the extent of the philosopher's fortune. Both of those apocryphal items are found in medieval lives of Aristotle which, though popular, have no basis in fact.

The absence of classical authority for Aristotle's baldness does not prevent Stephen from including that very bit of detail in the midst of other, more securely documented matters of the philosopher's life. In "Scylla and Charybdis" Stephen's opponents are trying to explain away Shakespeare's legacy of his "Secondbest Bed" to Ann Hathaway. Eglinton seeks to deflect the evident insult by suggesting "—Antiquity mentions famous beds. . . ." Stephen interrupts to inform his auditors, "—Antiquity mentions that Stagyrite schoolurchin and bald heathen sage, . . . who when dying in exile frees and endows his slaves, . . . wills to be laid in earth near the bones of his dead wife and begs his friends to be kind to an old mistress (don't forget Nell Gwynn Herpyllis) and let her live in his villa" (*U* 9.718–24; my ellipses). The "Stagyrite schoolurchin" is Stephen's exasperated distortion of an earlier slight by Eglinton who labeled Aristotle as Plato's "model schoolboy with his diploma under his arm" (*U* 9.59). Again, the phrase "bald heathen sage" comes from a medieval portrait of the philosopher that has no historical basis.[21] There is, however, ancient (if not eyewitness) testimony to the provisions of Aristotle's last will and testament. Diogenes Laertius quotes what purports to be that document in his third-century A.D. *Life of Aristotle*. All of the provisions that Stephen mentions are more or less accurately reported—including his benefice of money, servants, and housing for Herpyllis, his mistress and the mother of his son, Nicomachus.[22] The purpose of Stephen's retort to Eglinton in *Ulysses* is to contrast the generosity of the Stagyrite with the niggardliness of the Stratfordite. The testamentary detail of goods, chattels, persons, and places in his summary of the evidence is also an effective means of rebutting the ethereal claims of the Neoplatonists in the National Library.

Somewhat the same tactic is used earlier in the same episode. When Stephen recalls that he owes AE a pound, he decides to defer his repayment: "Wait. Five months. Molecules all change. I am other I now. Other I got pound. . . . But I, entelechy, form of forms, am I by memory because under everchanging forms" (*U* 9. 205–209; my ellipsis). Here Aristotelian philosophy prevails over notions from popular biology. However much the "matter" of Stephen Dedalus is physically altered, his essential "form" remains, and remains in AE's debt. Two *Paris Notebook* entries contribute to the logic of that passage: "The soul is the first entelechy of a naturally organic body" (*De Anima* 2.1.412a20; McKeon 555); "The intellectual soul is the form of forms" (*De Anima* 3.8.432a2; McKeon 595).

As for Joyce's allusion to Aristotle's sex life, information on that aspect of the philosopher's career is not found in the life by Diogenes Laertius or in any other ancient document. Nevertheless, in one of the initial scenes in "Circe" Lynch expresses his doubts about the philosophical point of a visit to a brothel: "Metaphysics in Mecklenburgh Street!" (*U* 15.108). Stephen responds, "Even the alllwisest Stagyrite was bitted, bridled and mounted by a light of love (*U* 15.111–12). The image suggested by the three verbs in that sentence is not intended as a metaphor. In the Middle Ages there was a legendary report of the humiliation of Aristotle by an Indian "light of love" named Phyllis. The philosopher had been sent to remonstrate with Alexander the Great, whom this woman had bewitched into neglecting the important task of conquering the world. Phyllis took out her revenge by vamping Aristotle, who was so smitten that he agreed to let her ride him like a horse. Phyllis placed a saddle on the philosopher's back and a bit in his mouth, then rode him as he crawled about on all fours. When Alexander demanded an explanation, Aristotle replied: "If a woman can make such a fool of a man of my age and wisdom, how much more dangerous must she not be for younger ones? I added an example to my precept, it is your privilege to benefit by both."[23]

The anecdote became a staple of medieval moralization and was a very popular topic for artists.[24] Whatever the specific source of this information was for Joyce, he accurately noted the details but transferred the humiliation to Leopold Bloom. Proof comes later, in "Circe," when Bella Cohen (transformed into a male Bello) mounts Bloom: "Gee up! A cockhorse to Banbury Cross. I'll ride him for the Eclipse stakes. . . . (*he horserides cockhorse, leaping in the, in the saddle*) The lady goes a pace a pace and the coachman goes a trot a trot and the gentleman goes a gallop a gallop a gallop a gallop" (*U* 15.2945–49).

The reference to the philosopher's personal susceptibility to drives of the flesh is not Joyce's only allusion to Aristotelian sexuality. *On the Generation of Animals* is Aristotle's four-book treatise on the biology of reproduction. Quite naturally it has left its mark on the "Oxen of the Sun" chapter of *Ulysses* in which conception, embryonic development, and birth are primary topics. There Stephen asserts "how at the end of the second month [of gestation of a foetus] a human soul was infused" (*U* 14.247–48). Commentators point out that this theory can be traced back to Aristotle, who distinguishes between the "nutritive" soul (present from conception) and the "sentient/rational" soul (acquired during fetal development). Moreover, the origin of the second soul is not human: "Reason alone enters in from the outside and it alone is divine, because physical, bodily activity has nothing in common with the activity of reason" (*Generation of Animals* 2.3.736b27; not in McKeon). Neither Aristotle nor, following him, Thomas Aquinas mentions the precise time when this "infusion" takes place. Joyce's use of a typically scholastic verb ("to infuse") and his specification of "the end of the second month" make it likely that he was following some traditional Catholic—but not dogmatically official—source here.

Later in the same chapter Stephen delivers a confused minisermon on ends and beginnings: "The adiaphane in the noon of life is an Egypt's plague which in the nights of prenativity and postmortemity is their most proper *ubi* and *quomodo*" (*U* 14.385–87). In that sentence the Aristotelian term "adiaphane" is jumbled together with an allusion to the Exodus and with two grotesque English neologisms and a pair of Latin scholastic terms ("where" and "how") in an attempt to create a tone of profundity. The result is turgid nonsense. Another similar sentence follows: "And as the ends and the ultimates of all things accord in some mean and measure with their inceptions and originals . . ." (*U* 14.387–89). This may be intended as a parody of the Aristotelian principle that "the defining formula (*logos*) of a thing and that for the sake of which it exists, considered as its end, are the same" (*Generation of Animals* 1.1.715a9; McKeon 665). This is expressed a bit more clearly in another summary passage: "For those things are natural which, by a continuous movement originated from an internal principle, arrive at some completion . . . . The end and the means toward it do not come about by chance" (*Physics* 2.8.199b15–19; McKeon 251). On the other hand, Stephen's statement may be nothing more than his none-too-sober iteration that things tend to have a beginning, a middle, and an end. A little learning in ancient philosophy is a dangerous thing.

The same concern for the ultimate reasons for actions or behavior appears in *Stephen Hero*. Cranly has failed his university examinations and seems to be at a loss about what to do with his life. Stephen asks, "—What mysterious purpose is concealed under your impossible prosiness?" Cranly evades a direct answer with some glittering generalities: "—Most people have some purpose or other in their lives. Aristotle says that the end of every being is its greatest good. We all act in view of some good" (*SH* 220). Statements like this—especially after examination results have been posted—need not necessarily be glossed by reference to a classical source. There are, however, two adjacent entries in Joyce's *Paris Notebook* that are directly to the point here. Moreover, even though it goes against probability in the circumstances, Cranly does specifically cite Aristotle. The pair of notes are "Nature always acts in the view of some end" and "The end of every being is its greatest good." They come from the same collection of minor works on natural science as the citation about color and the "diaphane," which immediately precedes these items in the note-book (*On Sleep and Waking* 2.455b17 and 2.455b24; not in McKeon). The somewhat self-conscious citation of Aristotle by Cranly is not typical of Joyce's technique, but the weaving of esoteric notebook items into "real-istic" dialogue or description is an absolutely persistent characteristic of his method of composition.

After those cosmic pronouncements about design in nature, human destiny, and the fact that our ends are our beginnings, it is a relief to turn to matters of biological science later in "Proteus": "Science, it cannot be too often repeated, deals with tangible phenomena" (*U* 14.1226–27). This turn of the topic especially suits Leopold Bloom, who poses a problem "regarding the future determination of sex": "Must we accept the view of Empedocles of Trinacria that the right ovary (the postmenstrual period assert others) is responsible for the birth of males or are the too long neglected spermatozoa or nemasperms the differentiating factors or is it . . . a mixture of both?" (*U* 14.1231–36).

Aristotle reports that Anaxagoras (not Empedocles) claimed that males come from sperm from the right testicle, females from the left—or, as for the uterus, males are in the right side, females on the left (*Generation of Animals* 4.1.763b34; not in McKeon). Since these claims contradict each other, scholars regard the second option as an addition to the original text. An alternative view, which Aristotle favors, involves active sperm and passive womb, but the determinant factor is the gender of the embryonic heart. What causes the difference in heart gender is not clear (*Generation of Animals* 4.1.766a31–b27).

At any rate, it seems clear that the preceding theories of biological phenomena do not stem directly from Aristotle. The odd compound "nemasperm" (*nema*, Greek, means thread) and the Latin phrases "*nisus formativus*" and "*succubitus felix*" (*U* 14.1238–39) point to some later, hybrid source of information. In fact, a crossed notesheet entry for "Oxen of the Sun" incorrectly attributes the theory that males come from the right ovary to Hippocrates, the father of Greek medicine (*UNBM* 251:46). "ʳEmpedocles of Sicily" is also found in the same cluster (*UNBM* 252:24), as are other conceptual entries for the same chapter: "ʳflagellary movt. Tail [of sperm]" (*UNBM* 251:83) and "ʳnemasperm head on" (*UNBM* 251:13).[25] Senn has a compact discussion of the "procreating function" (*U* 14.31) and origin of some of this material—with characteristically suggestive application to the larger issue of the interpretation of *Ulysses*.[26] More recently, Stephen Soud has produced an entertaining and graphic consideration of *Aristotle's Masterpiece,* that monument to pseudosexual and pseudomedical folklore.[27] Despite its title, this widely circulated work, which was certainly known to Joyce, has almost nothing to do with biological writings of the ancient Greek philosopher.

The two references to *Aristotle's Masterpiece* (*U* 10.586 and 14.973–77) are not the only acknowledgments in *Ulysses* of the contamination (and outright perversion) of the ongoing tradition of Peripatetic philosophy. In the same spirit of discredited biological theories as those cited above, Joyce reports that a woman could be impregnated "peradventure in her bath according to the opinions of Averroes and Moses Maimonides" (*U* 14.246–47). The former was a twelfth-century Spanish-Arab philosopher and physician; the latter was a Spanish-born philosopher and Talmudic scholar who became the chief rabbi of Cairo, also in the twelfth century. Both men attempted to reconcile the works of Aristotle to their respective faiths, and their writings and translations had a tremendous impact on the rise of Christian scholastic philosophy in Western Europe. Their linked names also flash across Stephen Dedalus's mind while he is teaching his class at Mr. Deasy's school early in the day (*U* 2.158).

When Bloom and Stephen are together in "Ithaca," Maimonides' "*More Nebukim*" (Guide of the perplexed) is cited as an example of the work of one of "Three seekers of the pure truth, Moses of Egypt, Moses Maimonides . . . and Moses Mendelssohn" (*U* 17.711–12). Bloom adds a "fourth seeker . . . by name Aristotle," with the claim that the last "seeker mentioned had been a pupil of a rabbinical philosopher, name uncertain" (*U* 17.715–19). The legend that both Plato and Aristotle had been instructed in the Law of Moses and in Jewish learning was a popular piece of medieval misinformation, but it is totally without historical foundation.

At least one of Joyce's "helpers" during the Parisian "Work in Progress" years also acknowledges the authority of Aristotle. In his study of *Ulysses,* Stuart Gilbert discusses the rhetorical techniques and figures that are so prominent in "Aeolus." He writes that "according to Aristotle, the foundation of argumentation is the enthymeme." Somewhat later he adds (with the Greek terms in parentheses) that there "are three types of oratory, appropriate respectively to the three kinds of bearer; the deliberative . . . the forensic . . . and the expository. . . ."[28] Aristotle stresses the persuasive significance of the enthymeme (a syllogism without a middle term) for oratory in the introductory section of his *Rhetoric;* the threefold division of oratory is frequently mentioned in his works (*Rhetoric* 1.1.1355a4–17 and 1.3.1358b7; McKeon 1327, 1335). Long before Stuart Gilbert came onto the Paris scene, however, Joyce had taken a long series of highly technical notes from Aristotle's *Rhetoric* (VI.A.5.23–25). None of these Zürich entries seems to have been reused in *Ulysses.*[29]

In the Library debate there appears what looks like a cluster of laboratory notes: "Touch lightly with two index fingers. Aristotle's experiment. One or two?" (*U* 9.296–97). That allusion was triggered by a passage in Aristotle's *Problemata* (Problems), a long series of loosely connected questions—with some answers—about every imaginable kind of physical and occasional psychological phenomena: "Why is the north wind strong?" "Why should one eat dried fruits?" "Why do we stop sneezing if we rub our eye?" The last problem in the section on "touch" is: "Why does one object feel as if it were two if it is grasped by fingers crisscrossed (*enallax*)? Is it because we are touching it with two sensitive areas? For when we hold our hand naturally, we cannot touch an object with the outside (or inside) of both fingers" (*Problems* 35.10.965a36; not in McKeon).

After numerous personal experiments, I cannot figure out what Aristotle is talking about here. The textual variant ("outside"/"inside") and the murky meaning of *enallax* do nothing to buck up my confidence in the possibility of an experimental verification of this scientific theory. Stephen's methodological hesitation ("One or two?") also signals some confusion on his part. Yet, the passage cited is without a doubt the source of Joyce's allusion in "Scylla and Charybdis." And Aubert is certainly correct when he suggests a causal connection between the form of Aristotle's *Problems* and the series of questions and answers with which Joyce concludes his *Paris Notebook* (*CW* 146).[30] That structural technique is imitated, with direct reference to the *Notebook's* entries, in the questions Stephen poses to himself in *Portrait:* "—I have a book at home, said Stephen, in which I have written down questions which are more amusing than yours were. In finding the answers to them I found the theory of esthetic which I am trying to explain. Here are some questions I set myself: '*Is a chair finely made tragic or comic? . . . Can excrement or a child or a louse be a work of art? if not, why not*'" (*P* 214).[31] It is obvious that the distinct pattern of problem presentation in Aristotle's treatise also had some impact on the catechetical structure of the "Ithaca" chapter of *Ulysses.*

Joyce's interest in Aristotelian psychology has previously been discussed as the foundation for a number of Stephen Dedalus's literary theories in *Ulysses*. Aubert has shown the influence of Aristotle's thought on the development of Joyce's earlier theories of art. Although the *Paris Notebook* contains a number of fundamental entries from *De Anima, Metaphysics,* and some minor scientific treatises, Joyce's main interest during this period was aesthetic theory. Thus, Aristotle's *Poetics* and *Rhetoric* are of great significance here. There is no reason to doubt that Joyce studied the complete translations of these works. At the same time, there is ample evidence that Joyce also consulted two well-known modern works on Aristotelian theories of art and poetry. The influence of Bosanquet and Butcher is pervasive in the *Notebooks* from Paris and Pola, *Stephen Hero,* and *Portrait.*[32]

The March 27, 1903, entry in the *Paris Notebook* begins with a transliterated flourish: *"e tekhne mimeitai ten physin—"* (*CW* 145). That brief Greek sentence is often taken as the fundamental synopsis of Aristotle's theory of art: "Art imitates nature." This statement, however, does not come directly from the *Poetics*. Rather, Joyce's conspicuous transliteration is an indication of where he came upon this citation: in the first interpretative essay ("Art and Nature") in Butcher's edition of and commentary on the *Poetics*. There Butcher cites the proposition in Greek and identifies its source (*Physics* 2.2194a21, McKeon 239; and *Meteorology* 4.3.381b6 [not in McKeon]). He also explains precisely how this proposition (originally applied in other contexts) can be brought to bear on fine art, which is distinctly mimetic in Aristotle's system.[33] Butcher observes that, for works of painting and sculpture, "their meaning is helped out by the symmetry, which in the arts of repose answers to rhythm, the chief vehicle of expression in the arts of movement."[34] That observation was the spark for the distinctions in Joyce's *Notebook* in the paragraph headed by the Greek citation from Aristotle.

The first and longest entry in the *Paris Notebook* discusses the feelings of desire and loathing, both of which urge people to do something. Joyce argues that pity and terror excited by tragedy do not excite loathing; nor does a proper work of comic art excite desire. Rather, comedy and tragedy excite the feeling of joy. Concerns of this sort were, of course, paramount in Aristotle's treatment of Greek tragedy. Butcher discusses the pleasure of dramatic performance in several of his essays. His chapter on "The Function of Tragedy" concludes: "The [Greek tragic] poets found out how the transport of human pity and human fear might, under the excitation of art, be dissolved in joy, and the pain escape in the purified tide of human sympathy."[35] Considerations of this type reappear, *mutatis mutandis*, in aesthetic portions of Joyce's fiction. In *Portrait*, for example, Stephen explains to Lynch that the emotion of drama is "static," whereas desire, urging one to possess, is "kinetic" (*P* 205; also see *P* 213). In *Ulysses* Bloom is consoled by the "candour, nudity, pose, tranquility . . . of a statue . . . , an image of Narcissus" (*U* 17.1427–28). Later in the same chapter Bloom contemplates "the necessity of repose, obviating movement . . . the statue of Narcissus, sound without echo, desired desire" (*U* 17.2031–34).

Nowhere in the primary *Notebook* paragraph cited does Joyce use the term that Aristotle employed to explain how pity and terror could be pleasurable emotions. Aristotle's famous definition of tragedy is: "through pity and fear effecting the proper *katharsis* of these emotions" (*Poetics* 6.2.1449b24–27; McKeon 1460). Exactly what Aristotle meant by *katharsis* (purgation, cleansing) has been the subject of endless debate. In the light of Butcher's essay on the topic, from which Joyce derived his basic points for the notebook entry, he has allowed Stephen Dedalus great latitude in asserting that "Aristotle has not defined pity and terror" (*P* 204).[36] Nonetheless, the opening couplet of "The Holy Office" is proof that Joyce understood at least the medical dimension of the crucial term: "Myself unto myself will give / This name: Katharsis-Purgative" (*CW* 149). After excoriating the members of Dublin's literary elite, Joyce specifies his contribution to the mission of the clique. He is their "sewer": "That they may dream their dreamy dreams / I carry off their filthy streams." That fundamental Aristotelian function is then repeated in less elegant terms:

> Thus I relieve their timid arses,
> Perform my office of Katharsis.
> My scarlet leaves them white as wool.
> Through me they purge a bellyful. (*CW* 151)

A *Ulysses* passage previously discussed also has an Aristotelian context. Stephen considers what might have happened if Pyrrhus or Caesar had not been killed. He then wonders, "But can those have been possible seeing that they never were? Or was that only possible which came to pass?" These two rhetorical questions are followed by two imperatives. Stephen completes his reverie with "Weave, weaver of the wind." As if he were reading Stephen's mind, one of the students pipes up, "—Tell us a story, sir" (*U* 2.51–54). This train of thought might be an echo of Aristotle's repeated advice that, in selecting his plot episodes, a "poet should prefer probable impossibilities to improbable possibilities" (*Poetics* 24.10.1460a27 and 25.1714b11; McKeon 1482, 1485–86). For a similar passage in the *Wake* the identity of its classical source is absolutely confirmed by Joyce, as he considers "where the possible was the improbable and the improbable the inevitable." To present "a sequentiality of improbable possibles," a fiction writer would have to brush up "his subject probably in Harrystotalies." That revelation is closely followed by approval for "his remark for utterly impossible as are all these events they are probably as like those which may have taken place as any others which never took person at all are ever likely to be. Ahahn!" (*FW* 110.11–21).

Another example of a critical application of Aristotle's *Poetics* involves an Irish writer who befriended Joyce during his Paris visits. In a March 9, 1903, letter to Stanislaus from the French capital, Joyce writes that John Milington Synge gave him the manuscript of a one-act play, "Riders to the Sea." He says that Yeats had told him "it was quite Greek." Joyce goes on to remark that Synge was not an Aristotelian (*Letters* II.35). A few days later Joyce writes to his mother that he criticized the play, and that Synge said he has "a mind like Spinoza" (*Letters* II.38). Years later in Zürich Joyce wrote the program notes for three plays produced in 1918 by the English Players. His brief remarks about Synge's "Riders to the Sea" end with this sentence: "Whether a brief tragedy be possible or not (a point on which Aristotle had some doubts) the ear and the heart mislead one gravely if this brief scene from 'poor Aran' be not the work of a tragic poet" (*CW* 250). In his definition of tragedy in the *Poetics* Aristotle specifies that the action must be "of a certain magnitude" (*Poetics* 6.2.1449b25; McKeon 1460). Butcher's essay on that definition emphasizes that the phrase refers to the actual length of the play, as is clear from Aristotle's subsequent discussion of this element: "the greater the length, the more beautiful will the piece be by reason of its size, provided that the whole be perspicuous" (*Poetics* 7.7.1451a10; McKeon 1463).[37] In short, Joyce used Aristotle to undercut his praise of Synge's play, a process that had begun fifteen years earlier in a garret in Paris.

Additional critical venom with an Aristotelian flavor is found in "The Holy Office" (1904), as Joyce warns his readers that he has assigned a patent of classical authority to his criticism:

> Bringing to tavern and to brothel
> The mind of witty Aristotle,
> Lest bad bards in the attempt should err
> Must here be my interpreter:
> Wherefore receive now from my lip
> Peripatetic scholarship. (*CW* 149–50)

That comic invocation of a whip-wit patron to lash his Dublin opponents—as well as the evidence of his study of the philosopher's works—testifies to Joyce's serious regard for Aristotle. It is quite odd, therefore, that there is at least one glaring misstatement of Aristotle's teaching in Joyce's early writings—and another dubious example of guilt by association in *Stephen Hero*.

In an essay composed during his first year at University College (1898–99), Joyce marshaled all sorts of valid reasons to recommend "The Study of Languages." One of his arguments is that "[t]he higher grades of language, style . . . poetry . . . rhetoric, are again the champions and exponents, in what way soever, of Truth" (*CW* 27). By way of an incidental refutation he almost immediately adds, "The notion of Aristotle and his school, that in a bad cause there can be true oratory, is utterly false" (*CW* 27). To assign that notion to Aristotle or to any of his disciples is equally and utterly false. In the introduction to his three-book treatise *Rhetoric,* Aristotle indeed grants, aphoristically, that "what makes a man a 'sophist' is not his rhetorical ability, but his moral purpose" (*Rhetoric* 1.1.1355b17; McKeon 1328). In the same prominent section he makes the following statement of purpose: "We must be able to employ persuasion, just as strict reasoning can be employed, on opposite sides of a question, not in order that we may *in practice employ it both ways (for we must not make people believe what is wrong)*, but in order that we may see clearly what the facts are, and that, if another man argues unfairly, we on our part may be able to confute him" (*Rhetoric* 1.1.1355a29–34; McKeon 1328; my emphasis).

In light of those disclaimers by Aristotle, the form (if not, technically speaking, the substance) of Joyce's accusation is disingenuous. Perhaps, however, Aristotelian logic is not the best means of pointing out Joyce's error here. What might be more effective is an appeal to historical precedent. On the night the young James Joyce read his famous paper, "Drama and Life," to the Literary and Historical Society of University College, the curfew on debate was ignored, "and Joyce kept on talking for at least thirty minutes. He dealt in masterly fashion with each of his critics in turn and to salvos of applause—even from the ranks of [his opponents]. When, at the end, Seamus Clandillion pounded him on the back and exclaimed: 'That was magnificent Joyce, but you are raving mad,' he probably voiced the opinion of many of those present."[38] Since Aristotle himself felt so strongly about the use of the rhetoric for false ends, we might pose a hypothetical question to Joyce: "Was he not obligated to stand and refute Seamus Clandillion on the night of January 20, 1900?"

A second misapplication of Aristotle involves method, not teaching. In *Stephen Hero* the hero and Cranly are engaged in one of their typically ad hoc Socratic dialogues. Cranly praises the scientific insight of Aristotle and points out that he was the founder of biology. Stephen counters that Aristotle is also "the special patron of those who proclaim the usefulness of a stationary march." He goes on to clarify his paradox: "Have you not noticed what a false and unreal sound abstract terms have on the lips of those ancients in college? . . . The toy life which the Jesuits permit those docile young men to live is what I call a stationary march. . . . And yet both these classes of puppets think that Aristotle has apologised for them before the eyes of the world. . . . Kindly remember the minute bylaws they [the Jesuits] have for estimating the exact amount of salvation in any good work—what an Aristotelian invention" (*SH* 186–187; my ellipses).

When one reads page after page of *De Anima* or *Metaphysics*—or the section on the respective functions of sperm as residue and sperm as coagulate in *On the Generation of Animals*—it is possible to sympathize with Stephen's outburst here. At the same time, logic and the scientific method espoused by Aristotle do not proceed in fitful leaps of intuition. His methods demand precise distinctions, which may appear to an ardently creative mind to be little more than intellectual marching in place. My intent is not to defend academic pedantry or Jesuitical logic-chopping, but Stephen should place the blame where it belongs. Neither Aristotle nor Plato is responsible for the abuse of his method by every small-minded marionette who claims to be his disciple. In the Library debate in *Ulysses*, Stephen Dedalus himself demonstrates that he is aware of that distinction.

Nonetheless, Aristotle's penchant for examining every aspect of a question, or for viewing each phenomenon of nature from every conceivable angle, cannot be denied. That is the perspective on the philosopher that Joyce chooses to emphasize in the only two direct allusions to him in *Finnegans Wake*. In "Night Lessons" the essay topic suggested by "*Aristotle*" is "A Place for Everything and Everything in its Place" (*FW* 306.L2 and 17–18). That tendency to categorize and distinguish, to anatomize and summarize everything from tragic poetry to the fetation of caraboid as opposed to cephalopod females,[39] cannot be ignored. Thus, the provident Ondt in the Wakean fable is described as "a conformed aceticist and aristotaller" (*FW* 417.16).

In Aristotelian logic and science, the concept of causality is of primary importance. To analyze and define an object or action, we must consider its causes. According to the philosopher's classical statement, the causes are four: the material, the formal, the efficient, and the final (*Physics* 194b16–195a3; McKeon 240–41). These causes can be exemplified by a practical case: In the production of a statue of Athena for the Parthenon, the bronze is the *material* cause; the shape and design of the statue is the *formal* cause; the sculptor is the *efficient* cause; the honor of the goddess (and the glory of Athens) is the *final* cause. Joyce displays his grasp of these essential distinctions and their universal application: "all up and down the whole concreation say, *efficient* first gets there *finally* every time, as a complex *matter* of sure *form*" (*FW* 581.28–30; my emphases). In "Night Lessons" there naturally occur some general technical terms from ancient Greek logic that may also have an Aristotelian source: "lemmas . . . akstiom . . . your apexojesus will be a point of order" (*FW* 296.1–11). A *lemma* is an assumed premise; an *axiom* is a self-evident proposition; *epexēgēsis* is a pointed explanation—like my application of Aristotelian causality to the production of a statue of Athena.

The essential definition of Aristotle's First Cause is the fact that it is an "unmoveable mover" (*Metaphysics* 12.8.1073a24–28; McKeon 881); another work discusses whether or not the Prime Principle might move itself and then stop its motion (*Physics* 8.5.258b4–9; McKeon 373). A Notebook entry in Greek—not in Joyce's handwriting—records "αυτοκινατον" (VI.B.20.56). This is a slightly misspelled form of the adjective *autokinēton* (self-moved). Variants of the word appear in three unrelated contexts in the *Wake*: "autokinotos" (*FW* 5.32), "autokinaton" (*FW* 235.27), and "autokinatinetically" (*FW* 614.30). Jaun is also reported to have been invigorated by "a power of kinantics in that buel of gruel" (*FW* 441.28). Here Joyce may be amusing himself with Aristotelian terms for the Prime Mover; more likely he allowed the Modern Greek word for automobile (*autokinēton*)—note the neo-Hellenic pronunciation at the start of "avtokinatown (*FW* 484.16)—some room to maneuver in his narrative.

During his thoroughly Aristotelian second visit to Paris, Joyce sent a series of book reviews and one interview back to Dublin for publication, primarily in the *Daily Express* (*CW* 90–108). Probably the most significant of these pieces was a dismissive evaluation of Lady Gregory's *Poets and Dreamers*. Joyce's six-paragraph review begins with a reference that reflects its author's current intellectual program: "Aristotle finds at the beginning of all speculation the feeling of wonder" (*CW* 103). Joyce uses this citation to make some snide comparisons between "wonder, a feeling proper to childhood" and "wisdom," a property of "the crowning period of life." In Lady Gregory's stories, he finds a confused view of Ireland's youth and its old age. Be that as it may, Joyce's initial citation comes from the opening section of the *Metaphysics,* in which Aristotle seeks to discover certain principles and causes, the knowledge of which constitutes wisdom. In his investigation of this process, Aristotle looks to the earliest Greek philosophers: "For it is owing to their wonder that men both now begin and at first began to philosophize. . . . And a man who is puzzled and wonders thinks himself ignorant (whence even the lover of myth is in a sense a lover of wisdom, for the myth is composed of wonders)" (*Metaphysics* 1.2.982b12–19; McKeon 692).

In *Scribbledehobble* Joyce noted that, whatever his ancient or modern reputation for omniscience might be, there were gaps in Aristotle's knowledge. Joyce's pertinent archival entry is composed in a manner that imitates a traditional Semitic formula found in Old Testament wisdom literature (compare Proverbs 30:15–31): "3 [things] Aristotle didn't know labour of bees, flow of tide, mind of women" (*Scribbledehobble* 99 [512]). Apart from those three areas, Joyce's Aristotle served him well, in both fact and fiction. When AE sniffed about the "speculation of schoolboys" (*U* 9.53) in the National Library, Joyce—and Stephen—missed a nice chance to remind the oracular Platonist of the following profoundly Aristotelian observation: "the beginning of all speculation [is] the feeling of wonder."

8

Minor Philosophers

In the histories of Western thought, philosophy (as a method of inquiry and a medium of discourse about ethics) begins with Socrates in the mid-fifth century. Before the advent of the "gadfly of Athens," however, there were thinkers—primarily from the Greek city-states in Asia Minor—who examined the nature (*physis*) of things. These Ionian "physicists" and their forerunners were mainly preoccupied with the origin and coherence of the universe. Their various theories usually attempted to identify some sort of prime matter or force. It is most likely that Joyce became acquainted with the pre-Socratics through general lectures, or a hand-book, on the history of philosophy. There is no indication that he studied their theories firsthand or in any depth; the same is true for several other ancient philosophers who are less well known than Plato and Aristotle.

Heraclitus

In a 1903 review of a book on the philosophy of Giordano Bruno, Joyce notes that "Coleridge should have set him down a dualist, a later Heraclitus" (*CW* 134). Heraclitus of Ephesus held that fire was the primary form of all matter. Thus, the universe is in a state of constant flux; only the *logos* (idea, thought, word) is stable. In the sensible world "everything flows" (*panta rhei*). Joyce composed a Latin version of this axiom in his Brunonian "Historiology" passage in the *Wake*: "*totum tute fluvii modo mund[um] fluere*" (the whole world flows serenely, like a river) (*FW* 287.25).[1] A distinct echo of the original Greek phrase can also be heard in "*Pantharhea*" (*FW* 513.22). Fritz Senn has pointed out a Joycean approximation of a second famous fluvial maxim by Heraclitus, "You never step into the same river twice."[2] Bloom wonders, "It's always flowing in a stream, never the same. . . . life is a stream" (*U* 8.93–95). That theme, of course, inundates *Finnegans Wake*.

Anaxagoras

Anaxagoras migrated from Ionia to Athens, where he became a teacher of the politician Pericles and the tragedian Euripides. He taught that intelligence (*nous*) was the formal cause, the shaper of all things in the universe. In the *Wake* he is linked with the famous mathematician Euclid, whose name has been slightly altered to make him sound like a modern atomic physicist: "Neuclidius and Inexagoras" (*FW* 155.32–33). That Joycean version of the philosopher's name may also allude to Anaxagoras's exile from Athens. When he was expelled from the city's main place of assembly and trade (the agora), he was literally driven *ex agoras*. At any rate, the *Wake* contains a topsy-turvy thematic allusion to *nous* (mind, intelligence): "(Nonsense! There was not very much windy Nous blowing at the given moment through the hat of Mr. Melancholy Slow!)" The very next sentence in the text is "But in the pragma what formal cause made a smile of *that* tothink (*FW* 56.31–32). In philosophical argument, the Greek noun *pragma* (matter, thing) is frequently opposed to *nous*; and even the wildest pre-Socratic could not have restrained a "smile" if something as concrete as *pragma* were proposed as a "formal cause"—to think of "*that*"!

Pythagoras

Pythagoras left the island of Samos for the Greek city of Croton in southern Italy. There he founded a brotherhood to study his philosophy and observe his ritual doctrine. His major scientific interests were mathematics and the extension of the consonance of the musical scale to the entire universe: Everything is number. For Joyce, however, Pythagoras's primary contribution was his teaching about the kinship of all living things through the transmigration of souls. Although the precise word is not found in the extant fragments of his works, *metempsychosis* is most definitely associated with Pythagoreanism. The term, along with its memorable facsimile "met him pike hoses," occurs ten times in *Ulysses*.[3] I suggest that it is possible to detect a veiled reference to the term *metempsy-chosis* in the pedantic phrase "the Pythagorean sesquipedalia of the panepistemion" (*FW* 116.30–31). As for the etymology of the two jaw-breakers in that phrase, the Latin adjective *sesquipedalis* (a foot and a half long) is applied by Horace to outrageously pompous verbal compounds (*Ars Poetica* 97). The Greek noun *panepistēmion* is composed of the ele-ments *pan-* (all, every), *epistēm-* (knowledge, understanding), and the suffix designating a place, or location. It is the equivalent of the English word *university,* which is composed of the Latin roots *uni-* (one) and *vers-* (turn); that is, a place where all branches of knowledge converge on a single goal, wisdom. And it is in just such a place that one most readily expects to hear long strings of polysyllabic jargon.

McHugh suggests that the alternative statement "woman formed mobile or man made static" (*FW* 309.21–22) is compounded from two elements in the Pythagorean table of oppositions: "male and female" and "rest and motion." A possible source for this Joycean blend of physics and sexism is the *Britannica* article on the philosopher (*EB* 22.699).

The well-known story of the loyalty of Damon and Phintias (frequently misspelled "Pythias") supplies a humanistic appendix to the primarily scientific and philological discussion of the philosopher-mathematician Pythagoras. The two young men were members of the Pythagorean community in southern Italy. On a trip to Syracuse, Phintias was arrested on trumped-up charges of spying and conspiracy, then condemned to death by Dionysius, the tyrant of the powerful Sicilian city-state. Damon offered himself as security for his comrade, who was given time to return home and settle his affairs. When Phintias's return was delayed, Diony-sius ordered the execution of Damon. Phintias arrived in the nick of time, but the loyal pair argued about which of them must pay the penalty. Dionysius was so impressed by their fearless devotion that he pardoned both and asked to be initiated into their Pythagorean brotherhood.[4] Joyce alludes to the willingness of each comrade to die in place of the other: "andens aller, athors err, our first *day man*" (*FW* 578.34; my emphasis). The italics identify Damon; the pair's mutual devotion is expressed in terms of Danish: *anden* (other) and *eller* (or). The phrase "andens aller" also alludes to Kierkegaard's famous treatise *Enten-Eller* (*Either/Or*), the title of which is repeated in phonetic English "athors err" (see *FW* 281.26–27).

Empedocles

In the search for prime matter, another pre-Socratic thinker, Empedocles, proposed Fire, Air, Earth, and Water, elements that were kept in
motion by Love and Strife. He also was famous for his medical expertise
and is cited as one of the authorities on conception in "Oxen of the
Sun"; there "Empedocles of Trinacria" is given as the authority for the
claim that males are born from eggs generated in the right-side ovary
(U 14.1232–33; also note UNBM 252:24). This theory and another para-
phrased at U 14.387–92 are actually found in Aristotle's On the Generation
of Animals. The attribution to Empedocles of the theory of origin of
monsters is accurate, but the statements on ovarian gender should be
assigned to Anaxagoras. In the latter citation, Joyce's use of the Latin
trinacria (three-cornered) as the name of Sicily is a clue that he might
have picked these bits of obstetrical speculation from a medieval or early
modern compendium of medical (mis)information.[5]

Zeno of Elea

Zeno was born in the early fifth century in a Greek city in southern Italy
already famous for its school of philosophy. Most probably to confute
radical Pythagorean doctrine, Zeno devised a number of paradoxes
designed to prove that motion and plurality were illusions. The best-
known two of these ingenious arguments are: First, swift-footed Achilles
can never overtake the hare, because by the time he reaches the point
from which the hare started, his slow but steady opponent will already
have moved to another point, and so on ad infinitum; second, since an
object is at rest when it occupies a space equal to its own dimensions, an
arrow in flight is at rest because, at any given moment in its flight, it occupies a space equal to its own dimensions. Aristotle quoted these paradoxes
of Zeno so as to refute them (Physics 239b14–32); Joyce alludes to them as
part of his zany encyclopedia of scientific information in "Night Lessons."
His exposition begins with "the zitas runnind hare and dart," and
concludes with "while the catched and dodged exarx seems himmul-
teemiously to beem (he wins her hend! he falls to tail!) the ersed ladest
mand and (uhu and uhud!) the losed farce on erroroots" (FW 285.3–13).
In my reading of this passage, the hare and the arrow dart from here to

there and the pursued moves from the starting line (*ex archēs*) so that its frustrated pursuer simultaneously arrives at the spot where it has just been. In this way, the first and the last assume their paradoxical positions—unless there is some radical error in Wakean logic. A clue to the source of that scenario of compressed action is found in "zitas," Joyce's casual spelling of the first Greek letter in Zeno's name, *zēta*.

Democritus

In the midst of a list of HCE's achievements are some highly suspect academic claims: "did I not festfix with mortarboard my unniversiries, wholly rational and gottalike sophister agen sorefister, life sizars all?" This mixture of sophists and scholarship students ("sizars" at Trinity College) includes "democriticos" (*FW* 551.28–31). The early Greek physicist-philosopher Democritus was a proponent of the theory that everything in the universe was composed of atoms. Atoms are tiny, indivisible bodies (*a-* is a Greek suffix for "not," "un-"; *tom* is the root of "to cut," "to split"), infinite in shape and number. As they fall at random through the void of space, they collide and combine to form every object in the universe. The combination takes place by chance; there is no divine wisdom directing the process, which is therefore completely explicable in rational terms. Roman writers often characterize Democritus as the "laughing philosopher," unable to restrain his amusement as he observes human folly. Heraclitus, on the other hand, is the "weeping philosopher," unable to hold back his tears at the same spectacle.[6] Perhaps Heraclitus's pathological despair over the absence of sustained rational behavior by his fellow humans is also part of the allusive play in a previously cited Wakean statement about the lack of "Nous blowing . . . through the hat of Mr Melancholy Slow" (*FW* 56.31–32).

As well as manipulating some of the pre-Socratic philosophers, Joyce also alludes to several later Greek thinkers.

Theophrastus

In the "Aeolus" chapter of *Ulysses*, the radical Hellenophile Professor MacHugh complains about the Latin language and culture that he is obligated to teach for a living. The Romans, he asserts, are "a race the acme of whose mentality is the maxim: time is money" (*U* 7.555–56). As a matter of literary and ethnic fact, that maxim is ascribed to Theophrastus, the prize pupil, and the successor as leader, of the Peripatetic school at Athens. The original version included in a list of aphorisms reported in a ancient "Life" of the philosopher: "He [Theophrastus] used to say that in one's budget the most expensive item is time."[7]

Theophrastus also appears fleetingly in the *Wake*. There Yawn/Shaun defends himself by asking his accusers, "Has not my master, Theophrastius Spheropneumaticus, written that the spirit is from the upper circle?" (*FW* 484.30–31). This question seems to me to be a rhetorical ploy, in which Yawn seeks to flummox the Four Old Men by pretending to be fantastically learned in classical metaphysics. His authority, "Theophrastius Spheropneumaticus," is spurious, and the proposition that the "spirit is from the upper circle" makes no sense, except as a literal translation of the two Greek roots in the pseudophilosopher's highfalutin cognomen: *sphair-* means sphere or circle; *pneumatikos* means windy or spiritual. I suggest that Yawn (and Joyce) are blowing etymological bubbles here, but why Joyce uses a variant of Theophrastus's name is not entirely clear. Thus I resort to a congenial method—one that has a hallowed ancient patent: conjecture based on the thinnest claim of bibliographical evidence. As Aubert notes, Bosanquet reports that, after taking the chair of Aristotle's school, Theophrastus exhibited "a positive and naturalistic tendency of reflection."[8] Among the prolific scientific output attributed to him by Diogenes Laertius (more than 465 books, totaling "in all 232,808 lines"), there is a treatise on windy spheres or inflated balls. (Upon reflection, it would perhaps be prudent to forget about an ancient source here and to allow Joyce his own creative moment of sesquipedalian puffery in dealing with Theophrastus.)

Antisthenes

Antisthenes was a pupil first of the sophist Gorgias, then of the avowed anti-Sophist Socrates. Eventually he attracted his own followers, who were called Cynics (from the Greek adjective *kynikos,* dog-like). They earned this odd name either because they first gathered in Athens at Cynosarges (white dog) gymnasium or because, in the opinion of the public, their philosophical positions were hostile and snappish. Antisthenes' teachings deprecated prior scientific and metaphysical speculations; the pursuit of virtue was all that mattered. Joyce alludes to both the metaphorical name of this school and its emphasis when he has Stephen berate Zoe in "Circe": "You would have preferred the fighting parson who founded the protestant error. But beware Antisthenes, the dog sage" (*U* 15.2641–42; also see *UNBM* 282:155). Earlier in *Ulysses* Professor MacHugh says, "—You remind me of Antisthenes. . . . It is said of him that none could tell if he were bitterer against others or against himself. . . . And he wrote a book in which he took away the palm of beauty from Argive Helen and handed it to poor Penelope" (*U* 7.1030–39; also see 7.621–32, 9.740, 10.816–17). Not a line of Antisthenes' work comparing Penelope and Helen survives, but this topic was a typical exercise in the debate among Greek rhetorician-philosophers in the late fifth and fourth centuries. There is a significant pre-*Ulysses* archival reference to Antisthenes (VIII.A.5.8), which comes from the compendium of classical mythology by Roscher that Joyce consulted in Zürich. That entry is a documentary source for Professor MacHugh's complaint about Helen's scorned beauty.

Diogenes

Judged by frequency of allusion, Joyce's favorite minor Greek philosopher is another Cynic, Diogenes. According to tradition, after an extravagant youth, he was converted by Antisthenes in Athens. To practice a life of extreme austerity, he lived in an overturned tub at the temple of the Mother of the Gods. When Alexander the Great visited Athens, he is said to have asked Diogenes if he could do anything for him; the Cynic replied, "Yes, you can stop blocking the sunshine." Another tale has Diogenes wandering the streets of Athens with a lantern, searching for an honest man. The latter anecdote supplied Joyce material for frequent allusion.

In "Circe" John Eglinton seems to have recanted his previous interest in literary matters. He is brought on stage: *"(produces a greencapped dark lantern and flashes it towards a corner: with carping accent)*. Esthetics and cosmetics are for the boudoir. I am out for truth. Plain truth for a plain man" (*U* 15.2257–59).

Variations on this scene are repeated several times in the *Wake*: "by the dodginess of his lentern" (*FW* 184.17); "and his washawash tubatubtub and his diagonoser's lampblick, to pure where they were hornest girls" (*FW* 290.21–22); "Your diogneses is anonest man's" (*FW* 411.28–29); "I be accentually called upon for a dieoguinnsis to pass my opinions" (*FW*

421.26). Another reference pivots around the components of the philosopher's name: *dio-* means "of Zeus"; *gen-* is the root of the verb "to give birth," "to be born." This is the reason for linking *"Diogenes"* to "Brother Jonathan" in "Night Lessons" (*FW* 307.L and 5), since the name Jonathan, in Hebrew, means "the Lord has given." An additional connection between the searching philosopher and Brother Jonathan might also be the fact that, as a nickname, it was applied by the British to earnest American colonials who, like Diogenes, sought honesty in their relations with the Crown. Among the other layers of allusion, Joyce connects personally with the Cynic philosopher. Ellmann reports that Joyce "told his friend Claud Sykes that, so long as he could write, he could live anywhere, in a tub, like Diogenes" (*JJII* 110). Years later, in 1931, during one of his frequent periods of searching for an ideal residence in Paris, Joyce wrote to Miss Weaver: "I am looking for a goodsized barrel in which to live, preferably a Guinness's one" (*Letters* I.300).

Epicurus

At the end of the fourth century B.C. (a generation after the death of Alexander the Great), Epicurus began to instruct the members of his philosophical community in Athens. Their meeting place was a garden; from this fact of location it would be easy to summarize Epicurus's ethical teachings as "the rosy path to pleasure." Such a characterization would be grossly unfair to the sophistication and the scientific and ethical interest of the school. The "physics" of Epicurus is simply the atomism of Democritus. It later served as the basis for Lucretius's Latin poem "On the Nature of the Universe" (*De rerum natura*). The basis of Epicurean ethics is its search for absolute freedom from pain and fear. This goal of perfect tranquillity is anything but the lush bower of hedonism that has become the caricature of the system. Joyce locates his only reference to Epicurus in an ambiguous context of luxuriant flowers: "spancelled down upon a blossomy bed, at one foule stetch, amongst the daffydowndillies, the flowers of narcosis . . . *epicures* waltzing with gardenfillers, puritan shoots" (*FW* 475.8–12; my emphasis). Allusions to Wordsworth ("a host of golden daffodils") and to the life of an early Christian ascetic (St. Paul the Hermit)[9] do not camouflage Joyce's awareness of the original location of Epicurus's philosophical community, in the "Garden."

In the descriptions of several of the various schools of ancient Greek philosophy, it is customary to use place names that were significant to the group. For example, Plato liked to meet with his disciples in a grove on the River Cephissius near Athens. This area, with its gardens and gymnasium, was known as the Academia; hence, Plato's followers are called the Academic philosophers. Aristotle's school is the Peripatetic because he and his students discussed important matters while walking around (*peripatein* in Greek) their meeting place, the Lyceum. Since Zeno taught his pupils at the Stoa (porch) in Athens, they are known as Stoics.

Zeno of Citium

I suggest that the "puritan shoots" (*FW* 475.8–12) cited two paragraphs ago are meant to represent the Stoics, who are regarded as the pleasure-shunning opposites of the Epicureans. The late-fourth-century thinker Zeno of Citium (a city on Cyprus) is traditionally regarded as the founder of the Stoic system at Athens. There is far more to this school of philosophy than the maxim *anechou kai apechou* (endure and renounce); at the same time, the pursuit of absolute wisdom and justice through a rigid adherence to duty is the hallmark of Stoic ethics. Joyce does not seem to have been personally attracted to this system as a guide to the good life. There is, however, hard evidence that he knew something about Stoic physics and metaphysics. The forming principles of all things are, according to this system, quite literally "pieces of god." These elements, separated from the whole and containing seeds of the divine fire, are *spermatikoi logoi* (seed-like thought-causes); the Latin equivalent is *seminales rationes*. In an early-1929 notebook Joyce jotted down the entry "logoi spermatikoi / ᵇrationes seminales"(VI.B.4.144). These two items were translated into the "Night Lessons" text of the *Wake* as a literal pair of "doubleviewed seeds" (*FW* 296.1). The Latin phrase is also conflated with a sailor's food, "semenal rations" (*FW* 296.4), whereas the Greek phrase is given an argumentative twist, "to be more sparematically logoical" (*FW* 296.25–26).

I do not know where Joyce picked up these technical terms, but a glance at the Notebook pages confirms the Greek philosophical context of these entries.[10] After a fairly long index of names and events in Gallo-Frankish history (VI.B.4.141–44), there follows a page and a half of terms from cross-cultural explanations of creation and generation.

Following the Stoic "logoi spermatikoi" come "ᵇdoubles / ᵇseed," "scarab / beetle" (VI.B.4.144); then "the holy ankh," "logos dharma," "Tao." The crossed "ᵇdot stigme" (VI.B.4.145) reappears in the text as "stickme punctum" (*FW* 296.3), a nice example of Joycean *figura etymologica*. Here Joyce's version of the Greek noun *stigmē* (point, period) is placed beside the Latin noun that means a small hole, a spot. Both words originate in the act of sticking a stylus into clay or making a tiny mark with a pen: punctuation. After these entries in the Notebook cluster comes the Greek "semeion" (sign, symbol), followed by "ᵇa/toms." Joyce's syllabic separation of the last term shows he is aware of its Greek components. The properties of atoms appear next in the Notebook list: "indivisible / unmanifest forms." Then comes "ᵇin Nun / (space)" (VI.B.4.145). Nun is the ancient Egyptian god of the watery abyss, the unformed "space" of chaos. Joyce inserted this Pharaonic divinity into his text just after the "doubleviewed seeds. Nun" (*FW* 296.1). The last item in this Notebook list is a marginal "Tiamat," the sea monster of Semitic and Phoenician mythology.

Whatever his immediate source of information, Joyce was obviously reading about ancient creation tales—Greek, Egyptian, Indian, Chinese, Semitic. Each of these systems of mythology or philosophy presents some story or explanation of how the world was originally generated and organized. The prime matter may have been a scarab beetle or a sea monster; the forming principle may have been materialistic atoms or Lao-tse's "Way" (*tao* in Mandarin). At any rate, from this diverse index Joyce selected a number of entries for inclusion in *Wake*. Pride of place must go, in my opinion, to Zeno's Stoic "seed-like reasons." Another item from the list shows up in a later, distinctly bicultural tale of creation: "We may come, touch and go, from atoms and ifs but we're presurely destined to be the odd's without ends" (*FW* 455.16–18). Here Adam and Eve from Genesis are linked with atoms randomly colliding in the void. Moreover, the reader is paradoxically reminded, by an echo from the catechism, that human beings were created by God and that their destiny, willy-nilly, is to live happily with Him for all eternity.

The foregoing excursus into a page and half of the *Wake* Notebooks demonstrates the importance of genetic evidence as a factor in the interpretative process. Before creating a critical universe or assigning a gratuitous formal cause, we must examine the prime material that the original Demiurge assembled.

Posidonius

The exclamation "Posidonius O'Fluctuary!" (*FW* 80.28–29) is most likely meant to apply to the Greek god of the sea, Poseidon, with an appropriate Hiberno-Roman patronymic, by which he becomes a "son of the waves." There was, however, a later Stoic philosopher named Posidonius. After study in Athens, he spent most of his career teaching at Rhodes, where he gained the reputation of the most learned man of his times. Although some of his innovations are interesting (notably the concept of the Divine Fiery Breath, emanating throughout the universe as its operative principle), Posidonius is mainly and marginally remembered—such are the fluctuations of fame—as one of Cicero's many philosophy tutors.

Archimedes

Archimedes of Syracuse in Sicily was a mathematician-engineer whose remarkable discoveries and inventions have earned him a place of honor in the history of science. He is probably best known for the shout that followed his solution of the problem of determining specific gravity. While entering a full bath he noticed water flowing over the edges, and observed that the volume of the displaced water would equal the volume of the object introduced into it. From that observation he deduced that certain weight-volume ratios could be calculated. These data could enable one to detect, for example, differences in the composition of a pure gold crown from that of a crown that had been hollowed out or merely plated. Even those who are not fully up to speed on the basic physics involved in that discovery remember Archimedes' shout, *Eurēka!* That word is the perfect tense of the Greek verb "to find," "to discover." The perfect tense is *not* a simple sign of past time. Rather it indicates that an action has taken place *and* that its impact is still being felt. The graphic example I use in elementary Greek classes utilizes the English verb "to die"; its parallel perfect form means not "I died," but "I *have* died—and *am* dead." Thus, Archimedes' shout announced a mid-third-century B.C. discovery that has abiding validity. Joyce testifies to that historico-linguistic fact in *Finnegans Wake:* "yoeureeke" (*FW* 230.1).

In *Ulysses* Buck Mulligan applies the word, characteristically in Greek, to an obscene situation. Stephen has concluded that "in the economy of heaven, foretold by Hamlet, there are no more marriages, glorified man, an androgynous angel, being a wife unto himself." Mulligan cries "*Eureka! Eureka!*" (*U* 9.1051–53). This shout announces the inspiration for a new play: "*Everyman His Own Wife / or / A Honeymoon in the Hand / (a national immorality in three orgasms) / by / Ballocky Mulligan*" / (*U* 9.1171–76).

Another claim by Archimedes in the field of physics was his assertion that, given another world to use as a fulcrum (and a long enough lever), he could move this world. That boast was made to King Hiero of Syracuse, who needed some wonder weapons to prevent a Roman fleet from capturing his city. Archimedes designed giant grappling cranes and all sorts of long- and short-range catapults.[11] He is also reported (but the tale is certainly apocryphal) to have constructed large mirror lasers to focus the light of the sun on the Roman sails and thereby cause them to burst into flame. Leopold Bloom recalls this feat when he speculates about a glass flashing on Howth: "That's how that wise man what's his name with the burning glass. Then the heather goes on fire. It can't be tourists' matches. What? Perhaps the sticks dry rub together in the wind and light. Or broken bottles in the furze act as a burning glass in the sun.[12] Archimedes. I have it! My memory's not so bad" (*U* 13.1137–42). In the previous citation Bloom's *eurēka* has been silently translated into English: "I have it." In the *Wake* the Greek verb is transposed into the name of an Icelandic explorer: "lief eurekason and his undishcovery of americle" (*FW* 326.30–31).

Joyce also re-creates Archimedes' boast about the fulcrum and the lever: "the archimade levirs of his *ekonome* world" (*FW* 230.34–35; my emphasis). The italicized word in that phrase seems to me to be a slightly off-kilter phonetic transliteration of two Greek roots, *oik-* (house, estate) and *nom-* (law, regulation). The literal meaning of *economy* is management of property. The term is sometimes extended to "human society as a whole." In that sense, Joyce's adjacent "ekenome world" can be seen as a pair of near synonyms. Another etymological link is *oikymenē,* which is transliterated in English as the basis of *ecumenical.* It is the standard Greek word for world.

This review of the impact of ancient philosophy on Joyce's work has moved from the pre-Socratic to the Hellenistic era. We leap ahead to the perpetuation of Greek thought and inquiry in the Roman world.

Epictetus

Among the most memorable episodes in the *Portrait* is the dialogue in the physics theater between the dean of University College and Stephen Dedalus. Stephen says that he works "at present by the light of one or two ideas of Aristotle and Aquinas"; he also says that if this source of light is not enough, "I shall sell it and buy another." The Jesuit replies: "—Epictetus also had a lamp, which was sold for a fancy price after his death. It was the lamp he wrote his philosophical dissertations by. You know Epictetus?" (*P* 187).

Epictetus was born in the Greek city of Hierapolis in Asia Minor; he lived as a slave in Rome, but was freed by his master. When the Emperor Domitian expelled all philosophers from the capital city, Epictetus went to Epirus and formed a school of disciples. After his death (about A.D. 120), his *Discourses* were compiled and published by his pupil Arrian. The teaching in them is primarily ethical and emphasizes the cheerful resignation of the human will to a transcendent divine providence.

Stephen replies to the dean's inquiry by stating that Epictetus was an "old gentleman . . . who said that the soul is very like a bucketful of water" (*P* 187). That coarse retort scarcely does justice to the Stoic's actual words: "The soul is something like a bowl of water, and the external impressions something like the ray of light that falls upon the water. Now when the water is disturbed, it looks as if the ray of light is disturbed too, but it is not disturbed" (*Discourses* 3.3.20–21).[13] The dean does not comment on Stephen's elision of the moral point of Epictetus's simile. At the same time Stephen has not permitted the "water" of his aesthetic soul to have become ruffled by the Jesuit's questions.

The dean's discourse is also undisturbed; he relates another anecdote about the philosopher. When an expensive iron lamp was stolen from the shrine of Epictetus's household gods, he replaced it with a clay lamp (*P* 187). This reflection comes from *Discourses* 1.18.15–16, where the topic is the provocation of others to crime: The just man ought not to be angry with those who act out of invincible ignorance of their moral flaws, since a true philosopher cannot be disturbed by any considerations that stand outside his own area of moral choice.[14] Again, neither the dean nor Stephen appears to be aware of the context or the ethical point of the anecdote.

I think it unlikely that Joyce intended his readers to wonder about the original intent of this pair of elided Stoic excerpts or to contemplate their "morals." Rather, the selections from Epictetus's *Discourses* serve another narrative purpose. They are designed to contribute to the psychological atmosphere of the text. The dean's example of the iron and earthen lamps is immediately followed by a paragraph in which Joyce takes the reader into his hero's mind: "The smell of molten tallow came up from the dean's candlebutts and fused itself into Stephen's consciousness with the jingle of the words, bucket and lamp and lamp and bucket. . . . Stephen's mind halted by instinct, checked by the strange tone and by the imagery and by the priest's face which seemed like an unlit lamp or a reflector hung in a false focus. What lay behind it or within it? A dull torpor of the soul or the dullness of the thundercloud, charged with intellection and capable of the gloom of God?" (*P* 187–88).

The interplay here between the occasion (kindling a fire in a physics classroom), the citations (about reflecting buckets of water and lamps), and the applications (two wills, two philosophical systems) is remarkable. Joyce's careful selection of imagery and diction leads, within a few paragraphs, to Stephen's concluding thought: "How different are the words *home, Christ, ale, master,* on his lips and on mine! . . . My soul frets in the shadow of his language" (*P* 189). The opposition of language and culture also has a nationalistic dimension. A bit later in the narrative, a student asks a stupid question about exam material in a science class. "The voice, the accent, the mind of the questioner offended him. . . ." Again Stephen reflects: "—That thought is not mine. . . . It came from the comic Irishman in the bench behind. Patience. . . . Patience. Remember Epictetus" (*P* 194). It is clear that Stephen is at home with neither the dean's English nor his classmate's Irish intonation. The Stoic philosopher cited as a guide counseled forbearance, yet he was expelled from home by the emperor. Stephen Dedalus practiced silence and cunning, then chose exile from a domestic culture that had become alien to him.

Marcus Aurelius

Marcus Aurelius was not only the emperor of Rome (A.D. 161–180) but also the author of a respected philosophical work, the *Meditations.* This highly ethical and relentlessly Stoical treatise was composed in Greek. The sole Joycean reference to the emperor-philosopher occurs in "Night Lessons": "*Marcus Aurelius*" is linked in the text to "What Morals, if any, can be drawn from Diarmuid and Grania" (*FW* 306.L3 and 27–28). The connection between a pair of lovers in early Irish saga and Marcus Aurelius lies in the report of his unflinching reconciliation with his wife, Faustina, who, according to a contemporary source, had betrayed both the imperial throne and the imperial bed. Finn MacCool also pardoned treasonous young lovers, one of whom was his wife. In selecting this Roman-Hibernian theme for an essay topic in the *Wake*, Joyce indicates his regard for the emperor's forgiveness of marital infidelity as the acme of Roman Stoicism.[15]

Joyce's work makes use of varied material from minor Greek philosophers, from Heraclitus's world in flux to Marcus Aurelius's humane *Mediations*. There are, especially in *Finnegans Wake*, some surprising allusions to matters as diverse as Anaxagoras's *nous*, Archimedes' inventive experiments, and Epictetus's expensive iron lamp. Although he was the most mathematical of the pre-Socratic philosophers, Pythagoras's major appearance in *Ulysses* is as an exponent of the transmigration of souls. One additional allusion serves to circumscribe the two primary areas of Joyce's literary use of ancient philosophy. Whereas Leopold Bloom is interested in both physical and metaphysical matters (hence his concern about "jawbreakers about phenomenon and science and this phenomenon and the other phenomenon" [*U* 12.466–67]), Stephen Dedalus's concern is ethics and aesthetics. Near the end of *Portrait*, Lynch disputes Stephen's claim that art must not excite desire: "one day I wrote my name in pencil on the backside of the Venus of Praxiteles in the Museum. Was that not desire?" (*P* 205). Several pages later Stephen refutes his irreverent friend: "How about the true [as well as the beautiful]? It produces also a stasis of the mind. You would not write your name in pencil across the hypothenuse of a right-angled triangle?" (*P* 207–8). Surely not; and it is probably a good thing that neither Shem nor Shaun considers that desecration of the hallowed locus of the Pythagorean theorem during their geometry exercise in the *Wake*.[16]

9

Tragedy

"It may be a vulgarism, but it is literal truth to say that Greek drama is played out. . . . Its revival is not of dramatic but of pedagogic significance" (*CW* 39). That iconoclastic judgment was pronounced by James Joyce in the first paragraph of his paper "Drama and Life," delivered to the Literary and Historical Society of University College, Dublin, in 1900. The same dismissive tone is found in most of his subsequent comment on the tragic theater of ancient Greece. We might wonder what access to the literature of the world's stage the eighteen-year-old student had. The popular verse translations of Greek plays by Gilbert Murray did not begin to appear until 1902; the English versions of the tragedies that were available earlier were usually in stilted, almost verbatim form, designed to help students struggling with the original texts.[1] The hero of *Stephen Hero* suggests, however, that his creator had been able to consult some sort of comparative material on Greek tragedy: During Stephen Daedalus's reading of Ibsen, he found that the only examples of "anticipations less distinct and attempts less successful" were "translations of the Hindu or Greek or Chinese theatres" (*SH* 40).

From the start, then, it is necessary to stress a biographical element in Joyce's reception of Aeschylus, Sophocles, and Euripides. His command of Latin and, even as a Dublin-bound student, of French and Italian was impressive, but he could not read a Sophoclean choral ode. Direct access to the original text is especially significant in the case of Attic drama. In Joyce's fiction there are references to this gap in his language training. Early in *Ulysses* Buck Mulligan unctuously rubs Stephen Dedalus's face in "*epi oinopa ponton*" and "*Thalatta!*" (*U* 1.78–80). Mulligan's model is Oliver St. John Gogarty. In life—as in the novel—there was rivalry between the two students, and Gogarty's flaunting of his Greek was part of the abrasion.[2] A parochial stand-in for Gogarty/Mulligan appears in *Stephen Hero* in an episode directly concerned with Greek tragedy. Stephen Daedalus has been informed that the college's president is reviewing his paper on Ibsen, submitted to be read before the Debating Society. "Whalen, the College orator came up to them. This suavely rotund young man . . . regarded Stephen now with mild envious horror and he forgot all his baggage from Attica:—Your essay is tabu, Daedalus" (*SH* 89). Whalen is wrong; Stephen does deliver his essay. But after the presentation, the college orator rises to comment: "It was with some diffidence that he ventured to criticise but it was evident that Mr. Daedalus did not understand the beauty of the Attic theatre. He pointed out that Eschylus was an imperishable name and he predicted that the drama of the Greeks would outlive many civilizations" (*SH* 101).[3]

The figure of the "suavely rotund" Whalen anticipates that of "[s]tately plump" Mulligan. Moreover, each is a literary Hellenosnob. In neither *Portrait* nor *Ulysses*, however, is there an episode featuring a debate between Mulligan and Stephen on ancient tragedy. That scene had already been played in *Stephen Hero*, with Stephen and Father President as the protagonists. The Jesuit speaks first: "—So far as I can remember . . . you treated Greek drama—the classical temper—very summarily indeed, with a kind of juvenile . . . impudence, shall I say?" The student replies: "—But the Greek drama is heroic, monstruous. Eschylus is not a classical writer" (*SH* 96–97). Presumably, Stephen's further arguments (see chapter 10, on Aristophanes) convinced the president to permit the paper to be delivered. After his fellow pupil's oratorical and critical triumph before the Debating Society, Whalen was not loath to fling his few barbs of Attic envy, as described. In Joyce's later versions of Stephen's academic career, this scene is discarded, and readers of *Ulysses* are denied the hypothetical privilege of hearing Mulligan's discourse on, say, the utter sublimity of the *anagnōrisis* of Xuthus in Euripides' *Ion*. Nonetheless, Mulligan's real-life model, Dr. Oliver Gogarty, would certainly have appreciated Joyce's epigrammatic dismissal of the entire enterprise: "Hellenism—European appendicitis."[4]

Another factor in Joyce's refusal to bow before the ancient dramatists is their hallowed status among the contemporary literary establishment. There are no overt references to Greek tragedy in the *Hamlet*-debate in *Ulysses*, but Stephen's primary opponents were the Dublin devotees of Attic tragedians. With the following couplets Joyce skewers George Russell (AE) and his ilk in the 1904 broadside, *The Holy Office*:

> But I must not accounted be
> One of that mumming company
>
> . . . .
>
> Or him who once when snug abed
> Saw Jesus Christ without his head
> And tried so hard to win for us
> The long-lost works of Eschylus. (*CW* 150–51)

Joyce's doggerel deflation of AE seems fully justified with respect to his classicizing pose. One of Russell's biographers reports that his mature subject had "forgotten most of the little Latin and Greek he had once known."[5] That probably did not stop him from making grand pronouncements about the drama of ancient Greece. Years later a barbed echo of Joyce's distaste for the topic and its affected enthusiasts is recorded in the *Wake*. A "*greak esthate*" appears, "*explaining aposteriorly*" what one needs to know about "all the quirasses and all the qwehrmin in the tragedoes of those antiants their grandoper" (*FW* 343.17–23).

The educational and social patent of Greek, along with Gogarty/ Mulligan's Olympian linguistic air and Joyce's stated preference for "Ibsen's New Drama" (*CW* 47), all contributed to the dismissal of Greek tragedy in his early essays and autobiographical fiction. For these reasons, presumably, the classical plays are a topic of very little serious concern even in the later works. Another relevant factor is basically aesthetic in nature. During the period when Joyce was a student in Dublin, the literary quality of the contemporary translations of Greek drama would have to be rated as very low. The task of producing English versions was a challenge: All the tragedies are written in verse, of differing meters and in two dialects; reference to the background of the complex mythological plots is often highly cryptic; the texts do not include stage directions, and even the character assignment of lines is sometimes ambiguous. There are also strict formal restrictions: No more than three speaking characters appear on stage at the same time; the plot action takes place in a single day; significant parts of the drama are designed to be sung and danced by a chorus; the Greek actors wore masks and conventional costumes.[6] Joyce was aware of these potentially alienating elements: "In speaking of Greek drama it must be borne in mind that its rise dominated its form. The conditions of the Attic stage suggested a syllabus of greenroom [actors' lounge] proprieties and cautions to authors, which in after ages were foolishly set up as the canons of dramatic art, in all lands" (*CW* 39). These idiosyncratic features—of language, structure, and production—are implicit and explicit in the text of every ancient drama. In any attempt at a translation of all such elements into another language—not to mention into another theatrical tradition—the obstacles to engagement are obvious and extensive.

The enormous popularity in North American universities of classics-in-translation courses, especially those featuring the Greek tragedies, may obscure the fact that such accessibility was not always the case. Comprehensible, gripping, producible versions of ancient drama have been available for two generations at the most. The Penguin Classics series and the University of Chicago *Complete Greek Tragedies* are the products of the postwar era. Before that time there were, of course, occasional translations that passed literary and dramatic muster, but these were the exceptions. The English prose versions of Sophocles' tragedies by Richard Jebb are almost parodically stiff. Gilbert Murray's acclaimed versions of Euripides (written at roughly the same time that Joyce was working on *Dubliners* and *Portrait*) were deliberately romanticized. In many places, especially in the choral passages, the English is a lush paraphrase of the original Greek. Murray's memorable collocation of "the Apple-tree, the signing and the gold" in the second choral ode of *Hippolytus* is a case in point. That line and the entire stanza in which it is embedded not merely distort the Greek; they also transform Euripides into Swinburne.[7] Before and after Murray, many of the English translations of an ancient tragedy or comedy read (thanks to pedantic intent or poetic incompetence) like grammar-vocabulary props for an unimaginative beginner in a gerund-grinding language class. That quality, perhaps designed to convince the readers that mastery of an inflected language was the only portal into the precincts of Hellas, did not attract large audiences. Nor were sophisticated readers likely to regard these academic exercises as having any place in world literature. Stephen MacKenna, the brilliant translator of Plotinus, summarized what must have been a common reaction to these versions of Greek tragedies: "the Verrall-Jebb pseudo-grand days-of-yore-ish sham."[8]

One of the offshoots of these contorted translations—a byproduct that Joyce surely admired—was parody. Among the best is the 1883 "Fragment of a Greek Tragedy," by A. E. Housman, himself a distinguished poet and classicist. The following excerpts are from the beginning and the end of his hilarious "version":

> CHORUS: O suitably-attired-in-leather-boots
> Head of a traveler, wherefore seeking whom
> Whence by what way how purposed art thou come
> To this well-nightingaled vicinity?
> My object in inquiring is to know.
>
> . . . .
>
> ERI: O, I am smitten with a hatchet's jaw;
> And that in deed and not in word alone.
> CHORUS: I thought I heard a sound within the house
> Unlike the voice of one that jumps for joy.
> ERI: He splits my skull, not in a friendly way,
> Once more: he purposes to kill me dead.
> CHORUS: I would not be reputed rash, but yet
> I doubt if all be gay within this house.
> ERI: O! O! Another stroke! That makes the third.
> He stabs me to the heart against my wish.
> CHORUS: If that be so, thy state of health is poor;
> But think arithmetic is quite correct.[9]

Support for my claim that Joyce was quick to mock the formal conventions of Greek tragedy is found in his reflection that one learns from Aeschylus's *Choephori* that "in ancient Greece brothers and sisters took the same size in boots" (*SH* 193). The point of that comment is mockery of the Greek poet's embarrassing example of a "recognition device" that is used to indicate to Electra that her brother, Orestes, has returned to avenge the death of their father, Agamemnon. Earlier in the same tragedy, a lock of Orestes' hair was discovered—with the same dramatic purpose—at the tomb of the murdered king. (Chapter 10 discusses Aristophanes' comic send-up of these dramatic conventions.) I am confident of the parodic intent of Joyce's double allusion to a popular song and to Aeschylus's strand of fraternal hair in "the kerl he left behind him" (*FW* 234.7–8).

In October of 1903 Joyce wrote a review for a Dublin newspaper of Arnold F. Graves's *Clytaemnestra: A Tragedy.* The evaluation dismisses in three sharp paragraphs this verse adaptation of the familiar "revenge-for-Agamemnon" theme. Joyce shows little respect for this "literary curio" or for the Trinity professor of classics, Robert Yelverton Tyrrell, who supplied an introduction. After lambasting the play's moralizing slant, structure, and diction, the review concludes with an irreverent citation from Graves's work, a speech by the seer Tiresias:

Beware!   Beware!
The stone you started rolling down the hill
Will crush you if you do not change your course. (CW 127)

Not long after Joyce wrote that review, Ireland's premier poet decided to try his hand at translating Sophocles' *Oedipus the King*. William Butler Yeats asked Gilbert Murray for a literal version of the Greek text. The Oxford professor declined the honor. Yeats then asked Oliver St. John Gogarty, who accepted. Almost three decades after the start of this cooperative project, Yeats revealed his procedure in a newspaper note: "I found a young Greek scholar [Gogarty], who, unlike myself, had not forgotten his Greek . . . [and] bought Jebb's translations and a translation published at a few pence for dishonest schoolboys. Whenever I could not understand the precise thoughts behind this translator's half Latin, half Victorian dignity, I got a bald translation from my Greek scholar."[10]

Since Yeats's *King Oedipus* was not performed until 1927, it is unlikely that Joyce (then hard at work on *Finnegans Wake*) bothered to read the highly lyricized text of this translation. On the other hand, one can hardly imagine Gogarty's failing to mention, with self-aggrandizing mockery, his involvement in Yeats's project at its very inception in Dublin. In fact, a casual sentence in a letter from Gogarty to an Oxford friend makes that "bald translation" sound a bit grander: "I am preparing a trans. (verse) of 'Oedipus Rex' for Yeats!"[11] Reports of the poetic-pedantic collaboration would not have impressed Joyce, especially since Yeats promoted his Sophoclean project with a dig at Latin poetry: "Greek literature, like old Irish literature, was founded upon belief, not like Latin literature upon documents. No man has ever prayed to or dreaded one of Virgil's nymphs, but when Oedipus at Colonus went into the Wood of the Furies he felt some of the creeping of the flesh that an Irish countryman feels in certain haunted woods in Galway and Sligo."[12] That characteristic slur on Roman literature from the Anglo-Irish literary establishment would have infuriated Joyce, who might justly have inquired, "Just what Vergilian nymphs, old boy?" The Greco-Gaelic prejudice and preference behind Yeats's statement do much, in my judgment, to explain Joyce's dismissal of ancient tragedy. Early evidence for this stance is articulated by Stephen Daedalus: "a great contempt devoured him for the critics who considered 'Greek' and 'classical' interchangeable terms" (*SH* 33).

On the other hand, it is clear from his critical comments that Joyce was familiar with many of the technical terms employed in criticism of Greek tragedy and with *the* classic commentary on Greek tragedy, Aristotle's *Poetics*. (Chapter 7, on Aristotle, discusses Joyce's creative use of the text and tenets of the *Poetics*.) The following is a brief property list of Wakean distortions of some traditional elements of the ancient theater.

The standard etymological explanation of the noun *tragedy* is that it is a compound of the nouns for he-goat (*tragos*) and song (*ōdē*). That odd combination of words is variously annotated as originating in the award of a goat as the prize in early dramatic competitions or in the goat costumes that members of the chorus wore in primitive productions. Joyce himself is unsure of the origins of the term and the genre: "What then agentlike brought about that *tragoady* thundersday this municipal sin business?" (*FW* 5.13–14; my emphasis). The Wakean performance referred to in that citation involves a protagonist who is "a *hegoak*, poursuivant, horrid, horned . . . Mister Finn, [who is] going to be Mister Finnagain" (*FW* 5.7–11; my emphasis). Perhaps Joyce is also implying that the plot action of his book will be like some archaic ritual in which a Year-god is slain to ensure fertility, and then rises again. Indeed, the theory of a seasonal festival associated with Dionysus is frequently mentioned as the origin of drama.[13]

Whatever their rustic genesis, the works of the fifth-century Athenian playwrights Aeschylus, Sophocles, and Euripides were most definitely staged at public expense during the Greater Dionysia, the city's annual spring festival. I detect an allusion to that civic occasion in the quoted phrase "municipal sin business" (*FW* 5.14). That is, as well as dealing with the matter of sins involving the city—twelve Athenian citizens to judge whether Orestes is guilty of matricide in *Eumenides,* the king's unwitting pollution of Thebes in *Oedipus the King,* Dionysus's punishment of the same city for refusing to acknowledge his divinity in *Bacchae*—the tragedies were also staged on a religious holiday, when all mundane affairs of the *polis* were suspended—"sin [Spanish for "without"] business." Another phrase is proof of Joyce's knowledge that wealthy Athenian citizens were "taxed" by being required to pay the expenses of producing a tragedy. The general technical term for such civic obligations was *leitourgia;* when the expenses involved the presentation of a tragedy at the festival, the duty was a *choragic* (leading/providing for a chorus) liturgy. Versions of both of these terms appear at the top of the same page of the *Wake:* "lethurgies" (*FW* 334.1) and "choractoristic" (*FW* 334.7), the second neatly combining the chorus and an actor.[14]

No discussion of tragic terminology can omit mention of *harmatia*. That Greek word, well known to all students of ancient drama, comes from the *Poetics.* The hero in tragedy is brought down "by some *error or frailty*"; in a well-constructed plot the reversal of fortune should come not from vice but "from some great *error or frailty*" (Aristotle 1453a3–4). The original Greek for the italicized words in the two key passages is *harmatia*, often translated as tragic flaw. That term has generated more heated discussion than any other word (except, perhaps, *katharsis*) in Aristotle's treatise and in the history of the criticism of dramatic literature. Butcher's classic commentary on the *Poetics* devotes almost twenty pages to various interpretations.[15] My focus is on the etymology of the term. It comes from the Greek verb *hamartanō*, the root meaning of which is "to miss the mark" in shooting an arrow or throwing a missile; other metaphorical meanings extend from that concrete base.[16] In the Septuagint and in Christian Greek, *hamartia* is most often translated as sin, as, for example the "great sins" of Sodom and Gomorrah (Genesis 18:20) or the "many sins" forgiven the woman who anointed Jesus' feet (Luke 8:47–48). I suggest that Joyce was aware of the wide range of possible translations of this Aristotelian critical term from the *Poetics:* a "miss," error, flaw, guilt, sin. When he applied the word to his own Wakean version of an ancient Greek drama, his Dublin Catholic background prevailed; thus, he opted for the most morally burdened choice: "that tragoady . . . this municipal sin business" (*FW* 5.13–14).

Joyce's command of the technical vocabulary of the classical stage extends to two items involved in the actual production of a play. In Greek tragedy the actors wore a thick-soled, high-laced boot, the *kothornos;* in English this sort of shoe is called a buskin. (Comic actors wore low, thin-soled shoes, called *socci* in Latin [socks in English]. Both Greek and English terms for tragic footwear are displayed as part of "Jaunty Jaun's" outfit in the *Wake:* "the first *cothurminous* leg of his nightstride" (*FW* 429.1–3) and "a bullock's hoof in his *buskin*" (*FW* 429.16–17; my emphases).

In the light of Joyce's overridingly negative critical statements about the enduring values of Greek tragedy, it is no surprise that there are in his correspondence or fiction very few direct references to Aeschylus, Sophocles, Euripides, or their works. Indirect allusions are also sparse. In an

August 7, 1924, letter, Stanislaus Joyce reminds his brother that he (Stanislaus) had pointed out "the resemblance between the 'Bacchanals' [*sic*] of Euripides and Ibsen's 'Ghosts'" (*Letters* III.104). This reference is made in a paragraph in which Stanislaus discusses some of the ramifications of the interplay between the imagination and the sexual instinct in "Circe." Joyce's Trieste library contains an Italian translation of Euripides' *Bacchae;* there are some late-1952 notes in it, in Stanislaus's handwriting, on that play's central character, the god Dionysus. But there is no archival or allusive evidence pointing to a Euripidean influence on *Ulysses.*[17] The only possible Wakean reference to works of the last of the Greek tragedians is a muted "bacchante" (*FW* 247.35) that appears as the second element in an alphabetical list of nicknames for Issy's pretty maids, all in a row.

Stuart Gilbert includes an apparently offhand remark about Euripides in his discussion of the "Hades" episode of *Ulysses.* The caretaker of Glasnevin Cemetery is the well-known Dublin character, "John O'Connell. . . . He never forgets a friend" (*U* 6.710). Gilbert comments that all the mourners at Dignam's funeral "are sure to have a good word for the caretaker—an echo of the Euripidean eulogy of Hades and such euphemisms as the designation of the *Eumenides.*"[18] The second point is right on the mark: The Greeks traditionally called the *Erynines* (the Furies, chthonic hags who avenged family blood) the "Kindly Ones" (*Eumenides).* The origin of this euphemism—and the conversion of the horrific goddesses into the guardians of family solidarity—is dramatically enacted at the end of the final play in Aeschylus's *Oresteia* trilogy. I am not, however, aware of any similar "eulogy" (literally, a good word) for Hades. Nowhere in Euripides' nineteen surviving plays and the fragments of numerous others does an appropriately ingratiating term occur. Gilbert's offhand display of philological finesse seems unfounded here.

For the annual productions of ancient Greek drama at the festival of Dionysus, each of the competing poets submitted a bloc of four plays. In addition to the three tragedies, there was a "satyr" play, so called because its chorus was always a troupe of these hairy, randy companions of the god. In a satyr play some aspect of theme or mythological source of the trilogy was presented in parodic form. The only complete example of the genre that has survived is Euripides' *Cyclops.* Its plot follows the rough outline of Homer's tale of the encounter between Odysseus and the Cyclops Polyphemus, with the distinctive addition of a wily Silenus and his shipwrecked crew of satyrs. The crude humor of the dramatic burlesque of this epic episode centers on the drunkenness caused by the potent skin of wine that Odysseus brings to the island of the Cyclops, where Dionysus's comrades have also been trapped in the monster's clutches.

In a little-known article H. D. Rankin pointed out twenty-two "similarities and parallels" between Euripides's *Cyclops* and Joyce's "Cyclops" chapter in *Ulysses*.[19] Even a cursory examination of the evidence cited reveals that Rankin's outlandishly phrased claim of "'isotropic' eruptions of similarity" cannot be sustained. None of his examples points exclusively to the text or the plot of the satyr play. All of the thematic parallels can far better be explained as prompted by Homeric—as well as Vergilian and Ovidian—monsters.[20] Finally, in the more than seven hundred lines of the "Cyclops" notesheets (*UNBM* 81–129) there is nothing that even hints that Joyce may have looked at the Greek text or an English translation of Euripides' 709-line *Cyclops*. Thus, as much as he may have hypothetically enjoyed this satyric reprise of Homer's famous episode, there are absolutely no grounds for the suggestion that Joyce knew or used that ancient Greek play. Indeed, in the Citizen's pub in *Ulysses* the drinking is quite restrained, and there is only a faint echo of the cannibalism that is the staple of Euripides' satyr play.[21]

Sophocles is twisted into "Suffoclose!" in "The Ballad of Persee O'Reilly," and the three adjacent masters of world literature are "Shikespower! Sendodanto! Anonymoses!" (*FW* 47.19).[22] The protagonist of Sophocles' most famous play is brought briefly onstage several times in the *Wake:* "an eatupus complex" (*FW* 128.36), "greedypus beautibus" (*FW* 445.23), "adipose rex" (*FW* 499.16), "*Oropos Roxy*" (*FW* 513.21). There are two references to the incident of infant mutilation that gave Oedipus (Swollen Foot) his ominous name. In the first, "Yet how lamely hobbles the hoy of his then pseudojocax axplanation" (*FW* 63.30–31), Oedipus's wretched mother-wife, Jocasta, also puts in an appearance. In another allusion the tragic hero is instructed to "Put your swell foot foremost (*FW* 434.19). In "Night Lessons," "*Edipus*" is keyed to the topic "If Standing Stones Could Speak" (*FW* 306.L and 22–23). The suggested essay would presumably deal with the Sphinx and her enigmas.

The detailed notesheets that Joyce assembled during the composition of *Ulysses* contain a minor reference to Sophocles. A five-item index dealing with the dance concludes with the following entry: "Soph. 16 nude, oiled lyre dance pean Apollo's altar" (*UNBM* 287:45). The reference is to the traditional report that the adolescent Sophocles was chosen to lead a chorus of Athenian youths in the city's celebration of the decisive Greek defeat of Xerxes' Persian fleet at Salamis in 480 B.C. The "pean" (*paean*) is a battle victory song dedicated to Apollo. The detailed specificity in Joyce's note indicates some sort of documentary source. *Smith's Smaller Classical Dictionary* (a copy of which was in Joyce's Trieste library) reports that Sophocles "was chosen to lead, naked, and with lyre in hand, the chorus which danced about the trophy, and sang the songs of triumph."[23] That description is quite close to the compact catalog of details in the note. Nevertheless, the absence of the term *paean* and a specific reference to Apollo in the *Dictionary* report prevent me from naming that work as the *direct* source of Joyce's information about Sophocles' first public appearance as an artist. The fact that the notesheet entry is found in a more general dance index also suggests another, less specifically classical source. Finally, the notesheet was made for possible inclusion in "Circe." That potential placement may explain Joyce's attention to the fact that the young dramatist was not only "nude," but also "oiled," another detail not included in Smith's *Dictionary*. Thus, the search for a source remains open. At the same time, Joyce's use of this note in *Ulysses* is clear: the only "naked . . . oiled" character in the text is Leopold Bloom, reclining in the bath, with his bar of lemon soap (*U* 5.567–68).

After the pair of scornful citations in *Stephen Hero,* the venerable tragedian Aeschylus does not appear in any of Joyce's critical work or fiction. There is, however, an uncrossed archival note in the Bérard material that was assembled for *Ulysses:* "Eschylus—slaughter of Persians at Salamine" (VIII.A.5.13). Aeschylus wrote the *Persians,* the only surviving Greek play with a historical (not mythological) plot. It deals with the return of the Persian King Xerxes to Susa and his reception at the royal court after the disastrous defeat of his fleet by the Athenians at the Battle of Salamis. There are no allusions to this play or any other by Aeschylus in *Ulysses*. Another unused *Wake* note, "green cloth carpet for tragedy" (VI.B. 28.143), is an Irish variation on the carpet that Clytemnestra unrolled with a flourish, ostensibly to welcome Agamemnon home from Troy. In Aeschylus's play, however, the fatal color of that carpet is royal—or better, blood—red (*Agamemnon* 910).[24]

Apart from that archival curiosity, Aeschylus is also conspicuous by his absence from the *Wake*. *Prometheus Bound* may be an exception. It is the only surviving play from a trilogy by Aeschylus that dealt with the enmity between the Titan and Zeus, the third-dynasty king of Olympus. In that tragedy Prometheus is bound to a crag in the Caucasus Mountains. Several visitors come to him there, one (the gadfly-maddened Io) to seek his advice, the others (notably the lackey-god Hermes) to urge him to cease his opposition to Zeus. Prometheus refuses to compromise, and Zeus sends an eagle to tear at his opponent's perpetually renewed liver. Eventually—but not in the surviving play—the two gods settle their differences in a way that will guarantee the Thunderer's eternal reign and Prometheus's freedom.

That, in bare outline, is the plot of the Aeschylean drama and its lost sequel. These events, however, are common to the traditional mythological tales of the birth and maturity of the Greek gods, in which Prometheus plays an important role. There is only one element (the eagles) in Joyce's treatment of Prometheus in the *Wake* that specifically binds these allusions to the text of the tragedy. Nonetheless, there follows here a review of other possible references, because Aeschylus's play is certainly the most dramatic and well-known version of the divine conflict.

The primary mythological feat of Prometheus, a first-dynasty Titan, is his gift of fire to mortals. The light and heat brought into the world by this benefice are symbolic of a great leap forward in human development and technology; there is a concomitant intellectual dimension to these advances: The god's name means Forethought. His nature and its benefits are explained in the margin of "Night Lessons": "*Prometheus or the Promise of Provision*" (*FW* 297.L2). The adjacent text specifies the expansively luminous and practical nature of the gift that Prometheus provides: "And light your mech" (*FW* 297.16–17); the Greek *mechanē* means resource, device. An archival note (from the same Notebook as the "green carpet" entry) confirms this interpretation—and points out the "hindsight" of his similarly named brother: "Prometheus forethought / Epimetheus after—" (VI.B.28.127). Two other Wakean phrases capture the etymological essence of Prometheus's function and name, "devine previdence" (*FW* 62.7–8) and "Devine's Previdence" (*FW* 325.1–2). However, since neither excerpt occurs in a context that hints of Greek mythology, I prudently assign the phrases to an indistinct echo of a classical name and a Christian term: divine providence is God's informed, but nonobtrusive supervision of the universe and its inhabitants.

The Titan reacts to Zeus's punishment by refusing to reveal his foreknowledge of the means by which the Thunderer can be knocked from his heavenly throne. Finally, an accommodation is reached between the intransigent gods, and Prometheus is unbound in exchange for the name of the potential deposer. The exchange of freedom for the secret seems to be alluded to in the following passage: "and by four hands of *forethought* the first babe of *reconcilement* is laid in its last cradle. . . . Give it over! And no more of it!" (*FW* 80.16–18; my emphases and ellipsis). This interpretation is strengthened by the nearby presence of the "Allhighest," "his nuptial eagles sharpened their beaks of prey" (*FW* 80.20–21; also note VI.B.1.103), and "Jove bolt" (*FW* 80.28).[25] At the end of Aeschylus's *Prometheus Bound,* Hermes reveals that Zeus will send his Olympian eagle to tear at the chained god's liver. The totemic predator will repeat his torture every day until the secret of the fated successor is disclosed. The divine reconciliation eventually takes place, and Prometheus's chains are removed. Joyce briefly alludes to that celestial concord in "Promiscuous Omebound" (*FW* 560.1).

The details of the restoration of Olympian civility and mutual understanding are also spelled out (in several languages) in the following passage: "the promethean partonnerwetter which first (Pray go! pray go!) taught love's lightning the way (pity show) to, well, conduct itself (mercy, good shot! only please don't mention it!)" (*FW* 585.11–14). The two belligerent gods are named in the opening of this passage. Prometheus is present in an adjectival form that marks him as a lightning rod (*paratonnere* in French) to attract the wrath of the divine king. Zeus is a stubbornly Teutonic god of Thunder (*Donderwetter* in German). Each then learns to say "Please" in Italian (*Prego*). In this way the Lord of Lightning recognizes that he must show some pity, say "You're welcome" (*bitte schön* in German), and conduct himself well. Thanks are also expressed in French (*merci*) by the unbound Prometheus. Finally the pair reassure each other that neither needs to mention the other's renunciation of immortal enmity.

This review of possible Joycean references to tragic drama mentions several times that some of the examples may come from other documentary sources than the texts of the plays. This caution is underscored by the first of the Wakean allusions to Oedipus: "an eatupus complex" (*FW* 128.36). There can be no doubt of a Freudian context for this phrase. As a matter of archival fact, a precise psychoanalytic source can be cited. Notebook VI.B.19, compiled in June–November 1925, has several clusters of entries taken from Freud's detailed "Case Histories."[26] One of the entries, "A Phobia in a Five-Year-Old Boy [Little Hans]," contains the following comment by the "Professor [Freud]": "Things were moving towards a satisfactory conclusion. The little Oedipus had found a happier solution than that prescribed by destiny. Instead of putting his father out of the way, he had granted him the same happiness that he desired himself: he made him a grandfather and let him too marry his own mother."[27] In his Notebook comment on this passage Joyce converts Freud's summary into "[makes ⊓ nonno" (VI.B.19.37). When the character-sigla are converted into names, that note means that Shem ([) makes HCE (⊓) a grandfather (*nonno* in Italian).

On top of the next Notebook page, two "tragic" names appear, one after the other: "Oedipus / Prometheus" (VI.B.19.38). The reference to the doomed king of Thebes was certainly prompted by Freud's comment on Little Hans. On the very next page of the "Analysis," there is a footnote in which Freud comments on the pregnant links that the word *borer* (the translation of a German term for screwdriver) has with both *born* and *birth*. Freud chooses not to make a definitive statement on the possibility of "a deep and universal connection between the two ideas . . . [in] German [and English]." Nevertheless, the Viennese doctor is quick to add a final sentence to the note: "Prometheus (Pramantha), the creator of man is also etymologically 'the borer'."[28] Setting aside psychoanalytic and etymological considerations, there can be no doubt about Freud's text as the immediate—and modern—source of Joyce's archival juxtaposition of Oedipus and Prometheus. That fact, and the growing importance of archival research, must be kept in mind when considering a possible impact of Greek tragedy on the imagination (and the Notebooks) of Joyce.

In summary, Aeschylus, Sophocles, and Euripides do not play major roles in Joyce's work. I suggest several plausible reasons for the paucity of allusion: Joyce's inability to read the original texts, in the face of Gogarty's advertised competence; his interest in the "New" dramas of Ibsen; the poor quality of English translations of ancient plays, many versions of which read like unintentional parodies. In some of Joyce's early essays and in *Stephen Hero* there are occasional references to ancient drama, but nothing that displays any real insight beyond a typical flash of humor. As for the later works of fiction, the virtual absence of the tragedians prompts me to suggest that, if he had ever stretched his imagination to consider using material from Aeschylus, Sophocles, or Euripides, Joyce may well have thought again—and then repeated, sotto voce, the following parodic prayer by Housman's CHORUS:

> Never may Cypris for her seat select
> My dappled liver!
> Why should I mention Io? Why indeed?
> I have no notion why.

10

Aristophanes

The eleven surviving Greek comedies of Aristophanes have long been noted for their zany plots, stretched language, thwacking insults, rampant scatology, and exuberant obscenity. In other words, just the sort of ostentatiously "classical source" from which James Joyce might have appropriated technical, verbal, and thematic elements for parts of *Ulysses* and all of *Finnegans Wake*. There is, however, no explicit mention of the Athenian poet in any of the works, and relatively few covertly Aristophanic references have been detected. This chapter presents a number of significant new examples of the roles that the ancient Greek comedies play in various phases of Joyce's fiction. It also offers some insights into how, when, and why his allusive imagination seized upon this flamboyant material and worked it into the design of the *Wake*.

Joyce could not read the original texts of Aristophanes' comedies, but with the aid of a dictionary and a commentary, he would have been able to isolate specific phrases and to analyze their lexical or rhetorical components. He may occasionally have done so, but the evidence suggests that most of the references to Aristophanes were derived from translations or plot summaries of the comedies.[1] A number of instances of parodic humor from *The Clouds* illustrate how he uses comic details that are not dependent on the Greek text itself.

The Clouds

A debt-ridden Athenian in *The Clouds* seeks to enroll in Socrates' "think tank" to get a degree in newfangled methods of argumentation that will enable him to flummox his creditors. On an admissions visit to the institution, the nontraditional student (the father of a compulsive gambler who haunts the racetrack) is taken on a tour of the research facilities. There he is told about a project of Socrates to determine whether a gnat's buzzing is caused by wind expelled through its trachea and mouth or through its intestines and anus. By means of a convoluted argument Socrates proves that the flatulent gnat "has a bugle up its ass" (*Clouds* 156–65).[2] In the *Wake* Joyce includes this bit of pseudoscientific hot air in his catalog of HCE's suspicious activities: "he being personally unpreoccupied to the extent of a flea's gizzard anent eructation" (*FW* 558.4–5). There is archival evidence to support the claim for direct allusion. In one of the Notebooks the following pair of nearby entries appears: "[b]flea's gizzard" and "louse or fleahop" (VI.B.4.248–49). The first phrase was transferred into the text of the *Wake*.[3] The second, uncrossed phrase also seems to have been lifted from the same episode of Aristophanes' *The Clouds*. Another scientific problem vexing the researchers in the think tank is "the number of fleafeet a flea could hop, skip, and jump." Socrates provides an ingenious protocol to unlock the mystery. He first obtains precise measurement of a "fleafoot" by encasing the insect's pedal appendage in wax. When the mold hardens and is removed, calipers reveal the exact length of the new standard (*Clouds* 144–52).

Although the second archival phrase cited above ("louse or fleahop") was not incorporated into the text of the *Wake,* an immediately adjacent Notebook entry does appear in the completed work. This item serves as a minor illustration of Joyce's re-creative mind in action. The entry is "[b]performing fleas / waltz they try to / escape from bar" (VI.B.4.249). It does not seem worthwhile to me to speculate about whether this dramatic anecdote is rooted in Joyce's experience at some seedy saloon in Nighttown or whether it is, perhaps, his reflection on ballet exercises at a "barre." What is more to the point here is the note taker's leap from a classical literary allusion to an amusing contemporary vignette about the liberation of some musical parasites. It seems fairly obvious to me that the one phrase triggered the other. Later, when Joyce returned to this Notebook, his imagination locked on to the unlikely performance—and ignored its Aristophanic genesis. The entry reappears in the *Wake* in two forms, neither of which has any connection with ancient comedy: "the foxtrotting fleas" (*FW* 180.18–19) and "when he walts meet the bangd. I will put his fleas of wood in the flour" (*FW* 320.10–11).

Joyce was definitely interested in another group of cloud-nine researchers who labor in Socrates' comic institution of higher learning.

They are crouched over a hole in the earth, plumbing deep geological secrets. When the prospective student inquires why their rear ends are pointed at the sky, he is informed that they are "minoring in astronomy" (*Clouds* 193–194). In another highly Latinate section of the *Wake,* Joyce allows Shaun to defend his own ground-breaking scientific curiosity; he works "under astrolabe from my upservatory" (*FW* 551.25). The suggestion of a direct allusion to *The Clouds* is reinforced by adjacent references to contemporary university scholarship, where one can hear the debates of "sophister agen sorefister" (*FW* 551.29). In *The Clouds* there is a bitter academic debate between Philosophy (or True Logic) and Sophistry. In Aristophanes' state-of-the-art polytechnic, the slick word twister humiliates his traditional rival. In Joyce's dream-fiction, allusion is as strange and as powerful as illusion.

I detect the direct borrowing of another brief episode from the same comedy. The scientific research at Socrates' institution has demonstrated that the gods of Greek mythology are figments of benighted imagination. The atmospheric activity of the clouds, for example, provides a natural explanation for Zeus's thunder and lightning. The prospective student is flabbergasted to hear a purely meteorological rationale for rain. Before this enlightenment, he admits, he thought the rains came when "Zeus pissed through a sieve" (*Clouds* 373). The Olympian god-king, rain, and the utensil reappear in the exclamation, "holey bucket, dinned he raign!" (*FW* 312.11–12). The entire bit of rigorous deduction is then condensed into a single compound noun, "peecieve" (*FW* 609.30). The context for that term is a discussion by *Muta* and *Juva* about the existence and power of the patriarch HCE, their fuming, thundering lord and master. The barbarian boy's cyclic solution to the question of traditional authority is expressed "[b]y the light of the bright reason which daysends to us from the high" (*FW* 610.28–29). The suggestion of classical source here is reinforced by the etymology of Zeus/Jupiter. The ultimate root for both names is the Indo-European *deiw,* "to shine." Thus, in his emphatically patriarchal forms, the supreme Olympian, *Zeus pater* or *Juppiter,* is literally "bright or day-sending father." The rationale of the argument in this section of the *Wake* is not unlike that which prevails in *The Clouds.* Hence, in Joycean terms Juva's coinage "peecieve" signals both a rejection of theocratic dogmatism and a perception of the primacy of muddled reason. Juva is not the first Joycean character to think along those lines. In *Ulysses* Leopold Bloom is presented as persistently interested in scientific phenomena. When a drop of rain falls on his hat on the way to Paddy Dignam's funeral, he observes "an instant of shower spray dots over the grey flags. Apart. Curious. Like through a colander" (*U* 6.129–31).

Lysistrata

Harry Burrell amply demonstrates the Wakean presence of another comedy of Aristophanes. Again the allusions come from a domestic source, Aubrey Beardsley's illustrations for *The Lysistrata of Aristophanes, Now First Wholly Translated into English.* In the *Wake* that work is clearly indicated in "It his ambullished with expurgative plates . . . Mr Aubeyron Birdslay" (*FW* 356.30–357.3).[4] It also seems likely that several adjacent phrases allude both to the fairly straightforward sexual theme of *Lysistrata* and—even in their expurgated form—the outrageously suggestive details of the illustrations. In Joyce's text, HCE comments on his reaction to the pictures: "as I have just been seeing, with my warmest venerections" (*FW* 356.33). Prominent female buttocks are a feature of both Aristophanes' verse and Beardsley's drawings. Burrell reasonably suggests references to this steatopygous fixation in "that preposterous blank seat" (*FW* 356.35) and "assasserted" (*FW* 357.31).

Grotesquely distended phalli are the subject of wordplay throughout the text of *Lysistrata.* (This element of plot and costume is also graphically emphasized in Beardsley's unexpurgated illustrations, which Joyce could not have seen.)[5] For example, when the young Athenian soldier returns from the front lines and wishes to make love to his wife, he announces his presence: "Oh! Oh! How this erection strains and convulses me! How I am being tortured on the rack." A messenger from the enemy camp reports that a similar condition affects the Spartans: "We are in misery!"[6] Joyce naturally takes note of the references to and puns on these painfully prolonged erections, caused by the women's Panhellenic sex strike: "a dard of pene" (*FW* 357.9–10). McHugh's glosses on this phrase are directly to the point: "*Per*[*sian*] dard: pain [;] *Sl*[*ang*] dard: penis[;] *It*[*alian*] pene: penis."

At the conclusion of his brief discussion of the parallels between the *Wake* and Beardsley's *Lysistrata,* Burrell also suggests that "[t]here are many additional correspondences" and that he suspects "most of the play is submerged in pages [*FW*] 363–66."[7] After combing that section of the text for possible allusions, I have been able to come up with only a couple of phrases that might plausibly correspond to the play's plot or themes. Early in *Lysistrata* the heroine's female forces occupy the Acropolis and repel an attempt by a troop of Athenian gaffers to drive them from the citadel. As they begin the battle, the female chorus invokes the aid of Athena, whose temple, the Parthenon, their sisters have seized. One of Beardsley's illustrations, "Lysistrata Defending the Acropolis," shows her second-in-command emptying a chamber pot onto the male Commissioner, with the city's citadel in the background. I suggest the entire siege scene is compactly re-created by Joyce in brief phrases. First, "inherdoff trisspass" (*FW* 363.26) expresses male outrage at the ineffable boldness of the women's takeover of the city's most sacred precincts; next, "I could have emptied a pan of backslop" (*FW* 363.29) neatly catches the warrior-woman in the act of dousing the Commissioner's martial ardor; finally, in "for the love of goddess and perthanow" (*FW* 366.12), I hear an appeal to the virgin (*parthenos*) goddess Athena and a reference to her temple (the Parthenon) on the Acropolis. It must be stressed that the immediate inspiration for Joyce's byplay here was Beardsley's illustration, since the Greek text is lacking the equivalent word for either Parthenon or chamber pot. The Acropolis and its sacred precinct are mentioned in prior scenes of the play. The filled pot, however, is the artist's reaction to the translator's imaginative expansion of another prop that is specified in the original. When Lysistrata dismisses the Commissioner at the end of their *agōn*, she says, "Take this garland [for your funeral]." The English version that Beardsley illustrated slightly adjusts the wording ("Take this as a coronal") and adds a stage direction "(*Throws water on him*)."[8]

The force of another cryptic—but clearly obscene—Joycean allusion requires more extensive comment. In his debate with Lysistrata, the Commissioner admits that he and his fellow citizens have asked for trouble by pampering their women. He gives an example of a hypothetical husband's oversolicitous concern for his wife's domestic pleasure: "Goldsmith, the pin of the necklace which you worked for my wife slipped out of the hole while she was dancing last night. . . . [I]f you have any time, by all means call about nightfall and fit the pin in."[9] Joyce condenses this Aristophanic vignette into two phrases: "our findest *grobsmid* among all their *orefices*" (*FW* 357.1; my emphases). The German word for goldsmith is *Goldschmied; grob* is a German adjective meaning crude, coarse, gross. The *Wake*'s "grobsmid" combines both terms, perhaps to specify a lewd precious-metals craftsman who is amenable to a request for a house call.

There he will rather grossly work a pin into a hole. The locus of that doubly intended service is probably the primary reason for "orefices," which sounds and looks quite a bit like the English word *orifices*. At the same time, *orefice* is the Italian word for goldsmith. The emphatic repetition of that key term from the original passage in *Lysistrata* cannot be mere coincidence.

All of the allusions from *Lysistrata* are used by Joyce in an episode in which the *Wake's* hero, HCE, defends himself, once again, against imputations of disgraceful misconduct. Since most of these allegations are sexual, the Aristophanic material is a gold mine. The "textual" source for this sort of thematically appropriate borrowing is not merely an English translation of the comedy, but also—and more significantly—the illustrations to that edition.

The Birds

The presence of a number of allusions to Aristophanes' *The Birds* in the *Wake* has been pointed out by Philip Graham.[10] In that comedy two politically and socially disgruntled Athenians seek to establish an entrepreneur's utopia, Cloudcuckooland, "by localoption in the birds' lodging" (*FW* 449.17–18). The aider and abettor of their scheme is a former human turned into a bird, the Hoopoe. As the chorus of the play assembles, the Hoopoe identifies the species and characteristics of each bird. Joyce introduces his avian swarm in fifteen lines of text that feature "warblers' walls . . . throstles and cloughs . . . the drummling of snipers . . . whippoor willy in the woody . . . crekking jugs," and so forth (*FW* 449.19–32). Another concentration of fabulous birds appears earlier in the *Wake:* "gnarlybird . . . bleakbardfields . . . pigeons . . . crows . . . peacefugle a parody's bird, a peri potmother . . . peewee . . . a flick . . . huemerambows" (*FW* 10.32–11.12; my ellipses).[11] Hidden within this avian cluster are rough approximations of several titles of Aristophanes' plays: "nubo" (*FW* 11.5)—*The Clouds* (*nube* in Italian); "peace-" and "pacts'" (*FW* 11.9, 12)—*Peace* (*pax* in Latin); "bird" (*FW* 11.9). In the next paragraph there are "knights" (*FW* 12.4) and "brekkers" (*FW* 12.14)—*The Frogs.* (See later section for further discussion of disguised references to titles.)

The close combination of comic characters and titles strengthens the case for the detection of several more subtle allusions to *The Birds* in the *Wake.* In his note on the primary passage, Graham points out that the presence of "Saint Jamas Hanway . . . lapidated" (*FW* 449.14–15) is meant to recall the occasion when stones were thrown at Jonas Hanway, the first male to dare to unfurl an umbrella on the streets of London.[12] The pseudohagiographical epithet "lapidated" (*lapis* is Latin for stone) links him with early Christian martyrs who were stoned to death for their unconventional beliefs. Graham also suggests a covert reference to *The Birds*. As Cloudcuckooland becomes established in the sky, the gods in the high heavens are furious that the new realm threatens to cut off their divine intercourse with earthlings. Prometheus, who has always supported human advancement, appears in the birds' camp and offers to betray the gods. He holds an umbrella (*skiadeion*) over his head so that his fellow divinities cannot witness his treachery (*Birds* 1509).

Shortly after that episode, the immortals send a three-god delegation, under a safe conduct, to negotiate with the birds. Heracles, whose appetite is as extensive as his laborious journeys, seeks to stay behind in Cloudcuckooland and enjoy a barbecue that has been prepared to tempt him to defect. When Poseidon urges him to return to Olympus, Heracles indicates that "he is willing to remain behind to supervise the roast meat" (*Clouds* 1689–90). Graham (correctly, in my judgment) suggests that this scene is echoed in the *Wake*: "but I'd turn back as lief as not if I could only spoonfind . . . my lady of Lyons, to guide me by gastronomy under her safe conduct. That's more in my line. I'd ask no kinder of fates than to stay where I am, with my tinny of brownie's tea" (*FW* 449.9–13).

Graham makes two other, equally cogent suggestions that involve the presence of real or fictional Irish politicians among the flock of Aristophanic civic adventurers on the same page of the *Wake*. Sir Boyle Roche (1743–1807) was an Irish M.P. noted for his "bulls." He is reported to have uttered the following excuse in the House: "Mr. Speaker, it is impossible I could have been in two places at once, unless I was a bird."[13] Joyce places "Peter Roche" (*FW* 449.16) in the company of the other bird-men in the passage. "Roche" might be Wakese for "roc" or "rook"; but there can be little doubt that there is also an intended allusion to the "bullish" Roche here, since the M.P. is described as "at this passing moment *by local*op*tion* in the birds' lodging" (*FW* 449.17–18). My emphases in the previous citation are designed to call attention to the Latinate noun "bilocation," which occurs almost exclusively in the miraculous lives of the saints. The preternatural ability to be in two places at once would therefore be regarded as a sign of sanctity.

A second local politician who may be covertly perched in this passage is John Hooper of Dublin. His name sounds something like the brashest entrepreneur in *The Birds,* the "Hoopoe." Moreover, in *Ulysses* the afore-mentioned alderman gave the Blooms a "matrimonial gift" of "an embalmed owl," which "stood on the mantlepiece" at 9 Eccles Street, next to another wedding present, "a timepiece of striated Connemara marble" (*U* 17.1335–39). In the *Wake* these objets d'art are commemo-rated as "that owledclock . . . has just gone to twoohoo the hour" (*FW* 449.24–25).

Even though he appears in a context that is only tangentially avian and Aristophanic, I suggest that Joyce worked into the *Wake* the third member of the gods' ambassadorial team from *The Birds.* At the beginning of II.3, HCE is introduced in terms that make him appear monstrous. One of his ogre-like characteristics is his "tribalbalbutience" (*FW* 309.2). One way of interpreting that polysyllabic term is to hear it (with McHugh) as an abstract noun from the Latin participle *balbutiens* (the stammering person), with a stammered repetition of *bal-* and an emphatic prefix *tri-* (three, triple). There is another possibility. Along with Poseidon and Hera-cles, the Olympians send a third delegate to negotiate with the leaders of Cloudcuckooland. He is Triballus, a god who is a completely uncouth barbarian (*barbarotatōn* [*Birds* 1573]). He can barely mutter a few words of gibberish-Greek (*Birds* 1572, 1615, 1628–29, 1678–79). In contrast to the graceful and melodious birds of the new utopian settlement, Triballus must appear to be the quintessential babbling ogre. That perspective is hinted at in the *Wake,* "from a bride's eye stammpunct" (*FW* 309.4).

Play Titles

As pointed out previously, commentators starting with Graham have noted a second cluster of covert titles of Aristophanes' plays in close prox-imity to one another. This wordplay also occurs in an ornithological context, which increases the likelihood of allusion: "birds'" (*The Birds*) (*FW* 449.17); "dwealth" (*Wealth* [*Ploutos* in Greek]) (*FW* 449.18); "night" (*The Knights*) (*FW* 449.22); "peacefed" (*Peace*) (*FW* 449.32); "grenouls" (*The Frogs*) (*FW* 449.34); "cloudscrums" (*The Clouds*) (*FW* 449.36).[14] It would be rash to argue against these identifications, but there may be more: What about the titles of the other five Aristophanic comedies, some of which are equally well known? If the net of allusions is extended for four lines, onto the next page of the *Wake,* I believe a case can be made for the nearly adjacent presence of several more titles.

The Great Idea of *The Assemblywomen* (*Ecclesiazusae*) involves a group of Athenian women who take over the city's legislative assembly. They vote that supreme political power should be placed in their hands and then throw a giant party celebrating the new regime. To avoid detection in their foray into the legislative arena, the women must first disguise them- selves by putting on their husbands' outfits. The two most emphatically visible of these props are the men's too-large shoes and the women's false beards. I see these items of feminist stagecraft in Joyce's text in the protest "my otther shoes, my beavery, honest!" (*FW* 450.3). Borrowed footwear and fake facial hair ("beaver" is 1920s' slang for "beard")[15] are combined here with a pair of fur-bearing amphibious mammals, an otter and a beaver.

In *The Women at the Festival* (*Thesmophoriazusae*) the tragedian Euripides learns that the Athenian matrons are planning to pillory him for antifem- inist activity at their annual "ladies' day" religious celebration. Euripides sends his kinsman, disguised as a woman, to the feast to defend his artis- tic reputation. This ploy fails, and the unmasked kinsman is about to be sacrificed. At the last moment, as in more than one of Euripides' own melodramas, he is rescued by the conniving poet himself, who also appears in drag. Joyce, I suggest, converted all of this pseudoritualistic slapstick into "a dace feast of grannom" (*FW* 450.4). In that phrase the first three elements sound like "a day's feast," which is the occasion for the comic action in the play. The last element suggests a group of older women, "grannies," or, in colloquial and obsolete English, "grannams."

Perhaps the most thoroughly camouflaged title is Joyce's idiosyncratic re-creation of plot and a central ploy of *Lysistrata.* In Greek, the chief char- acter's name literally means Disbander (*lysi-*) of the Army (*-strata*)." The Wakean phrase "melt my belt" (*FW* 450.3–4), then, can be interpreted in at least two ways: first, "cause my pugilistic clout to dissolve"; second, "loosen the sash of my robe." Lysistrata and her militantly pacific Athen- ian sisters mount a plot to refuse to engage in sex until peace is declared on every front. Their representative, Myrrhine, repeatedly outflanks her horny husband and his stratagems to undo the sash of her gown.[16] Hence, Joyce's brief phrase can be read as an encapsulation of both the theme of Aristophanes' comedy and one of its most theatrical episodes.

In a 1931 addition to an early post-*Ulysses* notebook, Joyce jotted the following entry: "Frogs vespers" (*Scribbledehobble* 145 [762]).[17] Separately, those two nouns could be the titles of two comedies by Aristophanes, *The Frogs* and *The Wasps*. In scholarly reference works, the latter play is designated as *Vespae*, Latin for wasps. The Notebook item reappears in the *Wake* changed to "Dogs' vespers" (*FW* 276.11). That faint allusion would not usually have prompted a search for other Aristophanic titles in the adjacent text. Yet, the presence of "Becchus" (*FW* 276.13) two lines below the putative titles caused me to pause. Dionysus/Bacchus is the patron-deity of the Greek theater; he plays a major role in *The Frogs*. My subsequent search through the same paragraph of the text flushed out four other fairly obvious allusive titles: "birds" (*FW* 276.19); "peace" (*FW* 276.27); "feaster's" (*FW* 277.5); "enclouded" (*FW* 277.15–16). Another reference to some Latinized (and diminutively homonymic) *Knights* may also be intended in "noctules" (*FW* 276.23). That makes a total of seven relatively plausible—or at least not outlandishly nebulous—titles on fewer than two pages of text. The archival note strengthens the force of the interpretive conjecture here. (If any of the four remaining titles is present in this paragraph, it has escaped the multilingual nets with which I have beaten the area on numerous hunts for allusions.) In short, Aristophanic titles were regarded by Joyce as fair game for a thrice-repeated inclusion in his own robustly comic universe.

The Frogs

It would be difficult to miss the initial—and the most obvious—borrowing of Aristophanic material by Joyce in the *Wake*. At the top of the second page of that work is an adaptation of the signature lines of the croaking chorus in Aristophanes' *Frogs:* "Brékkek Kékkek Kékkek Kékkek! Kóax Kóax Kóax" (*FW* 4.2). In a late 1926 Notebook Joyce jotted down a three-line entry to remind himself of the chant: "ᵒBrek Kek Kek . . . Oloo Quauoauh!" (VI.B.15.164). One commentator suggests that the emphatic trochaic rhythm of this onomatopoeic phrase imitates "the thrust-withdrawal of coital movements."[18] I see no reason for a sexual reference here; rather, the context is that of the celestial archetype for all tribal or national armed clashes—a war between the immortals, specified as "oystrygods gaggin fishygods!" The conflicts are then brought down to earth "the Baddalaries partisans . . . the Verdons catapelting the camibalistics out of the Whoyteboyce" (*FW* 4.1–5). Here Joyce neatly moves Aristophanes' chant out of the Underworld into the upper regions, where humans settle their differences in the light of day. In *The Frogs* the primary battle is a contest for the world's heavyweight championship in the composition of tragedy. That is why the patron-god of Greek drama, Dionysus, journeys into Hades—and across its frog-filled perimeter swamps[19]—to conduct a literary duel between Aeschylus and the recently deceased Euripides. This competition has its nasty moments, but none of them is violent or physical. Hence, I suggest that the martial context of Joyce's use of the phrase may indicate that he was aware that the Stygian cries of the Greek frogs had also been adopted as a cheer by football fans at Yale University.[20] The battle between Harvard and Yale is *the* game in the perennial gridiron rivalry between these athletic aristocrats of the Ivy League.

At this point it would be reasonable to inquire whether Joyce knew anything at all about American football. Stanislaus Joyce states that his elder brother "disliked football" (soccer) and "detested rugby."[21] Any awareness of a similar trans-Atlantic sport would seem highly unlikely. Yet Atherton has shown that the *Wake* contains several references that conflate Irish hurling, soccer (association football), and English Rugby Union football: "the foodbrawler, of the sociationist party . . . and all his fourteen other fullback maulers" (*FW* 144.5–7).[22] Atherton has also uncovered, thanks to an examination of archival drafts, an even more emphatic passage, in which rugby and soccer footballs refer, respectively, to Tristan's vigorous fondling of Iseult's buttocks and breasts. The following is his discovery, in the final version of the text: "the hero, of Gaelic champion . . . with his sinister dexterity, light and rufthandling, vicemversem her ragbags et assauayetiams, fore and aft, on and offsides, the brueburnt sexfutter" (*FW* 384.23–28). At one stage this read: "The handsome sixfoottwo rugger and soccer champion . . . with sinister dexterity he alternately rightandlefthandled fore and aft the palpable rugby and association bulbs."[23] There is a third, brief allusion to rugby and its tactical terminology in one of the bird passages: "the *rugaby* moon . . . amuckst the cloud*scrums*" (*FW* 449.34–36; my emphases).

But rugby, however similar, is not the same as American football. In another passage I detect several loud and clear examples of stateside gridiron jargon, and here again sport is a convenient metaphor for energetic sexual byplay between Tristan and Iseult. In this case, the specific cross reference is to "French" kissing, using the tongue: "as quick, is greased pigskin, Amoricas Champius, with one aragan throust, druve the massive of virilvigtoury flshpst the both lines of forwards (Eburnea's down,boys!) rightjingbangshot into the goal of her gullet" (*FW* 395.35–396.2). In those lines the emphatic "pigskin"[24] is the primary indicator of a figurative football thrust, through which the American champion, in a burst of power, flashes past the line of scrimmage, crosses the goal, and scores a touchdown. Joyce refers to the regional affiliations of the offense (both American and Breton) and the defense (Hibernian). Just as pseudo-Latin or an archaic French noun suggests the collegiate playing field ("Champius"; *campus*), so too is the climactic plunge to victory the act of a real man (*virilis*), and the line of teeth that he penetrates are of gleaming ivory (*eburnea*).

That interpretive double reverse leads to a final connection, involving competition on the playing field and on the comic stage. One of the most distinctive formal elements in Aristophanic comedy is a stylized debate. In this *agōn* (contest, match) a proponent and an opponent square off verbally to defend or rebut the Great Idea on which the plot of the play pivots. Thus, in *Lysistrata* the titular heroine lambastes an Athenian "Commissioner" who contends that women belong in the kitchen, not in the Treasury—much less should they be permitted to try to stop the Peloponnesian War. In *The Clouds* the long debate on traditional as opposed to innovative education pits Philosophy versus Sophistry. In a part of the *Wake* that contains several other references to incidents in *The Clouds,* Joyce alludes to this memorable battle of wits as "sophister agen sorefister" (*FW* 551.29). The choice of "sorefister" to characterize one of the opponents is Joyce's way of calling attention to the jab-and-parry, competitive aspect of the comedic *agōn,* just as the "Brékkek Kékkek" chant introduces the clash of "wills gen wonts" (*FW* 4.1).

Early Fiction

Prolonged exposure to *Finnegans Wake* (and to its critics) can result in extravagant responses to that polymorphous text. While it is reasonable to cast a rugby player as a two-handed fondler, a claim for a link between the comedic *agōn* and the collegiate gridiron may stretch the point. In a change of time and perspective, then, the final section of this chapter is a straightforward review of Aristophanic allusion in Joyce's earlier, more conventional fiction. There are two items that indirectly impinge on aspects of ancient Greek comedy. Portions of several "esthetics" passages from *Stephen Hero* were not included in similar sections of *A Portrait of the Artist as a Young Man*. In one of them Daedalus argues with the president of the college, who has rejected his paper on modern drama. The Jesuit indicates that in the essay "Greek drama—the classical temper" has been treated "with a kind of juvenile . . . impudence, shall I say" (*SH* 96; Joyce's ellipsis). Stephen counters: "—But the Greek drama is heroic, monstruous [*sic*]. Eschylus is not a classical writer! . . . By 'classical' I mean the slow elaborative patience of the art of satisfaction. The heroic, the fabulous, I call romantic. Menander perhaps, I don't know . . ." (*SH* 97; the final ellipsis is Joyce's).

At the time when Joyce was composing *Stephen Hero* (1904–6), Menander's works were known only through fragments quoted in ancient grammarians. The actual texts of his New Comedies were lost. Thus, although handbooks of the history of Greek literature would include entries on Menander's reputation as a stylist and a skillful creator of plots and characters, neither Stephen Daedalus nor James Joyce could have read anything like a scene—not to mention a complete play—by Menander (approximately 342–290 B.C.). It is true that his comedies were closely imitated, in Latin, by the Roman playwrights Plautus and Terence; but even in the face of uninformed Jesuit censorship, there was slim evidence indeed that would have permitted Stephen to establish Menander as the "classical" dramatist. Perhaps this lack of textual support caused the student-essayist to hesitate, then to allow the argument to trail off into a preciously modest ellipsis, "perhaps, I don't know. . . ." At any rate, there is little in the form, theme, and diction of Menander's New Comedy that is like Aristophanic comedy of the late fifth century B.C. In the context of Stephen's essay, then, I am not inclined to label his apotheosis of Menander as a juvenile critical "bloomer" by a budding Liffey artist; rather, it is an early example of the principle of hedged critical uncertainty in action.

The second item of Aristophanic interest in *Stephen Hero* also begins with a brief bit of Aeschylus-bashing. While supposedly studying his Italian homework text,[25] Stephen "devised the following question and answer for the pseudo-classical catechism":

> *Question*—What great truth do we learn from the *Libation Pourers* of Eschylus?
>
> *Answer*—We learn . . . that in ancient Greece brothers and sisters took the same size in boots. (*SH* 192–93; my ellipsis)

There are several items dealing with classical drama—both tragedy and comedy—that need comment here. First, the locus for this traditional dramatic device is indeed Aeschylus's *Libation Bearers,* the second play in his *Oresteia* trilogy. There Electra first deduces that a lock of hair found on Agamemnon's tomb must be that of her brother Orestes (*Libation Bearers* 167–80). Then she finds another sign: her foot exactly matches the footprints beside the tomb; the feet that made them must be those of Orestes. Joyce is not the first critic to mock this highly implausible attempt at a coup de theatre. In his tragedy *Electra* Euripides has the skeptical sister dismiss any suggestion of validity in this hackneyed Aeschylean "recognition device." She asks how any footprints could be left on rocky ground— and she states that a man's foot would of course be bigger than a girl's (*Electra* 532–37).[26] That parody of an earlier dramatist's work is found in a tragedy. Euripides' comments, however, are much like the mass of similar jabs that constitute the long *agōn*—a parodic "tragedy contest" between Aeschylus and Euripides—in Aristophanes' *The Frogs.* And, as a matter of fact, the "matching strands of hair" from Aeschylus's *Libation Bearers* did attract the comic poet's attention in another of his plays.

Another of the distinguishing formal features of Greek Old Comedy is the *parabasis.* In it the chorus would "step aside" from its role in the plot and "turn to" the audience to deliver a personal message from the playwright. In his revised version of *The Clouds* Aristophanes has his cumulus-chorus speak in defense of the drama in which they perform. They sing to the audience that in the current production of the play, there is none of the trite vulgarity of a typical comedy. The revised action, they claim, seeks chaste and prudent viewers, who will be recognized, "just as Electra in her play discovered her brother's strand of hair" (*Clouds* 534–36). This is a fairly tame example of Aristophanic literary send-up. Yet, the mention of Orestes' tress is clear evidence that, within a generation of Aeschylus's production of the *Oresteia*, this device was recognized as a hackneyed gimmick, ripe for derision by both tragic and comic poets. Joyce's sarcastic question-and-answer for his "pseudo-classical catechism" in *Stephen Hero*, then, is merely another exhibit in a long parodic tradition—as, most assuredly, is his phrase "the kerl he left behind him" (*FW* 234.7–8).

A final example of Joyce's use of Aristophanic humor comes from *Ulysses:* "Socratididion" (*U* 9.237). In Greek literature this diminutive form of Socrates' name appears most prominently in an early scene in *The*

Clouds during which the debt-ridden father is being shown around the think tank. He and his student-escort spot Socrates dangling above the stage in a basket, like some atheistic deus ex machina. They call to the Master several times; then the student uses the diminutive form as a token of collegial affection (*Clouds* 222).

In the "Scylla and Charybdis" chapter of *Ulysses,* Stephen Dedalus's use of "Socratididion" may be meant to be affectionate, or it may be intended as dismissive. He is delivering his *pronunciamenti* on the connected topics of Shakespeare, *Hamlet,* and paternity. Although he is ostensibly open to comment, the last thing Stephen wants to do is to engage in a Wildean, pseudo-Platonic dialogue with his auditors (*U* 9.1068–69). As he deflects an objection by Eglinton to his sophistic arguments, Stephen must briefly discuss the functions of the three important women in Socrates' life. From his shrewish wife Xanthippe, Stephen contends, Socrates learned dialectic. From his midwife mother, he derived the "maieutic" method, whereby the teacher assists at the birth (*maieuesthai*) of a student's idea. Finally, Stephen admits that he does not know what Socrates learned from his first wife (or mistress), Myrto (*U* 9.232–39). It is with reference to the last woman that Joyce uses the diminutive form "Socratididion." If it is meant to be an echo of pillow-talk by the philosopher and his lady love, then the word is affectionate, perhaps mockingly so. If it is Stephen's way of suggesting that even Socrates could be tied up in an exasperating sexual relationship, then the term is mildly censorious. At any rate, immediately after mentioning Myrto's name, Stephen injects a parenthetical wish "(*absit nomen*!)." The Latin means "Banish the presence of the term (or name)." This phrase is a variation on the more familiar apotropaic *absit omen,* which means "Banish the prophetic sign"; that is, "I hope that what has just been said or seen does not predict the occurrence of something I fear." What does Stephen want to banish here? "Myrtō" is a proper name derived from the Greek word *myrton,* meaning myrtle-berry. It also has an obscene meaning, "cunt"[27] (which may be the source of the reputed name of Socrates' wife-mistress).

It is not surprising that the most emphatic use of the word in its obscene sense occurs in Aristophanes' *Lysistrata.* The Spartan Herald, with his prodigiously painful phallus, has just arrived in Athens. He reports that, until their men agree to push for peace throughout all Greece, the Spartan women will refuse to allow even a "tweak of their cunts (*myrtō*)"

(*Lysistrata* 1004). In short, Joyce's placement of "(*absit nomen!*)" in the midst of his views on Socrates' women indicates his awareness of the sexually explicit twist to the name Myrto. By it he also allows Stephen to underscore the reason-melting potency that the name suggests. In my judgment, from either point of view the separation of two typically Aristophanic names ("Socratididion" and "Myrto") by the forfending Latin expletive is another covert indication of the clever adaptation of ancient Greek comic techniques in Joyce's work.

It is less difficult to suggest a general conclusion about the Aristophanic material in Joyce's abandoned *Stephen Hero* and *Ulysses* than it is to find a coherent matrix for the allusions in *Finnegans Wake*. Quite simply, when he radically reshaped *Stephen Hero* to form *A Portrait of the Artist as a Young Man*, Joyce eliminated any comparative comments on the Greek theater, tragic or comic. Perhaps he recalled a judgment he had rendered in a collegiate paper: "Greek drama is played out. . . . Its revival is not of dramatic but of pedagogic significance" (*CW* 39). More likely, he chose the Aquinian formulas "*Pulcra sunt quae visa placent*" (*P* 186, 207) and "*ad pulcritudinem tria requiruntur, integritas, consonantia, claritas*" (*P* 212) as better (and equally esoteric) emblems of Stephen Dedalus's new aesthetics. The Socratic material in *Ulysses* is limited to Stephen's theories about *Hamlet* during the debate in the National Library. Here the sexual aspects of these theories can be expressed discreetly in the form of classical allusion and etymology, however crude.

Although the term *agōn* appeared several times in my discussion, there is no hint that Joyce used any aspect of such an Aristophanic contest in his fiction. Neither the *Hamlet* episode just mentioned nor the occasional debates in the *Wake* ("The Mookse and the Gripes" [*FW* 152–59] and "St. Patrick and the Archdruid" [*FW* 611–13]) owe anything, in matter or form, to this feature of Greek comedy. That absence of intertextual parallels in structure and the avoidance of any consistent pattern of character identification hold true for the *Wake* in general. It is a fact that some of Socrates' absurd experiments from *The Clouds* are found in the catalogs of HCE's alleged offenses and that all of the Beardsley-*Lysistrata* references are appropriately applied to him. The significant factor here, however, is not Greco-Hibernian typology, but the timeless opportunity for comic sexual and scatological innuendo. The references to *The Birds* and the distorted titles of the plays seem to have been mutual stimuli for expansion.

I also detect a cross-cultural click between Aristophanes' comedy of utopian aggression and the actions of Shaun in the *Wake*, in a compact cluster of allusions near the end of the sermon to Issy and her flower girls (*FW* 449.9–450.4). Without doubt he is an entrepreneur, a poseur, and a self-serving emissary; his scheme to convince his sister of his innocent intentions is straight out of an Irish Catholic "Cloudcuckooland"—but that is as far as we can go with the comparison. The two other groups of Aristophanic titles (*FW* 11.5–12.14 and *FW* 276.11–277.16) have nothing to do with Shaun or seductive pseudosermons.

The *Wake* was in progress from 1922 to 1939. There are several distinct phases in that long period of composition, the details of which are complex and controversial.[28] None of the Aristophanic material discussed in this chapter entered the evolving text before 1926, when the basic shape, "plot," and characters of the *Wake* had been determined. (The only exception is the very early [1923] "pigskin" in the "Tristan-rugby" passage.) Many elements, of course, were to be restructured, added, and expanded before the final publication of the complete work in 1939. The comedies of Aristophanes made their contributions to the text at various stages during that period of creative augmentation; several elements, including most of the *Lysistrata* allusions, are very late (1937–39) additions. This type of accretion falls somewhere within the terminal categories of "allusive parallels," "key rhythmic clusters," and "foreign-language word clusters" as outlined by David Hayman in his schematic analysis of the *Wake's* "nodal infrastructure."[29] In short, nothing from Aristophanes was central to the conception or early growth of the *Wake*.

The reason why Joyce selected Aristophanic material to be part of this process is obvious. As indicated previously, two of the three lists of play titles detected in the *Wake* have absolutely no connection with the bogus utopian homilist, Shaun. Rather, both of those nonthematic clusters are allusive patches in the work's polychromatic space-time–scape. Their distorted presentation ("cloudscrums," "a dace feast of grannom") forms a small part of the work's comic design. The *Wake* was painted from a palette of world literature, history, geography, mythology, music, all applied in numerous languages and startling combinations. Whatever else the result of this controlled overlay of cultural and linguistic pigment may be, both the evolving and finished forms are certainly meant to be viewed as funny. Characteristically, in neither his Notebooks nor the text of the

Wake does Joyce acknowledge his obligations to the master of ancient Greek comedy. Nevertheless the muted presence of Aristophanes, his farting gnat, croaking frogs, and enthusiastically pin-setting goldsmith can be detected—with a little careful scraping—just beneath the surface of the final canvas.

11

Miscellaneous Writers

Two of the most accessible vignettes in the *Wake* are presented as fables: "The Mookse and the Gripes" (*FW* 152.4–159.23) and "The Ondt and the Gracehoper" (*FW* 414.16–419.10). The format of both tales is that of a narrated debate between the two animal/vegetable/insect stand-ins for Shaun and Shem. The most emphatic (but scarcely the exclusive) point of contention in the first fable is the primacy of the Roman Catholic Church over secular authority and Greek Orthodox theology. The Mookse, for example, is likened to "Quartus the Fifth and Quintus the Sixth and Sixtus the Seventh . . . [and] Lio the Faultyfindth," as he pontificates "with his unfallable encyclicling" (*FW* 153.26–34; also note VI.B.4.331). The Gripes reenacts the Emperor's genuflection to the Pope at Canossa (A.D. 1077) when he whimpers, "for all the rime on my raisins, if I connow make my submission, I cannos give you up" (*FW* 154.30–32). Issy sashays onto the scene as Nuvolleta; she watches the proceedings but cannot distract the disputants, who are too busy with that perennial male preoccupation, theological subtleties: "—I see, she sighed. There are menner" (*FW* 158.5).

The second fable does not seem to have any overt allegorical referents. As in the tale on which it is modeled, Joyce's provident Ondt (Shaun) shames, then saves the prodigal Gracehoper (Shem). The latter admits his errors and promises to amend his ways in a traditional "moral," here expanded to 34 lines, rhymed and italicized. The following couplets conclude the piece:

> *Your feats end enormous, your volumes immense,*
> *(May the Graces I hoped for sing your Ondtship song sense!),*

Your genus its worldwide, your spacest sublime!
But, Holy Saltmartin, why can't you beat time? (FW 419.5–8)

Its conventional form does not mean that this fable lacks a Wakean touch. It is crawling with references to every possible type of insect, in a hill of languages. Thanks to his state of spendthrift "joyicity," for example, the Gracehoper "was always making ungraceful overtures to Floh and Luse and Bienie and Vespatilla to play pupa-pupa and pulicy-pulicy" (*FW* 414.24–26). The German *Floh* means flea; the Danish for louse is *lus;* the German *Bienie* is bee; and the Latin for little wasp could be *vespatilla.* A pupa is a stage in the development of an insect, and "pulicine" is a pedantic adjectival form of the Latin noun *pulex, pulicis* (flea).

Behind the elaborate Joycean allusions and diction, there are obvious classical models for these animal morality tales: the fables of Aesop. In his Paris library Joyce had a copy of the fables translated by Vernon Jones, and there is clear evidence that his citations are based on that version.[1] According to tradition, Aesop was a freed slave who lived in the late sixth century B.C. No details of his life survive—in fact, the fables ascribed to him have been reworked, translated into verse, anthologized, and excerpted so constantly that it would be more accurate to refer to this traditional collection of works as Aesopian.[2] In the prologue to "The Ondt and the Gracehoper," Joyce shows his awareness of the cross-cultural, multilingual status of these pieces: "—I apologuise, Shaun began, but I would rather spinooze you one from the grimm gests of Jacko and Esaup, fable one, feeble two" (*FW* 414.16–18). The English noun *apologue* (allegory, fable) has been converted into a verb by Shaun in the passage just quoted. It is composed of the Greek elements *apo* (away, from) and *logos* (word, thought, story); as used here, an *apologos* is a tale of which the meaning must be derived from a subsurface reading of the plot. That, however, is as close as the rest of the citation gets to ancient Greek. There are other hints, in other languages, as to what Joyce is up to with his Ondt and Gracehoper. The French noun *gestes* means tales or adventures; Joyce modifies his "gests" with the adjective "grimm," in which the extra "-m" is meant to suggest the collection of German fairy tales of the Brothers Grimm. "Jacko and Esaup" here are only tangentially the sons of the patriarch Isaac: Jacob and Esau. Their prime referents are the two most important fabulists in Western literature, Jean (or John/Jack) de La Fontaine and Aesop. James Atherton suggests that Joyce's "fable one" refers, literally, to the first fable in La Fontaine's book, "La Cigale et la Fourmi" (The grasshopper and the ant).[3] The second verb in the passage, "spinooze," is clearly meant to sound like Spinoza. I am not aware that this seventeenth-century Dutch-Jewish philosopher wrote any fables; thus his presence in the text probably has more to do with arachnids than ethics—that is, like a spider, Shaun will spin out his fluidly cautionary tale of dutiful and negligent insects.

There are several other fairly direct references to Aesop in the *Wake*. The most straightforward is the marginal *"Esop"* in "Night Lessons." The essay topic keyed to his name is "Tell a Friend in a Chatty Letter the Fable of the Grasshopper and the Ant" (*FW* 307.L and 14–16). I take the "Chatty Letter" as a direct reference to the March 26, 1928, letter to Harriet Shaw Weaver, in which Joyce carefully explicated many of the entomological elements of the fable (*SL* 329–32). Several other Wakean allusions are formulaic: "Eset fibble" (*FW* 29.13); "esiop's foible" (*FW* 422.22); and perhaps "esoupcans" (*FW* 289.5).

Aesop writes that every person carries two bags filled with faults. The bag in front holds his neighbor's flaws; the one behind, his own short-comings (*Aesop* 60). Thus, people do not see their own faults, but never fail to see those of others. In the *Wake* Joyce makes what seems to be a similar report about the epic hero Finn MacCool: "prospector, he had a rooksacht, retrospecor, he holds the holpenstake" (*FW* 137.31–32). An oblique Aesopean allusion is certainly possible here. What is most likely being described, however, is not an updated version of the "Two Bags of Faults"; rather, Joyce is probably playing around with the strange denota-tions of two ancient Greek adverbial prepositions. (See chapter 13, on the classical Greek language at work in Joyce's fiction, for an explanation of the apparent paradox in their use.)

Finnegans Wake is not the first of Joyce's works in which the fables of Aesop appear. There are at least seven distinct allusions in *Ulysses*. One reference merely cites the traditional title, which introduces the two participants whose encounter constitutes the plot of the fable. In a Circean fantasy Bloom fends off an attach by THE NYMPH: "No prun-ingknife. The fox and the grapes, is it?" Bloom's assailant is dressed in a nun's habit. He fears that, if she had a suitable tool, she would slice off his penis and use it as a macabre dildo: "Crucifix not thick enough?" (*U* 15.3464–65). In Aesop's fable the hungry fox damns the unreachable grapes by muttering that they are not ripe. Moral? People who cannot get what they want blame the times and the circumstances—and pretend they do not care. Likewise, so it would seem even in Joyce's Nighttown vision, at least in Bloom's lurid imagination, for a nun in a *"white habit, coife and hugewinged wimples"* (*U* 15.3434).

In other instances the references are sufficiently brief to indicate that Joyce expected Aesopian plots and morals to be familiar to the reader. Bloom muses on the way the Irish public treated Parnell: "very effectively cooked his matrimonial goose, thereby heaping coals of fire on his head much the same way as the fabled ass's kick" (*U* 16.1398–1400). The last element in that cascade of clichés refers to the fable in which a Wolf agrees to pull a thorn from the hobbled hoof of an Ass. The Ass kicks his helper in the teeth, whereupon the Wolf reflects: "My father taught me to kill, and I ought to have stuck to that trade instead of attempting a cure" (*Aesop* 130).

During the same episode, Bloom reacts to the tirade of the proprietor of the cabman's shelter against the English taxes and the merchants who have drained the natural resources of Ireland. His situation is like that of James Fitzharris, "Skin-the-Goat," who drove a decoy cab in the Phoenix Park murders—in fact, the café owner trades on the rumor that *he* is that hero. The real Fitzharris, however, is now on the dole, and "the pseudo Skin-the-et cetera . . . had transparently outlived his welcome." Like English imperial entrepreneurs, local Irish chauvinists always went too far: "temperamental, no economising or any idea of the sort, always snapping at the bone for the shadow" (*U* 16.1070–75). The final phrase in Bloom's analysis is a not very informative attempt to summarize the plot of one of Aesop's fables. In it a dog crosses a river with a piece of stolen meat clamped between his jaws. When he sees his blurred reflection in the water, he imagines that another dog, with more meat, is nearby. He snaps at the phantom rival and loses both the substance and the shadow. Greediness—and blaming others for your problems—does not pay off (*Aesop* 75).

When Bloom sees a bat flying at twilight on Sandymount strand, his thoughts characteristically turn to science: "Wonder why they come out at night like mice. . . . Birds are like hopping mice. What frightens them, light or noise? Better sit still. All instinct like the bird in drought got water out of the end of a jar by throwing in pebbles" (*U* 13.1127–30). In the fable of "The Crow and the Pitcher" there is no mention of a drought, just a pitcher with little water in it. Bloom, however, attributes the bird's action to mere instinct; Aesop's moral attributes the clever plan to "Necessity, the mother of invention" (*Aesop* 17).

Just before lunch Bloom contemplates the abstemious frugality of some of his fellow Dubliners, the Methodist Mr. Purefoy, for example: "Selfish those t.t's [teetotalers] are. Dog in the manger. Only one lump of sugar in my tea, if you please" (*U* 8.366–67). Aesop's miserable cur slept in a manger, and growled to keep the horses from their food. He cannot eat oats, and therefore will not allow those who can to get near their fodder (*Aesop* 60). The traditional title of this fable reappears in the *Wake*, with a significant Joycean twist of character identity that resoundingly injects Bethlehem into the scenario: "Do you hold yourself then for some god in the manger, Shehohem, that you will neither serve nor let serve, pray nor let pray? (*FW* 188.18–19).

In "Aeolus," J. J. O'Molloy drops in at the newspaper office. The barrister's practice is in decline, and he now does some writing for various periodicals. There is an unassigned comment (by MacHugh? by Bloom?) on O'Molloy's state of affairs: "Funny the way those newspaper men veer about when they get wind of a new opening. Weathercocks. Hot and cold in the same breath" (*U* 7.308–9). In Aesop's model the two characters are "the Man and the Satyr," an odd couple who agree to live together. One day in the winter the Satyr sees the man blowing on his hands to warm them; later, at supper, the man blows his porridge to cool it. The Satyr leaves, unable to be friends with a man who blows hot and cold with the same breath. Joyce's use of this fable is highly appropriate to the overinflated chapter in *Ulysses*. His substitution of "in" for Aesop's "with" also imparts a cynically modern swerve to the original tale. In the ancient version the Satyr was merely too dense to tell which way the wind was blowing (*Aesop* 86).

Finally, in "Sirens" Joyce re-creates an entire Aesopean fable. It is put into the musical mouth of Lenehan and chanted to Miss "Girlgold" Kennedy: "—Ah fox met ah stork. Said thee fox too thee stork: Will you put your bill down inn my throath and pull uppah bone?" (*U* 11.247–49). In Aesop's tale the participants are traditionally a Wolf and a Crane, but the moral is the same: A bad man thinks he has done you a favor by refraining from hurting you (*Aesop* 106). Miss Kennedy apparently has enough sense and experience to recognize the underlying sexual threats in Lenehan's ditty. Thus, the mock-classical appeal falls, "plappering flatly," on deaf ears of the woman behind the Ormond bar.

Just as Phaedrus carried on the fable tradition by adapting and composing verse versions in Latin six centuries after Aesop, so too did later writers perpetuate the genre. In addition to the fleeting appearance of La Fontaine (*FW* 414.17–18), another French poet who published a collection of animal tales is clearly cited: "[Jean-Pierre de] Florian's fables" (*FW* 385.11). The Russian fabulist Ivan Krylov is also commemorated near the end of "the Mookse and the Gripes." There Nuvoletta/Issy realizes that the two insect-debaters have argued themselves into a tree and a stone without paying any attention to her; "she gave a childy cloudy cry: *Nuée! Nuée!*" That farewell line and her tears are summarized in an almost immediate reprise, "crylove fables" (*FW* 159.9–14).

In the early history of the Roman republic the plebeians revolted against patrician control and left the city. A senator was dispatched to convince the common citizens that their secession would destroy the entire state. His plea (as re-created by the historian Livy) was framed in the parable of the "Revolt of the Parts of the Body": When the hands, teeth, and other parts of the body fail to do their jobs, the belly cannot supply nourishment through the veins to all the members; thus the entire body wastes away. The plebeians understood the senator's message and agreed to return to Rome, where their interests were assured special protection.[4] At least two passages in the *Wake* exploit this fable: "As popular as when Belly the First was keng and his members met in the Diet of Man" (*FW* 26.28–29) and "—He's not all buum and bully.—But his members handly food him" (*FW* 550.4–5). Another reference combines this moment in Roman political history with the arrival of Christianity in Ireland: "hands his secession to the new patricius but plums plebmatically for the bloody old centuries" (*FW* 129.18–19). The Wakean vocabulary of this passage (the Greek *phleps, phlebos* [vein] combines with the Latin *plebs* [the common people] in "plebmatically") is certainly intended to echo the nutritional anatomy of the political parable. Joyce's immediate source for the extended analogy is probably Livy 2.32.9–12 or its close imitation in Shakespeare's *Coriolanus* 1.1.90–150. Behind both versions lies the fable "The Belly and the Members," which has the same general plot and message—but no veins (*Aesop* 128).

Joyce's grasp of the Aesopian tradition also includes the works of the American fabulist Joel Chandler Harris. His tales in dialect, published in the highly popular *Uncle Remus* series, are commemorated several times in the *Wake*. "Rere Uncle Remus" himself is partially transformed into what seems to be an Afrikaner slave master when he is called "the Baas of Eboracum [Latin, meaning York]" (*FW* 442.8) in a passage that also features an allusion to the War of the Roses. Br'er Fox appears twice in the ultracomplex religious controversy involving the Tangos and Pangos: "Brerfuchs" (the German *Fuchs* means fox) and "Breyfawkes" (*FW* 574.4, 36). Br'er Rabbit's habitat is also cited in conjunction with his comrade in the fables: "Brerfuchs and Warren" (*FW* 547.4).

Next in the category of miscellaneous Greek writers come several lyric poets, each of whom has a cameo role in the *Wake*. With the primeval Eve and the metamorphosed Procne and Philomela, "*Sappho*" of Lesbos is one of the few women posted in the list of essay topics in "Night Lessons." In addition to her passionate lyric poetry, Sappho is noted for the circle of girls and young women to whom she introduces the arts, behavior, dress, and attitudes that were expected from the daughters of the aristocracy in ancient Hellenic society. Thus her marginal name suggests to Joyce a discourse on "Should Ladies learn Music or Mathematics?" (*FW* 307.L and 21–22). On the same page of the text, the Hellenistic poet "*Theocritus*" also appears in the margin. His name is keyed to "American Lake Poetry" (*FW* 307.L and 11). That topic, *mutatis mutandis*, is generically appropriate, since Theocritus is regarded as the inventor of Greek pastoral poetry, though there are few lakes in his native Sicily.[5]

The late-seventh-century B.C. Alcman is the most famous poet in the Dorian dialect. According to a doubtful tradition he was born in Sardis in Asia Minor and was brought to Sparta as a slave. There the metrical innovations in his hymns, choral lyrics, erotic verse, and drinking songs earned him emancipation. The last of those genres and his period of bondage may have suggested an identification with the Scandinavian handyman at HCE's pub. The infamous Persian conquest and domination of the city of Sardis also seem to contribute to Joyce's brief but bibulous tribute to Alcman: "profusional drinklords to please obstain, he is fatherlow soundigged inmoodminded *pershoon* but *aleconnerman*" (*FW* 141.25–26; my emphases).

Another composer of ancient Greek *skolia* (drinking songs) lies behind the phrase "*anegreon in heaven*" (279.F32). The original title of this eighteenth-century song was "Anacreon in Heaven." (Its music supplied the tune for "The Star-Spangled Banner.") Anacreon (about 550–465 B.C.) was a lyric poet famous for his praise of wine and love. Only fragments of these poems survive, but a collection of imitations, the *Ana-creontica,* was widely circulated in antiquity and was later translated into Latin and various modern languages. Adaline Glasheen suggests a second, ingenious allusion in "seap*an nacre* buttons *on*" (*FW* 559.10; her emphases—my admiration).

The devil-may-care attitude of the Gracehoper in the *Wake* is compactly summed up in "harry me, marry me, bury me" (*FW* 414.31; also note VI.B.21.149). Although it is impossible to claim the following ancient Greek epigram, usually attributed to Hipponax, as the source of Joyce's rhymed imperatives, the sentiments are not dissimilar:

> Two days are the happiest of a man's wedded life:
> The day that he marries and the day that he buries his wife.

The study of geometry was once solidly established in the standard curriculum. Euclid and his propositions are more an inevitable feature of secondary education in America and western Europe than they are a paradigm of ancient Greek mathematics. As a matter of fact, Euclid's primary contribution to that field was not in theory or innovative solutions, but in his ability to organize and present the discoveries of others with dazzling clarity. He taught and wrote his *Elements* in Alexandria, the new intellectual capital of the Greek-speaking world, about 300 B.C.

Joyce's most memorable tribute to the father of geometric instruction is the diagram found at the apex of the "Night Lessons" episode of *Finnegans Wake.* The figure is composed of two intersecting circles in which are inscribed a pair of triangles: ALP/αλπ. The diagram, drawn to scale, is the graphic solution to "Problem ye ferst, construct ann aquilittoral dryankle Probe loom! . . . Concoct an equoangular trillitter" (*FW* 286.19–22). Those challenges are nothing other than the Joycean restatement of the first problem in Euclid's *Elements:* Construct an equilateral triangle on a given finite line. The solution begins with the line: "A is for Anna like L is for liv" (*FW* 293.18–19). Next, draw two overlapping circles, for each of which the line AL is a radius. Since all the radii of every circle of equal circumference (a given here, since both radii are line AL) are the same, then the lines described from A and L (which meet at P), being the radii of circles of equal circumference, are themselves equal. Thus, the resultant three-sided figure APL (and απλ) is an equilateral triangle. The following is the Wakean version of the final step of the problem: "Now, to compleat anglers . . . join alfa pea and pull loose by dotties and . . . eelpie and paleale by trunkles. Alow me align while I encloud especious!" (*FW* 296.22–28).

The process summarized by the text of the *Wake* is clearly demonstrated by the following diagram, lifted directly from a modern edition of Euclid's *Elements*.[6] Its similarity to the diagram in the middle of page 293 of the *Wake* is startling—and graphically illustrative of Joyce's use of documentary sources.

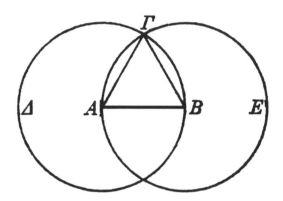

That is how the twins solve the "muddest thick that was ever heard dump" (*FW* 296.20–21). After the problem and its diagram are finished— since this is *Finnegans Wake*, not sophomore year at Central High—there is a practical, sexual application: "I'll make you to see figuratleavely the whome of your eternal geomater" (*FW* 296.36–297.1). If we keep an eye on the diagram, that corollary requires little comment. It is more a matter of sixth-grade imagination than anatomical specificity. "Quicks herit fossyending [*Quod erat faciendum*, Latin for "That which was to be constructed"]. Quef! "(*FW* 298.4–5). Joyce's perversion of the hallowed geometrical gerundive (the more familiar Euclidean form is *demonstrandum* [the thing that was to be shown]) adds to the salacious tone of the exercise. The pseudo-Latin "fossyending" can also be interpreted to mean that the problem ends at a *fossa,* the genuine Latin word for a ditch or pit; the French *fosse* also means hole or ditch. In both languages the terms are frequently used obscenely for the female genitalia. Joyce's "Quef!" can be read as the standard abbreviation, Q.E.F. (like Q.E.D.), for the entire phrase.[7] It is also meant to be reversed, to spell out a familiar English expletive. Joyce attempted the same sort of thinly disguised obscenity in *Ulysses:* "Books you were going to write with letters for titles. Have you read his F? O yes, but I prefer Q. Yes, but W is wonderful. O yes, W" (*U* 3.139–40).[8]

In a 1929 Notebook there is a series of three geometric figures that seems to be a practice exercise for the *Wake* diagram. The first shows two congruent triangles (another basic theorem in Euclidean geometry); the second is a semicircle with a line inscribed from the diameter to the circumference (it does not appear to illustrate any theorem) (VI.B.4.301). The third figure (VI.B.4.302) is a rough sketch (with only the radial line marked AB) of the diagram constructed in Joyce's text to demonstrate the first proposition in Euclid's *Elements*.

During his years at Belvedere College in Dublin, Joyce took the annual examinations set by the Intermediate Education Board for Ireland. The results were published and his scores in "Euclid" (600 possible points) are recorded: 230 (1894), 175 (1895), 180 (1897), 220 (1898).[9] These marks are not nearly as impressive as those for Joyce in Latin, modern languages, and English. Nonetheless, in comparison with the scores of other examinees, they seem about average and testify to an impressive span of years in which Joyce was asked to demonstrate his competence in geometry. In the context of his last work of fiction, that time was not wasted. Indeed, during his revisions of the geometric section of chapter II.2 of the *Wake*, Joyce wrote to Miss Weaver: "I have had too much to do, being up sometimes till 1.30 fooling over old books of Euclid and alegbra" (*Letters* I.280). It should also be noted that Leopold Bloom's wide scientific interests include Euclid. The last entry in the catalog of his books in "Ithaca" is a *"Short but yet Plain Elements of Geometry,"* with elaborate biblio-graphical and inscriptional annotation (*U* 17.1398–1407).

Apart from the laborious construction of the diagram in "Night Lessons," there are a number of other references to Euclid in the *Wake*. McHugh calls attention to an allusion to Todhunter's edition of Euclid—"toadhauntered"—in a footnote on the same page of the text as the diagram (*FW* 293.F2). When ALP prepares to give her presents, she consults "Casey's Euclid" (*FW* 206.12–13). Glasheen notes that John Casey, a mathematics professor at Dublin's original Catholic University, wrote *Sequel to Euclid*, a text noted for its demonstrations of the circle.[10]

The phrase "Casey's frost book" (*FW* 286.9) links that text with Percival Frost's *Treatise on Solid Geometry*. The latter work is where we should look for information on "comic cuts" (conic sections) (*FW* 286.8).

The Alexandrian geometrician himself appears, along with the early Greek natural philosopher Anaxagoras, in "Neuclidius and Inexagoras" (*FW* 155.32–33). In another passage, his most important work is linked with its author's name: "me elementator joyclid" (*FW* 302.12). The young students in "Night Lessons" are reminded of the importance of the study of the entire field of mathematics: "What signifieth *whole* that but, be all the *prowess of ten*, 'tis as strange to relate be, *nonparile* to rede, rite and *reckan*, caught allmeals dullmarks for his *nucleuds* and *alegobrew*" (*FW* 283.20–24; my emphases). Issy also gets some advice: "You may spin on *youthlit's* bike and *multiplease* you Mike and Nick with your kickshoes on the *algebrars* but, volve the *virgil* page and view, the O of woman is long" (*FW* 270.22–26; my emphases). (The last clause of that excerpt more or less summarizes the lesson that the boys can discover by solving Euclid's first problem.) Their sister is reminded that geometry, multiplication tables, algebra, and Latin grammar are fine, but a saucy ride on her bike probably does more than Euclid or Vergil can to expose the mystery of life to man.

On the subject of Euclid and ancient Greek geometry, there is a puzzling archival passage. A draft of material for the "Night Lessons" episode of the *Wake* preserves the following sentence: "As if that three could solve, singly or together, the twohornedheaded dulcarnon, handed round aurally since Euclid's patent, that stumped Alex among anders and drove him to pilfer turnips."[11] In that draft excerpt, "Euclid," "Alex . . . anders," and "turnips" make up a strange collocation. I know of no apocryphal tale about the boyhood of Alexander the Great that has him ditching a difficult geometry lesson to steal turnips. And since the Macedonian king died before Euclid wrote his *Elements,* he could not have been stumped by anything in that compendium. On the other hand, the tautological "towhornedheaded dulcarnon" has connections with *both* Alexander and Euclid. First, after his visit to the oracle of Zeus/Ammon in the Libyan desert, the Macedonian king was regarded as the son of that god; many traditional portraits show the two ram's horns of Ammon on Alexander's head.[12] Second, "dulcarnon" comes from an Arabic word meaning "lord of the two horns"; it is used in English to refer to a dilemma (on the horns of which one is stymied). A specific example of that connotation is the application of "dulcarnon" *either* to Proposition I.5 of Euclid: angles opposite the equal sides of an isosceles triangle are equal (because the problem was difficult for beginners to solve, it was called, in Latin, *pons asinorum* [the bridge of asses]) *or* to Proposition I.47: the Pythagorean theorem (because its diagram looks like a two-horned figure).[13] Joyce himself was aware of both connotations, as shown by the following adjacent notes: "ʳdulcaron = 2 horned / ʳ47th prop of Euclid or Alexander's 2 horn heads" (*Scribbledehobble* 7 [3]). In sum, Wakean logic forges a link that connects the horns with both Alexander and Euclid. (The relevance of the pilfered turnips remains enigmatic.)

As far as the published text of the *Wake* is concerned, the Euclidean and Alexandrian dimensions of the draft version of the passage are moot. Neither personal reference to the ancient Greeks was transferred into the final text. All that remains of the weird early version is an equally strange marginal note: "*Some is out for twoheaded dulcarnons but more pulfers turnips*" (*FW* 276.L1).

Born in Asia Minor and trained in Alexandria and Greece, Galen (second century A.D.) was regarded as the greatest practitioner of medicine in the Roman world. In addition to serving as private physician to several emperors, he wrote a large number of treatises on a full range of medical and pharmacological topics, including a commentary on the works of Hippocrates, the father of Greek medicine.[14] The language of these works (as well as Galen's cultural milieu) was Greek—hence his inclusion here. Joyce alludes to this famous physician at least twice, both in cryptomedical contexts.[15]

In his vilification of Shem, Shaun makes the following charge: "Then he went to Cecilia's treat on his solo to pick up Galen. Asbestopoulos! . . . arestocrank!" (*FW* 424.6–10; my ellipsis). Dublin's School of Medicine was on Cecilia Street. Asbestos does not seem to serve any therapeutic purposes, but the French noun *poule* is slang for whore, tart. I suggest that Shaun is accusing his brother of consorting with prostitutes who are unquenchable, insatiable (*asbestos* in Greek). This conjecture is supported by the fact that *galène* (French for sulphide of lead) was once used to treat venereal disease. That clinical application, in Wakean terms, is designed to stop the spread of the illness: "ar[r]est-" and the German *krank* (sick).[16]

The other allusion to Galen occurs in a passage that describes Shem cooking eggs in his closet-kitchen. First he goes to the "lithargogalenu fowlhouse for the sake of akes" (*FW* 184.13). The setting here is more chemical than gastronomical: The eggs are "brooled and cocked and potched in an *athanor*" (*FW* 184.17–18; my emphasis). The italicized word is a technical term for a conical smelting furnace used by alchemists. That context adds a medico-mineral dimension to "lithargogalenu": Not only was the coop one in which the hens (*gallinas* in Spanish) were lethargic, but also the compounds litharge (lead protoxide) and galena (lead sulphide) were present. The former is derived from the Greek roots *lith-* (stone) and *arg-* (silver); the latter is the Latin word for lead (*galena*). Both are ores from which lead is smelted. Again, there seems to be no chemotherapeutical use for either of these compounds. Perhaps then they are meant to foreshadow the concoction of the ink in the next paragraph; or maybe their colors, silvery-white and yellow, are meant to mimic those of the eggs being cooked in the passage. There are other possibilities. One of the Spanish terms for a medical doctor is *galeno*— derived, of course, from the name of the Greco-Roman physician Galen. Such an Iberian doctor might be inclined to prescribe a lithagogue, a medicine that serves to lead (from the Greek *agōgos* [a guide]) a stone (*lith-*) from a patient's kidney. If this medical application has any validity, it might also lead to a reexamination of the term by which Shem is introduced in the paragraph being discussed: "our low hero was a self valeter" (*FW* 184.11). The Latin verb form *valet* means "he is strong," "he is healthy." Could Shem be serving not only as his own valet but also as his own doctor or pharmacist? If so, that act of self-prescription would help to explain—in an era that knew nothing about cholesterol or holistic-organic therapy—both the large helping of eggs and the conspicuous piles of chemicals. Also note the nearby stock of "costive . . . antimonian manganese limolitmious" (*FW* 184.36).

A series of notes for *Ulysses* is a fitting emblem with which to conclude a chapter that has dealt, from a Hellenic perspective, with various authors and genres. In these archival lines Joyce shows that his creative imagination (like that of Leopold Bloom) is capable of bringing modern mathematical science into the family romance. The following are three of the four entries in the cluster:

^gspace reversible time no
Lobatschewky const. tot. curv. neg
Riemann " " " pos. (*UNBM* 474:85, 87–88)

The theories of two prominent nineteenth-century mathematicians, the Russian Nikolai Lobaschevsky and the German Georg Riemann, are essential to the development of non-Euclidean geometry. At the same time, Joyce was interested in a more traditional approach to the problems of space and time; his writerly and domestic concern is revealed in the second entry in the series:

Eucl. space not total curvature of the spine (Dilly) (*UNBM* 474:86)[17]

That note was transferred into the text of the "Wandering Rocks" of *Ulysses*. Mr. Simon Dedalus, on his way to the Ormond Hotel, has just encountered his daughter Dilly on the street. She has been waiting for him, since the family needs money for food. Mr. Dedalus assumes the offensive with a paternal shot: "—Stand up straight for the love of the lord Jesus" (*U* 10.657). When Dilly shrugs her shoulders, he continues, "—Stand up straight girl. . . . You'll get curvature of the spine" (*U* 10.662). There is a small measure of consolation for poor Dilly in this exchange—according to Euclid that curvature cannot be total. Q.E.D.

12

Modern Greek

Joyce's inability to read the original texts of ancient Greek literature—a gap in his otherwise extraordinarily broad linguistic background—chafed him. Budgen reports an incident from Zürich during World War I:

"I told him [Joyce] that I left school and went to work in my thirteenth year, but that the only thing I regretted about my lack of schooling was that I was never able to learn Greek. He thereupon regretted his insufficient knowledge of that language but, as if to underline the difference in our two cases (or so I interpreted it), he said with sudden vehemence: 'But just think: isn't that a world I am peculiarly fitted to enter?'" It was during this same period, his friend also remarks, that "Joyce associated a good deal with such Greeks as were available in wartime Zürich, for he thought they all had a streak of Ulysses in them."[1]

While there is no reason to doubt that Joyce admired the polytropic verve of his Greek associates, it is also true that he wanted to learn something of the language they spoke, the modern descendant of the mother tongue of Homer and Aristotle. His primary mentor in that project was Paul Phokas, another temporary resident in neutral Switzerland. Phokas's family was originally from Same, a harbor town on Cephalonia, an Ionian island just west of Ithaca. In 1900 the they went to Galatsi in Romania, where the men worked for a steamship company on the Danube. After being wounded in the Balkan wars, Phokas came to Zürich and found work in a commercial office. His path crossed Joyce's at the weekly meetings of the Club des Etrangers at the zum Weisses Kreuz restaurant and especially at the Café Odéon. Soon the two exiles began to help each other to learn their respective native languages.[2] Several notebooks of word lists, practice sentences, and translation exercises survive to testify to

Joyce's progress in the rudiments of Modern Greek. (On these sheets are also a few examples of Phokas's work in English, but they permit no real estimate of his success in that language.) There is, however, one document from the Zürich period that has special literary significance. It is the first translation of any of Joyce's work into another language.

On April 14, 1917, Phokas sent the author a letter enclosing eight francs for a copy of *A Portrait of the Artist as a Young Man*. At the top of the sheet containing this request is Phokas's handwritten copy of Poem XXXIV ("Sleep now, O sleep now") from *Chamber Music*.[3] The three stanzas on the left are in the original English; the right side is a line-by-line literal translation into Modern Greek. Only in the final two verses of his version does Phokas deviate slightly from Joyce's text: He uses *glyka* (sweetly) for "in peace," but he includes a verbatim alternative, a parenthetical—and archaizing—dative with iota subscript *en eirenē* (in peace); instead of his usual *kardia* (heart), he substitutes a *psychē* (soul) for Joyce's repeated "heart." Perhaps this translation was an exercise suggested by Joyce, who presumably supplied a copy of the text. At any rate, Phokas's request and the enclosed payment for *Portrait* are a personal indication that the pupil considered himself ready for the challenge of a longer and considerably more complex work by his teacher.

A phrase in *Ulysses* might be meant as a muted tribute to Joyce's language mentor during his years in the commercial center of Switzerland. In the Cyclopean catalogue of genuine and sham holy men in *Ulysses*, "S. Phocas of Sinope" marches in the procession immediately after "S. James the Less" (*U* 12.1690). I suggest that Joyce intended to join his first name with the last name of his Greek friend, thereby bestowing literary canonization on his drinking companion and language instructor.[4]

Hagiography aside, the Greek exercise notebooks can tell us something of the relationship between Joyce and Paul Phokas and of their method of mutual language instruction. Exhibit VIII.A.6.a consists of two separate pages, written by Phokas, containing several versions of the Greek alphabet, nine phrases relating to the weather ("βροντᾷ / it thundors [*sic*]"), and a series of paradigms for the declension of some masculine, feminine, and neuter nouns. These models are in fact far more grammatically schematic than is actual usage, but even so *eis* followed by the accusative replaces the more classicizing dative form. The basic information on these sheets must represent the earliest phase of instruction, sometime in 1916. Their format would have been familiar to Joyce from his study of Latin.

The next archival document is a thirty-two-page pocket notebook with an oval label on its cover. In that label Joyce drew a crude map of the islands of Great Britain and Ireland; over Ireland he wrote ἑλληνικὰ (Greek) (VIII.A.4 front cover). In the notebook itself Joyce's orthography is somewhat hesitant, and there are occasional corrections, presumably by Phokas, of forms and spelling. Most of the notebook consists of basic Greek-English vocabulary lists,[5] along with a few phrases of a practical nature: "Do you have a house to rent? How much does it cost a month?" (VIII.A.4.3). There are several reasons why I conclude that Phokas dictated the Greek words in this document and that Joyce supplied the best English equivalent. The items appear, not in alphabetical order, but in loosely logical clusters (contrasting adjectives and adverbs; words for "today," "tomorrow," "yesterday"; synonyms; adjacent terms for "prince" (*pringkips*) and "Prince of Wales" (*diadachos* [correctly *diadochos*]—literally, "successor"); groups of commercial terms; and so on. That sort of order strongly suggests a face-to-face, question-answer method of vocabulary building, not the private consultation of a dictionary.

In the same notebook Phokas wrote out the first stanza of the Greek national anthem. At the top of the next page Joyce wrote "*exoristos* = exile," followed by the Greek sentence "I am an exile from my fatherland" (VIII.A.4.16). The juxtaposition of a fellow expatriate's national anthem and Joyce's statement is not a function of pedagogical happenstance; it is an expression of the empathy between two comrades in an alien land.[6] Later in the same notebook Joyce copied out the words of a Greek patriotic song, "Dark Is the Night in the Mountains" (VIII.A.4.21); Phokas also reproduced the song, with his own interlinear translation into English, on a separate document (VIII.A.6.h) that includes a few incidental vocabulary items in Joyce's hand. The repetition of the two song lyrics is additional evidence of a process of mutual instruction. Another indicator that the instructor worked closely with his pupil is a pair of business letters written by Phokas to one of his firm's clients. Joyce copied the Greek texts of this correspondence into the notebook, so as to get the feel of a complete and practical document in that language (VIII.A.4.18 and 27).

Another notebook (VIII.A.1) begins with seven pages of Greek sentences written by Joyce, probably in response to dictation from Phokas. Here, the diffuse vocabulary, sometimes complex structure, and occasional corrections argue that a native-speaking mentor was at hand. The fluidity of Joyce's handling of the Greek script and the relative sophistication of some of the sentences mark this notebook as having been composed at a fairly advanced stage of instruction. There are also several internal indicators that the dictation technique being used is a variation on Berlitz aural-oral pattern practice, a method that Joyce knew well.[7] The following are examples that I have translated into English:

Do you like French cooking?
Yes, if the cook is good. (VIII.A.1.1)
May I please send three packages to Ireland?
I think so; I will get the information. (VIII.A.1.2)
Are you Mister Paul? Absolutely correct. (VIII.A.1.6)
Are you happy with my progress, Mister Teacher? (VIII.A.1.7)
Excuse me, it's necessary for me to go to the lavatory. (VIII.A.1.7)

There are also several extraordinarily crude sentences employing vocabulary that would be used only by two men who feel completely at ease with each other. In short, notebook VIII.A.1 demonstrates not only the method that Joyce and Phokas used to learn, respectively, Greek and English; it also is evidence of a considerable advance in the matter and form of those lessons. Several letters of correspondence in Greek were copied into this notebook; one of them includes Easter greetings from Phokas to Joyce's family (VIII A.1.12). It seems most likely, then, that the material was compiled in the spring of 1918 or 1919, in line with other indications that VIII.A.1. is from a later period than the other, more lexically oriented notebooks.

A page that appears to have been removed from another late notebook testifies to the fact that his mentor enjoyed randy humor and word games as much as Joyce did. Four lines in Greek in Phokas's handwriting appear at the top of the second page (my translation):

> *Soutsos*
> If you take away the initial "S"
> And put a "P" in its place,
> Then, with absolute certainty, dear lady,
> My name will please you.

The joke lies in the similarity between the Greek proper name Soutsos and the improper Greek word for penis, *poutsos* (prick). Joyce clearly saw the thrust of the wordplay and responded with characteristic linguistic curiosity. Just beneath Phokas's quatrain are four Greek nouns in Joyce's handwriting: *peos, psole, poutsos, poutsa*. The first could be translated as penis; the last three are definitely pricks. The next item on the page would generate reams of psychoreligious comment if it were better known to archival scholars whose interests lie in such matters. Soutsos's obscene name change and the four appended pricks are followed, in Greek, in Joyce's hand, by the doxology "Glory be to the Father and to the Son and to the Holy Spirit, now and always, and for ever and ever. Amen" (VIII.A.2.2). Amen, I say—or better, in the words of Phokas and Joyce: "*phanē* = basta" (VIII.A.4.5). Enough.[8]

The record of the four-year period of café camaraderie and shared language learning by Joyce and Phokas ends on a low note. In the autumn of 1919 the Joyces left Zürich to return to Trieste. Phokas went back to Galatsi in Romania. The Joyce archives at Cornell preserve a business card printed in Greek with Phokas's name and that of his hometown. Beneath his name Phokas wrote "with the compliments of the author" and included his home address. The top portion of the same side of the card contains a brief message in the writer's native language. It begins with Tί κανεις; τί γίνεσαι; (How are you? What's going on with you?). On the other side Phokas wrote in English:

> How are you? Why you dinnot ever write to me, although I wrote to you often? In every case I holde the best remembrance of you.
>
> Paul

The note is undated, although circumstances point to some time in late 1919 or early 1920. It seems unlikely that Joyce, who was busy completing *Ulysses* and preparing to move from Trieste to Paris, ever replied. There is no record of further correspondence from Phokas.

It might be possible for an specialist in the evolution of Modern Greek to make some general observations on the basis of the scanty linguistic evidence in the Joyce archives. But vocabulary lists, semiformulaic business letters, paragraphs copied from periodicals, isolated sentences, and a few personal notes do not offer material for sophisticated analysis. Moreover, the neo-Hellenic language itself was undergoing broad and deep changes during this period. Controversy between supporters of the "purified" (*katharevousa*) and the "*popular*" (*dēmotikē*) forms was fierce.[9] The vocabulary, spelling, and syntax of emigres from Greece, even those in the Balkans or Central Europe, can be distinguished from the language of those in Greece itself. It is clear that Phokas's Greek was that of the diaspora. Moreover, Joyce's method and motive for studying Greek were those of a linguistically adept student who clearly enjoyed learning and teaching languages—as long as he did not have to earn his living that way. Joyce's statement in a June 24, 1921, letter to Harriet Shaw Weaver, is an accurate evaluation of his own proficiency:

"I forgot to tell you another thing. I don't even know Greek though I am spoken of as erudite. . . . I spoke or used to speak modern Greek not too badly (I speak four or five languages fluently enough) and have spent a great deal of time with Greeks of all kinds from noblemen down to onionsellers, chiefly the latter. I am superstitious about them. They bring me luck"[10] (*Letters* I.167, *SL* 284). Another emigre whom Joyce met in wartime Zürich was Paul Ruggiero. They first became acquainted at the Club des Etrangers. Although he was born in Thessaloniki in 1887, Ruggiero was not an ethnic Greek, but Italian. He was Catholic rather than Orthodox and attended the French school in that northeastern Greek city. In 1912 his family moved to Istanbul, where he worked for the railroad company of the Ottoman Empire. In 1916 the Turks expelled many foreigners, and Ruggiero wound up in Zürich, where he became a clerk in a bank.[11] Ruggiero helped James and Nora Joyce find a more comfortable apartment in the city and remained a steadfast friend and correspondent for many years. In fact, when the Joyces sought to return to Switzerland during World War II, Ruggiero helped to make the arrangements. He and Madame Giedion-Welcker met their train at the Zürich station on December 10, 1940.[12]

As far as I know, no letters from Ruggiero to Joyce have survived, and it is thus impossible to determine whether he ever corresponded with his friend in Greek. I doubt that Joyce's basic command of the spoken language would have been good enough for him to have composed or followed a text involving any extended or important matters, especially after the passage of a number of years without practice. Published letters from Joyce to Ruggiero are written in Italian or French; there is a brief telegram in English (*Letters* III.501). In a short September 1938 letter from Paris, Joyce told Ruggiero that he had heard a French version of a song that his friend used to sing in Greek: "Epigha monos eis tin akrothalassia" (I walked out alone on the shore of the sea) (*Letters* III.430 and *JJII* 714).

A month or so later, on November 18, 1938, Joyce wrote another short letter to Ruggiero requesting his friend to write out the words of this song, "Un Rêve," in both French and Greek. Joyce wanted to sing that piece at the American Thanksgiving dinner that Maria Jolas was preparing for him. That note also includes an exclamation of some literary-historical significance: "Ho terminato il mio libro!!!" (I have finished my book). The book is, of course, *Finnegans Wake*. In the sentence immediately following that announcement, Joyce includes two words from languages other than Italian: "Thanksgiving (Εὐχαριστὶα)." Although the accentuation is characteristically askew, the meaning and the sentiments of Joyce's Greek translation are clear. For Ruggiero, the standard neo-Hellenic word for thank you or appreciation might not have had the same semiritualistic ring that *eucharist* would for an English speaker. Joyce, however, is clearly linking the spirit of the holiday with heartfelt thanks for the completion of his long-in-progress work. That solemn tone is muted by a another reference to the project: "Ho finito quel maledetto libro" (I have finished this cursed book).[13]

There are also several unpublished postcards that Joyce wrote to Ruggiero, sending short holiday greetings in Greek. One was sent from Locarno on December 23, 1917, with Christmas greetings: *Kala Christougenia*. Another, posted on December 31, 1919, from Trieste, thanks Ruggiero for his Christmas greeting and wishes him "many years." Joyce's signature is preceded by *o philos sas* (your friend). Another card, signed by the entire family, was sent from Paris on December 22, 1923. It testifies to the multiple languages in which these friends were able to communicate. The brief "Natale" message is written by Joyce in Italian, but he added his own wishes to the bilingual, French-English "Bonne Année / Happy New Year" greeting printed on the card. Under that Joyce wrote "Merry Xmas" and repeated the message in Greek, Italian, and German.[14]

There are also two items in his correspondence with Ezra Pound that are relevant to Joyce's occasional use of Modern Greek. The first is a calling card that was probably sent as a birthday greeting in 1923. Beneath Joyce's printed name, he wrote, in Greek, "To your good health and many years."[15] The second item is an illustrated postcard sent from Paris to Pound in Rapallo (forwarded to Syracuse in Sicily) on December 31, 1924. Joyce's usual New Year's wish, πόλλα κρόνια (many years), is misspelled, perhaps on purpose: *chronia* should begin with a chi, not a kappa; note the same "error" in *Ulysses*: "polla kronia" (*U* 12.600). What is significant about this document in the Joyce-Pound correspondence is not the formulaic Greek phrase but the illustration on the other side of the card. It depicts a pygmy elephant crowned with a giant wreath of leaves. A chubby little girl in a ruffled dress, carrying a bouquet of flowers, leans her left arm on the elephant's right tusk. Above this odd pair is the greeting "Bonne Année." Joyce's handwritten message on the other side of the card (which I paraphrase) facetiously interprets this scene as a picture of Pound introducing the animal to his American public. The elephant, which Joyce claims had just been decorated by the "Stockholm Thickhide Society," is identified as "*Ulixes*," Latin for *Ulysses*. Joyce obviously intended his comic New Year's card to be read by Pound as a jab at the Swedish Academy, which awards the annual Nobel Prize for literature.

There are several other "Good Luck" Greek friends of Joyce who deserve brief mention. Baron Ambrogio Ralli and Count Francesco Sordina were wealthy aristocrats of great influence in Trieste's Hellenic communities.[16] They were among Joyce's earliest language pupils and, in 1915, proved instrumental in securing an exit permit and lent funds so that the family could get to Zürich during World War I (*JJII* 255, 392). Joyce arranged to have a copy of *Dubliners* sent to Ralli (*Letters* II.455) and a copy of the baron's letter of thanks, in English, survives.[17] Later, Ralli was the only Triestine to subscribe to the first edition of *Ulysses* (*JJII* 506, 518). The baron's residence serves as a momentary backdrop to a chance meeting with Amalia Popper in *Giacomo Joyce*: "As I came out of Ralli's house I came upon her suddenly as we were both giving alms to a blind beggar" (*GJ* 15).

Another Triestine Greek whose friendship proved somewhat fortunate to Joyce was Nicolas Santos, a fruit merchant who seems to have acted as a low-volume bookseller. In a handwritten letter, with check enclosed, Joyce asks Grant Richards to send Santos six copies of *Dubliners*; the letter is dated June 6, 1914, one day after publication (see *JJII* 353).[18] (A far more enduring contribution to Joyce's literary enterprise was made by Nicolas's wife, Signora Gisela Santos, one of several women who were reputed to be models for Molly Bloom [*JJII* 376]).[19] And when the Joyce family got on the train from Trieste to Switzerland in 1915, the first person whom Joyce saw was a Greek pupil, Mario Megavis. Ellmann quotes from notes that Gorman made for his biography that to Joyce "this encounter seemed an omen that all would go well" (*JJII* 386).

Sometime during the 1920s Joyce composed a couplet on Myrsine Moschos, a young woman of Greek descent who was an assistant to Miss Beach in the Shakespeare and Company Bookshop:

Little Miss Moschos
Soft as a mouse goes.[20]

In Greek *moschos* means both a young shoot of a plant and a calf—and by extension "girl." Since Miss Moschos's first name means myrtle (*myrsine*), Joyce may have intended additional etymological fun to match his initial lines.[21]

Apart from the formulaic greetings on postcards, no original composition by Joyce in Greek has survived. There is no indication in his letters or notebooks that he ever read anything in neo-Hellenic literature. In neither *Ulysses* nor *Finnegans Wake* are there extended passages in Greek. Indeed, the Greek wordplay in the latter work looks as if it were mediated through a classical lexicon, not directly recalled from vocabulary drill in Zürich. Although there is a natural, genetic ancient-modern link in almost all of the word roots involved, it seems clear that Joyce never intended his lessons with Phokas to be a gateway to the *language* of ancient Greek literature. Rather, their basic oral-aural instruction gave him a feel for and some confidence in the ways that Homer's latter-day descendants used their evolving language. Perhaps his modest level of accomplishment in that endeavor helped to lessen the feeling of academic inferiority caused by his inability to perform standard exercises in the declension or conjugation of classical forms. At any rate, while I detect no traces of Joyce's study of *hellēnika* in *Ulysses,* there are some Modern Greek contributions to the polyglot sound and shape of his last book.

There are two fairly substantial clusters of Modern Greek in Joyce's Notebooks from the work-in-progress period in Paris. The first is a series of five sentences in Joyce's handwriting, most of which contain aphoristic statements about sleep. The following is the most pointed example: *"Tas nychtas ta kamomata ta blepe ē mera kai gela"* (The day sees the works/deeds of the night and laughs) (VI.B.18.137).[22] Another deals with the reputed advantages of a productive older man over an untested younger man. Even though both topics have thematic relevance to the *Wake,* these uncrossed notes do not reappear in that text in any form that I can detect. At the bottom of the same Notebook page, however, there is an index of related entries that were crossed out and used. The second verb in the Greek sentence quoted above is *gela* (laughs). Joyce experimented with the meaning and the pronunciation of this word in several notes: "[bk]yellaughter / [bk]yelaughter / gellaughter" (VI.B.18.137). The modern pronunciation of the letter gamma (*g*) frequently sounds like an

English *y*. Thus Joyce joined the pair of synonyms from different languages to produce a comic compound. In the *Wake* the process is taken one step further; the English component is replaced by its German equivalent, "yellachters" (*FW* 92.2–3).

Another archival cluster of neo-Hellenic material is found in a very late Notebook (dated late August to mid-October 1938). The two sections were written in an English transliteration of the Greek by Joyce. I suspect that he was transcribing the words of a Greek speaker who recited the passage for him. The first section, with its formulaic opening and emphatic rhyme, sounds like the beginning of a tale or song:

> *ena kairo kai ena semani*
> *ichane i turkoi ramassini*
> *kai eurassene to arni*
> *mes to kassani*

> (Once upon a time
> the Turks had a celebration
> and boiled the lamb
> in the big pot) (VI.B.41.157)

The English translation of the next section has a familiar ring: "It was a time once upon a time when I was small and they lived well and we even better" (VI.B.41.157). Those lines, which Joyce wrote out in transliterated form were, without doubt, copied from a reply to a letter he sent to Paul Ruggiero on September 4, 1938:

> Again I have to ask you for your help. How do you begin and end a fairy tale or a little story for children in Greek? To explain the matter to you: in English you begin:
>> Once upon a time and a very good time it was; and you end like this:
>> So they put on the kettle and they made tea and they lived happily ever after.
> The Germans say "Es war einmal" (It was once upon a time) and they end "Und wenn sie nicht gestorben sind, so leben noch heute!" (And if they have not died, they are alive even today!). Of course I do not want the Greek translation but something typically Greek (with the Italian Translation underneath). Each country has its own expressions for this purpose. I have finished my long book. Thanks to the Almighty. (*Letters* I.400)[23]

Joyce did not indicate to his friend what he intended to do with the Greek form of "Once upon a time," but the English version of that formula is the opening sentence of *Portrait* (*P* 7), and variations appear all over the *Wake*.[24]

Ioanna Ioannidou and Leo Knuth began to publish a list of Modern Greek elements in the *Wake* in the early 1970s.[25] That project stopped at the end of I.6, the episode of "Burrus and Caseous." (I assume that their efforts were superseded, a little over one-fourth of the way through Joyce's book, by the publication of O Hehir and Dillon, *A Classical Lexicon to "Finnegans Wake,"* in 1977, although that work takes only occasional notice of Modern Greek material.) Ioannidou and Knuth are quick to admit that it is a "tricky job" to establish limits of relevancy in compiling this type of word list. For example, unless the exact circumstances of composition are known, it is often virtually impossible to distinguish many neo-Hellenic elements from ancient Greek forms, or the latter from artificially generated but lexically domesticated English technical terms. In the case of Modern Greek the problem of paternity is compounded by several special factors. Throughout the twentieth century the spelling, transliteration, and pronunciation of the contemporary language (and its re-creation of ancient Greek forms) have been in flux (or is it *phlyks*?).[26] Since the standard French-Modern Greek dictionary (Pernot's *Lexique*) was not published until 1933, Joyce's primary sources of information during the first crucial decade of the *Wake*-in-progress would have been his memory or native-speaking Greeks whom he met in Paris. Of the greatest significance in this matter of etymological influence is a natural tendency to go too far in finding parallels. Although they guard against it, Ioannidou and Knuth too often succumb to the temptation to hear or see Modern Greek where it does not exist, in my judgment.

The following is a concrete example of their overextension of the linguistic and textual evidence. When Joyce reported that "the lass to be greeted rauchously . . . with houx and *epheus* and measured with missiles too" (*FW* 97.35–36; my emphasis), I doubt very much that he had "euches [efchés] blessings" in mind for the italicized word in the quotation. What he did have in mind are some linguistically festive "holly" (*houx* in French), "ivy" (*Epheu* in German), and "mistletoe" (English). Since the context calls for raucous greetings, there are also some "hoots" and cries of "alas" (*eheu* in Latin) to go with the missiles. But I can muster no contextual or acoustic support for supposing a Modern Greek pronunciation of εὐχή (*euchē/evchē/efhē*), "blessing," here.[27] As a matter of phonetic fact, Joyce *did* preserve the standard ancient pronunciation of the diphthong *eu* in the same root on at least one occasion in the *Wake*. Shaun responds to Issy's persistent courtesy to him: "Ever gloriously kind! And I truly am *eucherised* to yous" (*FW* 461.36–462.1; my emphasis). In Modern Greek, *eucharistō* (thank you) is pronounced *efharistó*. In his version of Shaun's appreciation, Joyce not merely reproduced the orthography (*eu*) but also emphasized the standard English pronunciation of this diphthong by ending his expression of thanks with an emphatic "yous."[28]

Next is a series of examples that are meant to highlight instances in which I think Ioannidou and Knuth have not missed the neo-Hellenic mark. Since the original format of their findings permitted only minimal comment, I expand the explanation by notching some of my own lexical arrows. Whenever possible I support these items with a reference from one of the Zürich notebooks.

- "You *phonio* saxo? Nnnn" (*FW* 16.7): There is an ingenious triple pun embedded in the emphasized word, and all of the possible meanings stem from two Greek roots. On the first level, the question is one of a series in which Mutt seeks to discover the language spoken by Jute. He has just asked, "You spigotty anglease? Nnn" (*FW* 16.6–7). The next inquiry uses a standard Greek verb for "to speak," "to make a sound," *phoneō*. The second level involves wordplay with a musical instrument, the euphonium, which produces its sounds well (*eu* in Greek). Finally, an appropriate insult is implied: *phonikos* is the Modern Greek adjective meaning bloody, murderous. The Jute is thus racially allied with a member of the two other Germanic tribes that invaded England in the fifth century, the Angles and the Saxons. In short, from an insularly Celtic perspective, Jute is a bloody Saxon. In a vocabulary list in a Zürich notebook Joyce recorded "*phonos/phoneuō* = murder" (VIII.A.2.3).

- "the tropic of Copricapron" (*FW* 26.12–13): Here Joyce has twisted the name of the constellation Capricorn (Latin for goat's horn) into a Greek phrase *koproi kaprōn,* meaning boars' shit. One of Joyce's practice sentences in a Zürich notebook reads "*Oi chiroi trogoun skata*" (The pigs eat shit). In a word list on the same notebook page appear "*skata* = shite / *kopros* = dung" (VIII.A.1.8); in another list "*kopros* = excrement" (VIII.A.4.24).

- "leadpencil . . . Molyydokondylon" (*FW* 56.12–13): This is one of the many instances in which the text of the *Wake* provides its own gloss for words from an unfamiliar language. Immediately following a notebook sentence that asks, "Do you have a pen?" Joyce wrote "*molybdokondilon* = pencil" (VIII.A.4.7; also note VI.B.45.149).

- "forken*pootsies*" (*FW* 77.32): My italicized conclusion of this bilingual compound points to its Modern Greek source, *poutsos* (prick). Joyce included this term in a list of synonyms in notebook VIII.A.1.2. I also suggest that the first element in the Wakean term is meant to be a rough approximation of the Dublin pronunciation of the all-purpose English participle, "fuckin'."

- "Guinney's Gap, he said, between what they said and the pussykitties" (*FW* 90.13–14): This excerpt appears in a passage that describes the celestial combat between the Good and the Bad Angels in terms of the terrestrial battle of the sexes. The synecdoche reduces all females to a pair of crude expressions for the external appearance of their sexual organs.[29] To reinforce his intent Joyce introduced the figure with a phonetic spelling of the Greek word for a woman, *gynē*. In Modern Greek the declensional form of the same noun supplies the term for wife, *gynaika*, as Joyce notes at VIII.A.4.7. An exercise sentence also reads *ē gynaika einai teras, einai alles ponēres* (A wife is a monster; they're all sly) (VIII.A.1.8).

The following set of citations has been selected to provide distinct examples of Modern Greek pronunciation at work. This was the Greek that Joyce heard from Phokas and Ruggiero in Zürich and that he would have heard from Hellenophones in Trieste or Paris. There is direct testimony to Joyce's interest in and problems with the pronunciation of Greek. An ear-witness in 1937 reports that Joyce "quoted long passgaes [of Homer's *Odyssey*] in his strange pronunciation where modern Greek coalesced with the Erasmus tradition and was flavored by English intonation."[30] In addition to the competing systems for re-creating the sound of ancient Greek, there would be differences in the way various members of the diaspora community, with varying levels of education, spoke their native language, which also had its own regional dialects. It must also be stressed that the language itself was going through a period of rapid and unstable transition. The following excerpt from the current *Blue Guide to*

Greece can be taken as equally applicable to Joyce's time: "No consistency can be attempted in the language or spelling of hotel names, since they are often chosen quite arbitrarily themselves. What is displayed on the building is likely not to correspond to the name listed in the hotel guide—only experience can help in the realization that (e.g.) Ilios, Helios, and Soleil designate the same hotel (Ηλιος)."[31]

One of the most noticeable differences between the pronunciation of ancient and Modern Greek is the vocalization of the second letter of the alphabet, beta. The classical, Erasmian pronunciation of that letter was equivalent to that given to a *b* in English. The neo-Hellenic pronunciation of β is *v*. Thus, the name of the English poet (and hero of the Greek war of independence), Lord Byron, is transliterated letter-by-letter as βύρων and pronounced "Víron." To approximate the sound of an English *b* contemporary Greek orthography uses the letters mu and pi (μπ [*mp*]). That explains why Greek scholars of English literature sometimes try to capture the original sounds, and spell Byron's name Μπάυρον (Baïron). Joyce was certainly aware of this phonetic shift: "that absurdly *bullsfooted bee* declaring with an even plainer *dummp*show than does the *mute* commoner with us how hard a thing it is to *mpe mporn* a gentleman" (*FW* 120.6–9; my emphases).

The following comment on the italicized elements is designed to translate Joyce's sound- and wordplay into intelligible English. McHugh cites a saying: "Knows not a B from a bull's foot"; it means "to be totally illiterate." The German noun *Dompfaff* means bullfinch; the adjective *dumm* means dumb. A dumbshow is a part of or interlude between parts of a play; it was originally performed without speech, literally a pantomime. In philological terms a mute is a consonant formed by a temporary stopping of the breath; *B* and *P* are both mutes. A person who cannot speak is also called mute or dumb. If the *Wake's* "mpe mporn" were pronounced as if it were a phrase in Modern Greek, the transliterated transcription would be "be born," which is its sense in the context of the citation.

There are several less obvious examples of the sound value of the neo-Hellenic beta in the *Wake*. In one of the Cad's encounters with HCE (apparently as related by Kate), it is made clear that she takes no guff from either party: "*Lave* that bloody stone as it is! . . . And, you, *take* that barrel back where you got it" (*FW* 80.29–32). I suggest that both of the imperatives that I have emphasized are connected. The first is Modern Greek, *labe* (pronounced "lave"), from the verb meaning "to take," "to grab." As uttered by Irish speakers of English, "lave" of course, means leave. The nearby—and narratively parallel—"take," however, argues that the two commands are not antonyms but synonyms. As additional evidence I offer another passage, in which HCE is defended against the various accusations: "if ever in all his exchequered career he up or *lave* a chancery hand to *take* or throw the sign of a mortal stick or stone at man" (*FW* 91.30–32). Here the two verb forms that I have italicized are not grammatically parallel, but their proximity argues for typically Wakean etymological play. Finally, two levels of allusion are at work in the following thematically emphatic sentences: "With a *bockalips* of finisky fore his feet. And a barrowload of *guenesis* hoer his head" (*FW* 6.26–27). The primary allusion is to Tim Finnegan's wake, in which the hero is laid out "with a gallon of whisky at his feet, and a barrel of porter at his head." The first allusive level is scriptural: The Bible of the Christian Church has the book of Genesis (Greek for beginning) at its head and comes to a finish with the Apocalypse (Greek for revelation). The second allusive level is spiritual: Guinness is the best-known brand of Irish stout; the Modern Greek word for bottle is *mpoukali,* pronounced "boukali." Joyce mixed the vowels up, but his intent is clear in "*Mpakoles*" (pronounced "Bakolis"), which heads a notebook page (VIII.A.4.5).

Since I do not wish to make a bull's foot out of a Greek *B,* I now turn to a few examples that illustrate how Joyce exploited other features of contemporary Greek pronunciation. In addition to being part of the sound-sense fun of the *Wake,* each citation contributes to a major theme in the book.

- In "Anna Livia" the washerwomen speculate about the extent of ALP's amorous encounters: "She had a *flewmen* of her owen. . . . *so aimai moe, that's agapo!*" (*FW* 202.5–6). The first word I have emphasized has its source in *flumen,* Latin for river. The second excerpt is a phonetically blended version of the Modern Greek sentence *Zōē mou, sas agapō* (My life, I love you!). The translation is cited in quotation marks because I have taken it directly from the author's own footnote to Byron's poem "Maid Athens, Ere We Part." The refrain that follows each of the five stanzas is written in Greek and glossed as a "Romaic [Modern Greek] expression of tenderness."[32] Joyce's literary source is confirmed by a previous allusion to "(meed of anthems here we pant!)" (*FW* 41.10).

- There is a Modern Greek version of the "Dark Man" question: "Men, teacan a tea simmering, hamo mavrone kerry O?" (*FW* 247.14). In the original the frequently repeated inquiry would be *Mēn, ti kanete sēmeron, ho mou mauro kyrio*? (How are you today, my dark sir?). The reply is given in the same language: "Teapotty. Teapotty" (*FW* 247.15), which reproduces the genuine ancient Greek *Tipote. Tipote* (So so. So so). The more modern and colloquial force of this all-purpose phrase (don't mention it) is recorded in a Zürich notebook: "ouden / tipote = nothing" (VIII.A.4.13) and the formulaic greeting/inquiry (*Ti kaneis*?) also begins Phokas's plaintive card to Joyce from Romania. The Wakean reply also appears in another multilingual passage, "Tippoty, kyrie, tippotty," where it is immediately followed by a question in Hindi: "Cha kai rotty kai makkar, sahib?" (Tea and bread and butter, sir?) (*FW* 54.12–13). But here even the Hindi nouns are connected by *kai*, the Greek word for "and."

- When HCE calls his children home as night falls, it begins to get cold: "Drr, *deff, coal lay on* and, pzz, call us pyrress!" (*FW* 244.17–18). The excerpt is one of a number of Joyce's evocations of the deluge motif. My italics highlight the neo-Hellenic pronunciation (eu = *ev* or *ef*) of Deucalion, who, with his wife, Pyrrha, survived the cosmic flood in Greek mythology.

- The following exclamation appears in an interlude in the Butt and Taff episode: "*By the hross of Xristos*" (*FW* 342.18–19). The twenty-second letter of the Greek alphabet is χ (chi), which is a voiceless fricative (as in the German *ich*) in Modern Greek. In fact, the fricative element is often so minimal that one hears only a slightly rough "h." Thus, "*hross of Xristos*" is meant to reproduce, phonetically, "cross" and, graphically, "Christ."

- The redemption motif is linked to an ophthalmological motif in the Wakeism "stavrotides" (*FW* 482.10–11). *Stauros*, the Greek word for cross, is given in its contemporary spoken form (αυ = *av* or *af*); the suffix -*ides* means "son of" and is a final component of many names in both ancient and Modern Greek. Here, however, I do not believe that Joyce's primary intent is to call Old Man John "Crosson"; rather, he can be identified by his "crossed eyes."

- The final verse of the Greek national anthem is "Hail, O hail, liberty!" The stanza that it concludes was written out by a native speaker in a Zürich notebook (VII.A.4.15). One of Budgen's notes for his book on the making of *Ulysses* rejects Joyce's suggestion that he quote the line in the original, just as it had often been sung at parties in Zürich by Joyce and Ruggiero.[33] In the *Wake*, the author, tenor, and student of Greek does not follow his own advice: instead of the notebook's χαῖρ' ω χαῖρε ἐλευθριὰ (which, according to the ancient pronunciation, would be transliterated as *chair' ō chaire eleutheria*), one finds a phonetic reproduction of the modern pronunciation of the first part of the verse: "Here Ohere" (*FW* 117.2). On the other hand, the Greek word for liberty is preserved in the ancient form and pronunciation in "(*Eleutherio*dendron! Spare, woodmann, spare!)" (*FW* 42.20; my emphasis). From these and other examples I deduce that Joyce's oral and graphic reproduction of Greek, ancient or Modern, was fluid.

• In September 1933 Joyce sent a postcard to Paul Ruggiero that deserves to be cited as a pedagogical coda to the preceding examples of Modern Greek pronunciation, especially of the aspirated consonants θ (theta), φ (phi), and χ (chi). Joyce wrote that he knew that the word for enemy was εχθρος (*echthros*), not εκτρος (*ektros*), but he was unsure where to place the accent. The whole point of his citing correct and incorrect English transliterations must be the fact that current pronunciation blurred the distinction between the aspirated (add "h") and unaspirated (no "h" sound) forms of the English letters *t* and *c/k*. Joyce, however, knew the right spelling because one of his mentors had corrected the pupil's error of "ektros" to "echthros = enemy" in a basic word list (VIII.A.4.9).[34] Joyce learned this lesson well; in the *Wake* Greek and English scripts are curiously mixed to produce the required double aspiration, "exthro" (*FW* 92.1).

In winding up the demonstration of neo-Hellenic elements in *Finnegans Wake*, all the examples that follow are ineluctably part of the modern—as opposed to the classical or Byzantine—vocabulary. The first two entered the Greek language during the nation's long occupation by the Ottoman Empire (1460–1832).

• The Turkish word *giaour* (pronounced "jour") is an Arabic term of scorn for non-Muslims; it means something like "infidel cur." Joyce must have heard it used, in less specific situations of abuse, by his

Greek friends. It is so deployed once in the *Wake:* "dug of a dog of a dgiaour, ye!" (*FW* 68.18). The other two appearances of *giaour* occur in distinctly religious situations, the first of which has a linguistic subtext that thrusts the Turkish word into an Armenian context: "we must grope on till Zerogh hour like pou owl giaours" (*FW* 107.21–22). The second passage compactly brings the world's three great monotheistic religions (and the Eastern Christian Church) into an uneasy state of toleration: "*jewr* of a *chrestend,* respecting the *otherdogs* churchees" (*FW* 312.32; my emphases).

- The Modern Greek word *soutzoukia* is borrowed from Turkish; in both languages it means smoked sausages (or stewed meatballs). Joyce uses the term correctly: "zootzaks for eatlust, including . . . rookworst [Dutch for smoked sausage]" (*FW* 77.31–32; my ellipsis). In the next line of text are the "forkenpootsies" (*FW* 77.32) discussed earlier. I suspect that, in colloquial discourse, that term might also be used for "sausage," or vice versa.

- One of the contemporary Greek words for house, *to spiti,* is used by Joyce in the phrase "tospite of the deluge" (*FW* 86.23–24). The lexical item is confirmed by a notebook entry "oikia / Speti } House" (VIII.A.4.30). The Wakean context suggests an Irish parallel to the American adage: "Please do not spit. Remember the Johnstown flood."

- A popular variety of Greek red wine is called *Maurodaphne,* literally dark laurel. Joyce acknowledges both elements in "Mavro! Letty Lerck's lafing light throw those laurals now on her daphdaph" (*FW* 203.29–30). The Mediterranean wine can also be ordered at a Dublin pub: "Mabhrodaphne, brown pride of our custard house quay, amiable with repastful, cheerus graciously, cheer us!?" (*FW* 406.25–27). A last appearance is in a sylvan setting: "in mauves of moss and daphnedews" (*FW* 556.18).

- As far back as the Homeric epics, the Greek word for smoke was *kapnos.* When Athena pleads Odysseus's case before Zeus, the goddess says, "He longs to see even the smoke (*kapnon*) raising up from his own land" (*Odyssey* 1.58–59). Just as the smoke from a hearth fire was a Homeric symbol for home, so too is there a colloquial Modern Greek expression for family unity: The members smoke together, *hēmikapnousi.* The components of this verb are *hēmi-* (half) and *kapnō* (to smoke). In the Eleventh Question in I.6 Shaun is asked by Shem if he would help save the soul of a poor, boozy, exiled poet. After all sort of evasions, Shaun says no, even if he and the petitioner were "bread by the same fire . . . , were we tucked in the one bed and bit by the one flea, homogallant [Italian for gentleman] and *hemycapnoise*" (*FW* 168.8–11; my emphasis). The italicized word is a reasonable facsimile of the Modern Greek verb form. In its metaphorical and etymological components, members of a family show their closeness by sharing a smoke, most likely with alternate puffs from a *narghile* (waterpipe).[35]

- The reason why Odysseus sits weeping on the shore of Calypso's island is his desire return home to Penelope. The beautiful goddess Calypso no longer pleases him: "At night he would lie beside her in the hollow caves because he had to, an *unwilling* man with a *willing* woman." In the original, a pair of emphatic Homeric participles close the verse, side by side: *par' ouk ethelōn ethelousē* (*Odyssey* 5.154–55). The primary ancient and Modern Greek word for "to will, "want," "wish" is (e)th*ēlō* (the *e* disappears in later usage). In the *Wake* Joyce plays with this verb, which is such an essential emblem of the human condition: "Be the lonee I will" (*FW* 88.14). I suggest that the second and third elements here be divided differently, into "thelo nee," which I hear as θέλω ναί, the neo-Hellenic equivalent of "I will, yes." The model for this statement is obvious: The Modern Greek translation of *Ulysses* ends with the following rendition of Molly Bloom's final affirmations, καί ναί εἶπα ναί θέλω Ναί (*kai nai eipa nai thelō Nai*).[36] My suggestion is also supported by Joyce's characteristic repetition of the same word or phrase in a different language, in this case English, "I will." A similar etymological figure is found near the end of the *Wake:* "Telle whish" (*FW* 597.36). Here the Greek verb is an imperative, and its initial theta has elided its "h." That echo of typical contemporary pronunciation receives, however, a compensatory aspiration in the first phoneme of "whish." In one of his pompous defenses of his behavior, Shaun cites "honorey causes through thelemontary channels" (*FW* 422.27–28). Here academic Latin (*honoris causa*) combines the elementary—and perhaps alimentary—means of warning someone to exercise correct choice (*thelemon*). This minatory and monitory etymological glide has taken us from Calypso's mythical island of Scherie to the smoggy squares of modern Athens.

Greek Orthodox Church

The religion of the vast majority of the inhabitants of modern Greece and the Greeks of the diaspora is officially known as the Holy Orthodox Catholic Apostolic Eastern Church. Its patriarch still resides in Istanbul, once known as Constantinople, the capital city of the Byzantine Empire. In 1054 Pope Leo IX excommunicated Patriarch Michael Cerularius and all members of his flock. That decree resulted in a permanent schism between the Western (Roman/Latin) and Eastern (Greek) churches. Since then the split has been widened by differences in theological and disciplinary matters, and exacerbated by the Crusaders' sack of Constantinople in 1204. The language, music, and art of the Orthodox Church were a mainstay of Byzantine and subsequent Greek culture, especially during the centuries of Ottoman domination.

Although Joyce was personally fascinated by aspects of Orthodox religious services (*Letters* II.86–87 and III.420), that interest was clearly more an exercise in choral appreciation than a demonstration of language competence or dogmatic approbation. On the other hand, Joyce emphatically introduced the Eastern Church into parts of his own inspired liturgy of the word in *Finnegans Wake*. The most conspicuous display occurs in the fable of "The Mookse and The Gripes" (*FW* 152.15–159.18). Among the roles those two characters represent are, respectively—but by no means respectfully—the Roman Catholic/Latin and the Orthodox/Greek and Russian churches. Many theological terms and the names of several patriarchal officials are interspersed throughout the fable.

Since almost none of this ecclesiological trivia is fundamentally linguistic, its presentation must defer to the following, strictly secular chapter that considers Joyce's devoutly comic abuse of the classical roots of Greek.[37]

13

Classical Greek

Although they do not neglect unearthed documents or inscriptions, archaeologists deal primarily with artifacts, things made by people. The final stratum of James Joyce's life offers an important artifact for the literary archaeologist. On his desk the day he died was a Greek lexicon (*JJII* 742). That work—or one like it—must also have been near at hand when Joyce was placing his Greek flourishes into the text of *Finnegans Wake*. A phrase like "during a chiliad of perihelygangs" (hundred-year period of close approaches to the sun) (*FW* 15.4–5) is not pulled out of the air. Neologisms like "Aletheometry" (truth-measuring) (*FW* 370.13) or "stigmataphoron (sign-carrying) (*FW* 606.27) are not recalled from casual conversations. The classical Greek contributions to the *Wake* are swotted up from a dictionary. The slang verb in the previous sentence is not meant to insult Joyce or to imply that his writing smacks of schoolboy pedantry. Rather, when it came to classical Greek, multilingual Joyce had to do what even advanced students of that language do—go to Liddell and Scott.[1]

The giant *Greek-English Lexicon* compiled by Henry G. Liddell and Robert Scott was first published at Oxford by the Clarendon Press in 1843. Numerous editions followed, and the 1996 volume (with the *Revised Supplement*) totals 2,446 quarto pages.[2] This work is the lexicon used worldwide by all serious scholars of the language and literature of ancient Greece. (An abridged version, in 804 octavo pages, is intended for use by intermediate-level students; its scope, portability, and cost mark it as the work that Joyce most probably consulted.) There is also internal evidence from the *Wake* that Joyce was familiar with the work of Liddell and Scott.

The references cited in Glasheen's *Census* are a starting point, but they must be examined with caution. In the river-swollen "Anna Livia" section of the *Wake,* two lads "in scoutsch breeches" appear slightly before a "leada, laida" lass (*FW* 204.6,10). Most readers would pass over the possibility of allusion here, regardless of Glasheen's comment: "the Liddell Water is a Scotch river."[3] True enough, but in my opinion it is a long, rough road that would link that bit of Highland geography to a classical lexicographer. A second reference needs some academic orientation: "Christ's Church varses Bellial!" (*FW* 301.9–10; note the crossed entry at VI.B.4.66). Liddell was Dean of Christ Church, and Scott was Master of Balliol—both positions at important colleges at Oxford. The university was sometimes called the Varsity, especially in terms of sports competition. On a more theological plane, the phrase also contains an allusion to the enduring battle between members of the Christian community and Belial, a name given to Satan or one of the fallen angels. A far more obvious instance, "What had she on, the liddell oud oddity?" (*FW* 207.26–27) is best understood, like "liddle giddles" (*FW* 448.25), as a reference to the learned Dean's daughter, Alice Liddell, who was a model for the feature character in Lewis Carroll's *Alice in Wonderland.* Lewis Carroll was the pen name of Charles Lutwidge Dodgson, a mathematics scholar at Christ Church.[4]

Since it is almost certain that a large number of the *Wake*'s roster of Greek words without obvious English derivatives came from a dictionary, one can often find enough information about them in O Hehir and Dillon's *Classical Lexicon* or McHugh's *Annotations.* My examination of the classical Greek linguistic elements in Joyce's last work deals with two broad categories of evidence: first, those words or phrases that involve details not evident in a mere citation of meaning, especially when their contribution to narrative context deserves more comment than a literal translation; second, the many examples of one of Joyce's favorite rhetorical devices, *figura etymologica,* that contain a Greek element as one of the comparative units. (*Figura etymologica* is a type of wordplay in which the same or similar terms, from two different languages, appear in close proximity to emphasize each other's lexical force. In political terms, a "catastrophic revolution" is a good example, since both words—one from Greek, the other from Latin roots—designate something that has been "overturned.")

Lexical Legerdemain

- *FW* 31.35: *"andrewpaulmurphyc* narratives." The commentaries correctly point out that this apparently Irish name is a phonetic representation of the adjective *anthropomorphic* (*anthrōpos,* human; *morphos,* shape, form). The term is most frequently applied to situations in which a being of greater (divine) or less (animal) than human characteristics is described in human terms. Yahweh's extraordinary meeting with Moses on Mount Sinai is a case in point. God placed Moses in a cleft in a rock and covered him with His hand; then, as God passed by, He removed His hand: "and you will see my back, but my face will not be seen" (Exodus 33.23). In this section of the *Wake,* the *"genesis"* (*FW* 30.2) of HCE's name "Earwicker" is being discussed. In the best traditions of the higher criticism of Scripture or other ancient texts, readers are alerted by Joyce to watch out for anthropomorphic aspects in the various explanations.

- *FW* 59.8: "lemonsized orchids." In the context of a nearby slang term for a large male sex organ ("lallance a talls" [*FW* 59.7]), it should be noted that the Greek word for testicles is *orchis;* small testes are *orchidia.* That interpretation is supported by "his own orchistruss accompaniment" (*FW* 128.26), where McHugh's gloss indicates that *orchestra* is a slang term for testicles. The same theme is also picked up by another phrase that occurs at the start of another highly genital passage: "the acoustic and orchidectural management of the tonehall" (*FW* 165.8–9). The Greek term for testicle is preceded by versions of both the Greek adjective *akoustikon* (hearing, auditory) and a phonetically disguised reference to the Greek word for scrotum, *kystis* (literally a bladder or pouch). The female genitalia appear several lines below in "isocelating biangle" (*FW* 165.13). Here the expected delta-shaped geometric figure has equal (*iso-*) legs (*skelē*), but just two (*bi-* in Latin) angles. The following curse from the Butt-Taff dispute is also relevant: "May his *boules* grow wider so his skittles gets worse!" (*FW* 341.12–13; my emphasis). The word I have emphasized is meant primarily to suggest some off-target balls in the English game of bowls (*boules* in French). The verb "grow" (not "go") suggests a vicious wish for the enlargement of someone's testes, or perhaps his bowels.

- *FW* 60.28–29: "striving todie, hopening tomellow." There are three levels to the lexical-intentional design of these phrases: the correlative contrasts between striving/hoping; to die/to mellow; today/tomorrow. The "hope" for "tomorrow" is reinforced by the Greek participial adverb, *to mellon,* which means the future.

- *FW* 131.30: "*hagion chiton eraphon.*" These three Greek words are certainly meant to echo the New Testament phrase that describes the garment stripped from Christ at the crucifixion, *chitōn araphos* (seamless cloak) (John 19.23). Joyce added an ungrammatically neuter Greek adjective, *hagion* (holy), and changed the first letter of the adjective for the sake of an HCE acrostic.[5]

- *FW* 137.12: "Kallikak." As McHugh indicates, this is a reference to the fictitious name assigned, in a nineteenth-century sociological study, to a family with a history of generations of abnormal and criminal behavior and disease. The coinage (perhaps unintentionally) also combines two basic Greek adjectives: *kalos* (good, noble, beautiful) and *kakos* (bad, evil, ugly).

- *FW* 137.31–32: "prospector, he had a rooksacht, retrospector, he holds the holpenstake." In this contrast of mountaineering points of view, the person who looks forward (*pro* in Latin) is equipped with a backpack (*Rucksack* in German); the climber who looks backward (*retro* in Latin) can stake his future in his hopes, at the same time that he keeps his balance with an alpenstock. Joyce's sense of place and time seems to be erratic here: front/future is linked to what is behind; back/past holds future prospects. Further confusion is injected into the scene by the fact that *Rücksicht* (literally a look back) is the German noun for consideration, respect.[6] When they first run across the adverbial prepositions *emprosthen* and *opisthen,* beginning students of ancient Greek face a similar spatial-temporal disorientation. With reference to place, *emprosthen* means in front of, before; in terms of time, it means previously, beforehand. Likewise, in terms of place, *opisthen* means behind, in back of; with reference to time, it means hereafter, in the future. Teachers of Greek love to deal with the cultural implications of the apparent paradox in that pair of terms. The explanation is that the ancient Greeks regarded what was in front of them (the future) as unknowable—it was in a position they could not see (behind them).

On the other hand, what had already happened (the past) was known and could be used as a guide in subsequent decisions—it was in a position they could see (in front of them). Having spent considerable time trying to put these distinctions in place in my students' vocabulary, I feel fairly confident that I am on the right track in orienting Joyce's prospective backpacker and retrospective optimist in the *Wake* passage cited.

- *FW* 159.5: "And Nuvoletta, a lass." At the end of the controversy between the Mookse and the Gripes, Issy sashays onto the scene to attract the attention of one of the rivals. They have just been described, in several languages, as a tree and a stone. Nuvoletta may contribute to the adjacent pile of "pietrous" (*FW* 159.4) references, since *laas* is Greek for stone. (See also "Parteen-a-lax Limestone [*FW* 100.13]).

- *FW* 174.19: "(*hemoptysia diadumenos*)." The literal meanings of the two parenthetical words are, first, spitting blood, and, second, slipping through or being slipped through (if from *diaduō*), or binding up one's hair or being crowned with a wreath (if from *diadeō*). The first word would seem to be a medical term; the second may refer to a famous statue of an athlete by the sculptor Polyklitos (fifth century B.C.). Even though these terms appear in a short index of Greek words in Notebook VI.B.46.59,[7] I am at a loss to explain their source or contextual purpose (see my comments on *FW* 353.6–8 just below).

- *FW* 229.20–24: "he too had a *great big oh* in the *megafundum* . . . that meataxe *delt her* made her *microchasm* as gap as down low" (my emphases). At the center of this exercise in transliteral obscenity lie two emphasized letters of the Greek alphabet: ω (omega) (big *o*) is a graphic representation of the rounded buttocks of the big bottom (*mega* in Greek; *fundus* in Latin) of Glugg's "guffer" (HCE); Δ (delta) is the pubic area where the small split (*mikro, chasma;* both Greek) of his "gummer" (ALP) is located.

- *FW* 340.25: "psychophannies." Against O Hehir and Dillon ("one who shows [*phan-*] the soul [*psych-*]"), I side with McHugh, who hears "sycophants" here. That Greek word is derived from *sykos* (fig) and *phantēs* (one who points out); the term was used, always with contempt, for public informers, who squealed on those trying to evade the prohibition against the export of figs from Athens. Lexicographers do not give the exact historico-economic circumstances of the embargo on the fruit, but there is no doubt that the term refers, scornfully, to Attic "fig-fingerers." That arcane bit of ancient legal terminology and its modern connotation appear in "the figger in profane . . . the flatter fellows" (FW 335.30–31) and "fig-blabbers" (FW 42.4); "sycopanties" (FW 94.16) is even more explicit.

- FW 353.6–8: "(*apoxyomenously*" . . . *euphorious*)." The two parenthetical words are derived from the Greek *apoxyomenos* (being scraped away) and *euphoros* (easily borne, healthy). They appear with "*hemoptysia diadumenos*" (FW 174.19) in the *Index Manuscript* (VI.B.46.59) and complete the four-unit Greek cluster there. Again, I have no clue as to their source or contextual force. But I detect the nearby reappearance of the two earlier words; "*hemoptysia*" (spitting blood) pops up as a more genteel English "scoffin," while "*diadumenos*" (more likely "wreathed," "with hair bound up" here) is lightly transformed into "diademmed" (FW 353.6–8).

- FW 376.19: "The eitch is in her blood, arrah!" In ancient Greek an initial ρ (rho, English *r*) was pronounced with slight aspiration, hence the English transliteration of ῥυθμός as *rhythmos* or ῥητορικός as *rhētorikos*. In the *Iliad* King Rhesus of Thrace loses his life and his fabulous team of chariot horses to Diomedes and Odysseus on a nighttime commando raid (*Iliad* 10.433–514). For some reason the title "Rhesus" was given to a group of Indian macaques (note "rhesus apes" [VI.B.21.71]). These small monkeys are best known because of an agglutinative factor in their blood that is also usually present in human blood. That "Rh factor" may cause serious blood problems during pregnancy or after transfusion for someone who is Rh-negative. In the phrase cited, Joyce combines chauvinistic sexology (there is an "itch" for Diarmaid in Grania's blood) and folkloristic hematology (her blood is positively "eitch . . . Arrah")."[8]

- FW 392.28: "kalospintheochromatokereening." O Hehir and Dillon give the Greek words for each element (*kalo-*, beautiful; *spinthēro-*, spark; *chrōmato-*, color; *krēnē*, fountain, spring), but it is not the purpose of their work to suggest the contextual force of this compound. Following the lead of the immediately preceding phrase, "amid the rattle of hailstorms," I propose a participial phrase as a translation: shooting off skyrockets; but I am unsure what that display of verbal pyrotechnics has to do with Old Man "Matt Emeritus" (*FW* 392.14), who leads off the paragraph.

- *FW* 416.12: "(*ichnehmon diagelegenaitoikon*)." This distinctly Greek parenthesis is easier to cope with than the two parallel examples at *FW* 174.19 and *FW* 353.5–7. Here the setting is the fable of the Ondt and the Gracehoper, so insects are obvious suspects. An ichneumon is a parasitic fly that infests the nests of wasps and feeds on their grubs. That function may explain the second word: *diagelaō* (laugh at), *genetikos* (giving birth, producing), *oikos* (house, hive); the compound term, then, designates the fly as an insect that "mocks the establishment of a wasp's nest." Another similarly beneficial parasite is the aphid-eating ladybird, a number of which appear right next to the "ichnehmon" in the *Wake:* "ladybirdies" (*FW* 416.12). The final Greek root in the second term (*oikos*) may also have been used by Joyce as a comment on the strange ways in which nature operates. That is, while the parasites destroy the wasps' household (*oikos*), they also perform a definite service to humans, as is noted in the article "Economic Entomology" in the edition of the *Encyclopaedia Britannica* that Joyce used. In fact, "Ichneumonidae" and "lady-birds" are mentioned three lines apart in the final paragraph of that piece. The next article, on the same page of the *Britannica,* is "Economics." It begins with a definition of the term: "from οἶκος [*oikos*], a house, and νόμος [*nomos*], rule,—the 'art of household management'" (*EB* 8.899). This cluster of etymology (true meaning of words), entomology (study of insects), and conspicuously Greek economics cannot be coincidence. Rather, Joyce's congenially encyclopedic source of information for this section of the *Wake* also supplied him with a polysyllabic description of the function of an economically beneficial bug.

- *FW* 478.32: "Is there cold on ye, doraphobian?" The Four Old Men are asking Yawn (who has assumed the persona of St. Patrick) why he is "shevering" with cold. It is because he is afraid to put on a fur-skin: he suffers from *dora-* (hide) *phobia* (irrational fear). That analysis of the Greek compound is given by McHugh and fits the context perfectly and is supported by archival evidence: "ᵍdorophobia (fear of fur)" (*Scribbledehobble* 161 [851]). O Hehir and Dillon suggest "*dōraphobia* (fear of gifts)," but do not comment on its appropriateness. In my book on Joyce's use of Latin, I cited this term as the author's ad hoc translation into Greek of Vergil's well-known statement *timeo Danaos et dona ferentis* (I fear Greeks, even when they bring gifts) (*Aeneid* 2.49).

- *FW* 481.22: "Salem, (Mass), Childers, Argos, Duthless." Joyce is distorting a series of Greek place names for the cities that traditionally claimed to have been the birthplace of Homer. Thus, Salamis becomes a city in Massachusetts solely on the basis of a similarity of sound; Chios and Childers begin with the same three letters in English (Chi-) and the same two in Greek (Χι [chi, iota]); Argos remains the same; but Joyce's catalog transforms Athens into "Duthless." Folk etymology is at work here. Athens was, of course, named after its patron-goddess, Athena. No satisfactory explanation of the meaning or root of the goddess's name has been given by scholars.[9] In the absence of a scientific etymology, I suggest that Joyce invented a plausible explanation for himself. He combined the Greek negative prefix and the common root *than* (death); then he translated his coinage (*athanēs*) into Wakean English. Thus, following that line of argument and deduction, the immortal Athena (and her city of Athens) is "Duthless."[10] Precisely the same mistaken derivation is recorded in a short archival index of words beginning with negative alphas: "a/thens / deathless / a = un, vide / °adriatic shipless / °atreeatric" (VI.B.12.91; see VI.C.6.61). The last entry is an "English" version of the preceding item (from *a-drios* [without a thicket, or woodless, in Greek]); following such folk etymology the Adriatic Sea is "shipless." Joyce inserted this coinage into the text: "beyond the outraved gales of Atreeatic" (*FW* 62.2).

- *FW* 511.16: "epexegesis." The correctly spelled Greek word for an additional explanation (as in an *epexegetical* infinitive, just to clarify things) is soon repeated in an English phonetic version, "a pigs of cheesus" (*FW* 511.18). Also note the phrase "your apexojesus will be a point of order" (*FW* 296.10–11), in which the term itself is both stated and defined.

- *FW* 522.7: "melanodactylism." This Joycean coinage means the "state having black (*melano-*) fingers (*daktylos*)," a condition that was literally true of Saint Sylvania (note the nearby "sylvan" [*FW* 522.17]). A bit more information about this eccentric holy woman is given later in the *Wake,* where she has undergone a change in gender: "Sylvanus Sanctus washed but hurdley those tips of his anointeds" (*FW* 570.32–33). McHugh supplies the source for this example of sacramental hygiene: "[Edward Gibbon,] *The Decline and Fall of the Roman Empire,* Ch. XXIX n. '[Saint] Sylvania. . . . At the age of threescore she could boast that she had never washed . . . any part of her whole body, except the tips of her fingers, to receive the communion'." (That last phrase is a perfect example of hagiographical epexegesis.)

- *FW* 599.19–20: "Nomomorphemy for me!" As dawn breaks and HCE rises from his bed, he may be asserting that his first task of the day will involve some form (*morphos*) of the law (*nomos*), or he may just be saying that he needs no more sleep. The Greco-Latin divine personification of sleep is Morpheus, because he causes "shapes" to appear in dreams. Ovid expresses this function in a neat Latin-Greek *figura etymologica:* Jupiter awakens "Morpheus who fashions phantoms" (*simulatoremque figurae / Morphea* [*Metamorphoses* 11.634–635]).

- *FW* 613.35–36: "Monogynes his is or hers Diander." McHugh points out the botanical and reproductive meanings that the capitalized terms have in Linnaean classification. The literal translation of the Greek roots in each word is "Single-woman" and "Double-man."

Figura Etymologica

Hellenistic (post–Alexander the Great) authors were especially fond of this technique, and they exerted a powerful influence on the etymological finesse of the Latin poets Vergil, Horace, and Ovid.[11] Wakean examples that can easily be detected by reference to McHugh's *Annotations* are not included here, nor are a number (such as "faroscope of television" [*FW* 150.32–33]) that should be obvious to those who scored well on the verbal portion of their SATs. Again, the etymological spring that trips this rhetorical device into action is covert tautology: the nearby presence of synonymous words having roots from different languages. When Milton wrote "with the sound / Of dulct symphonies and voices sweet" (*Paradise Lost* 1.711–12), he expected his readers to notice the acoustic saccharineness of his choice of words.

- *FW* 5.33: "basilikerks and aeropagods." Elaborate wordplay is involved here. The Greco-Roman *basilica* (from Greek *basilikos;* royal, kingly) was an administrative building with an aisled nave and apse; it became the standard form of a Christian church. *Kirk* is the Scotch word for church. In ancient Athens the most important court met on the *Areopagos,* the Hill of Ares; Joyce suggests that it also has something to do with the gods of the upper sky (*aero-*). The last Wakean element incorporates the Tamil word for temple (*pagavadi*), which probably came into English via the Portuguese *pagode.*

- *FW* 14.19: "excelsissimost empyrean." The Latin word for high (*excelsus*) is present in a double superlative (*-issimus* and "most"). That elevated adjective modifies the Greek word for "situated in the highest regions of the sky" (*empyrios*).

- *FW* 39.32: "hailfellow with meth, in." An elided form of the Greek preposition meaning "with" is *meth'*; *methy* is a Greek word for strong wine, with which a hailfellow (who is customarily "well met") is likely to toast his drinking companions.

- *FW* 41.30: "prothetic purpose." The Greek *prothesis* means purpose.

- *FW* 46.20: "Onesine . . . Boniface." This example of two synonymous proper names is clarified when "Onesine" is recognized as almost certainly a last-level typographical error in what should be "Onesime"—the French spelling of Onesimus, whom St. Paul mentions in his Epistle to Philemon 8–21. In that letter to an early Christian community in Asia Minor, Paul asks that Onesimus, freed from prison and slavery, continue to be regarded as "useful" by Philemon. The point of Paul's pun is that *onēsimos* is the Greek adjective that means useful. Joyce repeats that characteristic in the second name, "Boniface," a Latin compound that means doing good things, useful. (Also see "Obesume . . . Benefice" [*FW* 371.2]).[12]

- *FW* 119.3: "home homoplate." The Greek words *homo* (same) and *platē* (flat object) do not form a compound in that language. For an American baseball fan, however, the similar sounds, the adjacent definition, and the object itself naturally run together without any forced squeezing of the wordplay.

- *FW* 125.17–18: "Gopheph go." The Greek verb *pheugō* (pronounced "phefgo" in Modern Greek) means "I leave," "I flee."

- *FW* 160.21–22: "siderodromites and the irony of the stars." The Greek noun *sidēros* means iron; the plural Latin noun *sidera* means stars; a dromite is a kind of meteorite, often rich in iron. A far more likely reference to the Modern Greek *sidērodromos* (railway) is confirmed by "[t]the greek Sideral Reulthway" (*FW* 604.12) and an archival note: "soderodromos [*sic*] = railway" (VIII.A.4.2).

- *FW* 353.7–8: "*haloday . . . die and be diademmed.*" The Christian Greek term that is the equivalent of the English halo is *diadēma*. The "*-day*" is echoed by a Latin and a Spanish day, "*die*" and "*dia-*."

- *FW* 367.32: "an angel prophetethis? kingcorrier of beheasts?" McHugh glosses these two brief questions with a reference to the symbols of the four Evangelists. I am sure he is correct but his identifications are not precise: angel, Matthew; lion (king of beasts), Mark; ox (beast), Luke; eagle (messenger of the king-god), John. Moreover, in Greek an *aggelos* is literally a courier[13] and a *prophētēs* speaks on behalf of someone else, at his "behest."

- *FW* 403.17: "Apagemonite! Come not nere! Black! Switch out!" The first of these four commands lays down the same message as those that follow. The Greek *apage* is an imperative meaning "get out," "leave"; the second part of the injunction is a Latin vocative meaning "now that you have been warned."

- *FW* 425.31: "an immature and a nayophight." The Latin adjective *immaturus* means "not ripe," still growing; the Greek *neophytos* means newly planted, immature.

- *FW* 472.17–22: "photophoric . . . lampaddyfair." The Greek *photophoros* means light-bearing, more or less the same as the Greco-Latin *lampade-* (torch, light) *fer* (carrier, bearer). On the next page as this brilliantly illuminated passage, Joyce also wrote "lightbreakfactbringer" (*FW* 473.23–24), and two pages later, "phosphor" (*FW* 475.15) from the Greek *phōs* (light) and *phoros* (bearing, carrying).

- *FW* 551.15: "evangel of good tidings." The Greek *euaggelia* means good news, as in the Christian gospels (from the Anglo-Saxon *godspel*, good news).

- *FW* 555.11: "old time pallyollogass." The rare Greek verb *palaiologeō* (to talk about antiquities) supplied the name, Paleologos in English, for the last dynasty of Byzantine emperors (A.D.1261–1453).

- *FW* 619.2: "urogynal." This example of interlanguage wordplay is odd on more than one count: The two synonyms have been compressed into a single word, and both components appear to be from the same language. I suggest that Joyce intended *"uro-"* to be converted into the Greek adjective *euro-* (wide) and that that meaning be translated into the English slang word for woman, "broad." If so, it combines with the Greek root *gyn-* (woman) to form a *Wakean* adjective that is expansively and repetitively feminine. (Of course, since the coinage is Joyce's, it could concurrently mean "pertaining to the urination of a woman.")

In the preceding examples of Joyce's deployment of Greek vocabulary in the *Wake,* no instances from "Night Lessons" (*FW* 260–308) are included. There are, of course, Greek words scattered throughout that highly pedantic episode, but most of them can be figured out by looking at an English dictionary or by glancing at McHugh's glosses. Perhaps Joyce intends a bit of pedagogical realism here, since his pupils are concerned with a basic problem in geometry and fairly trite essay topics, not the intricacies of Greek grammar and literature. The four winds (*FW* 283.3–4) are probably from the *Odyssey* and are briefly discussed in my chapter on that epic. A sketch of a person thumbing his nose is drawn at the end of the "Night Lessons" episode. There Joyce informs readers who are not graphically oriented that the raised digit is an "anticherist" (*FW* 308.F1), Greek for thumb. The last book of the *Wake* also has very few Greek elements. After a dense flurry of highly artificial compounds in a paragraph that introduces the ultimate version of the Revered Letter (*FW* 614.27–615.10), almost no overtly classical words or roots appear in the text of that epistle or in Anna Livia's final hydrokinetic monologue.

Mechanics of Meaning

Joyce's long and thorough study of the grammar, syntax, and vocabulary of Latin left numerous conspicuous marks on his fiction. The declension of the demonstrative pronoun meaning "this" is a series of cases in point: "Hik! Hek! Hok! Huk!" (*U* 15.2599–2603) and "hicky hecky hock, huges, huges, huges, hughy, hughy, hughy" (*FW* 454.15–16). Since Joyce lacked anything like formal academic training in ancient Greek, there are few parallel examples from the mechanics of the language of Homer and Plato.

Short recitations of the Greek alphabet occur at least twice in the *Wake:* "alfrids, beatties, cormacks and daltons" (*FW* 19.9) and "alpilla, beltilla, ciltilla, deltilla" (*FW* 194.22–23); in both cases an Anglo-Latin *c* has been substituted for the Greek gamma in the third position. The entire alphabet, from alpha to omega, is compressed into "And me awlphul omegrims!" (*FW* 348.4–5). In one of the Notebooks Joyce took a stab at writing out the entire alphabet in Greek. He corrected an originally repeated epsilon for eta; xi is missing (though it may appear faintly in the margin); and the whole process stops at tau (VI.B.21 back cover verso).[14] The source and antiquity of these letters are described in the text as "creakish from age and all now quite epsilene" (*FW* 19.10–11). The last word in that citation is meant to recall the Greek letter ε (epsilon) and to remind readers that its ancient sound was that of an ε *psilon* (simple); that is, written with that character alone, not with αι, the diphthong that was pronounced the same as ε in later Greek.[15] The Modern Greek spelling of "b" (μπ/*mp*) is a topic of wordplay on the same page as the orthographic comment on "those superciliouslooking crisscrossed Greek ees" (*FW* 120.6–9, 18–19). In *Ulysses* Leopold Bloom disguises his writing in a letter to Martha Clifford: "Remember write Greek ees. . . . No, change that ee" (*U* 11.860–865).[16] Irish literary pretensions are cross-culturally mocked in "deltic dwilights" (*FW* 492.9). And the siglum (Δ) for ALP is the subject of frequent—and frequently obscene—wordplay, as in "Him her first lap, her is fast pal, for ditcher for plower, till deltas twopart" (*FW* 318.12–13). Joyce also reported to Harriet Shaw Weaver the reaction of editors to whom he submitted the "Anna Livia Plurabelle" episode: "New press opinions of Δ are : 'all Greek to us' 'unfortunately I can't read it' 'is it a puzzle'" (*Letters* III.131).

The correct placement of accent marks (acute, circumflex, and grave) on classical Greek words is an extraordinarily complex combination of memory, declension/conjugation, position, and the presence of enclitics/proclitics. The lesson on accentuation in an elementary Greek course causes the eyes of even the most dedicated student to glaze over. A major source of the perplexity is the outlandish jargon that has been invented to distinguish the various options for each accent. One example: When the circumflex accent (~) falls on the second-last syllable of a word, that word is a *properispomenon: pro-* (before), *-peri-* (around), *-spomenon* (something that is turned or circled); in other words, "a word that has something turned around the syllable in front of the last syllable." Joyce somehow picked up—perhaps from Stuart Gilbert—odd pieces of this terminology: "Oxatown and baroccients" (*FW* 288.11). An "oxytone" (sharp pitch) has an acute accent (´) on the final syllable; a "barytone" (heavy pitch) has no accent of any type on the final syllable. In the *Wake* the circumflex accent is bent out of shape, becoming "circumflicksrent" (*FW* 298.15).

In an attempt to practice what he rarely preaches, Joyce seems to have made a stab at correct Greek accentuation, "propenomen is a properismenon" (*FW* 59.15–16). The word "propenomen" is not genuine Greek but compressed Latin for "near the name" or "the name is near"). Since the form is not real Greek, it is impossible to determine what its appropriate accent might be. On the other hand, the *Wake's* only sentence in actual Greek—in "Night Lessons"—is correctly spelled and correctly accented: "οὐκ ἔλαβον πόλιν·" (*ouk elabon polin;* I/they did not capture a city) (*FW* 269.L2).[17] This sentence was well known to language-savvy schoolboys, since it can be pronounced to sound like an equally correct sentence in French: "Où qu'est la bonne Pauline?" (Where is the pretty Pauline?).

For a beginning or even advanced student of ancient Greek, the principles of metrics are just as formidable as the rules of accentuation. It is possible that the occasional appearance of metrical vocabulary in the *Wake* refers to Latin verse, which uses Greek terminology. Issy and her Rainbow Girls are seated "upon the brink*spondy* . . . all barely in their *typtap* teens, describing a charming *dactylo*gram" (*FW* 430.5–11; my emphases). The italicized words are terms used in classical versification. A *spondee* (——) and a *dactyl* (—⌣⌣) are the only two feet that occur in the hexameter line in Homer's or Vergil's epics. In Joyce's passage the twenty-nine young women are to be visualized sitting near a pond and tapping out a rhythmical message "with their eight and fifty pedalettes" (*FW* 430.9).

Not all dactyls in the *Wake* are metrical feet. Some are, literally, fingers, which is what *daktylos* means in Greek. Joyce indicated his awareness of this fact in a 1931 letter to Ezra Pound; its typed message closes with "herterodaktylographically yours, James Joyce" (*Letters* III.219). That jawbreaker of a concluding adverb means "hunting-and-pecking-with-two-fingers-wise." In his reply Pound signed off with "beg to remn. Autodidacicraticly, E.P."[18] Pound's typing was notoriously sloppy, but I detect a bit of a jab at Joyce's high-flown reference to his lack of skill at the typewriter. The Greek-based countercoinage just before his initials means "with the power that comes from teaching oneself."

Throughout the writings of Joyce, many of the examples of the ancient

Greek language in action were derived by the self-taught master from the pages of the Liddell-Scott lexicon. This chapter shows that sophisticated wordplay and fancifully appropriate tautology involving Greek elements are an important component of the "idioglossary he invented" (*FW* 423.9). One final etymology: *idios* (individual, peculiar, personal), *glossa* (tongue, language). A "peculiar tongue," sharpened by an autocratic creator of a cosmically "personal language"—not a bad way to sum up the entire enterprise.

"To pan! To pan!" (That's all! That's all!) (*FW* 466.1–2)

Notes

Chapter 1

1. Gilbert, *Study*, 71–72.
2. Horace celebrates Hypermnestra as *splendide mendax* (magnificently untruthful [to her oath]) in *Ode* 3.11.35; for comment on this phrase, see Schork, *Latin*, 148.
3. The phrase also recalls Vergil's *timeo Danaos* (I fear Greeks [even when they bring gifts]) (*Aeneid* 2.49); see Schork, *Latin*, 137.
4. Athena instructed Cadmus to sow dragon's teeth in the earth, from which sprang warriors who began to kill one another. Joyce may allude to this event at *U* 15.4680–81 and *FW* 134.4–6; more likely, however, the references are to a similar story that Ovid tells about Jason (see Schork, *Latin*, 179).
5. See Schork, *Latin*, 154–58.
6. The names of these two adventurers appear at the end of an archival list (VIII.A.5.31) of women and men named in the *Odyssey's* account of the trip to the Underworld. Homer says that Odysseus would have seen Theseus and Pirithous if not for the sudden fear that had gripped him and forced his return to the upper regions (*Odyssey* 11.630–31).
7. Plutarch, *Lives*, 4; hereafter all citations of Plutarch appear in the text.
8. One of the Press's readers suggested "string of his heart" or "thumb from his arse"; I appreciate that gesture of collegial ingenuity.
9. The archaeology of the period was not entirely neglected by Joyce: "Chamber cairn at Maeshowe in = tomb at Mycene / treasure chamber of Atreus— Ireland taught / them to make tombs" (*UNBM* 114:50–52).
10. An archival note indicates that Joyce himself sometimes thought in terms of "parallel lives": "cicero / demosthenes" (VI.B.28.5). One of his friends in Paris reports Joyce's enthusiasm for the *Lives*: "It is an artist such as Plutarch who makes them live again: the men of action and men of imagination are the complement of each other" (Power, *Conversations*, 73).
11. When the Athenians judged that one of the city's leaders was becoming too powerful, they voted to send him into exile for a specified period. The votes were recorded by being scratched on fragments of pottery (*ostraka*); hence the verb *ostracize*. Joyce has HCE allude to this ancient practice in his reply to charges of malfeasance: "I have been reciping om omominous letters and widely-signed petitions full of *pieces of pottery* about my monumentalness" (*FW* 543.6–8; my emphasis).
12. Gifford and Seidman (*"U" Annotated*, 343) suggest that Peisistratus the Tyrant may be intended because he is a participant in one of Walter Landor's *Imaginary Conversations*, a copy of which Joyce owned (Gillespie, *Trieste Library*, 143–44, no. 272).
13. A cross-cultural archival note is pertinent here: "ᒧ K's ear" (VI.B.18.208).

This entry appears in a cluster of material relating to ancient Persia, where an important official in the shah's court was called the Eye of the King. Joyce apparently noted the title and the function, but altered the titular organ—perhaps influenced by his awareness of the chamber in King Dionysius's palace.

14. Valerius Maximus, *Memorabilium* 6.2, extract 1; cited in Stevenson, *Macmillan Book of Proverbs*, 2153; for another instance of Philip's excessive drinking, see Plutarch, *Moralia* IX.99 ("Table Talk" 7.10.715).

15. The *Britannica* article on Demosthenes reports that he "declaimed as he ran up hill . . . [and] shut himself up in a cell" (*EB* 8:10).

16. See Canfora, *Vanished Library*, 66–70, 104–105.

17. One possible source of this wild piece of Irish ancient history is the legend of Partholan and that of a Scythian invader named Nemed, as recorded in the "Legendary Origins" section of the *Britannica* article on Ireland (*EB* 14:757).

18. Bauerle, *Songbook*, 431–34.

19. See Schork, *Latin*, 110–11.

20. These details are compactly laid out in a 1932 *Wake* Notebook: "Δ hair Berenice / dedicated to Arsinoe / wife of Phil. III. safe / back from Syria" (VI.B.35.101).

21. See Schork, *Latin*, 51–53.

22. Various versions of the Seven Wonders mention both the Hanging Gardens and the Walls of Babylon. In fact, early catalogs include the Walls far more often than the Lighthouse at Alexandria, but the latter is firmly enshrined in modern lists; see Clayton and Price, *Wonders*, 1, 169–70, and Romer and Romer, *Seven Wonders*, x–xii, 230–33. There is also an archival cluster, a truncated version, from Joyce: "Wonders of World / Hanging Gardens / Colossus of Rhodes / Pyramids of Egypt / Mausoleum / Temple of Diana" (VI.B.18.206, VI.C.8.168).

23. Clayton and Price, *Wonders*, 137.

Chapter 2

1. An accessible contemporary translation of *The Histories* is that in the Penguin Classics series; my citation is from Burn's introduction, 10.

2. Gilbert, *Study*, 78, 153, 395; for that last bit of information, Joyce's firsthand data came from the article on Penelope in Roscher's *Lexikon* III.1909–1910 as recorded in VIII.A.5.9 (see Herring, *Notes and Drafts*, 7–8, 17).

3. Rose and O'Hanlon establish that Joyce's immediate source for this note was Walter Leaf's 1912 book *Troy: A Study in Homeric Geography* (*Lost Notebook*, 38; for additional discussion of this source see chapter 4).

4. One of the early drafts for this section of II.2 (called "Scribbledehobbles") contains an expanded version of the material that was radically revised, condensed, and transposed into the text that appears in the printed edition of the *Wake*. The draft version reads, "He who will either be crowned or hanged scans history's error from the parrotbook of Datars, foully traduced for the use of dauphins of the meter of Herodotus or Noah's misbelieving Annalfabetter" (47478–248 [*JJA* 52.160]); also see Hayman, *First-Draft*, 29–31, 150, 154, and "'Scribbledehobbles.'" Herodotus, of course, wrote in prose, so the draft reference to his "meter" is not to be taken literally.

5. See the citations in the "General Index" in Bauerle, *Picking Up Airs*, 208.

6. As Gifford and Seidman indicate, the comment is modeled on a couplet from Byron's *Don Juan* (*"U" Annotated* 133).

7. For the Horatian dimensions of this phrase see Schork, *Latin*, 148; other aspects of treachery, Olympian and Homeric, are also embedded in this passage (see the section on Prometheus in chapter 3 and the "Cyclops" section of chapter 5).

8. According to ancient reckoning, the quadrennial games in honor of Zeus at Olympia were first held in 776 B.C.

9. The genetic history of the passage reinforces the suggestion of careful planning—and of Herodotean allusion—here. The "neighing" (47482b–104 [*JJA* 58:75]) and an original "deafmute" (47482b–104v [*JJA* 58:76]) were composed in November or December 1924; "deafmute" was changed to "surdumutual" (47487–224v [*JJA* 62:418]) between April 22 and May 31, 1937, the same very late stage of adjustment that added the key phrase "fall-ensickners aping" (47487–86v and 87 [*JJA* 62:168]).

10. There is a distinct, Latin source in the annals of Livy (the rape of the Sabine women) for this pair of superficially similar references; see Schork, *Latin*, 43.

Chapter 3

1. In the spelling of Greek proper names, phonological accuracy of transliteration has been sacrificed to the selection of forms likely to be most familiar to contemporary English-speaking readers of Joyce; the Roman form is usually added for important names. In citations from various sources, the spelling of the original document is retained.

2. For a clear and well-organized compendium of basic mythological data, I recommend Tripp, *Crowell's Handbook*.

3. Gilbert, *Study*, 398–99.

4. For emphasis on this linguistic provenance, see "S. George-le-Greek" (*FW* 569.7) in a list of Dublin churches in the *Wake*. That reference is to St. George's church on Temple Street, which has a classically Ionic facade; there is also a famous Orthodox church in Venice, San Giorgio del Greco.

5. There are several references to the Olympic games at VI.B.38.112 and in the post-*Wake* notebook VI.B.48.2, 13, 44.

6. See Schork, *Latin*, 77; in the *Wake* the minicatalog is introduced by "Every letter is a godsend" (*FW* 269.17).

7. Also see VIII.A.5.30, 32; these details were taken from Roscher, *Lexikon*, I.246–47.

8. Another famous mythical disguise used by Zeus is encapsulated in an archival note: "ᛒ swan / Δ leda" (VI.B.12.53).

9. The note "Amphitryon 38" (VI.B.31.242) refers to the Jean Giraudoux 1929 play of that title.

10. Corrections for *UNBM* appear in Herring, *Notes and Drafts*, 264, but this item (from *UNBM* 123, note to line 50) is not part of that list.

11. The translation quoted is that of Lang, Leaf, and Myers, 255; that version of the *Iliad* (and its companion, the Butcher and Lang *Odyssey*) are cited whenever the English words of the epics may have a bearing on the Joycean text.

12. Landuyt and Lernout, "Sources," 125.

13. Joyce was well aware of Athena's pervasive role in the epic, as shown in a 1920 letter to Budgen: "It [Hermes' gift of *moly*] is the only occasion on which Ulysses is not helped by Minerva but by her male counterpart or inferior" (*Letters* I.148; *SL* 272).

14. A convenient compilation of the schemata is found in Ellmann, *Liffey*, appendix after p. 187.

15. Ellmann, *Liffey*, 9, 20.

16. See *Commentary on "Odyssey,"* I.80.

17. See Herring, *Notes and Drafts*, 117.

18. Bishop, *Book of the Dark*, 226–37 and 433–36, n.15; Gottfried, *Iritis*, passim; Gordon, *"Wake,"* 96–98; Schork, "Nodebinding," 72–77.

19. Gilbert, *Study*, 51–56 (the primary textual references are *U* 1.176, 1.544, 3.38, 14.685; also note *UNBM* 309:59); Gilbert's emphasis on *omphalos* as navel is correct, but there is also a distinctly phallic instance in Mulligan's discourse in "Oxen of the Sun" (*U* 14.684–88).

20. See Forbes Irving, *Metamorphosis*, 53.

21. The translation is taken from Hesiod, *Theogony*, 46–47.

22. An archival note confirms this sophisticated example of typology (links between the Old and New Testaments): "°Judges/°Chap 6 / °v.36" (VI.B.37. 130).

23. See Havelock, *Aphrodite of Knidos;* there is an ancient epigram (often attributed to Plato) in which the goddess herself, on viewing the statue, asks, "Where did Praxiteles see me naked?" (*Greek Anthology*, 252–55 [Book XVI.160, 162]).

24. Vicarious titillation of this sort seems to have been fairly common in Victorian-Edwardian times. A biographer of H. G. Wells reports: "In the same [early teen] years, moreover, he was also discovering the compensating power of sexual fantasies. 'My own sexual life began,' he [Wells] wrote, 'in a naive direct admiration for the lovely bodies . . . of those political divinities . . . in *Punch* and . . . my first inklings of desire were roused by them and by the plaster casts of Greek statuary that adorned the Crystal Palace.' It was from the stimulus of these mythical ladies that Wells began to construct his image of the ideal woman—the 'Venus Urania', distant, unattainable, yet endlessly pursued" (cited in MacKenzie, *Wells*, 29).

25. It should not be thought that Joyce's interest in sculptural anatomy was limited exclusively to statues of females. A note for *Ulysses* displays a broader scope of archival research: "cf naked Apollo (balls) museum" (VI.C.7.223).

26. Senn cites Athenaeus in a note on an eighteenth-century Homeric parody of epic defecation and food ("Burlesque," 728–36).

27. The *Britannica* article on Aphrodite mentions that the Pandemos manifestation of the goddess was represented "as riding on a goat, a symbol of wantonness" (*EB* 2.168), an iconographic association that would have required no explanation to Joyce.

28. For the wordplay in a similar phrase, "ars all bellical" (*FW* 122.7), see Schork, *Latin*, 84.

29. Two recent articles explore Eleusinian contributions to chapters of *Ulysses:* Carpentier, "Archetypes," 221–38, and Brammer, "Mysteries," 87–124. A *Wake* note explains the reason for Persephone's detention in Hades (she

ate the sacred fruit of the Underworld): "pomegranate / diabolicity" (VI.B.34.49).

30. Ruck, "Documentation," 110–11; Mylonas, *Eleusis,* 291–94; Roscher, *Lexikon,* I.753.

31. Rahner, *Christian Mysteries,* 179–92; this book also contains a fascinating chapter on "Odysseus at the Mast" as a figure of Christ on the cross (328–86).

32. This is also an allusion to the magic texts included in the *Hermetica;* several specifically Odyssean references to Hermes are discussed in chapter 5.

33. Gilbert, *Study,* 159–76. Gilbert includes a note on the possible relationship between the Semitic root *k-m-r* (darkness) and the Homeric Cimmerians, who live in a "land shrouded in mist and cloud" near the entrance to the Underworld (*Odyssey* 11.14 and *Commentary on "Odyssey,"* II.77–79). Joyce introduces this gloomy realm into the *Wake,* where "Summerian sunshine" is contrasted with "Cimmerian shudders" (*FW* 504.6–7). The source of Gilbert's information is probably Bérard via Joyce.

34. I correct Herring's transcription, *Notes and Drafts,* 27; for Joyce's use of this phrase in "Wandering Rocks," see Schork, *Latin,* 126–27.

35. Gilbert, *Study,* 168; Joyce may have adapted the second archival epithet into "Entered into rest the Protestants put it" (*U* 6.943).

36. The Danish prince invokes the Irish saint in *Hamlet* 1.5.136.

37. Jolas, "My Friend," 15–16, and *Sur Joyce,* 81.

38. Ovid, *Metamorphoses* 2.304–28; for a discussion of Phaëthon, see Schork, *Latin,* 160–65.

39. Ellmann, *Liffey,* appendix after p. 187.

40. For additional comment see Senn, *Scrutinies,* 12, 21–22.

41. Ellmann, *Liffey,* appendix after p. 187; "simbouleutike" is more correctly transliterated as "symbouleutike."

42. V.A.8.19r; see Herring, *Notes and Drafts,* 166.

43. Another "me Ercles!" oath was unintentionally excised from the text at *FW* 162.35; see Higginson, "Notes on the Text," 453.

44. Rose and O'Hanlon, *Lost Notebook,* 35.

45. For an engaging review of Ulyssean references to boxers, see Mitchell, "Boxing," 21–30.

46. Rose and O'Hanlon, *Lost Notebook,* 35; for an exhaustive study of Tiresias's sex changes, see O'Hara, "Sostratus," 176–219.

47. Rose and O'Hanlon, *Lost Notebook,* 35; the Hebrew root *t-r-s* is found in the verb meaning "to contradict."

48. See Schork, "Apollinaire," 166–72.

49. West, *Hesiod,* 167–69; the phrase occurs in a similar context at *Iliad* 22.126; also see *Odyssey* 19.163.

50. *Homeric Hymn to Aphrodite* 5.218–38.

51. Ruck and Matheson, *Pindar,* 112.

Chapter 4

1. The quotation is from the prose translation of the *Iliad* by Andrew Lang, Walter Leaf, and Ernest Myers.

2. A retrospective review of the final, post-Iliad phases of the Trojan War occurs in the last book of the *Odyssey* in Hades, when the soul of Agamemnon tells the soul of Achilles about the funeral that the Achaeans gave for him. Joyce made a long index of notes from the Butcher and Lang translation of this passage (*UNBM* 496:53–64), but none was incorporated into the text of *Ulysses.*

3. Rose and O'Hanlon, *Lost Notebook,* xxviii–xxvi. Costello argues that Joyce learned about Bérard's theories from lectures during 1902–3 by Father Henry Browne, professor of Greek at University College (*Years of Growth,* 217–18). This is possible, but quite unlikely. There is no evidence that Joyce attended the Jesuit's talks; by the time Browne's *Handbook of Homeric Study* was published (1905), Joyce had left Dublin. I thank Elizabeth B. Cullingford for calling Costello's claim to my attention.

4. Rose and O'Hanlon, *Lost Notebook,* xxx.

5. Leaf, *Troy,* 329, and Rose and O'Hanlon, *Lost Notebook,* 38.

6. Leaf, *Troy,* 312, 321, 294, and Rose and O'Hanlon, *Lost Notebook,* 41, 39, 40; also see VI.B.16.1 and VI.B.18.253.

7. Autenrieth, *Dictionary,* 116, and Cunliffe, *Lexicon,* 157; forms of this verb occur only three times in the Homeric epics; its sole appearance in the *Odyssey* is in the hero's description of the construction of his bedroom (*Odyssey* 23.193).

8. This topic is discussed in some detail at the beginning of chapter 12, "Modern Greek."

9. Hyginus, *Fabulae,* 96.

10. Stanislaus Joyce, *Keeper,* 180; for a fictional application of "jackel" (but without the Homeric allusion), see *SH* 228.

11. Ellmann, *Liffey,* 110–16, 134, and *Consciousness,* 21, 67; also see Stanford, "Ulyssean Qualities," 125–36.

12. The documentary source for this entry is a study by Stefan Czarnowski on the cult of the hero (his specific example is St. Patrick); he notes that heroes were traditionally commemorated by poetic recitations and games (see Lernout, "Czarnowski," forthcoming). A second entry combines the truce during the celebration of Panhellenic contests (here the Isthmian games in honor of Poseidon) and the Welsh tradition of bardic and choral competitions: "Eistedfoddic Greeks of Is[thmia] their peace" (VI.B.9.73). Another crossed entry appears in a transcribed Notebook: "ᵇfuneral games" (VI.C.9.201).

13. Deasy's allusion is to "Cassandra," (*U* 2.239), the Trojan princess-prophetess whose warnings no one heeds. (He obviously fears that his bad news about the hoof-and-mouth disease will be ignored.) Agamemnon brought the captive Cassandra back to Mycenae with him, but failed to pay attention to her wild ravings about danger in the palace. Cassandra is mentioned twice in the *Iliad* (13.366 and 24.699–706). In the Underworld episode in the *Odyssey,* Agamemnon tells Odysseus that he heard the wails of the captive princess as she was killed at his side by Clytemnestra (*Odyssey* 11.421–23).

14. The Attic orator Isocrates' *Encomium on Helen* (around 370 B.C.) may have been composed as a reply to Antisthenes' piece.

15. Cited from the Scholes and Kain, *Workshop of Daedalus*, 83, it is the first entry in that notebook.

Chapter 5

1. In Socrates Kapsaskes' translation of *Ulysses* into Modern Greek, "cultured allroundman" is transformed into *enkyklopaidika morphomeno atomo* (Tzous, *Odysseas* [281]), a clever use of the root *kyklos* (circle, ring). Although I have not examined every line of this translation, I note *stripogyrizei* (94) for "swirls" (*U* 4.438, 440) and *gyrismenē sta phōtia* (95) for "with her [back] to the fire" (*U* 4.458–59). In Homeric Greek the epithet *polyplagktos* (much-wandering) is used of vagabond mariners, but not of the hero himself (*Odyssey* 17.425, 20.195).
2. Budgen, *Making*, 15–17.
3. Stuart Curran, "Bous," 167, and Senn, *Scrutinies*, 21–22.
4. Burkert, *Homo Necans*, 3; the Greeks, however, did not use the verb *stephanoō* for the wreathing of a sacrificial animal, with the possible exception of a simile in Euripides' *Iphigenia at Aulis* 1080 (see Friedrich, *Theological Dictionary*, VII.615–36).
5. For a fascinating discussion of the function of the middle voice in the *Odyssey*, see Peradotto, *Man in the Middle*.
6. Gillespie, *Trieste Library*, 120 [no. 219]; my thanks to Harry Ransom Humanities Research Center at the University of Texas at Austin for the opportunity of examining this text.
7. The lower case designation for the hero of Homer's *Odyssey* is not a lapse in copyediting consistency. Laërtes and Anticleia, the parents of Odysseus, are mortal; their stalwart son is, in both mythological and narrative terms, merely a hero.
8. See *Scribbledehobble*, 86 [361], and Schork, "Nodebinding," 69–77 and 82n.18.
9. See Gillet, *Claybook*, 55, and Gilbert, *Study*, 208.
10. See Dimock, "Name," 54–72; *Commentary on "Odyssey,"* III.97; and an extended treatment in Peradotto, *Man in the Middle*, 120–42. In her discussion of this topic, Clay discerns an active/passive, "trickster" dimension in the name (*Wrath*, 54–64).
11. Budgen, *Making*, 194–95.
12. Their source is Roscher, *Lexikon*, I.374; also note *UNBM* 278:3.
13. A curious point of Homeric animal husbandry should also be mentioned here. In the *Odyssey* the marvelous oxen of the Sun do not participate in two primary activities of the natural life cycle; they neither breed (*gonos d'ou gignetai autōn*) nor die (*Odyssey* 12.130–31). This exemption makes them an ironically appropriate symbol for the site, action, and tone of their title chapter in *Ulysses*.
14. Borach, "Conversations," 69–70; also see Budgen, *Making*, 16–17.
15. See Stanford, *Ulysses Theme*, 81–89 for comment on these works. Earlier studies with greater detail on the same topic include Andrew Lang, *Homer and the Epic*, especially the chapter "The Lost Epics of Greece," 323–348; another review of the material is "Homer and the Cyclic Poems," in Lang's *The World of Homer*, 197–221.

16. For more information on this American painter and his friendship with Joyce, see the index entries under his name in *JJII* 862; the "portrait" is also reproduced in *JJII* 443.
17. See Senn, *Dislocutions,* 121–37.
18. In the coronation scene in "Circe," however, "Bloom appears . . . in a crimsom velvet mantle trimmed with ermine" (*U* 15.1442–43). There is no indication of the maker of this regal garment, but Molly (and perhaps Lucia Joyce) undertake some archival knitting (*UNBM* 499:41 and 511:27).
19. *Commentary,* III.80–81.
20. See Gilbert, *Study,* 398–403 for extended comment on this motif.
21. See Schork, *Latin,* 194–95.
22. The Latin participial substantive is perfect passive, not (as sometimes translated) future active. For Joycean manipulation of similar grammatical and lexical items, note *"fututa fuere"* (have been fucked) and *"fore futura"* (will have been) (*FW* 287.26), and see Schork, *Latin,* 233–34. A *Wake* archival entry also casts doubt on Penelope's chastity: "she peneloped with all / love encounters = rendezvous" (VI.B.1.81).
23. Herring, *Notes and Drafts,* 4, 7–8, 17.
24. Doherty, "Reconsiderations," 344, 347, and 349 n.23.
25. For a comprehensive discussion of the figure of Penelope in ancient literature, see Mactoux, *Pénélope.* Recent works on Penelope in the epic tradition include Katz, *Penelope's Renown,* Felson-Rubin, *Regarding Penelope,* and Harper, "Fabric and Frame."
26. Throughout the rest of this chapter, I include page references to the Butcher and Lang translation (*B-L*) of the *Odyssey,* since Joyce's direct Homeric source is often critical to my argument. The edition I use is the Modern Library *Complete Works of Homer,* with separate pagination for the *Iliad* and the *Odyssey.*
27. There is no mention of Dublin circuses in Herr, *Anatomy of Culture,* or Kershner, *Popular Culture.*
28. Gilbert, *Study,* 270.
29. Ellmann, *Liffey,* 112–14.
30. For other aspects of this allusion see Schork, *Latin,* 148.
31. For a good discussion of the lexical legerdemain here, see Schein, "Odysseus and Polyphemus," 79–81.
32. Gilbert, *Study,* 271.
33. Scott, "Monster," 19–75.
34. *Burke's Peerage* (1970), 818: Flemyng was the grandson (second marriage) of fourth son of the second viscount.
35. Mondada, *Brissago,* 97–98.
36. Budgen, *Making,* 247; also see Suter, "Reminiscences," 62.
37. Mondada, *Brissago,* 80; I reproduce the epigraphical conventions of his transcription of the text.
38. Budgen, *Making,* 248; *JJII* 456–57.
39. Budgen, *Making,* 247; also see the baroness's June 9, 1920, letter, which mentions the "collection of my 'painted' Odyssey." I wish to thank the Carl A. Kroch Library at Cornell University for sending copies of four letters from the baroness (Scholes, *Cornell Joyce Collection,* 178 [no. 1204–1207]) and for permitting citation.
40. *JJII* 496, 788, and June 9, 1920, letter.

41. Mondada, *Brissago*, 117–18; the exact reference is *Journal of Royal Horticultural Society* 37 (1913): III.503–14.

42. For some details from Gilbert's perspective, see his *Paris Journal*.

43. Gilbert, *Study*, vi; cited parenthetically hereafter.

44. I have briefly examined Gilbert's Paris notebooks at the Harry Ransom Humanities Center at the University of Texas; they are packed with classical trivia.

45. In a May 18, 1918, letter to Miss Weaver, Joyce mentions the three major parts of his work: *"Telemachia"* (three episodes), *"Odyssey"* (eleven [*sic*] episodes), and *"Nostos"* (three episodes); a September 3, 1920, letter to John Quinn gives the Homeric names to each of the eighteen chapters (*Letters* I.113, 145).

46. For an outrageous Latin pun on the sexual connotations of the "use of the word 'Greek'," see Gilbert, *Study*, 364, n.2, and Levine, "Tattoo Artist," 297, n.12.

47. McCarthy, "Perplexed," 32.

48. Tagopoulos, "Return," 191–92; one of her conclusions is that Joyce did use the Butcher and Lang translation of the *Odyssey*.

49. Tagopoulos, 192–93; for an impressively nuanced discussion of this theme, see Austin, *Archery*, 244–53.

50. See Card, "Roses," 82–84, and the chapter "Why Does Molly Bloom Menstruate," in Ellmann, *Liffey*, 159–76. In the *Wake* Joyce creates his own pseudo-Greek term for the Feast of the New Moon, "Neomenie!" (*FW* 244.5); the process is both cursed ("maledictions and mens uration makes me mad" [*FW* 269.F3]) and accepted as a cyclic inevitability ("Deal with Nature the great greengrocer and pay regularly the monthlies" [*FW* 437.16–17]).

51. Childress, "Cicones," 80.

52. Klein, "'Womanly,'" 618.

53. For the classical evidence see Henderson, *Maculate Muse*, 131–32; for Joycean application see Conrad and Wadsworth, "Body Politic," 306 and 312, n.4. Dirk Vanderbeke delivered a paper on this topic at the 1996 International James Joyce Symposium in Zürich.

54. Also see *Letters* I.149 and Ferris, *Burden of Disease*, 69–70.

55. For the lexical evidence (and its ingenious application to Sophocles' *Oedipus the King*), see Rusten, "Triviality," 108–12.

56. Borach, "Conversations," 69–70.

57. Gillet recalls this anecdote in "Farewell," 168; Joyce also reported to his friend that the astounded priest objected, "but Ulysses is not a hero."

58. McCleery, "Lost Lamb," 635–39, and "Gathered Lambs," 557–63. At the 1995 Zürich James Joyce Foundation Summer Workshop on "Homer/Joyce/Homer," Freidhelm Rathjen made a presentation on a number of hitherto undetected verbal parallels between *Ulysses* and Lamb's book.

59. Giedion-Welcker, "Meetings," 276; the age parallel is not quite accurate— Stephen James Joyce would have been only about eight years old at that time.

60. Stanford, *Ulysses Theme*, 81–89.

61. I cannot claim to have checked the entire corpus, but I do admit to reading and enjoying a number of the usual suspects.

62. Lang's major professional works on this topic are *Homer and the Epic* (1893),

Homer and His Age (1906), and *The World of Homer* (1910). In 1907 he also wrote a children's book, *Tales of Troy and Greece*, dedicated to Rider Haggard. Two-thirds of this work is devoted to "Ulysses the Sacker of Cities" and "Wanderings of Ulysses"; the rest consists of chapters on Jason, Theseus, and Perseus.

63. Haggard, *The World's Desire* (hereafter cited parenthetically as *WD*) 14, and *Odyssey* 11.122–23.

64. Stanford, *Ulysses Theme*, 87–88; Lang also wrote a long narrative poem on Helen of Troy, which does not include the fantastically apocryphal details that energize the novel. In his autobiography Haggard records a parodic ballad, addressed to "Awdawcious Odyshes," that Robert Louis Stevenson sent to Lang after the publication of *The World's Desire*. Its second stanza deserves citation:

> Sic veerin' and sterrin'!
> What port are ye neerin'
> As frae Egypt to Erin
>   Ye gang?
> Ye ancient auld blackguard,
> Just see whaur ye're staggered
> From Homer to Haggard
>   And Lang! (Haggard, *The Days of My Life*, 8)

65. *Dictionnaire de biographie*, 5.1467–68.

66. Seidel, *Geography*, 4; the internal quote from Bérard, *Phéniciens*, II.557.

67. Bérard, *Navigations*, IV.473–74 (my translation).

68. Seidel, *Geography*, 9, 132–36, 149, 176–81, 218–27.

69. Seidel, *Geography*, 190–91.

70. See Austin, *Archery*, 90–97.

71. Seidel, *Geography*, 16–38, 178.

72. Stanford, *Odyssey* I.xli.

73. I refer to the three-volume revised edition of the *Commentary on "Odyssey"* (originally commissioned by the Valla Foundation) published by the Clarendon Press at Oxford (1988–92).

74. Senn, review of *Epic Geography*, 111–13.

75. Cope, *Cities*, 107–110.

76. Herring, *Notes and Drafts*, 3–4, 9.

77. Herring, *Notes and Drafts*, 4, and *UNBM*, 7–8.

78. Gilbert, *Study*, vii; *SL* 334.

79. The "article" was the French translation of "Proteus" in *La nouvelle revue française* 31 (CLXXIX, 1928): 204–26.

80. Colum, *Friend*, 89.

81. Herring, *UNBM* 57.

82. Budgen, *Making*, 309.

83. Childress, "Lestrygonians," 259–69.

84. Kenner, *Ulysses*, 27, 30; also see his "Sticks," 285–98.

85. Litz, *Art*, 37, 39, and additional comment on 25–26; also see Herring, *UNBM* 40.

86. Herring, *UNBM* 49–58; other pieces of similar genetic scholarship are col-

lected in his *Notes and Drafts*, especially the indispensable edition of Zürich notebook VIII.A.5.

87. *UNBM* 56, 57; his emphases, my ellipsis.
88. Austin, *Archery*, 225.
89. Kenner, *Ulysses*, 30.
90. Prescott, *"Odyssey* and *Ulysses,"* 427–44.
91. Gilbert, *Study*, 43, 297; the essential references in the novel are *U* 17.1447, *U* 14.129, and *U* 14.1472–73.
92. Kenner, "Sticks," 285–98.
93. Kenner, "Sticks," 296–97; Stanford, *Ulysses Theme*, 276n.6.
94. Gillespie, *Trieste Library*, 120 (no. 218).
95. Gillespie, *Trieste Library*, 63 (no. 90); Ellmann suggests that Joyce's interest in "metempsychosis" may have been triggered by an essay in Butler's book (see *Consciousness*, 91–92).
96. Budgen, *Making*, 358–59.
97. Heubeck, introduction, *Commentary on "Odyssey,"* I.3–23.
98. The documentary source for this note is not classical; it comes from Czarnowski's study of the heroic dimensions of the legend of St. Patrick (see Lernout, "Czarnowski"). The *Britannica* article "Homer" includes a summary of the findings of the "analytic" school and reviews epic analogues to oral songs (*EB*, 13.633–39); recitation at the Panathenaea is also discussed (*EB*, 13.627–28). Bosanquet mentions Wolf in his brief treatment of recent Homeric criticism (*Aesthetic*, 189–90).
99. Colum, *Friend*, 130–31; Gilbert, *Study*, 129; there is an archival index of terms from Jousse's book at VI.B.21.17–25.
100. Gillet, "Living Joyce," 199.
101. For a recent review of Joyce's use of Jousse, see Mailhos, "Preprovided Memory," 55–60, and Milesi, "Jousse. Joyce," 143–62; also note Weir, "Choreography," 313–25, and Hayman, "Language," 37–47.
102. See the number of entries under his name in the thirty-year (Fall 1963–Fall 1993) bibliography of the *James Joyce Quarterly* (*JJQ* 32 [Winter 1995]): 419–20; other lists of his publications are found in *Dislocutions*, 248–52, and *Scrutinies*, 248–52. A complete bibliography of Senn's Joycean publications is included in Frehner and Zeller, *Collideorscape*, xiv–xxiv.
103. Senn, "Turns," 29–46; reprinted in *Dislocutions*, 121–37; also see *Scrutinies*, 200–202.
104. Senn, *Scrutinies,"* 111–32.
105. Senn, "'Hamarte,'" 105–115.
106. Senn, "Long List," 31–76.
107. For a well-illustrated survey of the epic in classical painting and sculpture, see the recent Buitron and Cohen, *"Odyssey" and Ancient Art.*
108. Kestner, "Iconography," 565–94.
109. Budgen, *Making*, 15.
110. Schork, "Apollinaire," 166–72.
111. Budgen, *Making*, 188.
112. Langlotz, "Deutung," 72–99.
113. See Rose and O'Hanlon, *Understanding*, 281, and Atherton, "Sport," 52–64.
114. See Casson, *Mariners*, 120–24.

115. The *Odyssey* need not be the *direct* source of Joyce's meteorological information here; there is a pertinent note (from Bérard) in notebook VIII.A.5.16; also see VI.B.17.91.

116. Pausanius, *Guide,* 1.469–88 (10.25–31).

117. *Catholic Encylopaedia,* 5.176; the use of the term was abolished in 1882 (*CE* 8.25), but existing bishops retained their honorary designations.

118. Joyce also gives an odd spin to the rank in his 1907 Trieste lecture: he reports that "a bastard of the papal court" became ruler of Ireland, "a king *in partibus infidelium*" (*CW* 170). Another note may suggest an alternative stratagem for Odysseus: "had ill stayed at / home (demobbed)" (VI.B.10.45).

119. The lost VI.B Notebook is dated to "Aug–Sep 1926: Belgium"; see Rose, *Textual Diaries,* 28.

120. Loekle, "Dazibao," 127.

121. Note "Homerican" (VI.B.36.62).

Chapter 6

1. Throughout this chapter I supply parenthetical citations to Plato's dialogues using their standard titles and section references. Although the exact wording of these texts is rarely important in their Joycean mode, a reliable contemporary translation is Plato, *Complete Works,* ed. Cooper. Joyce owned two copies of the selected Platonic dialogues—and of Xenophon's *Memorabilia* (see Gillespie, *Trieste Library,* 185 [nos. 373–74]).

2. Whitehead, *Process and Reality,* 39. An aborted draft of II.2 in the *Wake* concludes with acknowledgment of the wisdom of the spokesman of the dialogues: "piling up sapience, an omnitude of jadg and daktar as sagely as Anisocrates" (47478–286; see Hayman, *First Draft,* 155).

3. For a discussion of a possible Gallic origin of this "Platonic" quotation, see the references to Flaubert later in this chapter.

4. Michels, "Revenge," 175–92, and Kimball, "Brainsick Words," 399–405.

5. Ellman, *Liffey,* appendix after page 187.

6. Curran, cited from Scholes and Kain, *Workshop of Daedalus,* 151.

7. Cited from the jacket of the third edition (1956) of Plotinus's *Enneads* by MacKenna.

8. *Joyce–Léon Letters,* 92.

9. James Stephens, whom Joyce saw in Dublin in late August 1909 (*JJII,* 333–34), was also a friend of MacKenna (see Dodds, "Memoir," in *Journal and Letters,* 39–40).

10. See the letter (sent sometime in 1921–22) from AE to MacKenna thanking him for a gift copy of the second volume of Plotinus. In it AE writes, modestly, "I owe whatever dignity of mind I possess to a study of Plato and the sacred books of the world" (Dodds, *Journal and Letters,* 163).

11. The specific details about Xanthippe's shrewishness are not found in the dialogues of Plato. Xenophon reports that her own son said "no one would have been able to put up with that most difficult woman" (*Memorabilia* 2.2.7), and the writings of the Cynic philosophers are filled with uncomplimentary anecdotes about her. An archival note (VI.B.1.16) records an unexpected fact about Socrates: One of his ancestors was the master craftsman Daedalus (see *Euthyphro* 11.b.9).

12. Earlier in the discussion Mulligan explicitly mentions "the charge of pederasty bought against the bard." That prompts the unattributed reflection "Catamite" (*U* 9.732–34).

13. Mr. Best has already been described as a "blonde ephebe [Greek youth]. Tame essence of Wilde" (*U* 9.531–32). Also see Kestner, "Youth," 233–59, and the figures.

14. For the suggestion of an allusion to an Irish comic song, see Meehan, "O'Grady," 512–13.

15. Aubert, *Aesthetics*, 99; some of the terminology used by Joyce in his 1902 talk on Mangan (*CW* 74) are also traced to a similar source (*Aesthetics*, 64, 71).

16. For a discussion of this process at work with Aristotelian material, see Aubert, *Aesthetics*, 86–99.

17. Allison, "Coincidence?" 267–82.

18. There were no translations of Plato's works in Joyce's Paris library; the Trieste collection included *Five Dialogues Bearing on Poetic Inspiration* and *Socratic Discourses by Plato and Xenophon* (Gillespie, *Trieste Library*, 185 [no. 373–74]).

19. For a "Platoist" interpretation of *Portrait*, see Feshbach, "A Slow and Dark Birth," 289–300; for possible influences on *Portrait* from D'Annunzio's "Socrates" and "Stelio," see Scholes and Kain, *Workshop of Daedalus*, 69–79.

20. Schork, *Latin*, 51–53.

21. Yeats, *A Vision*, 247; also see Jolas, "My Friend," 14–15, and *Sur Joyce*, 83.

22. Hart, *Structure*, 129–34.

23. Yeats, *A Vision*, 248; for comment see Rankin, "'Taylorised,'" 11.

24. See Rankin, "Joyce's Remove," 11–12; and note "P.t.l.o.a.t.o. . . . plates to lick one and turn over" (*FW* 286.13, 18).

25. For a discussion of Joyce's use of Wilde's "W.H." essay, see Burnham, "Love Triangle," 43–56. Another of Wilde's dialogues, "The Decay of Lying," features Percy who acts as Vivian's compliant straight man.

26. Wilde, *Letters of Oscar Wilde*, 868.

27. Ellmann, *Wilde*, 395–96.

28. See Stanislaus Joyce, *Keeper*, 155n.2; *JJII* 296; and *CW* 141.

29. Flaubert, *Correspondance*, II.691; his emphasis.

30. Bart, *Flaubert*, 48–49, 117.

31. Flaubert, *Correspondence*, I.358.

32. The passage from Flaubert's 1857 letter is discussed in several essays in Jacquet and Topia, *"Scribble" 2* and in Cross, *Flaubert and Joyce*. None of the authors questions its "Platonic" aspects or its contemporary Gallic source.

33. Aubert, *Aesthetics*, 127–28, 136–37.

34. See Gerson, *Companion to Plotinus*.

35. Scholes and Kain, *Workshop of Daedalus*, 143–44.

36. In the *Wake* Joyce emphasizes that "the hen" is resolutely "one": "the hen is not mirely a tick or two after the first fifth fourth of the second eighth twelfth" (*FW* 119.23–24); that assertion, however, is undercut by another: "not one hen only nor two hens neyther" (*FW* 256.5). T. S. Eliot was also attracted to this term: "Mr. Eliot's Sunday Morning Service" (1920) includes the lines "In the beginning was the Word. / Superfetation of τὸ ἕν, / And the

mensural turn of time / produced enervate Origen" (Eliot, *Complete Poems*, 33–34).

37. There is a fairly long index of vaguely theosophic terms in VI.C.7.255–62, but none of them seems to have made its way into any of Joyce's texts.

38. See Copenhaver, *Hermetica*, 95.

39. Atherton, *Books*, 46; Gilbert, *Study*, 44–45; McHugh, *Sigla*, 71.

40. Stanford, *Ireland and the Classical Tradition*, 8, 191–94.

41. Vincent Deane has discovered Joyce's source of this information: J. M. Flood, *Ireland: Its Saints and Scholars*, 95 (see Deane, "Wellspring," 24).

Chapter 7

1. An archival note joins these three philosophers in a strange union: "platonic wedding / of Aristotle / & Aquinas" (VI.B.35.87).

2. Theoharis, *Anatomy*, 1–35.

3. Aubert, *Aesthetics*, 83–137; in this section Bosanquet's *Aesthetic* (1892) is also frequently noted as an important intermediary source.

4. Feshbach, "Magic Lantern," 3–66.

5. See Armstrong, *Ancient Philosophy*, 66–113.

6. The first reminiscence is by Constantine P. Curran, the second by Felix E. Hacket; both are cited from Scholes and Kain, *Workshop of Daedalus*, 147, 149–50.

7. Stanislaus Joyce, *Dublin Diary*, 53.

8. Jones, "Essence," 291–311.

9. See Atherton, *Books*, 138–39; for a thorough discussion of the topic, see Noon, *Aquinas*, and a reevaluation by Staley, "Thomistic Encounters," 155–68.

10. The text of the *Paris Notebook* can be found in *CW* 143–46 or Scholes and Kain, *Workshop of Daedalus*, 52–55.

11. Aubert, *Aesthetics*, 16–17.

12. Gillespie, *Trieste Library*, 62 [no. 87].

13. Aubert, *Aesthetics*, 127–30, 131–37; Peterson ("More Grist," 213–16) picks up some additional material that Aubert overlooked.

14. Aubert, *Aesthetics*, 135.

15. Hereafter I cite not only the standard references to Aristotle's text, but also the page where any given passage appears in the accessible collection of material in English translation compiled by Richard McKeon, *The Basic Works of Aristotle*.

16. Theoharis, *Anatomy*, 17–22.

17. In this canto of the *Inferno* Dante has just visited the abodes of "pagan" poets and warriors; now he comes upon the philosophers and natural scientists, presided over by Aristotle. Others mentioned here are Socrates, Plato, Democritus, Diogenes, Anaxagoras, Thales, Empedocles, Heraclitus, Zeno, Euclid, Ptolemy, and Galen (*Inferno* 4:134–144).

18. In a September 1903 review of *Aristotle on Education*, Joyce first used the phrase from Dante (*CW 109–110*). Even though I cannot cite examples of their reappearance in Joyce's fiction, the diction in a pair of 1903 reviews demonstrates a precocious mastery of colorful phrases and philosophical wordplay: Bruno is praised for "his attempt to reconcile the matter and form

of the Scholastics—formidable names" (*CW* 133); a pragmatic professor is mocked for trying to put "to shame the ghostly forms of Plato" (*CW* 136). In the former phrase I detect a deliberate blurring of the distinction between the Thomistic concept of form and its degeneration into nominalism (*CW* 133); in the second phrase, Plato's necessarily real Ideas fade into antique specters (*CW* 136).

19. During the retreat in *Portrait* the student sinners are reminded of the power of the "fires of punishment": "Every sense of flesh is tortured . . . eyes . . . nose . . . ears . . . taste . . . touch" (*P* 122).

20. Diogenes Laertius, *Lives,* 183.

21. There is, however, Joycean archival authority for both aspects of the phrase: "ᵀArist. heathen sage" (V.A.2.31; see Herring, *Notes and Drafts,* 113) and "Aristotle bald lust" (VI.C.7.235).

22. Diogenes Laertius, *Lives,* 187–88; the *Britannica* article on Aristophanes also includes that testamentary information (*EB* 2.502).

23. See Sarton, "Aristotle and Phyllis," 8–19, for a general review of the material; Cohn, "Third Heat," 131–33, is the last of a series of *JJQ* notes on this topic.

24. Some iconographic evidence is cited by von Phul, "Phyllis Up," 180–81; also see the illustration in Ellmann, *Liffey,* after p. 158.

25. See Herring's introductory notes on these entries, *UNBM,* 35–37.

26. Senn, "*nisus formativus,*" 26–42; reprinted in *Scrutinies,* 58–74.

27. Soud, "Blood-Red," 195–208.

28. Gilbert, *Study,* 187–88.

29. See Herring, *Notes and Drafts,* 9–10; another pertinent archival note, "Ari La Rhetor" appears in Rose and O'Hanlon, *Lost Notebook,* front cover verso.

30. Aubert, *Aesthetics,* 93–94.

31. See Peterson, "More Grist," 215, for additional information.

32. For a full discussion of source texts and their adaptation by Joyce, see Aubert, *Aesthetics,* 83–140.

33. Butcher, *Poetics,* 116; Joyce owned this book (see Gillespie, *Trieste Library,* 62 [no. 87]).

34. Butcher, *Poetics,* 135.

35. Butcher, *Poetics,* 273; also 212–15, 266–93.

36. Butcher, *Poetics,* 240–73; Bosanquet, *Aesthetic,* 65.

37. Butcher, *Poetics,* 242.

38. The recollection is that of Eugene Sheehy, cited from Scholes and Kain, *Workshop of Daedalus,* 153.

39. That matter is discussed in Aristotle's *De Generatione Animalium* (On the generation of animals) (3.3755a11–21; not in McKeon).

Chapter 8

1. See Schork, *Latin,* 228–33, for a justification of this emendation of Joyce's text and the interpretation that flows from it.

2. Senn, *Scrutinies,* 198–99.

3. For the suggestion of a para-epic impulse (Samuel Butler's *The Humour of Homer*) for Joyce's use of this term, see Ellmann, *Consciousness,* 91–92.

4. The most accessible classical source for the story is Cicero, *De officiis* (*On duties*) 3.10.

5. That suspicion is confirmed by Benzenhöfer, "Embryology," 608–11; especially acute is the author's suggestion that the mention of "i condotti di Wolff [Wolffian ducts]" in the textbook lies beneath "a wolf in the stomach" (*U* 14.730).

6. Classical allusions to this pair are found in Juvenal, *Satires* 10.28–53; Horace, *Epistles* 2.1.194. Joyce's copy of Robert Burton's *The Anatomy of Melancholy* bears the pseudonym "By Democritus Junior," a precursor of Wakean reversal of psychic energy (see Gillespie, *Trieste Library*, 61 [no. 85]).

7. Diogenes Laertius, *Lives*, 198.

8. Aubert, *Aesthetics*, 98; Bosanquet, *Aesthetic*, 82.

9. See Schork, "Anchorite," 274–77.

10. These two phrases apparently occur in the introduction to an edition of a ninth-century *cento* (patchwork) of Homeric lines restitched into a moralizing Christian narrative. I cannot agree that Joyce knew and imitated this hyperesoteric work (see Fáj, "Probable Byzantine Model," 48–56).

11. Plutarch, *Lives*, 376–77.

12. There is archival evidence that Archimedes lies behind the physical details in this citation: "ᵇArchimedes: Sun flashing roof" (*UNBM* 101:31); "ʳWoods on burning hills not sparks but friction of twigs in wind: Archimedes" (*UNBM* 150:51–52).

13. The quotation is from Rolleston's translation of *Epictetus*, 60. Joyce had a later reprint of this work in his personal collection of books at Trieste (see Gillespie, *Trieste Library*, 92 [no. 155]).

14. Rolleston, *Epictetus*, 80; his note to this passage cites Lucian (a second-century A.D. Sophist and satirist) to the effect that, after the philosopher's death, the *clay* lamp was sold for the large sum of 3000 drachma (202, n.2). The *Britannica* article on Epictetus also records the anecdote about the posthumous sale of the replacement lamp to an antiquarian (*EB* 9.682).

15. For a full discussion of this cross-cultural allusion, see Schork, *Latin*, 72; Joyce owned a copy of the *Thoughts* (*Meditations*) of the emperor (see Gillespie, *Trieste Library*, 161 [no. 313]).

16. In the Eleventh Question of chapter I.6 in the *Wake*, Shaun huffs and puffs about "the more refrangible angles to the squeals of his hypothesis on the outer tin sides" (*FW* 150.34–35).

Chapter 9

1. Publication of Richard Jebb's prose Sophocles started in 1883; Theodore Buckley's literal versions of Aeschylus began in the 1860s. For a general account of the influence of Greek tragedy during this period, see Jenkyns, *Victorians*, 87–11.

2. See Schork, *Latin*, 28–39.

3. Whelan completes his statement with another pronouncement: "Greek art . . . is not for a time but for all times. It stands aloof, alone. It is 'imperial, imperious and imperative'" (*SH* 101). In *Ulysses* the Hellenophile Professor

MacHugh twists that figure into a charge against the crass conqueror of Greece: "We think of Rome, imperial, imperious, imperative" (*U* 7.485–86).

4. From Joyce's *Pola Notebook*, cited from Scholes and Kain, *Workshop of Daedalus*, 91.

5. Summerfield, *Myriad-Minded*, 6.

6. For a good introduction to the production aspects of Attic drama, see Arnott, *Public and Performance*.

7. Joyce's collection of books in Trieste included Murray's general introduction, *Euripides and His Age* (see Gillespie, *Trieste Library*, 175–76 [no. 346]; for comment on Murray see Highet, *Tradition*, 489–91.

8. Dodds, "Memoir," in *Journal and Letters*, 43.

9. Housman, "Fragment," 414–16.

10. My information comes from Stanford, *Ireland and the Classical Tradition*, 98; the interview appeared in the *New York Times* in January 1933. Stanford suggests that the literal translation that Yeats purchased was "perhaps one of Kelly's notorious *Keys to the Classics*, proscribed by high principled teachers." In his discussion of the project, Grab is skeptical of the 1904 origin of the play and he does not mention Gogarty's role as literal translator (see Grab, "Yeats' 'Oedipus,'" 336–540).

11. Gogarty, *Many Lines*, 73.

12. Yeats, *Letters*, 537.

13. Joyce could have found this information in the *Britannica* article on "Greek Drama" (*EB* 12.510–11). Whatever his source, as far back as his University College days he knew of this theory: "Greek drama arose out of the cult of Dionysos, who, god of fruitage, joyfulness and earliest art, offered in his life-story a practical groundplan for the erection of a tragic and a comic theatre" (*CW* 39).

14. The nearby presence of "chamber's ensallycopodium" (*FW* 334.2–3) and two archival references to *Chamber's Encyclopaedia* (VI.B.13.20 and VI.B. 18.256) suggest that work as the documentary source for these technical data. In the more frequently cited *Britannica* the terms are found in the articles "Drama" (*EB* 8.492) and "Choragic" (*EB* 6.269).

15. Butcher, *Poetics*, 316–33.

16. Senn, "Hamarte," 105–15; (also see relevant comment in chapter 5). Senn notes the presence of another key Aristotelian term "*anagnōrisis*," in *Scrutinies*, 83.

17. Franz Werfel's German translation of Euripides' *The Trojan Women* was in Joyce's collection; see Gillespie, *Trieste Library*, 92–93 [no. 157–58].

18. Gilbert, *Study*, 168; in remarks on Hades in chapter 3, I suggest a possible Joycean use of a euphemism for the Lord of the Underworld.

19. Rankin, "Satyr-Play," 3–12.

20. See Schork, *Latin*, 132–36, and Senn, "Gigantism," 561–77.

21. In fact, when the dog Gerryowen growls at Bloom's arrival at the pub, the Citizen is quick to say, "Come in, come on. . . . He won't eat you" (*U* 12. 409). Also see Stanford, *Ireland and the Classical Tradition*, 107–8, for comment on Joyce's use of Cyclopean cannibalism.

22. Those shouts echo an actual moment of Dublin literary enthusiasm. Padric Colum recalls telling Joyce about George Moore's reaction to a performance

of Ibsen's *Doll's House:* "Sophocles! Shakespeare! What are they to this!" (*Our Friend*, 47; also note the entry "Shakespeare, Sophocles and Ibsen" in Joyce's *Pola Notebook*, cited from Scholes and Kain, *Workshop of Daedalus*, 88).

23. *Smith's Classical Dictionary*, 472; see Gillespie, *Trieste Library*, 219–20 [no. 459].

24. There was a German translation of *Agamemnon* among Joyce's books in Trieste; see Gillespie, *Trieste Library*, 29–30 [no. 2]; Ellmann reports a production of Aeschylus's *Agamemnon* by Max Reinhardt in Zürich in 1917 (*JJII* 411–12).

25. The context of the final phrase suggests that Joyce was also alluding to a demythologized explanation of the origins of fire after a lightning strike in the forest: "the ward of the wind that lightened the fire that lay in the wood that Jove bolt" (*FW* 80.27–28).

26. Freud, *Collected Papers*, III.149–289; for discussions of these references see Ferrer, "Freudful Couchmare," 367–82; Rose, *Textual Diaries*, 87–88. Wim Van Mierlo has discovered several new clusters of archival references to Freud's case studies from which he draws important distinctions about their use by Joyce (Van Mierlo, "Revisited," 115–53).

27. Freud, *Collected Papers*, III.239.

28. Freud, *Collected Papers*, III.240n.1.

Chapter 10

1. There is nothing on or by Aristophanes in Joyce's Paris library. An English translation of four plays (*The Acharnians, The Knights, The Birds, The Frogs*) and an Italian translation of three others (*Le nuvole* [*The Clouds*], *I calabroni* [*The Wasps*], *La pace* [*Peace*]) survive from the Trieste library; see Gillespie, *Trieste Library*, 34–35 [nos. 15–16].

2. There is a similar example of cross-cultural scatology in Malacoda's trick in Dante's *Inferno* 21:139: *Ed egli avea del cul fatto trombetta* (And he had made a trumpet of his asshole). Joyce appropriated this line in a Miltonic-Dantean pastiche at the start of "Scylla and Charybdis" (*U* 9.32–34); for extended comment see Lobner, "Sounds," 43–54.

3. Immediately after the first phrase there is another crossed entry: "ᵇringing Latin" (VI.B.4.248); this may refer to the fact that "flea's gizzard" appears in a paragraph that contains thirty-four instances of the affectedly Latinate suffix *-ation*, including the adjacent "eructation" (*FW* 557.13–558.20).

4. Burrell, "Illustrator," 96–97.

5. Burrell traces the publishing history of various forms of this volume ("Illustrator," 97). It seems that the first general publication of the unexpurgated plates and text was *The Lysistrata of Aristophanes, Illustrated by Aubrey Beardsley*; the text of the comedy in that volume was translated into English prose by Samuel Smith.

6. Citations are from Smith's translation of *Lysistrata*, 42 and 51.

7. Burrell, "Illustrator," 97.

8. *Lysistrata* 602; Smith's translation, 32. See Aristophanes, *Lysistrata*, 147–148, for a good discussion of the props involved in this scene.

9. Smith's translation of *Lysistrata*, 27.

10. Graham, "Birds," 39.

11. For identifications of these, other nearby birds, and any other avian references throughout the *Wake*, see McHugh's *Annotations*.
12. Graham, "Birds," 39.
13. Graham, "Birds," 39.
14. The titles of many of Aristophanes' plays come from their choruses of elaborately costumed performers who sang and danced their roles in the circular orchestra in front of the stage platform. Although Joyce could not have known the following fact of Attic comedic history, he would have appreciated its relevance to the *Wake:* there is evidence for a chorus of "Rivers" (see Green, *Theatre,* 28).
15. See Deane, "Greek Gifts," 164, for a discussion of the source (*Irish Times,* October 20, 1922) of Joyce's amused interest in "beavers," as recorded in the very early (1922) Notebook, VI.B.10.2. Also see a section of Joyce's November 11, 1922, letter to Harriet Shaw Weaver about the current craze for a game involving the spotting of various types of "beavers" (*Letters* I.193).
16. The phrase "melt my belt" (*FW* 450.4–5) could also be genetically related to "zones asunder" (*FW* 328.8); and both phrases may echo a classical Latin source: Horace's *solutis . . . zonis* (with sashes unfastened) (*Odes* 1.30.5–6).
17. "25 Knights" (uncrossed) appears on the same page of *Scribbledehobble;* for the date of this entry see Rose, *Textual Diaries,* 31.
18. Wiggin, "Voice of the Frogs," 62.
19. For a complete discussion of this topic—with conclusive evidence that the croaks were part of a farting contest—see Wills, "Frogs in the *Frogs,*" 306–17.
20. It is also possible to suggest a source for this item of gridiron color: the *Britannica* article "Cheering" includes the entire Yale yell (*EB* 6.22).
21. Stanislaus Joyce, *Keeper,* 61–62.
22. Atherton, "Sport," 61.
23. Atherton, "Sport," 60–61; the correct designation for the first draft manuscript is 47481–94r (*JJA* 56.2); also note "Δ rugby ball / modelled on / her rump" (VI.C.5.92).
24. Another instance of "pigskin" (*FW* 603.20) appears in a paragraph packed with words and phrases that were common on American college campuses in the 1920s and 1930s. Although their source has not been discovered, these terms appear in the very late Notebook VI.B.46.44. For a transcription and commentary see Rose, *Index Manuscript,* 92–93; for the date of this index ("early Dec 1937–Feb 1938") see Rose, *Textual Diaries* 34. Since the "pigskin" in the football passage (*FW* 395.35) was added to the evolving text in April 1923 (47481–97v [*JJA* 56.15]), it cannot be derived from the late index. In fact, "pigskin" replaced "lightning" in a slightly earlier version (47481–95v [*JJA* 56.10]). In a much earlier Notebook there is another reference to American sport: "T's baseballs" (VI.B.3.123).
25. The text records that "Stephen was reading *Oreste*" (*SH* 192); I suspect that *Orestea* (Italian) was intended.
26. In his *Electra,* Sophocles uses two revelation or identification devices: a lock of hair (901) and a signet ring (1222–23).
27. See Henderson, *Maculate Muse,* 134–35.
28. The latest word in this frequently partisan field is Rose, *Textual Diaries.*
29. Hayman, *Transit,* 54–55.

Chapter 11

1. Vernon Jones, trans., *Aesop's Fables* (cited parenthetically in the text as *Aesop*); Connolly, *Personal Library,* 7 [no. 5].

2. *Oxford Classical Dictionary,* 29, 584–85; Stanislaus Joyce admired Velasquez's portrait of Aesop as "the wise old free slave, the *fier bourgeois*" (*Dublin Diary,* 78–79), but the "biographical" tradition that Aesop was once a slave cannot be verified.

3. Atherton, *Books,* 233; Vernon Jones, *Aesop,* 125.

4. See Schork, *Latin,* 60–61.

5. Just before "*Theocritus*" in the marginal list comes "*Jacob,*" the Old Testament patriarch who made his way first to Paddan-aram to find a wife (Genesis 28:5), then to Egypt to find his son (Genesis 46:6). The assigned essay topic is "Travelling in Olden Times" (*FW* 307.L and 10–11). In the course of composing this portion of the text, Joyce initially entered "Strabo" as the traveler, but eventually crossed him out in favor of a character from the bible (see Higginson, "The Text," 126–27). Strabo, a first-century B.C. Greek geographer, had expert qualifications for the slot; he traveled extensively in the Mediterranean and did considerable research on previous writers.

6. *Euclidis I,* 7; I thank Teubner Verlag of Leipzig for permission to reproduce this figure. Also note the article on geometry in the *Britannica,* which includes a prose summary of all of Euclid's work, but no diagram for Proposition 1 (*EB* 11.678). Joyce owned a copy of Hall and Stevens, *A Text book of Euclid's Elements: Books I. and II.;* see Gillespie, *Trieste Library,* 111 [no. 206].

7. For *fossa* see Adams, *Vocabulary,* 85–86; "quif" is English slang for a cheap prostitute (*Oxford English Dictionary*). Adjacent entries in his notes for the "Ithaca" chapter of *Ulysses* show that Joyce was aware of the distinction between the two Latin formulas that mark the completion of a Euclidean exercise: "Q.E.D. / ᵣQ.E.F." (*UNBM* 475.102–3).

8. See Schork, "Graphic," 351–54.

9. Bradley, *Schooldays,* 111, 117, 131, 141.

10. Glasheen, *Third Census,* 52.

11. The relevant draft stages are: 47478–242 (*JJA* 52.151) ("Scribbledehobbles" [1932]); 47478–290 (*JJA* 52.200) (extracted items crossed out [1934]); 47478–319 (*JJA* 52.211) (draft for Left Margin of what is now *FW* 276 [1934]). In the last draft mentioned, the first phrase of the marginal item "*Some is out*" could be read as an authorial comment on the process of excision. For a discussion of the evolution of this text see Hayman, "'Scribbledehobbles,'" 106–18.

12. Stewart, *Faces of Power,* 95–102, 314–23; color plate 8; figures 76–79, 87, 117–19, 122.

13. See the *Oxford English Dictionary* entry "dulcarnon." The Pythagorean theorem also appears in elliptical form in another passage: "refrangible angles to the squeals of his hypothesis on the outer tin sides" (*FW* 150.34–35).

14. There is a single archival reference to Hippocrates, but as far as I can determine, its information is incorrect. While he was interested in observing the eyes of his patients (*Prognosis* 2), there is no evidence that "Hippocrates dilated pupil" (VI.C.7.195).

15. An uncrossed archival note records this dubious psychosomatic advice: "Galen—balls more than heart / to live well not to love" (VI.B.1.72).

16. I owe this interpretation of Joyce's multilingual hijinks to Roy Arthur Swanson, who read my manuscript for University Press of Florida.
17. Although I have not examined the original British Museum notesheets, I have emended Herring's reading of the parenthetical proper name in this entry. He prints "(Milly)"; in my judgment the final application of the note to Dilly Dedalus is evidence that Herring probably—and slightly—misread Joyce's handwriting here.

Chapter 12

1. Budgen, *Making,* 358–59; there are more detailed remarks on 173–75.
2. Aravantinou, *Hellēnika,* 121–39, and *JJII* 407–408. Aravantinou's book must be used with caution (see the review by M. Byron Raizis in *JJQ* 16 [Summer 1979], 521–24), but it does reproduce the Zürich notebooks and related documents. Owen's dissertation on the same period (*Beginning,* 159–67) includes only a descriptive summary of this material.
3. *CP* 42; the poem was first published in 1907.
4. See Attwater, *Saints,* 286. According to tradition Phocas was martyred by Roman legionnaires in his garden on the southern shore of the Black Sea. Sailors in that area, in the Aegean, and in the Adriatic are reported to have sung chanties to honor this patron of mariners. The odd details of this pious tale are regarded with extreme skepticism by experts in the field of early Christian saint lore.
5. There are occasional words from other languages that Joyce knew: French *piste* (2), Latin *salve, vale* (3), Italian *basta* (5).
6. Budgen, *Making,* xvi; *Letters* II.299.
7. Gottfried, "Berlitz," 223–38.
8. Aravantinou dates this document to June 15, 1919 (*Hellēnika,* 159); I cannot determine her grounds for such precision, but Joyce's script and material mark it as the product of an advanced stage of instruction.
9. For a summary of the situation see Browning, *Greek,* 108–116. Bien, *Linguistic Revolution,* 13–146, analyzes the literary, political, and social dimensions of the controversy. A 1929 Notebook includes the entries "archaiki/demotiki/katervouse" (VI.B.4.210). Professor Peter Bien (Dartmouth) made several invaluable last-minute corrections; remaining errors and inconsistencies are mine—or Joyce's—not his.
10. It is interesting to note that one of Phokas's friends whom Aravantinou interviewed twice characterizes Phokas as "unlucky" in both Zürich and Galatsi (*atychos* and *den eiche tychē*); he prospered only when he went to Africa (*Hellēnika,* 132–33).
11. Aravantinou, *Hellēnika,* 121; the information comes from a 1976 interview with Mrs. Evangelia Ruggiero.
12. Ruggiero, "Last Days," 284, and *JJII* 739. One of his closest Zürich friends, Carola Giedion-Welcker, reports that Joyce told her in late 1940 that he "would like to write a drama on the revolution of the modern Greeks" (Kain, "An Interview," 97). Deep background for this project may be the reason for a long index of ancient Greek mythological and historical items in a post-*Wake* notebook, VI.B.48.42–49.
13. The text of the letter is in *Letters* I.402–3; also see *JJII* 714 for a translation of

the lyrics. Joyce reported to Ruggiero the mixed reception to his performance of the song at the dinner (*Letters* III.435).

14. My thanks to Robert Nicholson, James Joyce Tower, Dublin, for copies of
the last two items.

15. The card is dated "6.X.923"; Pound's birthday is October 28. My thanks to
Ellen R. Cordes of the Beinecke Library at Yale University for sending copies
of this and of Joyce's January 5, 1922, note to Valery Larbaud; he concluded
with thanks in a phrase of quite classicized Modern Greek (*Letters* III.52).

16. For a thorough and well-illustrated review of the ethnic Greek presence in
Trieste, see Pozzetto, *Nuovo Giorno*, and Hartshorn, *Trieste*.

17. Aravantinou, *Hellēnika*, 226–27; another letter from Ralli (May 27, 1920)
thanks Joyce for a copy of *Exiles* (231).

18. Aravantinou, *Hellēnika*, 221–22. The publisher's contract also called for
Joyce himself to purchase 120 copies (*JJII* 354, 392).

19. Aravantinou has much to say about Mrs. Santos; see *Hellēnika*, 77–82, and
an extract translated into French, "Amis grecs," *L'Herne: Joyce*, 58–64. An
April 2, 1920, letter to Joyce from Santos, who had become an importer-
exporter in Barcelona, is printed in *Hellēnika*, 232–34. In September, 1940,
Joyce asked Mrs. Jolas to see if the Greek consul in Marseilles had any information about the Santos family (*JJII* 734).

20. Joyce, "*Poems*," 88; Joyce refers to Miss Moschos on occasion in his "business" correspondence (*Letters* III.60, 66, 85, 12, 171).

21. There is evidence that, at exactly this period, Joyce was fascinated by a
university student "narrative" in which mythological proper names do
double duty in the plot as similar-sounding French words, many of which
are scatological or grossly obscene; see "Salade Mythologique" in *L'Herne:
Joyce*, 423–24.

22. Rose dates this Notebook to March–July 1927 (*Textual Diaries*, 28).

23. This letter was originally written in Italian, but only the English version is
printed.

24. See Hart, *Structure*, 236.

25. Ioannidou and Knuth, "Greek in 'The Mookse,'" 83–88 and 12–16, and
"Greek in FW," 39–54; they do not refer to the Zürich notebooks.

26. My play on transliteration options derives some support by a corrective
entry (in Phokas's handwriting) in a Zürich notebook: "Ξ = ks = ξ [*xi*] / Z =
z = ζ [zeta]" (VIII.A.4.19).

27. Ioannidou and Knuth, "Greek in FW," 49.

28. A Greek adverb from this same root appears in one of the Zürich notebooks:
"ευχαρίστως = avec plaisir" (*VIII*.A.4.19).

29. Some of the most frequently appearing items in McHugh's *Annotations* are
multilingual slang terms for the female genitalia.

30. Hedberg, "Parandowski," 443; the key sentence about Joyce's pronunciation does not appear in an earlier version of this memoir (see Parandowski,
"Meeting," 157). The "Erasmian" pronunciation (based on sound comparative linguistic evidence) is standard in academic instruction in ancient
Greek. The term falls from the lips of contemporary Greeks loaded with
skeptical scorn for pedantic perverters (especially Anglo-Saxon academics)
of their mother tongue.

31. Barber, *Blue Guide*, 73; the ancient breathing marks and tonal accents have

almost entirely disappeared in normal written and spoken Greek of the late twentieth century.

32. Byron, *Works*, 51; Joyce also manipulated Byron's own Latin-to-English translation of "[H]Adrian's Address to His Soul Whan Dying" (see Schork, "Butterfly," 403–5, and *Latin*, 184–87).

33. Budgen, *Making*, xvi.

34. The handwriting of the corrector is not Phokas's. If Ruggiero had once helped Joyce with the correct spelling of *echthros*, the point of the request, years later, for renewed tutorial assistance becomes sharper. I thank Fritz Senn for sending a copy of this card, which is among the memorabilia at the Zürich James Joyce Foundation.

35. Ioannidou and Knuth, "Greek in 'The Mookse,'" 16; none of the native speakers of Greek whom I consulted about this idiom could recall hearing it actually used.

36. Tzous, *Odysseas*, 816.

37. The Greek liturgical term *epik/clēsis* (the calling of the Holy Spirit to consecrate the bread and wine) has rightfully been excised from Joyce's critical vocabulary as a parallel to "epiphany" (see Steppe, "Merry Greeks," 597–617, and Schork, *Latin*, 6). Nevertheless, that hallowed word does appear—but uncrossed and unused—in a *Wake* Notebook (VI.B.22.141).

Chapter 13

1. Arkins's brief note ("Joyce and Greek," 444) educes inaccurate and inadequate evidence to suggest that "Joyce [knew] a certain amount of classical Greek."

2. For a compact review of the history of the *Lexicon*, see Lloyd-Jones, "Scott wrote that," 9.

3. Glasheen, *Third Census*, 257.

4. For the latest word on Dodgson/Carroll's relationship with the three Liddell girls, see Leach, "Wonderland," 15. Joyce comments on "the author of 'Alice'" in a March 28, 1928, letter to Miss Weaver (*Letters* III.174). In the *Wake* there is some wordplay involving Christ Church and Dodgson: "over at the house of Eddy's Christy, meaning Dodgfather, Dodgson and Coo" (*FW* 481.36–482.1); the Latin for Christ Church is *Aedes Christi* (literally, House of Christ); thus Oxford slang designates that college as "the House."

5. O Hehir and Dillon, as well as McHugh, incorrectly suggest *eripheios* (of a goat-kid) here; a pair of archival notes confirms the scriptural source: "Xiton araphon" (VI.B.12.51) and "χιτον ἄρραφον" (VI.B.17.40). The final paragraph of Joyce's 1909 review of Oscar Wilde's *Salomé* mentions this garment in English and Latin (*CW* 205).

6. An archival note may also add a moral dimension to the situation: "guilty looks back, conscience forward" (*Scribbledehobble* 88 [401]).

7. Rose, *Index Manuscript*, 119–20.

8. In hematology the initials *HR* are also used to designate a specific category of blood.

9. For comment on the origins of the goddess's name, see the article on "Athena" in the *Britannica* (*EB* 2.828). Bernal's argument "that both the city name Athenai and the divine name Athene or Athena derive from the

Egyptian Ht Nt (Temple or House of Neit)" (*Black Athena*, I.51–52) have not been accepted (see Jasanoff and Nussbaum, "Word Games," 193–94).

10. The comprehensive Liddell and Scott *Lexicon* lists only one occurrence in Greek literature of the adjective *athanēs*, in the works of Maximus of Tyre (16.2.). That reference, however, is incorrect; no such form appears there. I do not suggest that Joyce was tempted to check the original text of Maximus of Tyre; his rhetorical works are so inconsequential that he should be called "Minimus" of Tyre. Rather, this sort of inspired folk etymology smacks of a glance at a dictionary and a little imagination. On the other hand, it does seem that *athanēs* is a genuine *hapax legomenon;* it is used once by the famous Byzantine hymnographer, Romanos the Melodist, in one of his Easter *kontakia* (28.33.3).

11. For a fascinating discussion of the Greek background to and the Roman practice of name play (which "lies near the heart" of some aspects of contemporary Vergillian scholarship), see O'Hara, *True Names.*

12. This topic is treated in greater detail in Schork, "Significant Names," forthcoming in *JJQ.*

13. See the P.S. in Joyce's April 27, 1935, letter to Lucia: "E bene che gli angeli ti portino questo messaggio poiche angelo in greco significa messaggero" (It's a good thing that the angels are bringing this letter to you since "angel" in Greek means messenger) (*SL* 373–74).

14. Bill Cadbury's eagle eye has spotted alphas and omegas at *U* 15.3809–3813 (orgasmic) and in the draft stages of the *Wake* I.4 (genetic); see Cadbury, "Development," 217–19.

15. A brief archival cluster addresses issues of pronunciation and orthography of ancient Greek: "[b]lambdacism 'Melican' / rhotacism corpus, oris / [b]itacism Dai/e/dalos" (VI.B.17.99–100). Though two entries are crossed, I cannot identify their deployment in the printed text of the *Wake.*

16. Joyce's four surviving letters sent to Martha Fleischmann in Zürich, December 1918–February 1919, were written with Greek *ees* (for the texts, see *Letters* I.426–36; for photographic reproductions, see *Letters* I after page 440, illustrations 51–53).

17. Actually, there is a most minor error in the Greek: instead of a midline period (·), which is the Greek equivalent of a semicolon (;), the sentence should end with a Greek mark of interrogation (;). In this note I have attempted to make the source of the (printer's? proofreader's?) confusion about these fine points of diglossal punctuation as graphically obvious as possible.

18. Spoo, "Unpublished Letters," 560.

Bibliography

Abbreviations

AFWC   *A "Finnegans Wake" Circular*
AWN   *A Wake Newslitter*
EB   *Encylopaedia Britannica*
EJS   *European Joyce Studies*
JJLS   *James Joyce Literary Supplement*
JJQ   *James Joyce Quarterly*
JSA   *Joyce Studies Annual*

Adams, J. N. *The Latin Sexual Vocabulary.* Baltimore: Johns Hopkins University Press, 1982.

Aesop's Fables, trans. V. S. Vernon Jones. New York: Franklin Watts, 1969.

Allison, June W. "A Literary Coincidence? Joyce and Plato." *JJQ* 16 (Spring 1979): 267–82.

Aravantinou, Manto. Τὰ Ἑλληνικὰ τοῦ Τζαίημς Τζόυς (*Ta Hellēnika tou Tzaiems Tzous* [*The Greek of James Joyce*]). Athens: Hermes, 1977.

Aravantinou, Mando [*sic*]. "James Joyce et ses amis grecs." In *L'Herne: James Joyce,* ed. Jacques Aubert and Fritz Senn, 58–64. Paris: Editions L'Herne, 1985.

Aristophanes. *Lysistrata.* Ed. Jeffrey Henderson. Oxford: Clarendon, 1987.

Aristotle. *The Basic Works of Aristotle.* Ed. Richard McKeon. New York: Random House, 1941.

Arkins, Brian. "Joyce and Greek." *Notes and Queries,* n.s., 43 (December 1996): 444.

Armstrong, Arthur H. *An Introduction to Ancient Philosophy.* 2d ed. London: Methuen, 1949.

Arnott, Peter D. *Public and Performance in the Greek Theatre.* London: Routledge, 1989.

Atherton, James S. "Sport and Games in *Finnegans Wake.*" In *Twelve and a Tilly: Essays on the Occasion of the 25th Anniversary of "Finnegans Wake,"* ed. Jack P. Dalton and Clive Hart, 52–64. Evanston: Northwestern University Press, 1965.

———. *The Books at the Wake: A Study of Literary Allusions in James Joyce's "Finnegans Wake."* Carbondale: Southern Illinois University Press, 1974.

Attwater, Donald. *A Dictionary of Saints.* Harmondsworth, England: Penguin, 1965.

Aubert, Jacques. *The Aesthetics of James Joyce.* Baltimore: Johns Hopkins University Press, 1992.

Aubert, Jacques, and Fritz Senn, eds. *L'Herne: James Joyce.* Paris: L'Herne, 1985.

Austin, Norman. *Archery at the Dark of the Moon: Poetic Problems in Homer's "Odyssey."* Berkeley and Los Angeles: University of California Press, 1982.

Autenrieth, Georg. *A Homeric Dictionary.* Trans. Robert P. Keep; rev. Isaac Flagg. Norman: University of Oklahoma Press, 1966.

Barber, Robin. *Blue Guide: Greece.* London: A. and C. Black; New York: W. W. Norton, 1987.

Bart, Benjamin F. *Flaubert.* Syracuse: Syracuse University Press, 1967.

Bauerle, Ruth. *The James Joyce Songbook.* New York: Garland, 1982.

———, ed. *Picking Up Airs: Hearing the Music in Joyce's Text.* Urbana: University of Illinois Press, 1993.

Beckett, Samuel, et al. *James Joyce/"Finnegans Wake," A Symposium: Our Exagmination round His Factification for Incamination of Work in Progress.* New York: New Directions, 1972.

Benzenhöfer, Udo. "Joyce and Embryology: Guido Valenti's *Lezioni elementari di embriologia* as a Source for 'Oxen of the Sun'." *JJQ* 26 (Summer 1989): 608–11.

Bérard, Victor. *Les Phéniciens et l'Odyssée.* Paris: A. Colin, 1902–3.

———. *Les navigations d'Ulysse.* Paris: A. Colin, 1927–29.

Bernal, Martin. *Black Athena: The Afroasiatic Roots of Classical Civilization.* Vol. 1, *The Fabrication of Ancient Greece.* New Brunswick: Rutgers University Press, 1987.

Bien, Peter. *Kazantzakis and the Linguistic Revolution in Greek Literature.* Princeton: Princeton University Press, 1972.

Bishop, John. *Joyce's Book of the Dark: "Finnegans Wake."* Madison: University of Wisconsin Press, 1986.

Boardman, John, Jasper Griffin, and Oswyn Murray, eds. *Greece and the Hellenistic World.* Vol. I of *The Oxford History of the Classical World.* Oxford and New York: Oxford University Press, 1988.

Borach, Georges. "Conversations with James Joyce." In *Portraits of the Artist in Exile,* ed. Willard Potts, 67–72. New York: Harcourt, Brace, Jovanovich, 1986.

Bosanquet, Bernard. *A History of Aesthetic.* 2d ed. London: Allen and Unwin, 1904.

Bradley, Bruce. *James Joyce's Schooldays.* New York: St. Martin's, 1982.

Brammer, Marsanne. "Joyce's 'hallucinian via': Mysteries, Gender, and the Staging of 'Circe'." *JSA* 7 (1996): 86–124.

Browning, Robert. *Medieval and Modern Greek.* London: Hutchinson, 1969.

Buckley, Theodore Alois, ed. and trans. *Aeschylus: The Tragedies.* London: Bell, 1863.

Budgen, Frank. *James Joyce and the Making of "Ulysses" and Other Writings.* Oxford and New York: Oxford University Press, 1972.

Buitron, Diana, and Beth Cohen, eds. *The "Odyssey" and Ancient Art: An Epic in Word and Image.* Annandale-on-Hudson: Bard College, 1992.

Burkert, Walter. *Homo Necans: The Anthropology of Ancient Greek Sacrificial Ritual and Myth,* trans. Peter Bigg. Berkeley and Los Angeles: University of California, 1979.

Burke's Genealogical and Heraldic History of the Peerage, Baronetage and Knightage. Ed. Peter Townend. 105th ed. London: Burke's Peerage, 1970.

Burnham, Michelle. "'Dark Lady and Fair Man': The Love Triangle in Shakespeare's Sonnets and *Ulysses.*" *Studies in the Novel* 22 (Spring 1990): 43–56.

Burrell, Harry. "The Illustrator in the *Wake.*" *AWN,* n.s., 17, no. 6 (December 1980): 95–98.

Bury, J. B. *A History of Greece to the Death of Alexander the Great.* Rev. ed. London: Macmillan; New York: St. Martin's, 1963.

Butcher, S. H. *Aristotle's Theory of Poetry and Fine Art: With a Critical Text and Translation of "The Poetics."* 4th ed. New York: Dover, 1951.

Byron, George Gordon, Lord. *The Poetical Works.* New York: Hurst, n.d.

Cadbury, Bill. "The Development of the 'Eye, Ear, Nose and Throat Witness' Testimony in I.4." In *EJS* 5 (*Probes: Genetic Studies in Joyce*), ed. David Hayman and Sam Slote, 203–54. Amsterdam: Rodopi, 1994.

Canfora, Luciano. *The Vanished Library.* Trans. Martin Ryle. London: Hutchinson Radius, 1989.

Card, James van Dyck. "Roses and Camellias, Red and White." *JJQ* 23 (Fall 1985): 82–84.

Carpentier, Martha C. "Eleusinian Archetypes and Ritual in 'Eumaeus' and 'Ithaca'." *JJQ* 28 (Fall 1990): 221–38.

Casson, Lionel. *The Ancient Mariners: Seafarers and Sea Fighters of the Mediterranean in Ancient Times.* 2d ed. Princeton: Princeton University Press, 1991.

Childress, Lynn D. *"Les Phéneciens et l'Odyssée*: A Source for 'Lestrygonians'." *JJQ* 26 (Winter 1989): 259–69.

———. "The Missing 'Cicones' Episode of *Ulysses.*" *JJQ* 33 (Fall 1996): 69–82.

Clay, Jenny Strauss. *The Wrath of Athena: Gods and Men in the "Odyssey."* Princeton: Princeton University Press, 1983.

Clayton, Peter, and Martin Price, eds. *The Seven Wonders of the Ancient World.* London: Routledge, 1989.

Cohn, Alan M. "Phyllis on Aristotle: Third Heat." *JJQ* 9 (Fall 1971): 131–33.

Colum, Mary, and Padraic Colum. *Our Friend James Joyce.* Garden City, N.Y.: Doubleday, 1958.

A Commentary on Homer's "Odyssey." Ed. Alfred Heubeck et al. Oxford: Clarendon, 1988–92.

Connolly, Thomas E. *The Personal Library of James Joyce: A Descriptive Bibliography.* Buffalo, N.Y.: University of Buffalo Press, 1957.

———, ed. *James Joyce's "Scribbledehobble": The Ur–Workbook for "Finnegans Wake."* Evanston: Northwestern University Press, 1961.

Conrad, Kathryn, and Darryl Wadsworth. "Joyce and the Irish Body Politic: Sexuality and Colonization in *Finnegans Wake.*" *JJQ* 31 (Spring 1994): 301–13.

Cope, Jackson I. *Joyce's Cities: Archaeologies of the Soul.* Baltimore: Johns Hopkins University Press, 1981.

Copenhaver, Brian, ed. and trans. *Hermetica.* Cambridge: Cambridge University Press, 1992.

The Cornell Joyce Collection: A Catalogue. Comp. Robert E. Scholes. Ithaca: Cornell University Press, 1961.

Costello, Peter. *James Joyce: The Years of Growth: 1882–1915.* Schull, West Cork: Robert Rinehart, 1992.

Cross, Richard K. *Flaubert and Joyce: The Rite of Fiction.* Princeton: Princeton University Press, 1971.

Cunliffe, Richard J. *A Lexicon of the Homeric Dialect.* Norman: University of Oklahoma Press, 1980.

Curran, Constantine. *James Joyce Remembered.* London: Oxford University Press, 1968.

Curran, Stuart. "'Bous Stephenoumenos': Joyce's Sacred Cow." *JJQ* 6 (Winter 1969): 163–70.

Dalton, Jack P., and Clive Hart, eds. *Twelve and a Tilly: Essays on the Occasion of the 25th Anniversary of "Finnegans Wake."* Evanston: Northwestern University Press, 1965.

Deane, Vincent. "The Wellspring of the Saints: J. M. Flood in B.3." *AFWC* 7 (1991–92): 1–27.

———. "Greek Gifts: *Ulysses* into Fox in VI.B.10." *JSA* 5 (1994): 162–75.

Dictionnaire de biographie française. Paris: Librairie Letouzey et Ané, 1951.

Dimock, George E. "The Name of Odysseus." In *Essays on the "Odyssey,"* ed. Charles H. Taylor, 54–72. Bloomington: Indiana University Press, 1963.

Diogenes Laertius. *Lives of the Philosophers*. Trans. A. Robert Caponnigni. Chicago: Henry Regnery, 1969.

Dodds, E. R. *Missing Persons: An Autobiography*. Oxford: Clarendon, 1977.

——, ed. *Journal and Letters of Stephen MacKenna*. New York: William Morrow, 1937.

Doherty, Lillian E. "Joyce's Penelope and Homer's: Feminist Reconsiderations." *Classical and Modern Literature* 10 (Summer 1990): 343–49.

Dunleavy, Janet E., ed. *Re-Viewing Classics of Joyce Criticism*. Urbana: University of Illinois Press, 1991.

Eliot, T. S. *The Complete Poems and Plays: 1909–1950*. New York: Harcourt, Brace, 1958.

Ellmann, Richard. *Ulysses on the Liffey*. New York: Oxford University Press, 1973.

——. *The Consciousness of Joyce*. London: Faber and Faber, 1977.

——. *James Joyce*. New York: Oxford Press, 1982.

——. *Oscar Wilde*. New York: Knopf, 1987.

——, ed. *Selected Letters of James Joyce*. New York: Viking, 1975.

Epictetus. *The Teaching of Epictetus: Being the "Encheiridion" of Epictetus, with Selections from the "Dissertations" and "Fragments."* Trans. and annot. T. W. Rolleston. London: Walter Scott, 1905.

Euclid. *Euclidis I: Elementa I-IV.* Ed. E. S. Stamatis, after F. L. Heiberg. Leipzig: Teubner, 1969.

Fáj, Attila. "Probable Byzantine and Hungarian Models of *Ulysses* and *Finnegans Wake*." *Arcadia* (Berlin) 3 (1968): 48–72.

Felson-Rubin, Nancy. *Regarding Penelope: From Character to Poetics*. Princeton: Princeton University Press, 1994.

Ferrer, Daniel. "The Freudful Couchmar of ⋀d: Joyce's Notes and the Composition of Chapter XVI of *Finnegans Wake*." *JJQ* 22 (Summer 1985): 367–82.

Ferris, Kathleen. *James Joyce and the Burden of Disease*. Lexington: University Press of Kentucky, 1995.

Feshbach, Sidney. "A Slow and Dark Birth: A Study of the Organization of *A Portrait of the Artist as a Young Man*." *JJQ* 4 (Summer 1987): 289–300.

——. "The Magic Lantern of Tradition on *A Portrait of the Artist as a Young Man*." *JJA* 7 (1996): 3–66.

Flaubert, Gustave. *Correspondance*. Ed. Jean Bruneau. Paris: Gallimard, 1973–91.

Forbes Irving, P. M. C. *Metamorphosis in Greek Myths*. Oxford: Clarendon, 1990.

Frehner, Ruth, and Ursula Zeller, eds. *A Collideorscape of Joyce: Festschrift for Fritz Senn*. Dublin: Lilliput, 1998.

Freud, Sigmund. *Collected Papers*. Trans. Alix Strachey and James Strachey. London: Hogarth and The Institute of Psychoanalysis, 1925.

Friedrich, Gerhard. *Theological Dictionary of the New Testament*. Ed. and trans. Geoffrey W. Bromiley. Grand Rapids: William B. Eerdmans, 1971.

Gerson, Lloyd P. *The Cambridge Companion to Plotinus*. Cambridge: Cambridge University, 1996.

Gibson, Andrew, ed. *Joyce's "Ithaca."* European Joyce Studies 6. Amsterdam: Rodopi, 1996.

Giedion-Welcker, Carola. "Meetings with Joyce." In *Portraits of the Artist in Exile*, ed. Willard Potts, 253–80. New York: Harcourt, Brace, Jovanovich, 1986.

Gifford, Don, with Robert J. Seidman. *"Ulysses" Annotated: Notes for James Joyce's*

"Ulysses." Rev. ed. Berkeley and Los Angeles: University of California Press, 1989.

Gilbert, Stuart. *James Joyce's "Ulysses": A Study.* New York: Vintage, 1958.

———. *Reflections on James Joyce: Stuart Gilbert's Paris Journal.* Ed. Thomas F. Staley and Randolph Lewis. Austin: University of Texas Press, 1993.

Gillespie, Michael Patrick, with Erik Bradford Stocker. *James Joyce's Trieste Library: A Catalogue of Materials at the Harry Ransom Humanities Research Center, The University of Texas at Austin.* Austin: University of Texas Press, 1986.

Gillet, Louis. *Claybook for James Joyce.* Trans. Georges Markow-Totevy. London: Abelard-Schuman, 1958.

———. "Farewell to Joyce." In *Portraits of the Artist in Exile,* ed. Willard Potts, 165–69. New York: Harcourt, Brace, Jovanovich, 1986.

———. "The Living Joyce." In *Portraits of the Artist in Exile,* ed. Willard Potts, 170–204. New York: Harcourt, Brace, Jovanovich, 1986.

Given, Seon, ed. *James Joyce: Two Decades of Criticism.* New York: Vangard, 1948.

Glasheen, Adaline. *Third Census of "Finnegans Wake": An Index of the Characters and Their Roles.* Berkeley and Los Angeles: University of California Press, 1977.

Gogarty, Oliver St. John. *Many Lines to Thee: Letters to G. K. A. Bell, 1904–1907.* Ed. James F. Carens. Ireland: Dolmen, 1972.

Gordon, John. "Joyce's *Finnegans Wake.*" *Explicator* 50 (Winter 1992): 96–98.

Gottfried, Roy. "Berlitz Schools Joyce." *JJQ* 16 (Spring 1979): 223–38.

———. *Joyce's Iritis and the Irritated Text: The Dislexic "Ulysses."* Gainesville: University Press of Florida, 1995.

Grab, Frederic D. "Yeats' 'King Oedipus.'" *Journal of English and Germanic Philology* 71 (July 1972): 336–54.

Graham, Philip. "The Birds." *AWN,* n.s., 10 (1973): 39.

The Greek Anthology. Trans. W. R. Paton. Cambridge, Mass.: Harvard University Press, 1953.

Green, J. R. *Theatre in Ancient Greek Society.* London: Routledge, 1994.

Groden, Michael, et al., eds. *The James Joyce Archive.* New York and London: Garland, 1977–78.

Haggard, H. Rider. *The World's Desire.* New York: Harper, 1890.

———. *The Days of My Life: An Autobiography.* London: Longmans, 1960.

Harper, Margaret Mills. "Fabric and Frame in the *Odyssey* and 'Penelope'." In *Gender in Joyce,* ed. Jolanta W. Wawrzycka and Marlena G. Corcoran, 170–88. Gainesville: University Press of Florida, 1997.

Hart, Clive. *Structure and Motif in "Finnegans Wake."* Evanston: Northwestern University Press, 1962.

Hartshorn, Peter. *James Joyce and Trieste.* Westport: Greenwood Press, 1997.

Havelock, Christine M. *The Aphrodite of Knidos and Her Successors: A Historical Review of the Female Nude in Greek Art.* Ann Arbor: University of Michigan Press, 1996.

Hayman, David. "'Scribbledehobbles' and How They Grew: A Turning Point in the Development of a Chapter." In *Twelve and a Tilly,* ed. Jack P. Dalton and Clive Hart, 107–18. Evanston: Northwestern University Press, 1963.

———. *The "Wake" in Transit.* Ithaca: Cornell University Press, 1990.

———. "Language of/as Gesture in Joyce." In *Joyce: A Collection of Critical Essays,* ed. William M. Chace, 37–47. Englewood Cliffs, N.J.: Prentice Hall, 1993.

————, ed. *A First-Draft Version of "Finnegans Wake."* Austin: University of Texas Press, 1963.

Hedberg, Johannes. "Hans Kraus, Jan Parandowski, and James Joyce." *JJQ* 33 (Spring 1996): 441–46.

Henderson, Jeffrey. *The Maculate Muse: Obscenity in Attic Comedy.* New Haven: Yale University Press, 1975.

Herodotus. *The Histories.* Trans. Aubrey de Sélincourt. Rev. ed. Harmondsworth, England: Penguin, 1988.

Herr, Cheryl. *Joyce's Anatomy of Culture.* Urbana: University of Illinois Press, 1986.

Herring, Phillip F., ed. *Joyce's "Ulysses" Notesheets in the British Museum.* Charlottesville: University of Virginia Press, 1972.

————. *Joyce's Notes and Early Drafts for "Ulysses": Selections from the Buffalo Collection.* Charlottesville: University of Virginia Press, 1977.

Hesiod. *Hesiod's "Theogony."* Trans. Richard Calwell. Cambridge, Mass.: Focus Information Group, 1987.

Heubeck, Alfred. Introduction, *A Commentary on Homer's "Odyssey,"* ed. Alfred Heubeck et al., 1:3–23. Oxford: Clarendon, 1988.

Higginson, Fred H. "Notes on the Text of *Finnegans Wake.*" *Journal of English and Germanic Philology* 55 (1956): 451–56.

————. "The Text of *Finnegans Wake.*" In *New Light on Joyce from the Dublin Symposium,* ed. Fritz Senn, 120–30. Bloomington: Indiana University Press, 1972.

Highet, Gilbert. *The Classical Tradition.* New York and London: Oxford University Press, 1949.

Homer. *The Complete Works of Homer: The "Iliad" and the "Odyssey."* Trans. (*Iliad*) Andrew Lang, Walter Leaf, and Ernest Myers; (*Odyssey*) S. H. Butcher and Andrew Lang. New York: Random House, Modern Library, n.d.

Housman, A. E. "Fragment of a Greek Tragedy." *Yale Review,* n.s., 17 (January 1928): 414–16.

Hyginus. *Fabulae.* Ed. Peter K. Marshall. Stuttgart: Teubner, 1993.

Ioannidou, Ioanna, and Leo Knuth. "Greek in the 'Mookse and The Gripes' (FW 152–156)." Parts 1 and 2. *AWN,* n.s., VIII, no. 6 (December 1971): 83–86; X, no. 1 (January 1973): 12–16.

————. "Greek in Finnegans Wake." *AWN,* n.s., XII, no. 3 (June 1975): 39–54.

Jacquet, Claude, and André Topia, eds. *James Joyce 2: "Scribble" 2: Joyce et Flaubert.* Paris: Lettres Modernes, 1990. (*La revue des lettres modernes,* 953–58).

The James Joyce Archive. Ed. Michael Groden et al. New York and London: Garland, 1977–78.

James Joyce's "Scribbledehobble": The Ur-Workbook for "Finnegans Wake." Ed. Thomas E. Connolly. Evanston: Northwestern University Press, 1961.

The James Joyce–Paul Léon Letters in the National Library of Ireland. Comp. Catherine Fahy. Dublin: National Library of Ireland, 1992.

Jasanoff, Jay H., and Alan Nussbaum. "Word Games: The Linguistic Evidence in *Black Athena.*" In *Black Athena Revisited,* ed. Mary R. Lefkowitz and Guy McLean Rogers, 177–205. Chapel Hill: University of North Carolina Press, 1996.

Jebb, Richard C., ed. *Sophocles: The Plays and Fragments, with Critical Notes, Commentary, and Translation in English Prose.* Cambridge: Cambridge University Press, 1883–96.

Jenkyns, Richard. *The Victorians and Ancient Greece.* Cambridge, Mass.: Harvard University Press, 1980.

Jolas, Eugène. "My Friend James Joyce." In *James Joyce: Two Decades of Criticism*, ed. Seon Given, 3–18. New York: Vanguard, 1948.

———. *Sur Joyce*. Trans. Marc Dachy. Paris: Plon, 1990.

Jones, David E. "The Essence of Beauty in James Joyce's Aesthetics." *JJQ* 10 (Spring 1973): 291–311.

Joyce, James. *Finnegans Wake*. New York: Viking, 1939.

———. *Collected Poems*. New York: Viking, 1957.

———. *The Critical Writings of James Joyce*. Ed. Ellsworth Mason and Richard Ellmann. New York: Viking, 1959.

———. *Stephen Hero*. Ed. John J. Slocum and Herbert Cahoon. New York: New Directions, 1963.

———. *Letters of James Joyce*. Vol. 1, ed. Stuart Gilbert. New York: Viking, 1966. Vols. 2 and 3, ed. Richard Ellmann. New York: Viking, 1964.

———. *Dubliners*. Ed. Robert Scholes with Richard Ellmann. New York: Viking, 1967.

———. *Giacomo Joyce*. Ed. Richard Ellmann. New York: Viking, 1968.

———. *A Portrait of the Artist as a Young Man*. Ed. Richard Ellman; text corrected by Chester G. Anderson. New York: Viking, 1968.

———. *Exiles*. New York: Penguin, 1973.

———. *Selected Letters of James Joyce*. Ed. Richard Ellman. New York: Viking, 1975.

———. *Ulysses*. Ed. Hans Walter Gabler et al. New York: Random House, 1986.

———. *"Poems" and "Exiles."* Ed. J. C. C. Mays. London: Penguin, 1992.

Joyce, Stanislaus. *The Complete Dublin Diary*. Ed. George H. Healey. Ithaca: Cornell University Press, 1971.

———. *My Brother's Keeper*. Ed. Richard Ellmann. London: Faber and Faber, 1982.

Kain, Richard. "An Interview with Carola Giedion-Welcker and Maria Jolas." *JJQ* 11 (Winter 1974): 94–122.

Katz, Marilyn A. *Penelope's Renown*. Princeton: Princeton University Press, 1991.

Kenner, Hugh. "Homer's Sticks and Stones." *JJQ* 6 (Summer 1969): 285–98.

———. *Ulysses*. Rev. ed. Baltimore: Johns Hopkins University Press, 1987.

Kershner, R. Brandon. *Joyce, Bakhtin, and Popular Literature: Chronicles of Disorder*. Chapel Hill: University of North Carolina Press, 1989.

———, ed. *Joyce and Popular Culture*. Gainesville: University Press of Florida, 1996.

Kestner, Joseph A. "Before *Ulysses:* Victorian Iconography of the Odysseus Myth." *JJQ* 28 (Spring 1991): 245–58.

———. "Youth by the Sea: The Ephebe in *A Portrait of the Artist as a Young Man* and *Ulysses*." *JJQ* 31 (Spring 1994): 233–59.

Kimball, Jean. "'Brainsick Words of Sophists': Socrates, Antisthenes, and Stephen Dedalus." *JJQ* 16 (Summer 1979): 399–405.

Klein, Scott W. "Odysseus as 'New Womanly Man'." *JJQ* 26 (Summer 1989): 617–19.

Landuyt, Inge, and Geert Lernout. "Joyce's Sources: *Les grands fleuves historiques*." *JSA* 6 (1995): 99–138.

Lang, Andrew. *The World's Desire*. New York: Harper and Brothers, 1890.

———. *Homer and the Epic*. London: Longmans, Green, 1893.

———. *Homer and His Age*. London: Longmans, Green, 1906.

———. *The World of Homer*. London: Longmans, Green, 1910.

———. *Tales of Troy and Greece*. London: Faber, 1978.

Langlotz, Ernst. "Zur Deutung der 'Penelope'." *Jahrbuch des Deutschen Archäologischen Instituts* 76 (1961): 72–99.

Laubard, Valery. Review of "Protée" chapter of *Ulyssée*, by James Joyce; trans. August Morel and Stuart Gilbert. *La nouvelle revue française* 31 (1928): 204–26.

Leach, Karoline. "Ina in Wonderland." *Times Literary Supplement*, May 3, 1996, 15.

Leaf, Walter. *Troy: A Study in Homeric Geography*. London: Macmillan, 1912.

Lefkowitz, Mary R., and Guy McLean Rogers, eds. *Black Athena Revisited*. Chapel Hill: University of North Carolina Press, 1996.

Lernout, Geert. *James Joyce: Schrijver*. Leuven: Kritak, 1994.

———. "Czarnowski's *St. Patrick* in VI.B.14." Forthcoming.

Levine, Jennifer. "James Joyce, Tattoo Artist: Tracing the Outline of Homosocial Desires." *JJQ* 31 (Spring 1994): 277–99.

Litz, A. Walton. *The Art of James Joyce: Method and Design in "Ulysses" and "Finnegans Wake."* London, Oxford, New York: Oxford University Press, 1968.

Lloyd-Jones, Hugh. "Scott Wrote That." *Times Literary Supplement*, November 1, 1996, 9.

Lobner, Corinna Del Greco. "'Sounds are Imposture': From Patronymics to Dante's *Trombetta*." *JSA* 4 (1993): 43–54.

Loekle, Simon. "Dazibao: Homer Alone!" *JJQ* 33 (Fall 1996): 127.

Lohmann, Dieter. *KALYPSO bei Homer und James Joyce*. Tübingen: Stauffenburg, 1998. (*Ad Fontes* 5.)

The "Lysistrata" of Aristophanes, Illustrated by Aubrey Beardsley. London: Academy; New York: St. Martin's, 1973.

MacKenzie, Norman, and Jeanne MacKenzie. *H. G. Wells, a Biography*. New York: Simon and Schuster, 1973.

Mactoux, Marie-M. *Pénélope: Légende et mythe*. Paris: Belles Lettres, 1975.

Mailhos, Jacques. "'Begin to Forget It': The Preprovided Memory of *Finnegans Wake*." In *"Finnegans Wake": "Teems of times,"* ed. Andrew Treip, 40–67. European Joyce Studies 4. Amsterdam: Rodopi, 1994.

McCarthy, Patrick. "Stuart Gilbert's Guide to the Perplexed." In *Re-Viewing Classics in Joyce Criticism*, ed. Janet Dunleavy, 23–35. Urbana: University of Illinois Press, 1991.

McCleery, Alistair. "The One Lost Lamb." *JJQ* 27 (Spring 1990): 635–39.

———. "The Gathered Lambs." *JJQ* 31 (Summer 1994): 557–63.

McHugh, Roland. *The Sigla of "Finnegans Wake."* London: Edward Arnold, 1976.

———. *Annotations to "Finnegans Wake."* Rev. ed. Baltimore: Johns Hopkins University Press, 1991.

McKeon, Richard, ed. *The Basic Works of Aristotle*. New York: Random House, 1941.

Meehan, Jane S. "I Owe Three Shillings to O'Grady (*U* 103.07–08)." *JJQ* 16 (Summer 1979): 512–13.

Mercanton, Jacques. "The Hours of James Joyce." In *Portraits of the Artist in Exile*, ed. Willard Potts, 206–52. New York: Harcourt, Brace, Jovanovich, 1986.

Michels, James. "'Scylla and Charybdis': Revenge in James Joyce's *Ulysses*." *JJQ* 20 (Winter 1983): 175–92.

Milesi, Laurent. "Vico . . . Jousse. Joyce . . Langue." In *"Scribble" 1: Genèse des textes*, ed. Claude Jacquet, 143–62. Paris: Minard, 1988. (*La revue des lettres modernes* 834–39).

Mitchell, J. Lawrence. "Joyce and Boxing: Famous Fighters in *Ulysses*." *JJQ* 31 (Winter 1994): 21–30.

Mondada, Guiseppe. *Le Isole di Brissago: Nel passato e oggi*. 2d ed. Locarno: Armando Dadò, 1990.

Mylonas, George. *Eleusis and the Eleusinian Mysteries*. Princeton: Princeton University Press, 1961.

Noon, William T. *Joyce and Aquinas*. New Haven: Yale University Press, 1957.

O'Hara, James J. *True Names: Vergil and the Alexandrian Tradition of Etymological Wordplay*. Ann Arbor: University of Michigan Press, 1996.

———. "Sostratus *Suppl[ementum] Hell[enisticum]* 733: A Lost, Possibly Catullan-Era Elegy on the Six Sex Changes of Tiresias." *Transactions of the American Philological Association* 126 (1996): 176–219.

O Hehir, Brendan, and John M. Dillon. *A Classical Lexicon for "Finnegans Wake": A Glossary of the Greek and Latin in the Major Works of Joyce*. Berkeley and Los Angeles: University of California Press, 1977.

Owen, Rodney W. *James Joyce and the Beginning of "Ulysses": 1912–1917*. Ph.D. diss. (UMI 8026693), University of Kansas, 1980.

Oxford Classical Dictionary. Ed. Simon Hornblower and Andrew Spawforth. 3d ed. Oxford: Clarendon, 1996.

Parandowski, Jan. "Meeting with Joyce." In *Portraits of the Artist in Exile*, ed. Willard Potts, 153–62. New York: Harcourt, Brace, Jovanovich, 1986.

Pausanias. *Guide to Greece*. Trans. Peter Levi. London: Penguin, 1979.

Peradotto, John. *Man in the Middle Voice: Name and Narration in the "Odyssey."* Princeton: Princeton University Press, 1993.

Peterson, Richard F. "More Aristotelian Grist for the Joycean Mill." *JJQ* 17 (Winter 1980): 213–16.

Pindar. *Pindar: Selected Odes*. Trans. Carl A. P. Ruck and William H. Matheson. Ann Arbor: University of Michigan Press, 1968.

Plato. *Complete works*. Ed. John M. Cooper with D. S. Hutchinson. Indianapolis: Hackett, 1997.

Plotinus. *The Enneads*. Trans. Stephen MacKenna. Rev. ed. London: Faber and Faber, 1956.

Plutarch. *The Lives of the Noble Grecians and Romans*. Trans. John Dryden. Rev. ed. New York: Random House, Modern Library, 1932.

———. *Moralia*. Vol. 9. Trans. Edwin L. Muir, F. H. Sandbach, and W. C. Helmbold. Cambridge, Mass.: Harvard University Press, 1961.

Potts, Willard, ed. *Portraits of the Artist in Exile: Recollections of James Joyce by Europeans*. New York: Harcourt, Brace, Jovanovich, 1986.

Power, Arthur. *Conversations with James Joyce*. Ed. Clive Hart. Chicago: University of Chicago Press, 1982.

Pozzetto, Marco, et al., eds. *Il nuovo giorno: La comunità Greco-Orientale di Trieste: Storia e patrimonio artistico-culturale*. Udine: Instituto per l'Enciclopedia del Friuli–Venezia Giulia, 1982.

Prescott, Joseph. "Homer's *Odyssey* and Joyce's *Ulysses*." *Modern Language Quarterly* 3 (September 1942): 427–44.

Rabaté, Jean-Michel. *James Joyce, Authorized Reader*. Baltimore: Johns Hopkins University Press, 1991.

Rahner, Hugo. *Greek Myths and Christian Mysteries*. Trans. Brian Battershaw. London: Burns and Oates, 1963.

Raizis, M. Byron. Review of *Ta Hellēnika tou Tzaimes Tzous*, by Manto Aravantinou. *JJQ* 16 (Summer 1979): 521–24.

Rankin, H. D. "'Taylorised World' ([*FW*] 356.10) and Platonism." *AWN*, n.s., 2, no. 6 (December 1965): 11.

———. "Joyce's Remove from Aristotle to Plato." *AWN*, n.s., 2, no. 4 (August 1965): 10–13.

———. "James Joyce's Satyr-Play: The 'Cyclops' Episode in *Ulysses.*" *Agora* 2 (Fall 1973): 3–12.

The Roman Missal in English. 3d ed. New York: Benziger Brothers, 1925.

Romer, John, and Elizabeth Romer. *The Seven Wonders of the World: A History of the Modern Imagination.* New York: Henry Holt, 1995.

Roscher, W. H. *Ausführliches Lexikon der griechischen und römischen Mythologie.* Leipzig: B. G. Teubner, 1884–1937.

Rose, Danis. *The Textual Diaries of James Joyce.* Dublin: Lilliput, 1995.

———, ed. *James Joyce's The Index Manuscript: Finnegans Wake Holograph Workbook VI.B.46.* Colchester: *A Wake Newslitter* Press, 1978.

Rose, Danis, and John O'Hanlon. *Understanding "Finnegans Wake": A Guide to the Narrative of James Joyce's Masterpiece.* New York and London: Garland, 1982.

———, eds. *James Joyce. The Lost Notebook.* Edinburgh: Split Pea Press, 1989.

Ruck, Carl. "Documentation." In *The Road to Eleusis: Unveiling the Secret of the Mysteries,* ed. R. Gordon Wasson, Carl Ruck, and Albert Hofmann, 75–126. New York; Harcourt, Brace, Jovanovich, 1978.

Ruggiero, Paul. "James Joyce's Last Days in Zurich." In *Portraits of the Artist in Exile,* ed. Willard Potts, 283–86. New York: Harcourt, Brace, Jovanovich, 1986.

Rusten, Jeffrey. "Oedipus and Triviality." *Classical Philology* 91 (April 1996): 97–112.

Sarton, George. "Aristotle and Phyllis." *Isis* 14, no. 1 (1930): 8–19.

Schein, Seth. "Odysseus and Polyphemus in the *Odyssey.*" *Greek, Roman and Byzantine Studies* 11 (Spring 1970): 73–83.

Scholes, Robert, and Richard M. Kain, eds. *The Workshop of Daedalus.* Evanston: Northwestern University Press, 1964.

Schork, R. J. "A Graphic Exercise in Mnemotechnic." *JJQ* 16 (Spring 1979): 351–54.

———. "Apollinaire with Tirésias in the *Wake.*" *Journal of Modern Literature* 17 (Summer 1990): 166–72.

———. "Buck Mulligan as a *Grammaticus Gloriosus* in Joyce's *Ulysses.*" *Arion,* 3d ser., 1, no. 3 (Fall 1991): 76–92.

———. "'Nodebinding Ayes': Milton, Blindness and Egypt in the *Wake.*" *JJQ* 30 (Fall 1992): 69–83.

———. "The Emperor's Butterfly." *JJQ* 29 (Winter 1992): 403–5.

———. "Aristophanes and Joyce." *International Journal for the Classical Tradition* 2 (Winter 1996): 399–413.

———. "Significant Names in *Finnegans Wake* 46.20 and 371.22." *JJQ* 34 (Summer 1997): 505–16.

———. *Latin and Roman Culture in Joyce.* Gainesville: University Press of Florida, 1997.

———. "The *Wake's* Hairy Anchorite: st humphrey/onuphrius." In *A Collideorscape of Joyce: Festschrift for Fritz Senn,* ed. Ruth Frehner and Ursula Zeller, 270–77. Dublin: Lilliput, 1998.

Scott, Shirley C. "Man, Mind, and Monster: Polyphemus from Homer through Joyce." *Classical and Modern Literature* 16 (Fall 1995): 19–75.

Seidel, Michael. *Epic Geography: James Joyce's "Ulysses."* Princeton: Princeton University Press, 1976.

Senn, Fritz. "Book of Many Turns." *JJQ* 10 (Fall 1972): 29–46.

——. Review of *Epic Geography: James Joyce's "Ulysses,"* by Michael Seidel. *JJQ* 14 (Fall 1976): 111–13.

——. *Joyce's Dislocutions: Essays of Reading as Translation.* Ed. John Paul Riquelme. Baltimore: Johns Hopkins University Press, 1984.

——. "Ovidian Roots of Gigantism in Joyce's *Ulysses.*" *Journal of Modern Literature* 15 (Spring 1989): 56–77.

——. "In Quest of a *nisus formativus Joyceanus.*" *JSA* 1 (1990): 26–42.

——. *Inductive Scrutinies.* Ed. Christine O'Neill. Dublin: Lilliput, 1995.

——. "A Note on Burlesque Bloom." *JJQ* 32 (Spring/Summer 1995): 728–36.

——. "'Ithaca': Portrait of the Chapter as a Long List." In *Joyce's "Ithaca,"* ed. Andrew Gibson, 31–76. European Joyce Studies 6. Amsterdam: Rodopi, 1996.

——. "Dispersion of 'Hamarte'." In *Papers on Joyce,* no. 2, ed. Francisco García Tortosa and José A. Álvarez Amorós, 105–15. Compobell: Spanish James Joyce Society, 1996.

Skeat, Walter W. *An Etymological Dictionary of the English Language.* Oxford: Clarendon, 1953.

Smith's Smaller Classical Dictionary. Ed. E. H. Blakeney. London: J. M. Dent and Sons, 1910.

Soud, Stephen E. "Blood-Red Wombs and Monstrous Births: *Aristotle's Masterpiece* and *Ulysses.*" *JJQ* 32 (Winter 1995): 195–208.

Spoo, Robert. "Unpublished Letters of Ezra Pound to James, Nora, and Stanislaus Joyce." *JJQ* 32 (Spring/Summer 1995): 533–81.

Staley, Thomas F. "Religious Elements and Thomistic Encounters: Noon on Joyce and Aquinas." In *Re-Viewing Classics of Joyce Criticism,* ed. Janet E. Dunleavy, 155–68. Urbana: University of Illinois Press, 1991.

Stanford, W. B. "Ulyssean Qualities in Joyce's Leopold Bloom." *Comparative Literature* 5 (Spring 1953): 125–36.

——. *The Ulysses Theme.* Ann Arbor: University of Michigan Press, 1968.

——. *Ireland and the Classical Tradition.* Dublin: Allen Figgs; Totowa, N.J.: Rowman and Littlefield, 1976.

——, ed. *The "Odyssey" of Homer.* London: Macmillan; New York: St. Martin's, 1964.

Steppe, Wolfhard. "The Merry Greeks (With a Farewell to *epicleti*)." *JJQ* 32 (Spring and Summer 195): 597–617.

Stevenson, Burton, ed. *The Macmillan Book of Proverbs, Maxims, and Famous Sayings.* New York: Simon and Schuster, 1973.

Stewart, Andrew. *Faces of Power: Alexander's Image and Hellenistic Politics.* Berkeley and Los Angeles: University of California Press, 1993.

Summerfield, Henry. *That Myriad-Minded Man.* London: Colin Smythe, 1975.

Suter, August. "Some Reminiscences of James Joyce." In *Portraits of the Artist in Exile,* ed. Willard Potts, 61–66. New York: Harcourt, Brace, Jovanovich, 1986.

Tagopoulos, Constance. "Joyce and Homer: Return, Disguise, and Recognition in 'Ithaca'." In *Joyce in Context,* ed. Vincent Cheng and Timothy Martin, 184–200. Cambridge: Cambridge University Press, 1992.

Taylor, Charles H., ed. *Essays on the Odyssey: Selected Modern Criticism.* Bloomington: Indiana University Press, 1963.

Theoharis, Theoharis C. *Joyce's "Ulysses": An Anatomy of the Soul.* Chapel Hill: University of North Carolina Press, 1988.

Tripp, Edward, ed. *Crowell's Handbook of Classical Mythology.* New York: Thomas Y. Crowell, 1970.

Tzous, Tzaiems. *Odysseas* [Joyce, James. *Ulysses*]. Trans. Socrates Kapsakes. Athens: Kedros, 1990.

Van Mierlo, Wim. "The Freudful Couchmare Revisited: Contextualizing Joyce and the New Psychology." *JSA 8* (1997): 115–53.

von Phul, Ruth. "Aristotle, Phyllis Up." *JJQ* 8 (Winter 1971): 180–81.

Weir, Lorraine. "The Choreography of Gesture: Marcel Jousse and *Finnegans Wake*." *JJQ* 14 (Spring 1977): 313–25.

West, M. L., ed. *Hesiod: Theogony*. Oxford: Clarendon, 1966.

Whitehead, Alfred North. *Process and Reality*. Ed. D. R. Griffin and D. W. Sherburne. New York: Free Press, 1978.

Wiggin, L. A. "The Voice of the Frogs: An Analysis of *Brekkek Kekkek Koax* from *Finnegans Wake*." *AWN*, n.s., 6, no. 4 (August 1969): 60–63.

Wilde, Oscar. *The Letters of Oscar Wilde*. Ed. Rupert Hart-Davis. New York: Harcourt, Brace, and World, 1962.

Wills, Garry. "Why Are the Frogs in the *Frogs*?" *Hermes* 97 (1969): 306–17.

Yeats, William Butler. *The Letters of W. B. Yeats*. Ed. Allan Wade. New York: Macmillan, 1955.

———. *A Vision: A Reissue with the Author's Final Revisions*. New York: Macmillan, 1956.

Index

Since Joycean reference or allusion to the original Greek texts is extremely rare, I have not included the "works/citations/pages" or "citations/works/pages" tables that are part of the Latin companion volume. Throughout this Greek volume, the chapter divisions, subheadings, and citations of original sources are conspicuous and clear.

R. J. Schork is professor emeritus of classics at the University of Massachusetts–Boston. He is the author of *Sacred Song from the Byzantine Pulpit: Romanos the Melodist* (UPF, 1995) and *Latin and Roman Culture in Joyce* (UPF, 1997).